MW00770556

AROUND the WORLD in FORTY YEARS

AROUND the WORLD in FORTY YEARS

Barbara Smith

ISBN 978-1-7353753-0-4

CONTENTS

This book is dedicated to my husband Wayne, a frequent travel partner, and our daughters, Elizabeth and Emily.

INTRODUCTION

MY JOURNALING BEGAN on my first visit to Europe in 1980 when I wrote of my overwhelming first impressions in a descriptive letter to my in-laws. Several more trips followed to magical places. It wasn't until I traveled through Southeast Asia in 1986 that more extensive writing began. Capturing the essence of the places I visited in words became a passion and I continued to journal each overseas trip. Sharing them with fellow travelers led to lasting friendships.

Growing up in a small town in Michigan as the oldest of six in a middle-class family, travel consisted of an occasional summer vacation in a nearby cabin on a lake. My maternal grandparents lived on the north side of Chicago and I stayed with them on several occasions. Those visits seemed exotic. The thought of international travel never crossed my mind.

That all changed when my husband accepted a position in a company in the Los Angeles area in 1979. Frequent overseas travel became his routine and I occasionally accompanied him. Our first joint trip in 1980 took us to Holland, Paris and London. I was captivated and the travel seed was planted.

This book covers sixteen trips I took with my husband, our daughters, friends, or on my own. In more recent years, you'll notice a gap. Having traveled through so much of the world, my husband and I opted for two extensive tours of the western United States, visiting many National Parks and significant landmarks. Although I wrote about these trips, this book concentrates solely on international destinations. Rounding out my forty years of travel would have included a few days in Denmark followed by a Baltic cruise from August 26th to September 9th, 2020, but the trip was canceled due to the COVID-19 pandemic. Africa and India remain on my bucket list.

I've included many positive experiences along with some that were less satisfying. Each adventure offered something new and exciting and added to my understanding of the fascinating world in which we are so fortunate to live.

THE BEGINNING OF
40 YEARS OF OVERSEAS ADVENTURES
England, The Netherlands, and Paris

May 1980

This letter was written in long-hand to my in-laws during our return flight to California as I chronicled the impressions of my first overseas experience.

May 17, 1980

Dear Mom and Dad,

We are now flying over the many islands off the coast of NW Scotland, a beautiful sight in the late afternoon sun and a lovely ending to my first European trip. These past two weeks have been a dream come true for me and I want to share some of my impressions with you.

London was a wonderful city. One could sense centuries of history in its heart. We stayed in the Dukes Hotel close to Buckingham Palace. Although impressive in size, the palace had the appearance of a museum rather than a royal residence. Saint James's Park, which leads up to it, was spotlessly clean and filled with small ponds filled with ducks and swans. Its flower beds had more tulips than I've ever seen and the gardens were beautifully tended.

We were just a short walk from Parliament, Big Ben, and Westminster Abbey, a burial place for many English monarchs. We also toured St. Paul's Cathedral, designed by Christopher Wren. Although it was spectacular, I preferred the history tucked into Westminster Abbey.

My three favorite landmarks in England were the Canterbury Cathedral, Windsor Palace and the Tower of London. Canterbury was simply awesome—and enormous. The little village of Canterbury leading up to it charmed us. Wayne and I were both glad that we decided to make the day trip to it by train.

We had a delightful stay at the Compleat Angler in Marlow. Located adjacent to a weir, a low dam built across the river, it was a favorite fishing spot of Sir Izaak Walton. An outstanding dining room overlooking the weir added to the charm and the small village of Marlow enchanted us.

Nearby Windsor Castle, which I toured while Wayne worked in Marlow the next day, truly took my breath away as I approached it. Situated on a rise, the enormous structure showcased over nine hundred years of history. The staterooms were so elegant that finding the right words to describe them is almost impossible. They were embellished with gold leaf, elaborate carvings, marble, Savonnerie carpets, portraits of royalty by artists such as Van Dyke and Reynolds—it just went on and on. I couldn't fathom so many treasures in one location.

Queen Elizabeth currently likes to spend more time at Windsor than at Buckingham Palace and this didn't surprise me at all. Fortunately, she wasn't in residence on the day that I visited, enabling me to tour the interior of the castle.

Returning to London, we took a boat ride on the Thames from Parliament to the Tower of London on a Sunday afternoon. Since the lines to enter were blocks long, we chose to walk along its exterior. One had the feeling of going back hundreds of years in time. The iron bars on the prison walls coupled with the moats and heavy gate guarding the entrance added a sense of foreboding intrigue.

On our way to Broadway in the Cotswolds, we stopped briefly in Oxford. We walked along some of the streets bordering the colleges and then toured Christ Church. Its stained-glass windows are exquisite. The highlight, however, was a tour given spontaneously by a charming priest we happened to meet. He told us that Lewis Carroll, a pen name, had been a priest at Christ Church and Alice, the daughter of the gardener who played in the courtyard, inspired Alice in Wonderland. He showed us the tree where Carroll imagined the rabbit hole to be.

From Oxford we drove to Blenheim Palace, a magnificent structure built by the first Duke of Marlborough. The equally remarkable grounds were designed by Capability Brown. Filled with art and history, it rests near a small lake. The story of a love-hate relationship between Sarah Marlborough and Queen Anne fascinated us. In more recent times, Winston Churchill was born at Blenheim Palace.

The Cotswolds and our two nights in Broadway at the Lygon Arms were very special. The inn dates to the 16th century and our room was in the original section. It had heavy beamed ceilings, leaded windows and was filled with English antiques and a canopied bed. I loved this stay.

Surrounded by soft rolling hills, the Cotswolds were dotted with quaint villages and streams. Lovely stone houses with bright gardens will remain a favorite memory. We had two days to wander through Upper and Lower Slaughter, Bourton-on-the-Water and many more charming villages.

On our way to Birmingham's airport for our flight to Amsterdam, we had time to tour Warwick Castle. Although much smaller in size than Windsor, the tour of the 12th-century dungeon and torture chamber served as a reminder of those cruel times.

Amsterdam is a city of contrasts. Its canals remain in place after 600 years. Parts of the city were elegant; others seemed to be in various stages of decay. The streets were filled with weird-looking characters and graffiti covered many buildings in the centrum, the city's center.

After breakfast the following day, we took a canal boat ride for an hour before visiting the Rijksmuseum. We saw Rembrandt's Night Watch and many other important works of art before visiting the Van Gogh Museum and its incredible collection. That night we had dinner at an Indonesian restaurant and goat meat was served. It was a first for me and it actually was good.

The next morning Wayne had business meetings in Leiden and I went on to the The Hague, a lovely and very proper city. I visited a number of museums during our three-day stay, one with a panoramic view of a North Sea fishing village painted in 1880 by Hendrik Mesdag. He created a 360-degree work of art on the walls of a large circular room and enhanced it with real sand, driftwood, old oars, and other seaworthy items.

I also took a short train ride to Delft, a miniature Amsterdam with lovely small canals, and then climbed to the top of the bell tower in a 400-year-old Lutheran church. Wonderful views! The palace where William of Orange was murdered is also in Delft but it was closed for repairs.

On Wednesday night we took a train to Paris, traveling through Antwerp and Brussels while it was still light enough to see these cities. We arrived at our hotel, the Meurice, just after midnight. Our spacious room had a window overlooking much of Paris, including the Eiffel Tower brightly lit at night.

Thursday was a French holiday so Wayne and I walked through the enchanting city all day long. We began at the Arc de Triomphe, strolling down the Champs-Élysées enhanced with its rows of chestnut trees in bloom. After walking along the exterior of the Louvre, which was closed due to a strike, we crossed the Seine to the Left Bank. We toured Notre-Dame located on Île de la Cité and admired its magnificent stained-glass windows before returning to the Right Bank, walking past the Opera and the Palais Royal.

That evening we had dinner with an American banker and his wife in their spectacular apartment overlooking the Seine. She had worked for *Gourmet* magazine and both enjoyed cooking. We were the recipients of their talents and we enjoyed hearing of their experiences in and around Paris.

On Friday I strolled through more of the city and popped into a number of the small boutiques. The fashions were beautiful but very expensive and I enjoyed every minute of browsing sans making a purchase.

We had dinner with a Paris business acquaintance of Wayne's who spoke English and his charming wife who only spoke French. We managed to communicate with smiles and with translations from her husband. They took us to Tour d'Argent, one of the most famous restaurants in Paris. With a table near a window overlooking Notre Dame, we enjoyed our numbered duck dinner before saying goodnight and walking along the streets of Paris to our hotel.

The next morning was a Saturday and we took the Metro to Montmartre to visit Sacré-Cœur. This area has historically been an artists' mecca and we spotted a number of them in the square painting and selling their works. Sacré-Cœur, visible from much of Paris, is simply magnificent.

We returned to the Arc de Triomphe for a final walk down this inspiring boulevard before leaving Paris. Coupled with a good business trip for Wayne, this was a fabulous first European experience for me. We had some lovely times together and I leave with treasured memories and a better understanding of where Wayne visits on his overseas business trips.

Love,

Barbara

P.S. We just reached Canada. We're halfway home!

SOUTHEAST ASIA
South Korea, Jakarta, Bali, Singapore, Bangkok, and Hong Kong

October 16–27, 1986

BRAVE! DARING! Are you crazy? These were just a few of the remarks we heard as our group of fourteen gals prepared for the adventure of a lifetime. In the mid-1980s, not many women even dreamed about traveling through Southeast Asia on their own. Our group did just that.

After months of planning, and with the support and encouragement of our husbands who took on the roles of mother and father for our pre-teen and teenage children, we met at LAX on a crisp October morning to begin our tour throughout Southeast Asia. Ten of us hailed from San Marino and Pasadena. Three others came from Stockton, and one from Phoenix. Although we all knew some of the group well, no one knew everyone. As our travel progressed, we became a cohesive and compatible group.

We boarded Northwest Orient's flight to Seoul, South Korea, for a connecting flight to Hong Kong. After twelve hours in the air, our pilot announced that a typhoon threatened Hong Kong and we would spend the night in Seoul. We now could add another country to our travel itinerary.

The Northwest Orient representative informed us that because the 1986 Asian Games were taking place in Seoul, almost all hotels were booked. That necessitated a one-hour nighttime bus ride through Seoul to the Green Park Hotel, located in a wooded area on the outskirts of the city. As we drove through the city at 10:00 p.m., we noticed that it was bustling with people in suits and dresses, many carrying briefcases. It appeared they were just leaving their workplaces.

Our time in Seoul began and ended in the dark. After a very short night's sleep at the Green Park Hotel, we departed at 5:00 a.m. for our ride back to the airport. A spectacular eclipse of the moon made our early wake-up call worthwhile.

The typhoon had subsided enough for our flight to safely resume, and we arrived at Hong Kong's International Airport mid-morning, losing a day due to the international time change. Across the harbor, which was filled with barges and junks, Kowloon glistened in the rain, its rows of white high-rise buildings lining the shore, bordered by distant mountains.

With a six-hour wait in the airport for our flight to Jakarta, we spent the time wandering through the duty-free shops, writing postcards and lunching in the airport coffee shop. Cell phones were only a dream in 1986, so some of us called our families from the international phone booths. As novice travelers, we made the mistake of cashing our travelers' checks for Hong Kong dollars and Indonesian rupiah at the airport's expensive exchange rates.

We left Hong Kong at 3:30 p.m. for our flight to Jakarta, stopping briefly in Singapore for a transfer. The evening sky was alive with flashes of lightening. Jakarta by night bustled with activity; the streets were packed with bicycles, pedicabs and small food stalls. A canal in the city's center reflected the earlier Dutch influence in Indonesia.

En route, we passed a large park with an obelisk topped with a gilt flame. The 433-foot tower in Merdeka Square is the national monument of the Republic of Indonesia. Our hotel, the Sari Pacific, stood a block from the square. After our meager hotel in Seoul, this four-star winner was a welcome sight.

Pat, my roommate for the tour, discovered that her suitcase had been soaked by the heavy rains in Hong Kong and some of her clothes were irreparably damaged—not a good beginning for her. My suitcase must have been at the bottom of the cart, as it had remained dry.

After a quick sightseeing tour the next morning, we headed for the airport. In daylight, the overwhelming poverty just outside the city of Jakarta was evident. Small huts with zinc sheets for roofing lined the canal. Oblivious to their living conditions, the residents smiled and waved to us as we passed.

While flying to Bali on Garuda Airlines, we noted looming volcanic peaks through the intermittent shroud of clouds over the island of Java. One of the volcanoes in the process of erupting spewed plumes of smoke and lava high above its dome. We wished the day had been clearer for an unobstructed view of the volcano.

We arrived early in the afternoon at the Bali Beach Hotel in the village of Sanur. As we entered the lobby, our attention instantly focused on four tiny, wizened Balinese men sitting cross-legged on the floor in front of strange-looking hammered instruments. They sat perfectly still with straight backs, giving the appearance of statues. Within moments, the men picked up their hammers and began to play haunting rhythms. We later learned that this music forms the foundation of Balinese culture. We would hear Gamelan music often during our stay on Bali.

The first room assigned to Pat and me faced a courtyard. After a call to reception we were given a room with an ocean view. However, it was right next to the main power generator, which produced a constant buzz. One of our traveling companions who doubled as our tour coordinator somehow managed to get every one of us into quiet rooms with full views of the Indian Ocean. With four days to spend on Bali, we appreciated her effort.

The people on Bali are soft-spoken and friendly. Tranquil best describes them. Bali's population is ninety percent Hindu with a mix of Buddhist and other religions composing the remaining ten percent. For most residents, life revolves around the Balinese concept of Hinduism combined with music, dance, art, and architecture.

Our group attended an Indonesian buffet in one of the hotel's gardens. We enjoyed skewered beef, chicken, pork, and fish accompanied by rice, vegetables and a variety of dipping sauces. After dinner, we were treated to an hour of Balinese music and colorful folk dancing. The women wore ornate costumes in deep greens and purples with touches of gold. At the end of the performance, the dancers invited us to join them on stage. No one wanted to be the first, so I accepted. Once on stage, however, I was too embarrassed to turn around and face the large audience. So much for my debut as a Balinese dancer.

The next morning, our guide Surya met us at the hotel and we boarded a passenger van shortly before 9:00 a.m. He was surprised when he saw us and admitted that we were the first all-female group he had ever led. Surya, a Buddhist, accompanied us for the next several days along with our driver, Made, a Hindu. On one of our days, Surya included a guide-in-training, a convert to Fundamentalism. All got along in harmony. We girls often sang songs to Surya and Made, and they in turn sang Balinese songs for us. Surya was a patient soul and put up with our frequent questions and numerous requests for photo stops.

One of our destinations was a Hindu temple in Batubulan, home of the Bali Barong Dance Center, where we watched an hour-long performance of the Barong, the Hindu story of good versus evil. In this episode of the ancient Sanskrit epic *Ramayana*, good, represented as a dragon, battled evil, a witch-like figure. In this musical dance-play, good wins but evil always lurks in the shadows.

After the dance performance, we drove to Celuk, the village of the silversmiths. Each village on Bali showcased a unique craft or skill passed on from generation to generation. I bought silver rings for my daughters and a fruit spoon for myself. Our next stop was Mas, the village of woodcarvers. We listened to one of the master carvers explain the types of wood he used, and then toured the shop. Although I only purchased a bracelet, I was fascinated by the ornately carved masks and statues.

The Balinese were celebrating the holiday of Galungan, marking a time when ancestral spirits visit the Earth. Towering bamboo poles bent over at the top stood in front of each housing complex. Ornately carved bamboo decorations hung from the ends of the poles. We saw hundreds of them as we traveled from village to village.

Families lived collectively in housing complexes built of narrow, orange-red bricks. Elaborate stone carvings decorated the entrances and the interior buildings. Surya stopped at one of the complexes belonging to a family he had never met. It was considered an honor to have guests tour one's home on Bali. The residents seemed proud to have a vanload of women arrive unannounced for a tour of their complex. I can't even imagine a group of strangers randomly asking to walk through my home and gardens.

Just inside the complex, we noted designated areas for livestock, a vegetable garden, and the wells that provided water. The first building within the compound was a storage shed for supplies and beyond it, an outdoor kitchen. A long room that doubled as living and sleeping quarters spanned the back wall. There were one or two separate bedrooms, very small with only a bed in each, used by the head or heads of the household. Across from the storage shed stood a series of three small temples with offerings of flowers and rice on the altars, intended to ward off evil.

We were fortunate that our first day of touring coincided with Galungan, a major festival day. As we traveled further, a long procession of Hindu Balinese women lined the roadways with offerings of food and flowers high atop their heads. They wore colorful apparel and the offerings they balanced, some almost three feet high, were artfully arranged with tiers of rice cakes, chickens, pastries, fruits, and vegetables. It was a sight that would become even more meaningful later in the day.

Our next destination, the top of Mount Batur, showcased Lake Batur and a volcano that last erupted in the 1960s. Like so much on Bali, the views were breathtaking. Shortly after we arrived, a thick bank of fog drifted in and we were thankful that we had taken our photos earlier. Lunch in the remote village of Kintamani, patterned after the Indonesian Rijsttafel, offered an array of dishes complemented by the ever-present bowls of rice. It is said that an Indonesian meal is not complete without rice.

Except for unpeeled fruits and raw vegetables that we had been warned not to try, we ate well throughout our stay on Bali. We had fresh papaya and pineapple for breakfast and a variety of steamed vegetables came with every lunch and dinner. It was a delightful surprise to eat so well for so little money.

After our mountaintop lunch, we boarded the van in the midst of a swarm of peddlers selling postcards and other trinkets. The street merchants were like locusts whenever a tour bus would appear. In contrast to the villages where time seemed to have stopped a century ago, this was not a pleasant experience.

We made our way to the village of Tegalalang to visit the Holy Spring Temple. Because it was a festival day, the complex overflowed with Balinese Hindus who brought offerings to be blessed. Artfully arranged rice cakes and food adorned the altars as more and more women entered with offerings atop their heads, some walking for miles to reach the temple. Although we felt intrusive being there on this holiest of days, it was a moving spiritual experience for each of us.

Built around a natural spring, the temple rested near the purest water in all of Bali, yet it was not used for drinking. The water was divided into three separate areas—a bathing spot for men and another for women, while a third area supplied holy water for the blessing of the offerings. Since Western tourists frequented the temple, the two bathing areas were no longer used, although we did spot a group of young boys splashing in the buff.

As part of the spiritual ritual, people leaving the temple had bits of rice stuck to their faces, most likely a symbolic gesture similar to receiving communion in Christian religions. I wanted to photograph some of the children in their colorful clothing with decorative patterns of rice on their faces but it seemed inappropriate at a religious ceremony.

During his 1945-1967 reign, President Sukarno built a massive modern housing complex on the hill just above the Holy Spring Temple. It still stands in stark contrast to the ancient temple below it and I can only imagine how the worshippers must have felt to have this unholy intrusion looking down upon them.

From there we traveled a short distance to one of the most spectacular sights in all of Bali, its tiered rice fields. We stood along a bridge high above a river, entranced by the terraced plantations surrounding us on all sides. This view alone merited a trip to Bali. I'll always cherish the memory.

We drove on to Ubud, the village of artists. Having just seen the massive tiered rice fields, I purchased a small oil painting of several Balinese harvesting the rice. It hung in our living room for years and it now graces a wall in the home of one of my daughters.

As we drove through Ubud, Made had to stop our van while another long procession marched toward the temple. As before, all the women carried offerings on their heads. For the first time, we noted men in the procession playing native instruments as they marched along the roadway.

Our final stop was a batik shop in Sanur. Colorful pieces of art, clothing, scarves, handbags, and fabrics filled every inch of the building. I resisted making a purchase but returned at a later time to buy a shift and a beach wrap.

We met Surya the next morning and drove a short distance to Denpasar, the capital of Bali. Compared to yesterday's small villages, it bustled with activity; clusters of cars, scooters and pedicabs filled the streets, causing traffic jams at some of the busiest intersections.

Our first stop in Denpasar was the Art Center, built not long ago in Hindu style to house Bali's most significant treasures. The rooms featured Balinese paintings, silver, batiks, and sculptures of wood and stone. Our next stop took us to the palace of the last Balinese king, who was assassinated along with his family and servants in 1906 during a Dutch uprising. The palace was now a museum, housing collections of military and household pieces.

From there, we visited an open market located in the main square of Denpasar. It looked seedy and many in our van opted to stay put. Earlier, I had mentioned to Surya that I regretted not purchasing some batik fabric the day before and he assured me that I would find some in the market. That said, I decided to brave it. The market proved fascinating. Stall after stall in the lower section sold fruits, vegetables and other foods. Women arranged flowers on palm fronds and sold them for temple offerings. Even daily offerings could be purchased at the market. Additional stalls upstairs sold fabrics and household goods. I bought five yards of fabric in a deep green with gold designs in a diamond pattern for less than US$10. Driving away from the market, we noticed a truck with live pigs tucked into baskets. As I mentioned earlier, food is fresh on Bali.

We traveled quite a distance to Kuta Beach on the opposite side of Bali, a favorite of Australians, which had one of the island's best swimming beaches. We noticed Balinese women sitting under trees along the beach offering massage services to visitors, as well as a few topless sunbathers working on maximum exposure to the sun—or just maximum exposure.

After driving a bit further along the coast, we came to the Monkey Forest in Tanah Lot, which featured a temple built high on a cliff overlooking the ocean. We encountered only a few other people as we made our way up the path. Looking down from the temple, we understood why the Balinese Hindus selected this stunning location, isolated as it was. Monkeys sat in groups along the walls or in trees. Surya advised us to hold on to our purses and cameras so the monkeys wouldn't try to steal them.

Our next stop stood in sharp contrast to the Monkey Forest. Just ten minutes away, we arrived at the Nusa dua Hotel, the most famous and glamorous on Bali at the time. Located on the island's arid side, it was noticeably hotter and dryer here. The hotel, constructed to resemble a Hindu temple, gave one the impression of entering a sacred shrine. Once inside, the lobby exuded luxury. We enjoyed lunch at the hotel and spent a leisurely hour wandering through its elegance and its beautiful gardens. Like all our meals on Bali, our lunch cost almost nothing.

Afterwards, Pat and I perused our hotel's gift shop. We had an early dinner and then strolled the hotel grounds, listening to Gamelan music playing at a private party in one of the gardens. Back in our room, Pat and I talked for hours, just like a couple of college roommates, before calling it a night.

Although some of our group took cabs to various shopping locations the next morning, Pat and I opted for a day of leisure. We ordered coffee in our room at enjoyed it on our balcony with views of the tranquil ocean. The spell was soon broken by Australians in the room next to us playing pop music full blast on their radio.

We opted for Plan B and headed back to the hotel shops. In one of them, we found cassettes with recordings of the haunting Gamelan music that had become such an important part of our visit to Bali. After my return to the States, I listened to the tape often and it brought back special memories.

Most of our days on Bali were a mix of sunshine and clouds, and this day was no exception. After a late lunch, we donned our swimsuits and headed for the beach in front of the hotel. As soon as we arrived, clouds obscured the sun. In spite of this, we sat for a full two hours, knowing this would be our only opportunity to enjoy this lovely Balinese beach.

Later in the day, our group met in the lobby for a ride to Denpasar to see the Monkey Dance. Another episode of the *Ramayana*, this one was called the Kecak. We sat in seats above a sunken stage filled with nearly a hundred men. Representing monkeys, they sat in a circle and swayed while chanting. No musical instruments were played. The story told of how the monkey army saved Cita, Rama's bride, from evil. The hypnotic hour-long performance enchanted us and we particularly enjoyed the varied rhythmic drum-like sounds that the men produced. What a perfect ending to our time on Bali!

The next day we flew to Singapore. Our guide met us at the airport and took us to our hotel, the Marco Polo, not far from the heart of the city. En route, we marveled at the spotless beauty of Singapore. With no specific dinner plans, Pat and I decided to do a little exploring on our own. We left the hotel at nine in the evening and headed for Orchard Road, known for its shops. Since it was after hours, we could only look in windows. Even this late at night, the heat overwhelmed us. While Bali had ample trade winds to temper the heat, in Singapore it was close to ninety degrees without a breeze to offset the high temperatures. We California girls were used to evenings that cooled down from high daytime readings.

We spotted the Mandarin Hotel and decided to have a late dinner in its top floor revolving restaurant, offering changing views of the city and harbor. Our meal was good and the sights even better. The platform completed a full rotation as we dined.

When we all met the next morning for a tour of Singapore, we soon discovered how pampered we had been on Bali with a private van. We boarded a full-size bus filled with several other groups for our sightseeing tour of Singapore. This morning's short drive took us to both the Indian and Chinese sections of the city. A highlight was an ornate Hindu temple in the Chinese section standing in glowing contrast to the simple Hindu architecture on Bali.

Upon entering the temple, we were reminded by our guide to remove our shoes. As we observed a religious ceremony in progress, a young priest lifted up a silver plate holding a flame. He passed it to worshipers who put coins around the flame. White rice paste was then placed on each worshiper's forehead and holy water was poured into outstretched hands. After drinking the holy water, flower petals were applied to the sticky rice on their foreheads. We commented on the similarity of this ceremony to the Christian communion service.

Our next stop, Mount Faber, rose 240 feet above sea level. It offered panoramic views of Singapore and its harbors. Our last stop was the Botanic Gardens, sixty acres showcasing a variety of tropical flowers and plants. Established as a plantation in the middle of the city more than a century ago, it was now a UNESCO World Heritage site. We wandered through it and admired the array of plants and orchids.

Although Singapore residents hail from China, Malaysia, Indonesia, Thailand, and India, the Chinese were the first to settle here, bringing their Malay wives. The cooking developed by the Malay women is still some of the hottest and spiciest in the world, and Chinese men prize the cooking ability of their wives. After our morning tour, Pat and I sampled a Malay dish similar to bouillabaisse, enjoying our delightful, tearful lunch in the park across from our hotel.

After lunch, we joined two gals in our group for a tour of some of the shops in city hotels. My quest was for pearls. After looking in a number of boutiques, we found high quality pearls at reasonable prices in one at the

Hilton Hotel. I bought enough unstrung pearls from a reputable jeweler to make two opera-length strands, as little to no customs fee is charged when unstrung pearls are brought into the States.

We all met at 9:00 p.m. at the Raffles Hotel, home to numerous writers and artists in its heyday, and birthplace of the famous Singapore Sling. We sat in the Palm Court with our drinks, then enjoyed dinner in the Elizabethan Room for a grand total of US$22 per person. Ah, affordable elegance!

The next morning, I took a cab to Lucky Plaza, Singapore's equivalent of Hong Kong's Nathan Street. A multi-level, plain vanilla building, it was filled with shops selling watches, jewelry, electronics, shoes, and just about anything else. I came armed with some hot tips from the shoppers in our group who had been there the day before. With only forty-five minutes to cruise this vast array of shops, I found a jewelry shop where, after some negotiating, I bought two sapphire and diamond rings for my daughters.

At noon we met to embark on the next leg of our adventure, a three-hour flight to Bangkok, Thailand. Although my first impression of the city was a bit disappointing, Bangkok's secrets soon revealed themselves. The books I had read described Bangkok as a city of contrasts—luxury and poverty, beauty and filth, and sophistication and crime with pockets of antiquity tucked in among the modern. All proved to be true; Bangkok had a seediness coupled with a seductive allure.

After getting situated in our hotel, the Montien, not far from the famed Jim Thompson silk shop, we took cabs to the Dusit Thani Hotel for dinner. The hotel's restaurant, traditionally decorated, had walls covered in blue-green raw silk and pillars flecked with gold. Its artfully prepared native dishes looked almost too pretty to eat. But eat we did! Every dish arrived with exquisitely hand-carved vegetables cut to resemble flowers and leaves. We enjoyed Thai soup, chicken curry and a custard for dessert for US$14, tip included. As we dined, a man played Thai music on an instrument similar to those on Bali but with a softer, mellower sound.

We were met early the next morning by our Thai guide Prwya. She led us along the Chao Phraya River to the flower market where orchids spilled from baskets in each stall. Soon we arrived at the outer walls of the Grand Palace, a complex of buildings in the heart of Bangkok, which has served as the official residence of Thai kings since 1782. My camera could only capture bits and pieces of this magnificent complex begun by King Rama I, and added to by successive rulers. Inside the surrounding walls were ornately bejeweled buildings and temples. The glistening jewel-like effect was created using thousands of pieces of small, colored tiles and mirrors painstakingly set into pillars and walls. We were told that every fifty years, each piece is removed and replaced. The last replacement process was completed just four years before our visit.

Since the Chinese were some of the earliest settlers of Bangkok, the Buddhist religion dominates. The Temple of the Emerald Buddha reflected this influence and we stood in awe staring at its namesake statue before entering. Dating as far back as the mid-1400s, the figure is carved from jasper, a semi-precious stone. Emerald refers to its color rather than its composition. We removed our shoes before entering and admired the temple's paintings and murals. High above us was the Emerald Buddha seated in the lotus position, dressed in appropriate costume for the rainy season. The Buddha also had costume changes for summer and winter, which were displayed in the Palace Museum. At the beginning of each of the three seasons, the king would climb a ladder to the Buddha to assist in the clothes-changing ceremony.

That afternoon, most of the group went with Prwya to a local gem market. Having fulfilled my jewelry wish list, I opted to visit the Jim Thompson silk shop with four fellow travelers. Two-sided folding picture frames covered in raw silk caught my attention and I purchased several. From there we walked to the magnificent Orient Hotel, situated on the bank of the river directly across from the Grand Palace. We enjoyed an exquisitely prepared lunch as we watched small barges float along the river. Even at this world-renowned hotel, the price of our meal was reasonable.

Prwya arranged dinner at a tourist restaurant that featured Thai music and dancing. Although the dances varied considerably from Bali, we found the colorful costumes and intricate use of hand movements fascinating. Unfortunately, the food didn't match the quality of the performance.

On our return trip to the hotel, Prwya talked our bus driver into taking us into an alley that ran through Patpong, Bangkok's red-light district. While traversing the narrow alley, the bus became wedged between a brothel and a newsstand, and it took some time and skillful maneuvering to free it. We imagined the headlines reading, "Pasadena Ladies Trapped in Bangkok's Red-Light District".

The final leg of our journey began with a 6:00 a.m. wake-up call. After breakfast, we boarded a van for our ride to the airport, and headed for Hong Kong. Our relatively low flight path took us over Viet Nam, which had not yet opened its doors to American tourists. We flew over the Mekong River and had a clear view of villages along it. Before heading out to sea, our flight path took us over Da Nang. The mouth of the river and delta were visible but the city of Da Nang was obscured by clouds. It felt eerie to look down on a country where so many Americans and Vietnamese had perished a decade earlier.

After long lines in customs at the Hong Kong airport, coupled with several other delays, we arrived at our hotel in Kowloon, the Holiday Inn Harbor View. True to its name, we had a room with a clear view across the bustling harbor into Hong Kong. With only a few remaining hours to shop and sightsee, Pat and I made a beeline for the city streets. At the China Arts and Crafts along the waterfront, we discovered a variety of treasures, many from mainland China. Pat bought linens and I found a few pieces of exquisite cloisonné from Beijing.

Our next stop was the Peninsula Hotel, where we enjoyed high tea before heading for Nathan Street and its renowned bargains. For the first time during our travels, we felt uncomfortable and did just a quick perusal of shops along this crowded street before returning to our hotel.

The evening's dinner at The Plume, in Kowloon's stylish Regent Hotel, provided the perfect setting for our final gathering. Located on the second level, this elegant dining room overlooked the harbor, offering a stunning nighttime vista. Perfection best described the service, food and view, offering a memorable finale evening of our journey through Southeast Asia.

HOLLAND, PARIS AND LONDON
Wassenaar, Gouda, Delft, Kerkrade, Maastricht, Antwerp, Paris,
and London

October 19–November 4, 1988

I ALWAYS LOOKED FORWARD TO occasionally accompanying Wayne on business trips to Europe, and this one promised to be memorable. Not only would I have an opportunity to explore while Wayne worked, I would also visit my first cousin, Dana, now living in the Netherlands with her husband. Then on to Paris and London…

Our plane to New York City departed from LAX on schedule on a clear Wednesday morning. We then boarded a plane for our flight to Amsterdam and, allowing for the time change, arrived at 8:40 a.m. on Thursday. After renting a car at the airport, we drove to Wassenaar, a toney suburb of The Hague. Our destination was The Wittenberg Aparthotel, an old castle converted into a small private hotel. To our delight, our room overlooked a pond filled with ducks.

In spite of jet lag, Wayne headed for his office in Leiden. After a three-hour nap, I ordered lunch in our room. Ham sandwiches on a silver plate arrived, piled with enough to feed an army. Then I called my cousin Dana who now lived in Wassenaar. We had seen her a year earlier when she and her husband, Ed, were based in London, and we see more of each other overseas than we ever did in the States.

Dana met me at the hotel and we drove to Wassenaar's centrum, or town center, to walk along the short blocks of shops. It was a pedestrian-only area featuring a variety of stores—clothing, sporting goods, food, pastries, and, of course, flowers. An earlier light drizzle had all but ceased and I called attention to myself as a tourist with my opened umbrella. The Dutch consider a light rain a good day and not worthy of one.

We then drove to a nearby beach along the North Sea. The landscape reminded us of the communities bordering the central coast of Lake Michigan. Looking at the sand dunes and sea grass along this North Sea beach, it could easily have been my home town. It explained why so many Dutch immigrants settled in western Michigan. With its similar topography and temperatures, it must have felt almost like home to the Dutch who settled there.

Wayne and Ed joined us at dinnertime and Dana, a superb cook, presented us with veal, tiny roasted new potatoes, green beans, and a salad. She then served a Dutch cake decorated with meringue and marzipan, a work of art from one of the local bakeries. We chatted until 9:30 p.m. when the jet lag set in for us and we said goodnight.

The next morning, Wayne and I enjoyed a Dutch breakfast in our room with fresh rolls, meats and cheeses. At Dana's earlier suggestion I added yogurt, the best I have ever tasted. Wayne, in his quest to be a regular guy, ordered prunes. Again, our food arrived on silver serving platters. What a lovely hotel—quiet with elegant charm.

After packing our bags and checking out of the hotel, Wayne again drove me to Dana's home on another day of light rain. Although Dana had only been in Holland for a couple of weeks, she was ready for a drive to Delft with map in hand. Somehow, we missed the exit and ended up in Gouda. Since we were there, we decided to take a quick look. What a delightful surprise! We passed a cheese shop with enormous rounds of Gouda stacked along the sidewalk, and explored the central square with its gothic Town Hall built in 1450 AD, the oldest in the country. Then we toured the 18th-century St. John's Church, the longest in the Netherlands, best known for its seventy spectacular stained-glass windows. Our trip to Gouda was a mistake with a silver lining.

After rechecking the map, we headed back to Delft for lunch and a quick stroll through the central square. I had visited Delft a few years earlier and enjoyed seeing this charming city with its canals once more. As we headed back, we found ourselves on an unfamiliar ring road and it took quite a bit of time and maneuvering through wall-to-wall traffic to spot the exit sign to Wassenaar.

Wayne and his business associate Charles arrived at Dana's home later in the afternoon and, after saying goodbye to Dana, we followed Charles in our rental car to the Rotterdam airport to return it. Charles then drove us to his nearby home. His wife Carla joined us for a weekend in the Limburg region of the Netherlands, where the borders of Holland, Germany and Belgium meet. The four of us had talked about taking this trip for several years and now we were making it happen.

With Charles at the wheel, it took two and a half hours to reach Kerkrade, a small village in the southwest corner of the Netherlands. Our hotel for the weekend, the Kasteel Erenstein, originated as a castle and farmhouse built in 1485 AD. Our charming room in the old farmhouse had two-foot-thick walls and a staircase leading to an upstairs sitting room.

After getting situated, we dressed for dinner and walked to the castle, which was just across the roadway. As we came to the bridge which crossed the canal leading to the entrance, a forty-piece band lined the walkway playing for guests who were attending a special party. A bit later, we again heard them perform from our table in the elegant dining room.

We enjoyed an incredible three-hour, six-course dinner that began with a deer and goose liver pâté in a wild berry sauce. Then came a wild mushroom and hazelnut tart followed by a langostino mousse. The main course featured duck with ginger, then an assortment of cheeses from the Limburg area arrived. A chocolate mousse was presented as the grand finale. Sharing a spectacular meal with dear friends made the evening even more memorable.

We awoke at 8:00 a.m. and called for room service coffee. It arrived in one minute. We're talking top-rate service! A short time later, we met Charles and Carla for a Dutch breakfast in the farmhouse dining room. Afterward, we walked around Kasteel Erenstein to get a better look at it in daylight. It was a perfect fall day with a bright blue sky, cool, crisp temperatures hovering in the sixties and trees sporting brilliant fall colors.

Next, we drove through a hilly countryside to the village of Maastricht. Yes, Virginia, there really are hills in the Netherlands—but only in this region. Our route took us through small villages and farms. We stopped in Wittem to look at another lovely castle hotel, Kasteel Wittem, with only eight guest rooms and known for its dining facilities. Charles and Carla enjoyed an earlier stay here in the turret room. Two black swans graced the moat surrounding the castle and one of them kept pace with us as we walked.

Our next stop was the Margraten Memorial, home of the Netherlands American Cemetery, where 8,291 American soldiers were buried in 1944–1945 during the final years of World War II. Two long walls in this park-like setting formed the entrance and were inscribed with 1,722 names of Americans missing in action. Once inside, a reflecting pool welcomed visitors to row after row of crosses and Stars of David commemorating those who were buried here. We were deeply moved by this emotional site. My father flew missions near here and more than likely some of his buddies were remembered at Margraten.

We drove on to Maastricht, the most important city in the Limburg region, divided by the River Maas. Walking toward the centrum, we stopped at a sidewalk café for coffee. Wayne, Charles and Carla also ordered vlaai, pronounced fly, a fruit tart made in this part of the country. Charles and Carla then gave us a guided tour, taking us past St. Servaas, the oldest Roman church in Holland, built in the 10th century. After wandering past lovely old homes and buildings, we stopped for lunch at 't Klaoske, where we dined on sorrel and watercress soup and incredibly fresh salmon. We sat at a window table facing a small square and the passersby took delight in staring at us and our selections. We all had a good laugh along with a good lunch.

Afterward, I purchased a small black and white sketch of a bridge over the Maas with Maastricht in the background, and Carla bought a beautiful calendar with pictures of the area as a gift for us. People swarmed the shopping area. The pedestrian traffic was so thick that it was difficult to walk. At one intersection, a group of Peruvian musicians performed—a strange sight in this part of the world.

From Maastricht, we drove a few miles to another castle, Château Neercanne, built in 1698 AD, just inside Holland at the Belgian border, and the only terraced castle in the country, built into a hillside. As our dining destination for the evening, I hoped to take some photos in daylight. Unfortunately, much of the structure rested under scaffolding, awaiting work to be done on its decaying stonework.

Caves dotted the hillside behind the castle and one was used as its massive wine cellar. The caves dated back to Roman times when a particular type of yellow limestone was mined for the construction of buildings. During World War II, Rembrandt's *Night Watch* and other precious artworks were hidden in these caves. Tours used to be given but they no longer were available to the public.

We drove through more small villages along the Maas and inland. After stopping for coffee in one of them we went on to Vaals, located on the highest hill in the Netherlands, just over a thousand feet. A monument at the top marks the intersection of Holland, Belgium and Germany. In three short steps around it one can literally walk in three different countries. As typical tourists, this was exactly what we did. With its small villages and rolling hills, this area reminded me of the Cotswolds in England.

Once back at our hotel, we all rested for a couple of hours before taking a taxi back to Château Neercanne for another evening of decadent dining. Our hotel provided the taxi service and made the reservations for us. It took about thirty minutes to reach the château.

When we arrived, we were given a tour of the wine cellar in the cave and offered a glass of Dutch white wine produced using grapes from a nearby vineyard. The cave was lit with many candles and in the several rooms we wandered through, we noticed cases of French wines.

Once inside the Château, we were pleasantly surprised by the ambience of the dining room. Although the exterior of the building was far from restored, the interior had been extensively redecorated. While Kasteel Erenstein had rustic charm, Neercaans radiated elegance with its grey silk-fabric walls hung with bright impressionist paintings of local landscapes. A woman played soft piano music throughout the evening, albeit without passion. Dinner lasted four hours. We were again treated to a multi-course extravaganza with scallops in a fresh tomato sauce, salmon tartare on a bed of leeks, pheasant, Roquefort mousse, cheeses, a plate of four desserts, coffee, and another small cake for a finale.

In a room adjacent to us, a group of about twenty men attended some sort of celebration. When the pianist took a break, one of them took over the piano and played everything from Mozart to New Orleans jazz. He played with a passion and the diners adored him. The evening flew by and we finally took a taxi to our hotel at 1:15 a.m.

We decided on a late breakfast and, with bags packed, Charles drove through the countryside to Antwerp, Belgium. The second we crossed the Belgian border we knew we had entered another country. Housing looked simpler and farms lacked the manicured appearance of those in Holland.

Since Antwerp rests in the northern part of Belgium, it is Flemish. When we arrived in the city, Charles drove us to our hotel, the De Rosier, and we all said our goodbyes. Charles and Carla departed for their home and Wayne and I checked into our newest old hotel. From the street it appeared quite simple with only a plain green door to welcome guests.

Once inside, the interior was exquisite. With only ten guest rooms, there must have been just as many common rooms on the first floor. The building dated from the 1600s, when it was the residence of Antwerp nobility. In more recent times it served as a training residence for nuns working in the Belgian Congo. The nuns painted the walls in dark shades of brown and black and wallpapered over all the windows to protect their privacy.

In 1972, three men with backgrounds in antiques and decorating purchased the home and restored it even beyond its former glory. With jewel tones in the main rooms, marble floors, antique rugs and furnishings, and walls filled with art, the home-turned-hotel simply wowed us. A bar/restaurant faced the central courtyard. An indoor pool resembling a Roman bath looked inviting after our long weekend but we hadn't packed bathing suits. When we mentioned this, we were assured that it wasn't a problem. We could have the key to the pool and use it at our leisure with or without a swim suit. Our elegant room had fabric-covered walls, velvet trimmed drapes, an antique settee and armoire, and lovely oil paintings. We never heard a sound from any of the other guests. Seemingly unrelated to the ambience of the room, it was named the Hiawatha.

We unpacked once again and, with a map in hand, went into the streets in search of a restaurant for a late lunch followed by some sightseeing. The hotel's dining room was closed on Sundays but did offer a simple room service menu. We opted for a walk and stopped at the Preud'homme. I ordered salmon with a light pear sauce and Wayne opted for turbot. Both choices were delicious.

After lunch we toured the imposing Cathedral of Our Lady of Antwerp, built between 1352 and 1521 AD. Dominating the city's skyline, it featured impressive paintings by Reuben and other famous Flemish artists. From there we walked to the Royal Museum of Fine Arts, a neoclassical building housing another fine collection of Flemish art. The second floor showcased more works by Reuben than anywhere else in the world. Paintings by renowned artist such as Rembrandt, Van Eyck, Van Dyke, Ruysdael, and many more graced the walls. Hung in one of the rooms were fifteen paintings by Breughels, one of our favorites. His art offered the viewer a detailed glimpse into life from the late 1500s to the early 1600s AD. Just as we completed our self-guided tour, the lights began to flash signaling the museum's closure.

One of our hotel's owners booked an 8:00 p.m. dinner reservation for us at Relais Esterel located just a few blocks from us. When we arrived on this Sunday evening, we saw only one other couple, who left by 8:30 p.m. Talk about having the restaurant to ourselves! A full staff of waiters guided us through our five-course dinner. Wayne's scallops and my casserole of wild mushrooms received top marks from us. We also enjoyed the trout pâté, lamb and au gratin potatoes. The inevitable cheese course followed, topped off by a delicious chocolate mousse.

The next morning, Wayne left at 7:00 a.m. for a business meeting in Turnhout. I slipped back into bed and slept until his call at 11:00 a.m. Exhaustion from our varied travels caught up with me. After a very late breakfast, I made my way to the central square in the old part of Antwerp and bought two aprons and small boxes of hand-shaped chocolates.

The chocolates tell an interesting tale. It is said that in Roman times a landowner along the river stopped each boat that passed and demanded an exorbitant tax. If the boat owner couldn't pay, the landowner chopped off his hand and tossed it into the river. Finally, a Roman soldier confronted the landowner and, in retaliation, chopped off the landowner's hand. This grisly story—some say nothing more than a fairytale—is believed to this day by many residents of Antwerp. A massive statue of a Roman soldier holding a severed hand serves as the focal point in Antwerp's town square. The hand-shaped candies pay tribute to the legend and the name Antwerp literally means hand-throwing.

With just a little time to spare before Wayne arrived for our ride to the airport, I returned to the Cathedral of Our Lady of Antwerp. Although Reuben's *The Elevation of the Cross* and *The Descent from the Cross* were under restoration, *The Assumption of the Virgin Mary*, part of the tryptic, graced the main altar in brilliant reds, blues and greens. The back half of the cathedral was also undergoing major restoration but a glassed viewing area gave visitors a glimpse of the work in progress.

Wayne returned at 3:30 p.m. and we drove to the airport for our short flight to Frankfurt, Germany. We arrived just after 6:30 p.m. and met Wayne's Dutch business friends Coen and Charles a few minutes later. A cab ride took all of us to the Hotel Monopol across the street from the train station. Although the rooms had recently been restored, plaster dust covered the hallways. Workmen appeared at 7:00 a.m. the next day to work on the hallway. Coupled with the construction of a building just beyond our window, it made our stay unmemorable.

The next morning, Wayne departed with Charles and Coen for bank meetings and I left shortly afterward armed with a book touting a self-guided six-hour tour. As I've done since my first trip to Europe, I explore each new city on foot. My guide book pointed out that Frankfurt was not meant for tourists; it primarily functioned as a financial center. World War II took out most of the city's historic buildings and, in my opinion, the post-war replacements looked starkly plain. Only one square block of the old city had been restored to its former glory.

My guide book mentioned a good shopping area, so I headed toward the Zeil. I stopped in a few shops along a side street that featured designer boutiques. A red strapless cocktail dress priced at US$100 tempted me but I resisted. I also oohed and ahhed over a black velvet cocktail suit with hand beading and silk flowers priced at US$800. The prices were bargains compared to what I could find in the States and I had a good time browsing.

Finding my way to the old section of Frankfurt near the Main River, I visited the reconstructed Romberg Square. Buildings damaged during the war had been painstakingly restored using city records and photos as guides. I found this small but historically significant area charming. Near the square sat the 13th-century Nikolaikirche with its high red stone tower, a survivor from the war. In contrast to its exterior, the interior of the church had an ultramodern design. A second church, the Cathedral of St. Bartholomew, stood just off the square. I chose an outdoor café on the old Romberg Square called the Standefamtchen for a typical lunch of sausages, sauerkraut and potatoes.

I returned to the hotel to meet Wayne, Charles and Coen for a ride to the airport. One of the banks the men visited today offered their personal driver and they accepted. Little did they realize that this meant a speedy ride to the airport, a substantial distance from our hotel, cruising at 130 miles per hour. We're talking a very fast trip! I'm happy to report that there were no American tourists around any of the turns cruising at a reasonable seventy miles per hour. We would have taken them out on impact.

Our one-hour flight to Paris went smoothly and we taxied to the Élysées Hotel on Rue la Boétie located just a few blocks from the Champs Élysées. This relatively small hotel is quiet and comfortable and, for Paris, reasonable. Although it didn't measure up to the Meurice where we stayed on our first Paris visit, it satisfied all our needs.

Charles, who is fluent in five languages, took us for pre-dinner drinks at a nearby bar/restaurant called Le Boeuf sur le Toit. That translates to *The Steer on the Roof*. The décor was 1930s Art Deco and enormous baskets of mussels on ice greeted us at the entrance. Wall to wall with diners, the restaurant exuded gaiety and contentment. To add to the atmosphere, a piano player churned out memorable tunes. We could easily imagine Edith Piaf singing here as she played the piano.

We then went to a restaurant a few blocks away called the Alain Raye for the ultimate French feast. On one of his Paris visits, Charles had asked his taxi driver for restaurant suggestions and this topped the list. Portions were small, thank heavens. We began with a dish of scrambled egg with salmon and red caviar topped with a trout mousse. Baskets filled with mouthwatering rolls were passed frequently. Next came lobster and shrimp in a light curry sauce with white beans. We enjoyed grilled carp followed by sweetbreads on a bed of couscous. The inevitable cheese trolley filled with French selections arrived and was followed by an elaborate dessert presentation with tray after tray offering cream puffs, cakes, sugared grapes, caramel with honey, a custard-filled chocolate cake, and more. We literally tried these temptations until we had to admit defeat and could not be tempted to indulge any further. This evening's fare was sinfully divine. I'd dined and gone to heaven.

Can you believe that I actually ordered a continental breakfast the next morning? I just can't resist rich French coffee and perfect pastries, and the service in this hotel was perfection. When the waiter returned for my tray, he brought a fresh pot of coffee.

The day's beautiful weather proved ideal for walking. I had planned to master the Paris underground railways but not on a day like this. Since I am somewhat dyslexic and have absolutely no map-reading skills, I walked the three blocks I had memorized to the Champs Élysées. Once there I realized I had the location of the Residence Champs Élysées all wrong and was surprised to find that the Arc de Triomphe was on my right and not on my left. Once I got my bearings, I went on to the Place de la Concorde and backtracked on the Rue du Faubourg Saint-Honoré. On my previous trips to Paris I hadn't spent much time window shopping and the Rue Saint-Honoré was one of the places to find the best in fashion.

After stopping in several boutiques, I popped into the Ted Lapidis shop in quest of a deal on sunglasses. Almost immediately a salesman approached me holding a US$10,000 leather jacket that he assured me I couldn't live without owning. I slipped into it and although it was beyond fabulous, I decided life would go on without it. The salesman then brought out a red dress with large black buttons, the picture of simple elegance. At his insistence I tried it on and, although it did look sensational, I resisted. Telling him that I had just begun my day of shopping, I thanked him and left the boutique.

At noon I headed back to the Place de la Concorde and crossed a bridge to the Left Bank on a quest to locate a maritime antique shop for a friend in San Marino, California. He purchased an expensive antique maritime globe five months earlier and it hadn't arrived. He couldn't find his receipt and he had no idea what the shop's name was or precisely where it was located. My mission was to find the shop and ask why the globe had not been delivered to our friend.

All the information he could give me was that the shop sat on an angle on a corner in the antique district not far from the Musée d'Orsay. I found my way to Rue de Bac and utilized this as a starting point. Deciding to walk in a concentric circle around the nearest block, I spotted a small shop situated on an angle on the corner. Delighted that my sleuthing assignment had been successful, I crossed the street and discovered a furniture store. When I asked the saleswoman if the shop replaced a maritime antiques business, I soon realized she spoke no English.

I began to walk around block after block and noted that each corner had an angled shop situated on it. An hour later, after circling what seemed like countless blocks, I was about to give up my quest. I turned the final corner and there stood a small maritime antique shop. Voila! Feeling like a spy, I ducked around the corner and wrote down the name of the shop and of the intersecting streets where it stood. If the salesman had pulled a fast one on our friend, I wanted to have information to give him when I returned Stateside.

Entering the shop, I asked the elegantly dressed owner the ultimate ugly American question, "Do you speak English?" He paused and answered,

"A little." Very slowly I began to explain how our friend purchased an expensive globe and it never arrived. That was all I had to explain. He threw his arms into the air and, grinning from ear to ear, said, "At last you are finally here!"

It turned out that his English was good. He explained how another frequent client from Connecticut had written to him around the time that our friend bought his antique globe. This client purchased a smaller globe valued at a tenth the price of the one our friend bought. By mistake, the shop owner sent our friend's globe to his Connecticut client COD. The poor client nearly had a heart attack when he saw the price and refused to accept the globe.

In the meantime, the antiques dealer had cashed our friend's check and, with no address for him, had no idea how to make contact. Knowing that our friend resided in California, he sent the globe to San Francisco for storage, hoping our friend would contact him. The dealer had already paid more than US$300 in storage fees and that added to his delight in making contact with me. He was so excited that he insisted on calling my friend even though it was very early in the morning in California. Needless to say, my friend did not mind a 5:00 a.m. wake-up call with news that the globe mystery was solved.

Since my globe quest brought me almost to the doorsteps of the Musée d'Orsay, I backtracked to it and entered the museum. Constructed between 1898 and 1900, this magnificent Beaux-Arts edifice is worth seeing on its own. Once inside, one can visit a vast collection of Impressionist and post-Impressionist works by Cezanne, Monet, Manet, Pissaro, Renoir, Degas, Van Gogh, and Tissot, just to mention a few. Whistler's famous portrait of his mother also graced the walls. In 2014, this painting came to Pasadena's Norton Simon Museum as part of a temporary art exchange with the Musée d'Orsay and we drove to Pasadena to revisit it.

Leaving the Musée d'Orsay, I crossed the Seine and walked through the Tuileries located between the Louvre and the Place de la Concorde. Created by Catherine de Medici as the garden of the Tuileries Palace in 1564 AD, it opened to the public in 1667 AD and became the first public park after the French Revolution. As I strolled through the Tuileries, colorful leaves dropped from trees, children played and outdoor cafés bustled on this sunny October day. Having missed lunch, I walked on to the Rue de Rivoli and found a spot for a slice of strawberry tart and an espresso. So civilized!

That night, Wayne and I walked along the Champs Élysées with Charles and Coen to Le Lord Gourmand, another restaurant on Charles' list of favorites. We started with escargots followed by delicious warm goat cheese on a bed of braised greens. Wayne ordered fish and I opted for guinea hen. After the inevitable cheese trolley, two dessert trolleys featuring a wide array of sweets arrived at our table. I chose a chocolate gâteau and a floating island, my all-time favorite dessert. Our skilled waiter arranged each selection artistically and, when he presented them, they were almost too pretty to eat. To our delight we all managed to calorie our way through them. Afterward, we walked along the Champs Élysées savoring the aroma of roasting chestnuts.

The next morning, Wayne learned that his business meeting was canceled. After packing our suitcases, we strolled along the streets of Paris. Security around the Élysées Palace was in full force. Trucks with machine-gun-armed military personnel lined the street. We never did learn the reason for their presence. As we walked further, a gorgeous chocolate gâteau caught my attention in the window of a small bakery and I bought it to take to London to share with our friend Faye and Claudia, her German housekeeper.

The duty-free shops in the Paris airport are simply sensational and I bought a beautiful faux pearl and rhinestone necklace. I simply could not resist it. The jewels look authentic and to this day I enjoy wearing it.

When we arrived at Heathrow, we hailed a taxi for a ride to Faye's flat in the heart of St. John's Wood. Our driver practiced the block, tackle and brake approach as he sped out of the airport and onto the street of London. It was a harrowing experience, to say the least, as he wove in and out of the lanes of traffic packed with cars and buses.

Faye had invited us to be guests in her charming flat located directly across from Regent's Park and her Vizslas, Randy and Magic, were the first to greet us. Faye hailed from the San Diego area and named her dogs before her move to London, not realizing that the term randy had a negative connotation in England. Magic was named after Magic Johnson. I adored Faye's beautiful dogs and looked forward to a stroll through Regent's Park with them while she and Wayne attended bank meetings.

After a series of hotels, a stay in Faye's charming flat delighted us. Arriving while Faye was still at work, we sipped coffee and chatted with Claudia, who came to London to study English and hotel management. She lived with Faye and walked the dogs, cooked dinners and did light housekeeping in exchange for a place to reside while she studied.

When Faye returned, we all enjoyed a delicious dinner prepared by Claudia. She served chicken in a mushroom cream sauce with rice and my favorite, Brussels sprouts, which she remembered from an earlier visit. A lovely almond torte with raspberry sauce followed. Claudia cooks without recipes which absolutely amazes me. Later that evening we sampled the chocolate gâteau we brought from Paris and it, too, was divine.

Faye and Wayne departed very early for a day of business so Claudia and I had breakfast by ourselves. I then showered and did the plug-the-hairdryer-in-the-hall routine. My plan for today was to connect with my American friend Karen who now lived in London. She met me at Faye's flat and we taxied to the Royal Academy of Arts to view two special exhibits.

The first, a retrospective of the works by sculptor Henry Moore, filled an entire floor of the Academy. After a number of years in the planning stages, the exhibit was intended as a tribute to the sculptor on his ninetieth birthday. Unfortunately, he died two years before his birthday and missed this impressive celebration. The retrospective represented the largest collection of Moore's sculptures ever assembled in one show. I marveled at the weight that the floor we stood on had to be capable of holding. Karen and I rented tapes that led us through the exhibit and, to our delight, much of the commentary had been recorded by Moore just prior to his death.

The next exhibit was a collection of works by Toulouse-Lautrec, a delightful display of his sketches and colorful finished pieces. I had visited a show in Chicago but seeing the sketches of his famous posters displayed next to the finished works made them even more meaningful.

Karen and I had a light lunch in the museum's cafeteria and then crossed the street to Fortnum and Mason. I purchased some tinned shortbread for a future stateside tea. We then walked through the Burlington Arcade to New Bond Street. A David Hockney exhibit that was first shown in Los Angeles now was at the Tate Museum in London. Karen had heard that an art dealer had a few of his works. We found the shop and concluded that the works were substandard for Hockney. It appeared as though he had produced them hurriedly in hopes of sales to the British during his Tate showing. One of the works on display had drips of paint that looked accidental rather than planned. Nevertheless, Hockney's fabulous use of color did shine through.

Tonight's dinner with Karen and her husband Bill at Le Gavroche in Mayfair delighted us, both for the exquisitely prepared food and the company. We ordered a five-course menu that began with goose liver and truffles. A dish of langostinos and scallops was followed by breast of pheasant with mushrooms. After the cheese course we were presented a vanilla soufflé topped with an apple sauce. Gourmet dining was alive and well in London.

The next morning, Faye and Claudia left the flat early. Since it was a Saturday, I went into the kitchen to make a pot of coffee. I put four spoons of what I thought were coffee beans into the grinder and soon discovered from the strange smell that I had dipped into the dog food container.

Wayne and I took a taxi to the General Trading Company, a favorite of the royals as well as the upper crust of London. Charming! Next on our agenda was Beauchamp Place, pronounced "Beech-ham" by the Brits. This one-block-long street featured a number of boutiques and specialty stores. At one of them, the Reject China Shop, I found a teapot to match our Cottage Garden demitasse cups that I had purchased at Harrods on a previous trip. Its flaw was so miniscule that it was almost unnoticeable and it was a bargain.

We made our way toward Harrods and passed the International Amateur Athletics Federation's London headquarters. Since it was a Saturday, the offices were closed. I had stopped to say hello to friends I had met from the 1984 Summer Olympics in Los Angeles on my last trip to London and they were so surprised to see me. They said most volunteers do not take the time while in town to pay a visit. I had worked closely with the staff from London in my role as Assistant Protocol Manager of Athletics and enjoyed seeing them on their home turf.

Returning to Regent Street, we were overwhelmed by throngs of Saturday afternoon shoppers. We popped into a Liberty shop and found it just as packed with people. Our next quest was to find 84 Charing Cross Road and the bookstore from the novel with the same title. It is no longer there but a plaque commemorating it remained.

After another wonderful dinner cooked by Claudia, Faye drove us to the Globe Theatre. We saw *Lettice and Lovage*, a delightful comedy about an overly zealous tour guide with a flair for the dramatic and her overly prim and proper employer. We concluded the evening with coffee and dessert in Faye's flat. What a pampered life we were living!

The next day the four of us headed for the Embankment via the tube for a boat ride to Greenwich. It was a bright sunny Sunday but the temperature had dropped considerably overnight and it was cold. We boarded the boat and headed along the Thames past the Tower of London and other significant sites. When we docked at Greenwich, we noted a sailing ship that now served as a museum. With not much time, we opted to tour the National Maritime Museum, an impressive complex in the heart of the town opened in 1937 by King George VI. The building, completed in 1807 as a school for the children of seafarers, displayed ship models and plans dating from the 17th century, as well as globes, chronometers, navigational instruments, and a fine collection of Dutch and British maritime artwork.

A Sunday flea market covering several blocks caught our attention. Faye bought some books and Claudia purchased a few prints. After our early afternoon leisurely boat ride to Greenwich we opted for a train ride back to the Embankment and then took the tube to Faye's flat.

Following a romp for the dogs and hot coffee for us, we walked a few blocks to Tina's, a new restaurant just off the High Street. At Faye's suggestion, I ordered broiled Dover sole and it was outstanding. During dinner, Faye and Claudia told us about the raincoats and boots they have for the dogs. When we returned to the flat, Claudia dressed Magic in foul-weather gear and we all had a good laugh. Magic was a good sport and pranced around like a trotter.

With full sunshine the next day, I applied Barbara's Rule of Travel—when the sun shines, take advantage of it. I bought an all-day tube pass and headed out to explore. My first stop, Gray's Antiques, housed a number of stalls featuring silver, china and art. I spotted a small floral print from a book published in 1843. It came with a provenance—a paper of authenticity. Since the price was reasonable, I bought it as a memento of our 1988 trip. I have always found that art makes the best souvenirs and we have a number of small pieces commemorating our travels.

I took the tube to Green Park and walked along Piccadilly to Fortnum and Mason to purchase some tea. From there I returned to the Burlington Arcade. Karen and I had rushed through it on Friday and it appeared to be a good place to window shop. The shops featuring Irish linens were lovely, as were the price tags.

Claudia prepared another delicious meal for our final evening in London. We all sat in Faye's living room and chatted until almost midnight. It was such a treat to stay with Faye and we thanked her and Claudia profusely for their hospitality.

And so ended another memorable overseas adventure.

FAMILY TRIP TO LONDON AND EUROPE

London, Amsterdam, Munich, Wallgau, Berchtesgaden, Salzburg,
and Paris

August 10–28, 1989

THE SMITH FAMILY trip to London and Europe that we all had dreamed about for years was about to become a reality. Liz, age 17, and Emily, just shy of her 16th birthday, had traveled vicariously through us for years as we shared memories of our overseas adventures. It was finally time for the girls, Wayne and me to take a family trip abroad. We all did our last-minute packing and managed to stay within our one-suitcase limit—at least for the time being.

We checked our bags and managed to get to our departure gate at LAX just in time for our flight to Dallas, then boarded a plane for an eight-hour connection to London's Gatwick Airport. All went well until we arrived at Gatwick. We encountered a series of long delays, beginning with a gate for the plane to disembark, a tram to take us to the baggage claim area and then an hour's wait to clear customs. In all my travels, this was the worst entry we'd ever experienced, but we were finally about to begin our London adventure.

On our way to the flat we'd rented for a week, our driver took us through Wimbledon and past the famed tennis club, through Chelsea and Battersea Park, and we arrived at 2:00 p.m. Liz and Emily were exhausted and slept for a few hours after unpacking. Wayne and I, old troopers that we were, headed for the Safeway on Kings Road and bought basics along with some scones and jars of Devonshire cream and jams. Lugging our purchases took some doing but we'd be in good shape for breakfasts and snacks.

Located at 15 Sloane Gardens, our flat was situated at the top floor of a four-story red bacon brick building. Nicely furnished in English chintz, it offered us plenty of space with two bedrooms, a full bath, living room, and kitchen. Cozy and quiet, it was perfectly situated close to the Sloane Square tube. Beauchamps Place, Cadogan Square and Harrods were just short walks from us.

Wayne and I had our English non-tea with coffee and some biscuits from our food run and then took a one-hour nap until 6:00 p.m. The girls woke reluctantly and the four of us left the flat for a walk and dinner. The summer's six weeks of record-breaking heat had ended the day before we arrived, following a much-needed rain storm. With temperatures hovering between sixty-five and seventy degrees instead of the ninety-plus that we anticipated, we considered purchasing a sweater or two.

We wandered through Sloane Square and on to Knightsbridge. Our girls fell instantly in love with London as Wayne led us through small side streets and along the shops on Beauchamps Place. Since the pubs we passed were full this Friday night, we opted for the Spaghetti House Ristorante on Knightsbridge near Harvey Nichols. After a pasta/pizza fix we walked back to our flat. On the way, Emily bought fresh flowers at an outdoor market to brighten our home for the next week.

Everyone was up by 8:30 a.m. the next day, and after breakfast and showers we headed down Kings Road to Buckingham Palace. A crowd had already formed for the Changing of the Guard. We stood with the masses of humanity only to learn that the ceremony had just been rescheduled for every other day and today wasn't one of them. We'd have to catch this impressive ceremony at another time.

We walked through St. James's Park and its gardens before reaching #10 Downing Street. On my first visit to London in 1980, we could walk right up to the Prime Minister's dwelling but, with political disruptions abounding, one now had to view #10 from a guarded barricade placed at the street's entrance which remains in place to this day.

Our next stops were Big Ben and Parliament. We listened to Big Ben strike noon and then crossed the street to Westminster Abbey. Still suffering from jet lag coupled with the absence of hamburgers, her favorite food, Emily turned ghost white as we entered the cathedral. Wayne sat with her while Liz and I viewed the tombs of British monarchs and watched a number of visitors making brass rubbings.

When Emily felt better, she and Wayne joined us in the Poets' Corner. Buried here are Robert Browning, T.S. Eliot, Rudyard Kipling, Charles Dickens, Louis Carroll, Alfred Tennyson, and many more. The girls were in awe.

We then took a taxi to Harrods and spotted a Wolfe's Restaurant across the street. Since Emily was in dire need of a burger fix, we opted for Wolfeburgers in lieu of the Harrods cafeteria. Although the burgers cost a small fortune, they were very good.

Next, we walked along the first two levels of Harrods. I led everyone through the food hall and we bumped into friends from Wayne's company. Small world! We made plans to meet them for dinner the following evening.

From there we walked back to our neighborhood and strolled along the boutiques on Sloane Street. Emily spotted a pair of black leather boots she couldn't live without in the Pied a Terre shop and we bought them for her as an early birthday gift. While the girls popped into a couple more boutiques and bought some English makeup in a small pharmacy, Wayne and I headed back to the flat for another non-tea with coffee and shortbread.

Faye, our American friend living in London, appeared at 5:00 p.m. with tickets for tonight's Bolshoi Ballet, her welcome-to-London treat for the four of us. Although she was not able to join us for the ballet, we were delighted by her visit and generous gift.

We hailed a taxi to the Royal Opera House in Covent Garden. Thank heavens we allowed enough time! After discovering that the venue for tonight's performance was actually the London Coliseum, we quickly walked the few blocks and managed to be in our seats by curtain time.

The night's performance of *Swan Lake* was danced to perfection. We all agreed that the dancer playing the jester stole the show with his charismatic leaps. The twenty-four women portraying swans performed in perfect unison and the applause at the end of the ballet lasted fifteen minutes. The stage seemed to transform into a flower garden with layer upon layer of bouquets tossed on the stage. We would always cherish the memory of this evening.

Not far from the theatre we spotted a café that was still open. Emily read the menu posted at the entrance and noted that it served hamburgers. We were in business! With no taxis in sight when we finished, we took a tube ride back to our flat and agreed that our first full day in London met all our expectations and then some.

The next day we took the tube to Covent Garden. Emily, always spotting deals, bought a skirt and blouse in Boules. We then wandered around the Covent Garden Market for an hour and the girls purchased some English soaps to bring to their friends.

Our next stop was the British Museum. I had previously visited on a weekday in October and encountered very few visitors, but throngs of people crowded the museum on this August Sunday afternoon. In spite of the crowds, we managed to see the Rosetta Stone, ancient Egyptian sculptures, the Elgin Marbles from the Parthenon, and some Assyrian friezes. We ventured upstairs to see the Egyptian mummy display and, although the room overflowed with visitors, our girls were fascinated.

With a sudden burst of energy—funny how shopping could spur them on—the girls decided to check out more of the shops on Kings Road. We all window shopped for four blocks before heading to the flat for our late afternoon coffee and shortbread.

Tonight's walk to meet friends Ann and Bob at their London flat on Walton Street near Hyde Park had its challenges. As we walked along their street, the even-numbered addresses ascended in number, so we assumed that their single digit, odd-numbered flat was located in the opposite direction. We turned around and still couldn't find the flat. As it turned out, one side of the street listed even numbers from low to high and the opposite side, odd numbers from high to low.

The evening's dinner at one of London's newest hot spots, Scalini, had it all—ambience, service and good food. The choices included everything from free-range chicken and veal to a variety of pasta dishes. Hamburgers were not on the menu, but Emily thoroughly enjoyed her pasta selection.

The next day marked the twentieth anniversary of British military presence in Northern Ireland when troops were sent in to quell the IRA uprisings. The Brits beefed up security in London anticipating a potential reprisal and we had been warned by our British friends to avoid significant tourist spots within the city.

Deciding that it made no sense to be in the right place at the wrong time, we postponed our London sightseeing for the day and opted to visit Hampton Court Palace. We took the tube to the Waterloo station and then a train to Hampton Court. This marked my second visit and the first for Wayne, Liz and Emily. Hampton Court Palace offers one of the finest examples of Tudor architecture. In 1689 AD, a baroque addition designed by Christopher Wren was commissioned by William III who felt that the palace built for Cardinal Wolsey in 1514 AD was outdated. You may recall that Henry VIII removed Cardinal Wolsey from Hampton Court Palace and brought all six of his wives there. Queen Victoria opened the palace and its hedge maze to the public in 1838 and it has remained a draw for millions of visitors, including the four of us on this day.

We toured the Tudor kitchens, envisioning the well-fed Henry VIII feasting on whole legs of lamb. We then visited the royal apartments and the dining hall with its magnificent Flemish tapestries from the 15th and 16th centuries. My favorite was *The Triumph of Fame over Death*.

The original chapel had a magnificent two-story altar that arrived in pieces by barge and was assembled on site much like a giant jigsaw puzzle. It sat below a vaulted ceiling, also prefabricated and assembled in much the same manner. The gilt sparkled against the vibrant royal blue background.

In 1986, the baroque addition commissioned by William and Mary was nearly destroyed in a fire. Now, three years later, it was being painstakingly reconstructed at a cost of twelve million pounds. Every effort had been made to duplicate the original craftsmanship, although fireproofing was discretely added. The work was expected to take ten years to complete.

Suddenly we were hustled out of the palace by a guard who quite calmly told us that there was an alert and we needed to exit quickly. Naively, we had assumed that Hampton Court was far enough outside of London to merit a worry-free visit today. From what we later heard, there had been an idle threat but one not to be ignored at the time. We were grateful to have been able to see most of the palace before being asked to leave.

Once safely outside, we headed for the maze, a complex system of hedgerows. We wound our way along the high rows of boxwood and became thoroughly entangled in the maze. To complicate matters, a light rain began to fall. Boy Scout Wayne skillfully led us to the entrance by making left-hand turns at the end of each row. Brilliant!

We hopped on the train to London and the girls asked us a question about Wales. A delightful woman in front of us turned around and told us she was from Wales. By the time we reached London, she had mapped out a tour that we all hoped to follow someday. She suggested that we enter the north of Wales at Chester, a walled city near Liverpool and explained that "chester" always referred to a Roman walled city. She recommended the Blossom Hotel with its beamed ceilings and old-world charm.

From there we should visit Caernarfon Castle, pronounced Carnarvon, where the Prince of Wales is crowned, and then take the mountain road to Snowden. She described the northern mountain region as breathtaking and told us the Mt. Everest team of thirty years ago did their training on the peaks of Tryfan. From there, she suggested a trip through the Wye Valley with a stop at Hay on Wye to visit one of the world's largest book markets.

While in southern Wales she told us not to miss Beddgelert, where a dog's grave commemorates the tale of a dog saving a child from a wolf, only to be shot by his owner when it appeared with a foaming mouth. After the owner found his young son sitting next to a dead wolf, he realized the dog was a hero. She also recommended the town of Laugharne, pronounced *Larn*, the home of Dylan Thomas, whose boathouse at the time served as a museum/tea room; Tenby, home of famous Welsh painter Augustus John; and a stop at Tintern Abbey, the gothic masterpiece founded in 1131 AD on the bank of the River Wye. Not many years later, Wayne and I followed many of her suggestions on a trip through Wales but in reverse order, beginning at Tintern Abbey.

Once in London, we took the tube to Piccadilly Circus, which lived up to its name. It was an absolute mob scene and we opted to return to Sloane Square. Wayne and the girls cruised Kings Road while I put my feet up and wrote in my journal.

There wasn't one word on the evening news about a bomb threat at Hampton Court Palace. I wondered how many other venues experienced similar evacuations today. We will never know.

The next day would long be remembered as the Smith Family Marathon Day. We met our driver, John, at 9:00 a.m. in front of the flat and headed out of London for a drive to Eton College and Windsor Castle. Although no formal Changing of the Guard took place today, the girls were able to watch a small ceremony in the castle's courtyard just as the gates opened to the public at 10:00 a.m. We viewed Queen Mary's Dolls' House and toured the State Apartments, enjoying the looks of awe on our daughters' faces as they viewed the splendor of Windsor Castle. We then visited the Albert Memorial Chapel and St. George's Chapel with tombs of Henry VIII, Jane Seymour and Charles I, and a resplendent display of the banners and crests of the Order of the Garter.

Our next stop, the Compleat Angler in Marlow, tops the list of favorite inns for Wayne and me. We wanted to share it with our girls, even though we were not staying there on this trip. Situated on the Thames, it was a favorite fishing spot for Izaak Walton who wrote the book, *The Compleat Angler*. The inn's name pays tribute to him. We found a table with a lovely view and had coffee before moving on.

We then drove to Oxford. After a light lunch at the Poor Students' Café, we toured Christ Church College, Queens College courtyard and New College, dating from 1397 AD—not really so new after all. I had toured Christ Church College nine years earlier but had forgotten that it was founded and built by Wolsey from 1525-1529 AD and had been originally named Cardinal College. As he had with Hampton Court, Henry VIII snatched the college from the powerful Wolsey and rededicated it as Christ Church College in 1546 AD.

On our earlier visit to Oxford, an elderly priest we randomly met offered to take us through the Christ Church Chapel and then to a tree on the grounds which he said had inspired Louis Carroll to write *Alice in Wonderland*. We wanted to show the tree to Liz and Emily on this trip but the area where it stood was no longer open to the public.

After purchasing Oxford sweatshirts for the girls, we rejoined our driver and headed for Blenheim Palace in Woodstock. Dating to 1722 AD, it was another memorable place Wayne and I had visited previously. The residence of the Dukes of Marlborough, it was the only non-royal country house in England to hold the title of palace. We noted that the entrance now stood at the back of the palace along Capability Brown's lake and landscaped grounds. On our first visit in 1980, much of what we saw today was not open to the public and there was now an exhibit featuring Winston Churchill, who was born at Blenheim. It was almost like seeing the palace for the first time.

At 5:00 p.m. we left Blenheim and drove to Bourton-on-the-Water in the Cotswolds. From there we visited Upper Slaughter and went on to Lower Slaughter where we walked along a small stream meandering through the village. Nine years before, Wayne and I stopped at the Lower Slaughter Manor House and chatted with the owners. We learned that they had sold the manor house in 1987 and it had been meticulously restored by the new owners. What we had dubbed charming nine years ago now emanated elegance.

We hopped into our limo at 6:45 p.m. for a return ride to London. Although we were tempted to go through Stonehenge, an additional two hours' drive persuaded us to skip it. When we arrived at our flat just after 8:00 p.m. we all agreed that our long day had been filled with truly memorable experiences.

It brought Wayne and me so much joy to share many of the places so special to us with Liz and Emily. We provided them with a large dose of history, architecture and spectacular views and they kept pace throughout the day. Years from now they wouldn't believe how much we accomplished in just eleven hours.

Having promised the girls a dinner at London's Hard Rock Café, we chose to make that happen tonight. We headed for the restaurant at 9:00 p.m. and stood for nearly an hour before being seated. Our burgers and fries arrived at 10:45 p.m. What a day!

After a leisurely start the next morning, we purchased all-day tube passes and joined the Tower of London queue just before noon. Although the line stretched for almost a block, it moved quickly and we entered in less than half an hour. The Tower of London dated to the 1200s and it stood as a top attraction. Since this was Wayne's and my second visit, we conducted our own tour, including the Traitors' Gate, the Bloody Tower, the block where Anne Boleyn was beheaded, and the recently reopened Crown Jewels exhibit. The jewels on display, now easier to view, included the Star diamond and a collection of royal crowns and scepters—all magnificent. We then visited the torture room and the White Tower, filled with armor and weapons used through the centuries.

It was mid-afternoon when we left the Tower of London in search of a spot for lunch. After walking a few blocks with no success, we opted for the tube to Green Park and the Richoux Tea Room. I had stopped for a late lunch on a previous trip and knew it would be open. We were all ready to rest and to Emily's delight she spotted hamburgers on the menu. Liz was far easier to please.

After lunch we walked through the Burlington Arcade to Regents Street and the famed Liberty shop. We made a few small purchases and then went on to Carnaby Street. It was wild and crazy and the girls loved everything about it.

On impulse we hopped on a double-decker bus and sat on the upper level. The bus exited Regents Street onto Oxford. When we reached the Marble Arch we hopped off and took the tube back to our flat, arriving at 8:00 p.m. After another long day of sightseeing we all agreed that our late lunch counted as dinner and we looked forward to an early bedtime.

We found it difficult to believe that the next day, beautifully bright and sunny, was our last full day in London. Liz and Emily wanted to see where Charles and Diana had wed, so we traveled by tube to St. Paul's Cathedral, Christopher Wren's masterpiece begun in 1675 AD. As none of us had the energy to climb the 259 steps to the Whispering Gallery, we sat in pews and admired the exquisite altar and dome.

Our next stops were Green Park and Buckingham Palace. We arrived at 11:30 a.m. just as the military band marched down the Mall announcing the Changing of the Guard. Standing on a fence rail across from the Palace, we had a better view than most of the spectators packed in front of us.

Walking back toward our flat we noticed a pub in Cadogan Square and decided to give it a try for lunch. Since day one in London I'd tried to convince the girls that a pub lunch was not to be missed. With no other options they finally agreed. Wayne and I ordered our usual plowman's lunch consisting of a roll with cheese, chutney and pickles. Liz chose a chicken casserole and Emily ordered a baked potato and French fries, her two favorite foods after hamburgers.

We headed on to Beauchamps Place and the Reject China Shop. Liz hoped to find a miniature tea set to add to her collection and, sure enough, she did. Emily bought a china tea cup and saucer and I purchased an Irish Belleek vase. We then stopped at the General Trading Company which, as always, was filled with beautiful china and gift items. While Wayne kept himself busy in the luggage room, the girls and I made a complete loop through the shop before returning to our nearby flat.

After a short rest and a change into fancier clothes, we went to the Savoy for high tea. We thoroughly enjoyed the tea sandwiches, scones with clotted cream and the lovely tray of small desserts. The ambience was exquisite and we all agreed that this experience was, as the English say, lovely!

For our final evening in London we hailed a taxi and headed for the theatre district. With tickets in hand, we entered the Palace Theatre for a production of *Les Misérables*. The musical was everything we had hoped for and more. We had excellent seats and enjoyed seeing the musical in this intimate venue.

Afterward, we walked a few short blocks to an Italian restaurant called Café Rossini on Green Street. Having chosen this spot for no particular reason we were delighted by the quality of the dishes and the exceptional service. We were so full after our entrées that we passed on the tiramisu and when we mentioned that we regretted our decision not to give it a try, the owner brought a large slice and four forks. It was the best we had ever tasted.

We asked the owner to call a taxi and a driver in a Mercedes limo soon appeared. Our driver was a friend of the owner and we were sure it would cost a small fortune. He was charming and drove us directly to our flat, charging us the going taxi fare.

Next morning's packing proved to be difficult with all our additional London purchases. We dashed back to the General Trading Company and purchased large canvas carry bags that Wayne had spotted a day earlier. Now we had room for all our recent acquisitions and then some.

After a taxi ride to Heathrow at noon, we cleared customs quickly for our flight to Amsterdam. We relaxed during an almost two-hour delay and eventually boarded. Apparently, airline delays are commonplace during July and August.

With a one-hour time change we landed in Amsterdam at 5:00 p.m. and arrived at our hotel less than an hour later. The Hotel Ambassade, located at 341 Herengracht on the second ring canal from the centrum, was one Wayne and I had noticed on a trip in 1980 and which was actually a collection of seven row houses. Nine years later, here we were with our daughters. Our building, one of the original homes along the canal, offered charming views of the narrow Dutch houses on the waterway directly across from us.

After getting situated in our two-story room, we had coffee in the lounge and then walked a few blocks for a 7:30 p.m. canal ride. Since the sun set very late during the Dutch summers, it proved a perfect time for the hour-long ride. The canal tour was a repeat for Wayne and me but we knew it would provide a good introduction to Amsterdam for our daughters. Sharing a camera, we snapped a full roll of film as we glided through the canals.

There are more than a hundred canals in Amsterdam. On the few we traversed, we saw a church built in 1614 AD, some of the three thousand houseboats, the Amsterdam Harbor with a floating restaurant that seated nine hundred, the narrowest house—only a window's width in size, the cat boat with more than twenty felines living on board, a 15th-century bridge, the narrowest canal with houses built into the water as in Venice, and finally a canal where one could view seven bridges in a row. Our daughters were fascinated.

The girls had asked about the Red-Light District, so after the canal ride we walked to the area. Liz and Emily were as amazed as we had been when we first saw the scantily clothed sex-for-sale sirens sitting in windows along the walkway in hopes of snaring customers. We cruised through quickly just as the sunlight faded.

One of Emily's Amsterdam pursuits was a T-shirt from a bar/restaurant called the Bulldog. We passed it and she made her purchase. Liz found a miniature tea set nearby that looked like Delft. Returning to our hotel, we asked the man at the desk for a restaurant suggestion and he recommended the Haesje Claes located in an old home with various rooms for diners. We took his counsel and walked the few blocks to the restaurant. Our well-prepared steak, veal and pork were accompanied by steaming bowls of potatoes and vegetables to share. We ate well and the price was more than reasonable. Returning to the hotel just after 11:00 p.m., we all agreed that Wayne's map-reading skills had provided us with a memorable tour of Amsterdam.

The next day began with a full Dutch breakfast of rolls, cold meats, cheeses, and boiled eggs. Our daughters, in the room below ours, admitted they were having a difficult time keeping up with their parents but eventually joined us.

Just as we began our day with a walk along the canal leading to the Rijksmuseum, a bee landed on Wayne's back. Since he is allergic to them, he decided to return to the hotel for his bee sting kit. While waiting for him to return, the girls and I entered a nearby flower shop. The freshly cut flowers and arrangements, all reasonably priced, made us wish we were staying in Amsterdam long enough to justify a purchase.

As we all walked on toward the museum, we passed through an antique district and stopped in a couple of the shops out of curiosity. In one of them we admired several 300-year-old pieces of Delft in perfect condition priced at around US$1,000. In retrospect, I wish I had purchased one of the pieces.

Wayne and I had visited the Rijksmuseum on a previous trip and we enjoyed sharing the art it showcased with Liz and Emily. Topping the list was Rembrandt's *Night Watch*. We also admired works by Vermeer, Steen, Hals, and Brueghel for an hour before heading to the Van Gogh Museum.

Our first order of business was a lunch stop on the museum's patio. Learning that life does go on without hamburgers, Emily ordered shish kabobs, a baked potato, rolls, and pudding. Liz tried some Dutch yogurt.

To our dismay, much of the permanent collection in the Van Gogh Museum was on loan to a museum in São Paulo, Brazil. The good news was that a collection of Impressionist art hung in its place, including pieces by Modigliani, Manet, Cezanne, and Degas. Monet's 1890 *Boating on the Epte* was a highlight along with Renoir's *Marthe Berard* and *Pink and Blue*, the painting of the d'Anvers sisters. Of the many works by Van Gogh that remained, some of our favorites were *Bridge in the Rain, Courtesan, Bedroom in Arles, Vase of Flowers, Field with Irises*, and *Wheatfield with Crows*. We all agreed that the Norton Simon Museum in Pasadena just a few miles away from our San Marino home offered an impressive collection of Van Gogh's art.

We then made our way along more canals to the home where Anne Frank and her family lived from 1942 to 1944. Anne's famous diary described her life as she hid in constant fear of discovery by the Nazis, and we all felt the emotional impact as we stepped beyond the bookcase that disguised the entrance to the cramped quarters where the Frank and Van Pels (a.k.a.Van Daan) families sequestered. The rooms were so small that it was difficult to imagine so many people confined here for two years before their discovery in August of 1944. Only Anne's father survived life in the concentration camps; Anne and her sister perished in a typhoid epidemic. Her diary remains one of the most compelling accounts of the plight of Jewish families during World War II.

That evening, the girls were tired and opted for a room service dinner and a good night's sleep. Wayne and I charged on and walked around the corner for dinner at Casa di David, located on the smallest canal with its narrow buildings set into the water. Although the décor lacked charm, our meal measured up to the best Italian food we had tasted outside of Italy. The restaurant was packed with locals—always a good sign. In spite of extremely slow service, we thoroughly enjoyed our dinner.

Afterward, we walked along the narrow streets and canals for another half hour. On this spectacular evening we walked slowly, admiring the buildings with their gabled rooftops. Our hotel exemplified some of the best architecture in Amsterdam and its collection of buildings looked magnificent lit at night.

I had had a love-hate relationship with Amsterdam over the years. On my first visit in 1980, I was sad to see graffiti and decay on almost every street. Mobs of young dropouts filled the centrum and gathered near the palace. What should have been one of the most beautiful cities in the world looked as if it wouldn't survive. Nine years later it was much cleaner and almost all the graffiti had disappeared. Mobs of young people no longer congregated.

Walking through the streets tonight with stars above and the remarkable buildings softly lit along the canals, I had now fallen in love with Amsterdam.

The next morning, we headed for Schiphol Airport for our flight to Munich. My cousin Dana, her husband Ed and son Mark met us at the airport, making a special trip to have coffee with us before our flight. As always, it was a treat to see them and our gals enjoyed touching base with this part of their family after many years.

Our flight was delayed for almost an hour so we did the next best thing and wandered through the duty-free shops at Schiphol, some of the best in the world, and the girls managed to find some bargains before we boarded. Wayne upgraded us to business class and we had a nice lunch en route to Munich. With clear weather for the entire flight we could see the Rhine and Main Rivers, farms and villages, forests, and finally the Bavarian Alps as we approached Munich.

Following a quick stop at passport control, we soon had our luggage and our rented Mercedes. With only a few unwanted side trips, we arrived at the Conti Hotel on Max-Joseph-Strasse in time to drop off our luggage and head outside for the 5:00 p.m. Glockenspiel performance at the Town Hall. Arriving with just minutes to spare we joined the throngs who had gathered. The music began on the hour and five minutes later the lower tier of figures made their appearance. A series of carved male dancers rotated as their platform revolved. However, the top tier had a mechanical issue and never did move. Emily summed up our collective sentiment afterwards when she said, "You mean we raced all the way over here for this?"

Munich's Town Hall was an extraordinary building dating back to King Ludwig's reign during the late 1800s. It resembled a giant sandcastle with elaborate spires, gargoyles and intricate ornamentation. Since the doors to the courtyard remained open, we walked through and discovered a café with a series of tables with umbrellas. We enjoyed coffee heaped with rich whipped cream as we took in the many interior details.

Crossing the Marienplatz, the city's main square since 1158 AD, we went into the Roman Catholic Peterskirken dating to 1368 AD. Its Renaissance steeple and baroque choir were added in the 17th century. We admired the elaborate altar and then noticed a jeweled skeleton complete with a crown on a side altar. I thought it was a sculpture but Wayne and the girls assured me it was the real deal. Could it be St. Peter set in jewels?

After a short rest, we took a ten-minute taxi ride to the Seehaus in the English Garden, located just off Englanderstrasse. We were charmed by the building's carved wood paneling and frescoed ceiling. It featured Continental cuisine cooked with a German flair. Staying true to her tastes, Emily ordered a steak and baked potato and the rest of us opted for the specialties. Three of us added apple strudel and Emily had vanilla ice cream topped with whipped cream. Each to his own!

The next day began with a very early morning tapping of hammers at the Conti Hotel. It was undergoing a major renovation and the rooms directly across from ours seemed to be the prime targets. In the States, a hotel would close to the public during a major upgrade, but apparently this was not the case in Munich.

We opted for breakfast in our room and did our now-familiar get-the-girls-up-and-packed routine. While they experienced another slowdown, Wayne and I decided to scout for a shop selling hair dryers, as Emily had fried my trusty Italian overseas hair dryer in London. Success! We bought two Braun hair dryers and added a nylon suitcase. Having mastered the art of pyramid packing with everything rising to a mysterious and un-closable peak at the center of our suitcases, we three ladies needed the new bag to alleviate over-crowding.

I returned to our hotel while Wayne looked for a bank where he could cash some travelers' checks. The hammering had turned into all-out banging and the hall was filled with dust and workmen, so we all decided to meet in the lobby for coffee as we waited for our luggage and rental car.

With only a couple of brief wrong turns, we exited Munich and headed into the Bavarian countryside via the autobahn. Our destination was Schwangau to visit Neuschwanstein, the hilltop castle of Ludwig II, completed in 1886, and the inspiration for Walt Disney when he built Sleeping Beauty's castle at Disneyland. With me as chief map reader, a dubious honor at best with my dyslexia, we exited the autobahn and drove through the small villages of Weilheim, Peissenbert, Steingaden, and Fussen.

Judging from the nearly filled parking lots, we had arrived too late in the day for any hope of avoiding the lines into the castle. After a quick lunch in one of the cafés, we queued up for a pony cart ride up the steep hill. We stood behind the Dumpling family, so named by me because each weighed at least three hundred pounds. After a long wait, a cart finally arrived and stopped well beyond the front of the line. A mob scene ensued. We were able to board the cart but the driver refused to start up the hill until some of us exited. I could understand his thinking since all the Dumplings were on board. Knowing that we were in far better shape to walk the quarter mile uphill, we not so graciously exited and began our trek up to the castle.

If we had thought that the cart line was long, the one to enter the castle was horrendous. Once inside, another line formed for those wanting a tour in English. Seeing that the German line was much shorter, we opted for it.

Joining us was a group from France. Although very crowded, we enjoyed seeing the castle and the views of the countryside from its windows.

It really didn't matter that the tour was in German. The castle's majestic beauty spoke for itself. Ludwig had selected the location perfectly. As an aside, I was glad that I had chosen to visit Neuschwanstein in May on an earlier visit when I had the castle almost to myself, as August was a far different story.

Our next stop took us to the small village of Wies to visit the Wieskirke, an exquisite rococo church. Much to our dismay, we discovered that its exterior was covered in scaffolding. Even more disappointing was the interior. Only the front altar and two of the stunning pink marble pillars were visible. Green mesh covered almost every inch including the wonderful frescoed ceilings. A photo board displayed pictures of the interior so our girls could see just how beautiful it would be when the restoration was completed.

We then drove through Oberammergau on our way to the Linderhof, the smallest of Ludwig II's palaces, which also opened in 1886. I was surprised by the charm of Oberammergau, home of the famed *Passion Play*. Although it was a tourist town with an abundance of souvenir shops and restaurants, it nevertheless showcased some of the most beautiful Bavarian buildings in all of Germany.

Arriving at the Linderhof at 5:40 p.m. we learned that the last tour for the day had started ten minutes earlier. Although we missed seeing the interior, we walked around the exterior of Ludwig's small hunting palace and enjoyed the beautifully manicured grounds and spectacular fountains. Ludwig had been fascinated by Versailles and it was reflected in the Linderhof, his favorite palace, with its breathtaking views of the Alps.

We continued on through a mountain pass to Garmish-Partenkirchen and then to Wallgau to visit Claudia, the young woman Wayne and I had met in London when she lived with our friend Faye. After completing her classes last January, she returned to her home in Wallgau and took a position at the Post Hotel in this small Bavarian village. She had encouraged us to visit and here we were.

Claudia greeted us as we arrived just after 7:00 p.m. telling us she had chosen special rooms for us in this charming inn. Ours consisted of two stories with a balcony in the loft and the girls had a balcony with a magical view of the Alps. Our meal in the dining room was equally outstanding and Claudia translated the menu from German to English for us. Emily chose broiled chicken and Liz ordered veal. Wayne and I shared a rack of lamb. Emily had actually survived for a number of days without a hamburger— a small miracle.

At 10:00 p.m. Claudia met us at the hotel entrance and walked us up the mountainside to her family's home. She wore a charming Bavarian dress and had her long hair in a braid. Our girls were enchanted and Wayne and I felt honored to accompany her. Originally a farmhouse with an attached barn, her home was built two hundred years ago. Unfortunately, the barn no longer exists and the original kitchen was recently remodeled with modern cabinetry. A collection of family steins rested on a ledge above the handmade kitchen table.

Claudia's mother, a beautiful woman, also wore a Bavarian dress. Even though we spoke only a few words of German and she knew very little English, we could feel her warmth and instant friendship. We were sure Claudia had filled her in on the time Wayne and I spent with her in London. She served slices of delicious cake topped with blueberries that came from the eastern part of Germany near the Czechoslovakian border where she had been raised. Claudia's family moved to Wallgau two years ago when her father, a forester, was offered a government job in this beautiful area.

Before returning to the inn, Claudia toured us through her home and she and her father led us to a large unheated room used for processing fresh game. A deer hung from the rafters and in its mouth was an evergreen branch, the traditional last meal placed there by a hunter to show his respect for the animal. We were fascinated and each of us appreciated the significance of this traditional rite.

This night proved to be one of the most memorable of our journey. As we walked down the hill to the inn in this tiny village with no street lights and only bright stars shining above us, Emily said, "This is just like *Heidi*!"

Claudia took the next day off and met us at 8:30 a.m. for breakfast at the inn, followed by a drive through Garmish-Partenkirchen to a nearby town at the foot of the Alps named Eibsee where we boarded a cable car that took us to the 9,000-foot level of the Zupspitze. Our luck with the weather continued and from the top we had expansive views of the German, Austrian and Italian Alps.

In the winter, skiers used the cable car to reach the summit but during the summer it was strictly for sightseers and sunbathers. We noticed a number of people enjoying the warm day while sitting on rocks in shorts or bathing suits. A few of the women were basking topless in the sunshine, not seeming to care about the passersby. Our daughters encountered their first topless sunbathers on this mountain peak.

On our way down we took a train that traveled almost three miles through a tunnel in the mountain. Funneling downward, the train emerged halfway to the base, meandered through upland meadows, and eventually stopped at a station next to where we had boarded the cable car. It was interesting to ride by cable car on our way up and by train on our descent.

We had lunch at the Eibsee Pavilion at the far end of the parking lot. Our table was situated on the patio' overlooking a lake surrounded by evergreens and picturesque mountains. In a word, stunning! Swarms of bees were the only drawback and at this time of year they were everywhere. Since Wayne is deathly allergic to bee stings it was a bit disconcerting. This lakeside setting would have made the perfect background for our holiday card photo but we decided that Wayne had pushed his luck far enough.

After returning to the inn to collect our bags, we bid farewell to Claudia and began our autobahn drive. We passed Innsbruck, Austria and drove on through the Tyrol and back into Germany at Berchtesgaden. Wayne drove a rather tame 150 klicks—about 95 mph— on the autobahn. We had a bit of a scare when we came to the top of a rise and discovered that the traffic on the other side had come almost to a standstill. A truck in the right-hand lane was engulfed in smoke and everyone slowed as they passed to look at it. Some things never change and gawking at disabled vehicles seems to be universal.

At the halfway point, we left the autobahn and drove along two-lane roads through mountain passes the rest of the way. Villages with ski areas tucked into the peaks appeared before us. This two-and-a-half-hour drive proved to be one of the most scenically beautiful we had ever taken.

Arriving at Berchtesgaden, we were surprised by the town's size. With visions of an easy drive to our hotel we soon discovered that it would take some time to find it. We stopped at one point near an inn and Wayne and I popped in to ask for directions. The door closed behind us and not a soul came to greet us. We decided to leave, only to discover that we were literally locked in the building. One could enter but it required a key to get out. The girls were in the car oblivious to our situation.

Desperate, we rang a doorbell outside of one of the guest rooms. A man who spoke no English came to the door and from our descriptive pantomime he got the picture and unlocked the door for us to exit. Showing him the name of our hotel, he pointed in its direction. We soon arrived at the Geiger, several miles further along the roadway. Our rooms were plain but offered postcard perfect views of the Watzmann peaks from our balconies. Before dinner the four of us sat on our balcony watching misty clouds drift over the mountaintops. We didn't realize at the time just how fortunate we were to take advantage of the magnificent views.

We were all abruptly awakened during the night by a tremendous thunder and lightning storm, and the next morning awoke to the first real rain in almost two weeks. While we ate breakfast, the rain diminished and was nothing more than a drizzle as we began the half-hour drive to Salzburg.

By the time we arrived, the sun shone brightly. Wayne found a spot to park on the street just a few blocks from our first stop, the Mirabell Palace, built in 1606 AD. Liz and Emily thoroughly enjoyed the palace and its gardens enhanced with a multitude of dwarf statues carved from stone.

While wandering toward the town center we noticed an advertisement for a Bach chamber music performance scheduled for 5:00 p.m. Salzburg plays host to myriad musical performers during August and we hoped to take advantage of some of them. Our first move was to buy tickets for the Bach concert later in the day.

We crossed a footbridge over the river to the center of Salzburg. Street performances abounded and we stopped to listen to a number of them. One young man had an assortment of thirty or forty water-filled glass jars of various sizes. As he struck them, the sounds they produced reminded us of a xylophone. The range of notes he was able to coax out of the jars was remarkable and he performed both show tunes and classical pieces to perfection.

Wayne and I had enjoyed lunch at a restaurant in this area on an earlier visit but neither of us remembered its name. Emily spotted a place that looked interesting and it turned out to be the Tomaselli, our old favorite. It was still packed at 2:30 p.m. but we managed to find a table and enjoyed our omelets and desserts.

After lunch we boarded a tram that took us to the impressive hilltop castle that dominates Salzburg. Then we toured the house where Mozart was born before returning to the Mirabell Palace for the late afternoon chamber music concert. To our delight we had second row seats in this small, ornate concert hall. The young trio played three Bach concertos on violin, cello and concertina. Wayne and I had attended a concert in this same room on our first visit and we enjoyed sharing today's experience with Liz and Emily.

Following a stop for pastries and coffee we drove to Königssee, a dramatic lake just a few miles outside of Berchtesgaden. At 7:30 p.m., the pre-sunset hues made it magical. With only a few remaining tourists it was a perfect time to be here. Although we saw only a small part of the eastern end of the lake it was enough to absorb its beauty. Surrounded by soaring mountain peaks, it was fed by water from the melting snow. Only electric boats were permitted on the lake to keep the water crystal clear and the girls watched ducks dive for their dinner along the shore.

Liz and Emily struggled to keep up with our pace and opted for a quiet night at the hotel, so Wayne and I drove to an Italian restaurant called Gran Sasso. At this storefront spot we enjoyed another one of the best dinners we've had outside of Italy. After sharing a carpaccio appetizer, we ordered risotto con funghi and scaloppini. All were excellent and the service earned an A+. With only twelve tables in this small restaurant, we were happy to get in with such a late reservation.

Berchtesgaden is perhaps best known as the home of Hitler's Eagle's Nest, his mountaintop retreat. Interestingly, no one talked about it and we were not able to find it on any of the hotel's maps or locate a brochure describing it. It seemed to be something that the town would like to forget. We never did spot it, even from a distance.

The next morning, we met in the dining room for breakfast before checking out and driving to Munich for our flight to Paris. Entering the autobahn just across the Austrian border, traffic moved well for about half the trip before coming to almost a dead stop. Convinced that there had been an accident we would soon pass, we crawled along for another hour before we realized the autobahn simply could not handle the August tourist traffic. Concerned that we might miss our flight, Wayne exited the autobahn, opting for small country roads.

I became the chief map reader, a skill I barely qualify for, and with a couple of exceptions did a credible job. We drove through the countryside filled with verdant woods and farms. Our normal two-hour drive took three hours and would most likely have been much longer had we stayed on the autobahn.

We reached the airport exactly one hour before our flight to Paris. Wayne turned in our rental car and we hurried to the terminal with our heaps of luggage. Looking for our tickets, Wayne realized that the envelope holding them was missing, yet he still had the car rental forms. He raced back to the rental desk and traded the car forms for our plane tickets. All's well that ends well and we were soon on our way to Paris.

Not able to squeeze the four of us and our suitcases into a taxi, Emily and I took one and Liz and Wayne took another. We somehow arrived at the hotel at the same time in spite of taking different routes. Our home for the next four days, Hôtel de l'Université at 22 Rue de l'Université, rested on the Left Bank. Wayne and I had always stayed on the opposite side of the Seine and we decided to try something different on this trip. Our hotel was close to the antique district and the Musée d'Orsay; the Louvre and the Tuilleries were just across the river. We would begin tomorrow with the Louvre after a good night's sleep.

We woke up to the aroma of freshly brewed coffee and homemade croissants, and enjoyed them in our hotel's breakfast room before an early start at the Louvre. The long line we encountered moved swiftly and we did the ugly American quick tour beginning with da Vinci's Mona Lisa and ending with Michelangelo's sculpture of Venus. We allotted two hours for our Louvre tour, hardly enough to encompass its vast collections, and we concentrated on its Italian works.

After a quick lunch stop at a café on the Rue de Rivoli we crossed a bridge to the Left Bank and let our girls lead the way on a shopping excursion. The boutiques around the Boulevard St. Germain offered a variety of items from clothing to unique household goods and much more. We enjoyed wandering through many of them as we made our way back to our hotel.

With quite a bit of walking under our belt, we three gals opted for a nap before dinner. Wayne did a quick scouting mission for a restaurant and returned with information about an area near the Sorbonne that looked promising. We all walked about five blocks along Rue de l'Université to Rue de Seine and encountered a bustling area filled with street vendors, boutiques, patisseries, and restaurants. Liz spotted a small café just off the main street called La Citrouille that offered steaks as well as French cooking. She ordered what she thought was a veal dish and after a couple of bites discovered that she was eating liver. I passed my duck dish to her in exchange for the liver.

As lovely as our little hotel seemed, we discovered that the street noise was deafening and went on well into the early morning hours. None of us slept until it finally quieted and we didn't get up the next morning until 9:00 a.m. The girls showered and washed their hair and fried another hairdryer in the process.

We took the Métro to visit Notre-Dame. Although we encountered a slight drizzle it didn't merit umbrellas. On this misty day Notre-Dame's stained-glass windows looked magnificent and we sat for some time in the center of the cathedral taking in all its glory.

Next, we took the Métro to the Champs-Élysées and found a café on a side street for lunch. Emily, the hamburger queen, got her wish and the rest of us ordered French fare. Emily's hamburgers in Paris were served with no bun and a fried egg on top. She ate the egg first and then savored the meat. Whatever works.

The rain had ended after lunch as we walked along the Champs-Élysées. The girls popped in and out of several shops, finding no bargains but enjoying this unique experience. We then made our way to Rue du Faubourg St. Honoré with its blocks of designer boutiques. We bought fruit tarts at Dalloyau, my favorite patisserie in Paris, before walking through Place Vendôme en route to the Meurice Hotel's lounge for a much-needed coffee break. Wayne and I had previously stayed in the hotel and knew it would be a perfect place to stop. Its elegant décor and intricate tile patterns on the floor simply charmed us.

We were wearing out our daughters! Liz and Emily decided to call it a day and have their fruit tarts for dinner in their room. Wayne and I headed out at 9:00 p.m. and retraced our way to the area where we had been the night before. At our hotel's recommendation we tried a restaurant called l'Échaudé St. Germain and, for a reasonable price, we enjoyed our three-course dinner. With a small table by a window in this romantic little restaurant, we had a perfectly delightful evening. Wayne's salmon and my veal were exquisitely prepared and the apple tarte tatin that followed was simply the best we'd ever had.

We awoke knowing this was our last day in Paris and the end of our European adventure. With that in mind we walked to the Musée d'Orsay. I had visited this mighty museum on a previous trip but this was a first for Wayne, Liz and Emily. We spent several hours enjoying the museum's collection of Impressionist art before having a light lunch on the museum's rooftop. The views of Paris were spectacular and we asked a passerby to take a family photo with the city in the background.

After lunch we boarded a train to the Eiffel Tower. Liz and Emily wanted to see it up close while we were in Paris. Wayne had been to it on a previous trip and I always put it off thinking I'd visit it the next time I was in the city. It seemed a trifle touristy to me and, quite honestly, I would have skipped it once more had it not been for our girls.

I was right. It was touristy. It was also an awe-inspiring structure. Standing in proximity to the Eiffel Tower and fully grasping the enormity of it simply has to be experienced to be understood. We waited in line at the north platform and finally boarded a car operated by pulleys. The ride to the second level was almost a vertical climb as we soared above the city.

A fairly strong wind prevented us from continuing to the top level and it was just as well. We were awestruck by the panoramic vistas and by the distance we had ascended to this point. We spotted all the places we had visited in Paris. The series of bridges spanning the Seine looked like miniatures as did the Arc de Triomphe and the Opera House. We stayed on the platform for almost forty-five minutes before descending to the ground.

After our final coffee and pastry at a sidewalk café, we returned to the hotel to organize our burgeoning suitcases before heading out for dinner. One of Wayne's and my favorites, Le Boeuf Sur le Toit, has a sister restaurant on the Left Bank called La Coupole located on Boulevard du Montparnasse. When we arrived we were a bit disappointed. Unlike its more intimate sister, the brightly lit interior in this cavernous space had row after row of tables.

Once seated, we found the food and service exceptional. We muddled our way through one more menu in French, which by now we could interpret fairly easily. The food had a French country flair, and after two and a half hours at La Coupole we were ready to return to our hotel.

We said farewell to Paris early the next morning and took a limo to the Orly Airport under a bright blue sky. While waiting to board, we talked about the many and varied experiences we had shared. Traveling as a family made our adventures so special and we would all have wonderful memories of our time in London, Amsterdam, Munich, Wallgau, Berchtesgaden, Salzburg, and Paris.

EUROPE

Paris, Hamburg, The Netherlands, Bruges, and Luxembourg

March 18–31, 1992

WAYNE SPOTTED AN AD offering two tickets for the price of one on an airline's new route from Los Angeles to Paris. Never able to turn down a good deal, we were once again off for two weeks of business and pleasure. Translated, that meant work for Wayne and play for me.

The departure was delayed for forty minutes because of an excess of three thousand pounds on board the plane. Our captain announced that we would be on our way as soon as the overage was offloaded and I said a little prayer that our luggage wasn't part of the deal. Once airborne for our eleven-hour flight we relaxed in our comfortable business class seats and actually managed to sleep for a few hours. We awoke over Scotland just before dawn to a spectacular high-level view of a full moon.

With a nine-hour time change we landed at Charles de Gaulle Airport at 7:30 a.m. on a Thursday. After exiting passport control and collecting our luggage we met our driver for a more-than-leisurely drive in rush hour traffic into Paris and the Élysées Hotel at 92 Rue la Boétie.

After a three-hour rest we decided to be adventurous and headed out to find the Brasserie Poncelet where Richard, a chef and the son of San Marino friends, prepared the main courses each day. By the time we arrived all of Richard's special dishes were no longer available but we enjoyed a lovely Niçoise salad, crusty bread and slices of apple and pear tart. As we were savoring our late lunch, Richard stopped at our table to say goodbye. When it was time to leave and we asked our waiter for the bill he told us that our lunch was Richard's treat. What a lovely welcome to Paris!

Walking around the corner after lunch we discovered several blocks of pedestrian-only street markets filled with butcher shops, fish markets, produce and flower stands, and the inevitable array of baked goods. The French can make the most ordinary pastries appear extraordinary and we always enjoy seeing and sampling them.

It seems that there is always some sort of renovation going on in Paris and this trip was no exception. Walking along the Champs Élysées we noticed that the sidewalk near the Arc de Triomphe had been removed and new paving stones were being installed. We watched the stone masons cut each piece *sans* safety glasses. Dust and particles of stone filled the air and created an enormous mess.

We exited onto Rue du Faubourg Saint-Honoré, the Madison Avenue of Paris. Along it rest the finest boutiques with some of the world's best designs accompanied by outrageous price tags. Although I always enjoy window shopping along this elegant street, this season's fashions seemed a bit bizarre. Denim was accentuated with lace. Lengths were either very short or very long. It wouldn't be difficult for me to take a pass on sampling Parisian haute couture this spring.

From there we walked to the Hotel Meurice in hopes of a late afternoon coffee in its exquisite lobby. Because of fashion industry showings this week in Paris, the salon was closed to the public. With balmy weather we crossed the street to the Tuileries and enjoyed our espressos in this enchanting park.

We then crossed the Seine on the Pont Royal and walked along the Left Bank. Our self-guided tour took us past the little Hôtel de l'Université, where we stayed in 1989 with Liz and Emily, bringing back wonderful memories. A sudden spurt of energy took us along Boulevard St. Germain and a few side streets to l'Échaudé St. Germain, a bistro where we'd dined on a previous trip. We made a reservation and continued looking into shops.

Returning to the restaurant, we discovered that history doesn't always repeat itself. Instead of a quiet table for two near a window we were escorted to a basement room packed with tables. Smoke filled the air in this poorly ventilated room. America's policy of offering diners a non-smoking area hadn't yet reached Paris.

After dinner we walked a few more blocks to a Métro stop on Boulevard St. Germain. Looking at the map in the underground station, we realized just how far we had walked on our first day in Paris. We took the train back to our hotel at 10:00 p.m. and were ready for a good night's sleep.

When I awoke, Wayne had left for his business meeting so quietly that I never heard him. I decided to start the day at a leisurely pace. With another spectacular day to sightsee I headed away from the construction along the

Champs Élysées toward the parks near the Élysées Palace, filled with people young and old all enjoying the unseasonably warm weather. Jonquils and flowering trees fooled by two weeks of intense sunshine bloomed everywhere. What a day for Parisians and tourists alike! As the French would say, "C'est magnifique!"

In the fall of 1991, I enrolled in a French class for adults through a local community college. We met every Wednesday evening for three hours. Our professor did her best to impart the basics to her twenty students. However, she loved to chat in English about her life in Brussels, her political views or whatever other topic she stumbled upon on a given evening. Consequently, our French developed at a snail's pace. I had promised that I would not return to Paris without learning the basics and here I was on shaky ground once more.

Wayne's business was complete by mid-afternoon and we took the Métro to the Paris Opera House. He had not had an opportunity to tour this magnificent structure. Tours were over for the day so we entered the lobby and admired the exquisite grand staircase. I remember how impressed I had been when I saw it duplicated in the Palace of Justice in The Hague.

We had plans to meet Jean-François, a business associate of Wayne's, at 8:00 p.m. in front of our hotel. After waiting for forty-five minutes we suspected that we had our signals mixed and returned to our room. Keep in mind this was the pre-cell phone era. At 9:00 p.m. Jean-François called and apologized for the delay, having been caught in an enormous traffic jam. He had already called to ask that our table be saved and he suggested that we meet him at the restaurant, La Fermette Marbeuf, a ten-minute walk from our hotel. The meal was well worth the wait and we enjoyed fresh oysters, sole, sweetbreads, and memorable desserts including a chocolate gâteau for Wayne and a chestnut charlotte with a warm bitter chocolate sauce for me. Voila!

The next morning's rain persuaded us to opt for indoor activities. We decided on this Saturday morning to take the Métro to the Pompidou Museum, a first for both of us. The Pompidou, an uber-modern structure, featured a show with paintings by artists from Prague and Brno dating from 1910 to 1915 and very interesting furniture and pottery collections. We boarded an escalator encased in a plexiglass tube that took us up along one side of the building. At the top, the fifth floor, we were treated to a bird's-eye view of Paris. To our right we could see the Sacré-Cœur Basilica, straight ahead stood the Eiffel Tower and to our left, the spire of Notre-Dame.

Working our way down we discovered an exhibit of models and drawings by American architect Louis I. Kahn. Then we came to the museum's permanent collection of Impressionist and Fauvist art. We particularly enjoyed a grouping of bronzes and paintings by Matisse and works by such notables as Bonnard, Derain, Braque, and Picasso.

After a quick peek at the museum's contemporary art we exited into bright sunshine and walked with throngs of weekend wanderers to Les Halles. Filled with young people, it reminded us of Carnaby Street in London with its carnival atmosphere. The day was so lovely that we decided to tour the Latin Quarter on the Left Bank.

Since it was mid-afternoon, we bought ham and cheese baguettes and crossed the Seine near Notre-Dame. We enjoyed our baguettes while sitting on a park bench along the river directly across from the cathedral and marveled at our al fresco lunch in mid-March. We watched a young father and his son toss a football while we battled a flock of pigeons for exclusive rights to our sandwiches. Wayne calls them flying rats and I've never understood the fascination that some people have for these pesky birds.

Wayne led us on a two-and-a-half-hour tour of the Latin Quarter. We had not been in this section of Paris, so named because the university students who lived in this area were expected to converse in Latin until the turn of the twentieth century. The narrow streets, many of them inaccessible by car, charmed us. The area was filled with ancient churches, quaint shops, patisseries, small hotels, and many small restaurants featuring Greek cuisine. Our favorite find was the Hôtel Colbert on Rue de l'Hôtel Colbert. It had an appealing little courtyard, an attractive lobby and, best of all, rates were approximately US$160 a night. We'll try it on another visit.

Our next stop, the Musée de Cluny, originated as a 15th-century mansion adjacent to the ruins of a Roman bath. Filled with French and Roman religious artifacts and sculptures, it also featured an impressive collection of tapestries. Most notable were those of the *French Lady with a Unicorn* series dating from the 15th century. The brilliant reds and blues of the tapestries and the intricate detail in each were remarkable. Another highlight was a passageway connecting the mansion to a Roman rotunda with a massive vaulted ceiling constructed from bricks.

We found our way to the Sorbonne, founded in 1257 AD. After a brief look at the exteriors of some of the university's buildings we headed back to the Seine and again crossed the river near Notre-Dame, still filled with tourists even at this late hour. We boarded the Métro at 5:00 p.m. and heard an announcement in French that I didn't understand (so much for my three months of French lessons...) and everyone pushed their way out of the train. By the time the next train arrived, it was sardine city. Nevertheless, we made it to our hotel with two hours to rest until dinner.

Just before 8:00 p.m. we walked to Chez André. Wayne had his first

Parisian dinner at Chez André eighteen years earlier and he thought it would be fun to give it another try with me. That Saturday night it was filled to capacity with only a table or two available. The tables, right on top of each other, had to be pulled into the aisle to seat one of us against a wall. Smoke filled the room and we were elbow to elbow with the diners on either side of us. We decided to say adieu and retraced our steps to another restaurant we'd passed en route where we had a rather nondescript but nevertheless quiet dinner. As we left the hostess gave us a card with the restaurant's name, Sébillon Élysées, and matches printed with Chez André. Sister restaurants? Even in Paris, it was indeed a small world.

Since the next day was a Sunday, we opted not to set our alarm and enjoyed a late continental breakfast in our room. The long velvet drapes hadn't closed well last night so Wayne did his own home improvement act and safety-pinned them together. This morning he stood on a chair to undue his handiwork and the chair lurched forward into the window. Fortunately, he wasn't injured. We reported the broken window and malfunctioning drapes before heading out for the afternoon.

Our first stop was the lounge at the Meurice. Its intricate white tile floor inset with a motif of blue ribbons and elegant classic furnishings made it one of my favorite rooms in Paris, offering an ideal place to relax for an hour or so. The Paris fashion show had ended and the lounge was open for guests once more. While enjoying our espressos, people-watching, as always, played out before us.

Crossing the street to the InterContinental's Café Tuileries, we had a late afternoon lunch. I enjoyed a fabulously light bream and pistachio soufflé on a bed of field greens and Wayne had a seafood crepe wrapped in a pastry pouch placed on top of tomatoes and greens. The presentation was beautiful and the taste, even better. A chocolate mousse cake and a sinful meringue torte capped off our lunch. At nearly 5:00 p.m. we exited for a Métro ride to our hotel.

We met Coen, a Dutch business friend, at 8:00 p.m. for a short walk to Le Boeuf sur le Toit, one of the few places open on a Sunday evening. Our table, situated near the front, gave us full view of all who arrived. Wayne and I had had pre-dinner drinks at the restaurant in 1988 and were fascinated by its ambience. Tonight's dinner was all I had hoped for and more. We passed on the vast selection of mussels, opting for a vegetable pâté and tomato coulis followed by steak frites. Wayne's and my favorite dessert, floating islands, elevated our dinners to perfection.

The next morning Wayne slipped out of our room for his business meetings without a sound and I slept until 10:30 a.m. This decadence was getting to be a habit! I spent the morning packing and reading my travel books about Bruges and Luxembourg, two new places for me, before taking a taxi to the airport to meet Coen and Wayne for our flight to Hamburg. I gave myself a little extra time for some duty-free shopping but, with a weak dollar, there were no bargains. No purchases this time...

We all met and boarded for a smooth flight to Hamburg. After we landed, Wayne informed me that the Folker aircraft we flew in was the same model that had crashed into the New York Harbor just a few days earlier killing a number of passengers. This was not exactly comforting information and I was glad he waited until after we landed to share it with me.

Arriving at Hamburg's Vier Jahreszeiten, The Four Seasons, just after 7:00 p.m., we were given a fabulous suite on the inner courtyard. Although the view of the lake at the front of the hotel would have been beautiful, the busy street below made our room much more appealing. This elegant hotel is one of the world's finest. When we returned later that evening, a vase filled with a dozen roses greeted us. What a lovely touch!

At 8:30 p.m. we met Coen in the lobby and the three of us took a taxi to Bistro Canard, a top Fodor choice, about a ten-minute drive into an area filled with exquisite mansions. When we entered the restaurant, it appeared unpretentious and ordinary but we soon discovered that looks can be deceiving. Bistro Canard provided a delightful dining experience and a woman who spoke some English could not have been more helpful. The French cuisine menu offered outstanding selections. Wayne and I ordered duck prepared three ways. Salads had finally made their way onto the European scene and we enjoyed lettuce topped with bacon and avocado. The bread and almond pudding with a vanilla sauce was superb and we all agreed that Fodor scored another win.

Here's to German efficiency! I am married to one, so I know only too well. We awoke at 2:00 a.m. to a phone call from the front desk announcing that Wayne had received a fax marked RUSH. He assured the man that it could wait until morning and, although I went back to sleep, Wayne never really did. He left quietly and a few minutes after 9:00 a.m. it was my turn for reveille. I awoke to incredibly loud drilling and hammering that sounded like it was coming from our suite's living room. When it continued, I called the front desk and learned that we were located one floor above a major hotel renovation. Could this explain the lovely bouquet of roses?

I ordered in-room breakfast and suffered through another hour of constant disruption while getting ready for my day in Hamburg. It was obvious that the noise would continue throughout our three-day stay so I called the desk and asked to be moved to a quieter spot. The move took us up one floor and while still on the courtyard, the new room offered about twenty-five less space. We'd take the quiet over more space. When I returned later in the day, I discovered that our roses were moved to the new room.

As an aside, this was the third time we had a room right in the midst of reconstruction in a German hotel. Each hotel had a high rating. It appeared to be standard operating procedure to book rooms in the direct path of reconstruction in Germany, but this American tourist was tired of staying in top German hotels while drilling and hammering were in progress.

I finally headed outside into a cold drizzle and decided to explore a vast covered shopping area not far from the hotel. Entering at the Hamburger Hof, I wandered through a maze of shops for a couple of hours. Many of the gift and candy stores were filled with Easter items and I purchased some handmade marzipan eggs and bunnies for our daughters.

Wayne returned to the Four Seasons just after 5:00 p.m. and discovered that I had moved to a new room. With tickets for a 7:00 p.m. performance of Rossini's *Marriage of Figaro* at the Hamburg Opera House, we opted for a light dinner in the hotel. The Opera House was only a couple of blocks' walk and we found our seats easily in this relatively small venue. We commented on how much it reminded us of a miniature Dorothy Chandler Pavilion. As in Los Angeles, super-titles flashed across a screen above the stage with translations of tonight's performance, this time in German. We knew this opera fairly well and followed it with relative ease. Returning to the Four Seasons just after 11:00 p.m., we ended our evening with a cappuccino in the hotel's elegant lounge.

We were grateful to have been moved to a quiet room and slept until mid-morning. Ah, decadence! After a continental breakfast I led Wayne to the Hamburger Hof and a shop where I had seen some adorable hand-glazed metal bunny ornaments. I convinced him that although they were pricy they would become a new Smith Family Easter tradition. He agreed and we purchased ten unique bunnies. The tradition continues and I hang them on a branch secured in a wooden base every spring.

Returning to the street we walked to the town square for a closer look at the elaborate Rathaus, or Town Hall. From there we entered St. Peter's Church, a centuries-old cathedral now supporting a Lutheran congregation. A bone-chilling wind coming from the lake prompted us to walk quickly to a coffee shop in the arcade. The lake that dominated central Hamburg was actually formed by a river that was dammed to create it. A fountain spewing water at the end of the lake near our hotel added to the picturesque view.

After warming ourselves with coffee we collected our bags and taxied to the airport for a short flight to Amsterdam. Once there, Wayne rented a car which turned out to be the car from hell. More on this later. We drove to our next hotel, the Auberge de Kieviet, in Wassenaar. Located just outside The Hague, this elegant wooded suburb is home to the Dutch elite, international businessmen and dignitaries from around the world.

Our hotel room, a suite at the back of the inn overlooking the charming estate garden, suited us perfectly. Wayne had stayed at the Kieviet on several business trips but this was a first for me. The former Italian owner had mysteriously been disenfranchised from the hotel and restaurant a few years earlier, but the small inn, now in Dutch hands, continued its top-notch service.

Tonight's dinner at the Seinpost, a restaurant on the North Sea in Scheveningen, won raves. Although too dark to see the sea, our window table in the center of the round room was ideal. Our waiter suggested we order the fixed-price menu, which began with shrimp in a pastry crust followed by a warmed raw tuna salad and a small portion of sea bass in a vegetable cream sauce. After our main course of roasted lamb, a trio of chocolates—ice cream, mousse and a cake—appeared in small but sinfully rich and entirely satisfying portions. Wayne had voiced his praise for the Seinpost for so many years and I now knew why.

Ah, the perils of travel! Wayne had again slipped out silently and my morning wake-up call came from a golden retriever barking loudly in the garden just a few feet from our bedroom window. Quite obvious that it was a puppy, this little barker presented problems for those of us staying at the inn. The tethered dog continued to bark while a housekeeper folded laundry outside and a chauffeur stood nearby, equally oblivious to the noise. When I later mentioned the barking to the concierge, he told me in a tone of deference that the estate directly next to the inn belonged to the Spanish Ambassador to the Netherlands, inferring that the dog had diplomatic immunity.

I met my cousin Dana, now living in Wassenaar with her husband, in front of the Kieviet just before 10:00 a.m. We drove in a light rain to the town's shopping district to purchase food for tonight's dinner at her home. It was one of the highlights of our trip for me and I thoroughly enjoyed going from one specialty shop to another for meat, vegetables, salad greens, bread, and dessert. Although it took us nearly an hour, we now had a take-out dinner that would rival the finest restaurant.

Our last stop was a local florist. The owner had recently been named one of the five top floral designers in Holland. In a country known for its flowers this was indeed a distinguished honor and once inside I understood why this florist earned the tribute. The tables were covered with fresh arrangements and, as in Germany, we found a treasure trove of Easter decorations. I bought a charming papier-mâché rabbit to hang from a light fixture in our entrance. Another Smith Family Easter tradition was born!

We then drove to the American Women's Club located near the Kurhaus Hotel in Scheveningen. Each Tuesday a team of two or three gals would prepare a luncheon for approximately thirty guests and for a small fee, members could drop in for food and friendship. Today's team made pasta rolls with two sauces, a tossed salad and crème caramel. It was delightful to have an opportunity to experience a slice of life in another country and I enjoyed meeting many of Dana's friends.

After lunch we stopped at Dana's home to deposit our evening's dinner—marinated pork, potatoes au gratin, asparagus, bread with a cheese crust, a mixed salad, and for a finale, tiramisu. We then drove to the village of Lisse to tour the Keukenhof Gardens. Open only a few weeks each year, the park with its acres of flowers opened today. Although it was a bit too early for some of the gardens, we saw ample beds of daffodils, early varieties of tulips, hyacinths and many other flowers offering first-day visitors a breathtaking array of spring color. Because it was cold and overcast, we had the gardens almost to ourselves. Dressed in our wool jackets and gloves, I felt sorry for the two girls in lightweight traditional Dutch costumes who greeted us.

The park-like setting of the Keukenhof awed us with its meticulously tended grounds. In every direction we saw a sea of color. As we walked through the park, we came to a large windmill with blades that rotated as they caught the breeze. Beds in long wide strips spread for what seemed like blocks planted in singular rows of reds, blues and yellows resembled an Impressionist painting on acres of canvas.

We returned to the Wassenaar shopping center at 4:00 p.m. for a cappuccino, a warm welcome following our cold, wet walk through the Keukenhof. Dana then dropped me off at the Kieviet to freshen up and meet Wayne for our return to Dana's home to enjoy our gourmet take-out dinner. Dana entertains beautifully and it is always a special treat for us to relax in a home while we are traveling abroad. We enjoyed reminiscing with Dana and Ed.

Wayne had the leave-the-room-quietly routine down pat but the honorable pup managed to wake me with its familiar bark. I called to order room service for breakfast and before I could say a word the hotel captain asked if I would like orange juice, rolls and a large pot of coffee delivered. He remembered every detail from my order the day before. The Dutch always include a plate of cold meats and cheeses. Knowing that Wayne and I had some traveling to do in the afternoon, I made sandwiches to pack as a picnic. After breakfast I spent a leisurely morning rearranging my suitcase and catching up on my trip notes.

Wayne arrived with the leased Audi. The car had an overwhelming smell, something like a mix of dead rat and rotting fruit. We drove with the windows down hoping it would alleviate the smell. It didn't work and we froze. I was not looking forward to a trip to Bruges in the odiferous auto. After some urging from me, Wayne decided to drive to the Rotterdam Airport for an exchange. I felt justified when the Hertz agent opened the door of our car and backed away in disgust. We exchanged the Audi for a Mercedes and were soon on our way, arriving at the outskirts of Bruges two hours later in a maze of traffic. It took us another hour to reach our hotel. Having had it with cars in general and driving in Bruges in particular, we parked the car in a garage not far from the hotel for the rest of the weekend.

Our hotel, the Duc de Bourgogne, rested on a canal at Huidenvettersplein 12 not far from the town center and the centuries-old fish market square. With only twenty rooms, the three-story building had a charming brick façade with a Dutch-style tiered roof. Even though we booked our room more than two months before arriving, we were told that we would have to change rooms during our stay. Someone who liked the room had booked it ahead of us. Our first room, #3 on the second floor, had a large bathroom and a picture window overlooking the canal. The next night's room would be #14 on the third floor, which had a much smaller bathroom and a window so tiny that we had to stretch to see anything out of it.

As both rooms were quiet and comfortable, I later asked the receptionist which were her favorites. She mentioned #3 and #4 on the second floor and #17 on the third. All faced the canal with excellent views. She also mentioned #2 at the front of the hotel. I preferred the canal view.

Our trusty Fodor guide touted the Karmeliet as the only two-star restaurant in Bruges and we booked our reservations well in advance. After a slightly circuitous taxi ride, we arrived at an elegant mansion-turned-restaurant. Dinner was a three-hour extravaganza. We began with drinks and complimentary appetizers in a glass-enclosed solarium overlooking a courtyard garden. The menu was in French and very unusual at that so we relied on our waiter for advice. After sampling two starters we were ushered into an elegantly appointed dining room for the next part of the evening.

The room, decorated in a rich deep green with accents of gold, sported high ceilings with exquisitely carved crown moldings. Unlike most of our European dining experiences there was a conspicuous absence of ashtrays. Diners could smoke in the anteroom and the bar area but it was obviously discouraged here. Having been in so many smoke-filled rooms on this trip, it made me realize how offensive my smoking must have been to others and I am grateful that I quit.

Our dinner was indeed unique. Each course arrived on a different setting of china. We began with fresh white asparagus coupled with wild mushrooms and shrimp in a pastry shell. Then came hop sprouts, a delicacy only available for a couple of weeks each year, topped with salmon and a quail egg. The taste of the hops was sharp and interesting. The next course, a very rare pigeon breast infused with truffles and wrapped in spinach and bacon, was delicious. This was followed by wafer-thin ravioli stuffed with truffles. Then came a salad of field greens. We finished with a warm chocolate tart with fresh orange and grapefruit compote and a grapefruit sorbet.

After two hours of dining we were led back to the solarium for coffee and two small trays offering delicate pastries and homemade candies. We were treated like royalty and we marveled at the impeccable service and attention to detail. When our bill arrived, Wayne was a bit taken aback but, as he always says, "I don't go on vacation to save money."

For breakfast the next morning we sat in a window booth overlooking the canal. As we watched the first tour boats form a line, we decided to give one a try. We were assured by the man at the front desk that everything would be transferred to our second room while we were sightseeing.

In brilliant sunshine we boarded a boat just a few yards from our hotel for a tour in English. As it later turned out, our timing was perfect. We sat in front seats for the thirty-minute ride and Wayne took photos as we cruised through the canals that transformed this charming city into a miniature Amsterdam. The tour put Bruges, one of the best-preserved medieval sites in the world, into perspective. We were ready to roam the streets when we docked.

Walking in the direction of the Church of Our Lady with its *Madonna and Child* sculpture by Michelangelo, we discovered that it closed daily between 11:30 a.m. and 2:30 p.m. The temperature continued to drop and Wayne decided to return to the hotel for warmer clothes. When we arrived, our luggage had already been moved.

Heading toward Market Square we stopped at Tearoom Poeskaffee's on Steenstraat for a lunch of Belgian waffles with strawberries and a cappuccino. This was my second visit to Belgium and somehow I'd missed an encounter with a Belgian waffle. Not this time! This charming café knew how to make them to perfection.

While wandering just a few blocks from the hotel last night we passed several shop windows filled with Easter candies. One in particular featured exquisite chocolates and delicate woven baskets decorated with silk flowers and ribbons. I decided that they were special enough to chance getting them back to the States intact for Liz and Emily. Wayne thought I was crazy but soon realized that a woman obsessed cannot easily be dissuaded. I then bought candies in several small shops and marveled at the beautiful workmanship that went into each piece.

At 2:30 p.m. we returned to the Church of Our Lady, a Catholic church built in the 13th to 15th centuries, to see Michelangelo's awe-inspiring sculpture, *Madonna and Child,* created between 1504 and 1505 AD. We stood at the altar only a few feet from this priceless work and took in every detail. We felt fortunate to add this sculpture to other Michelangelos we had visited in the Vatican, Florence, Milan, and Paris.

We then walked a short distance to St. John's Hospital, dating from 1188 AD. It was the oldest medical facility in Europe and continued to function into the twentieth century, only recently becoming a museum. In the midst of an array of medical implements and rows of closet-like beds we were surprised to find a room with an exhibit of small sketches by Rembrandt. On display were sixty-seven tiny ink drawings created between 1630 and 1650 AD. We marveled at the intricate detail captured in each work. These included self-portraits, portraits of friends and family, scenes of villages with churches and windmills in the foreground, nudes, and religious scenes. Most were a mere five or six square inches. We spent ample time perusing the works and Wayne noted that one of them appeared to be of a golfer. I had my doubts since the scenes dated to the mid-1600s. Ice hockey, perhaps?

On our morning canal trip an area with small footbridges leading to a quaint group of buildings surrounding a courtyard was mentioned as a destination to see. A short while later we came to the Begijnhof, a monastery featuring blocks of medieval residential buildings bordering a square. Much to our delight, springtime jonquils, daffodils and bright blue flowers covered the entire plaza. The flowers, now at their peak, painted a breathtaking picture on the grounds before us. Wandering in the direction of our hotel we found a lovely linen shop tucked into a narrow street and I bought some lace sachets. For the next hour we strolled through a maze of streets and somehow ended up at my favorite confectionery shop where we sampled late afternoon tarts and coffees before returning to our hotel.

We opted to have dinner in our small hotel's dining room. Dinner was good; not great. The Flemish menu challenged us but our waiter deciphered it for us. Finishing in record time we headed to our third-floor retreat for a good night's sleep.

After a quick breakfast we walked to the Groeninge Museum. It featured works by 15th-century painters Jan van Eyck, Hugo van der Goes and Hans Memling, the Flemish artist who introduced oil painting to the world. Memling had traveled to Italy to teach oil painting to artists. A rather gruesome painting by Gerard David entitled *The Judgement of Cambyses* depicted the skinning of a man. The last room featured panels covered with bizarre abstractions by Hieronymus Bosch called *The Last Judgment.* Bosch must have filled his pipe with more than tobacco when he painted them.

We then visited the Gruuthusemuseum. The architecture of this 15th-century House of Lords is worth seeing, including its two-story entrance with ornate carved wooden ceiling. Weapons, armory, crests of silver and gold, tapestries, pottery, and china from Belgium, Luxembourg, Rouen, Delft, and the Orient filled room after room. Additional rooms displayed weights and measures, compasses, sextants, tools, musical instruments, and a large music box with the most melodic sound we had ever heard. When it began to play music in this medieval setting it actually gave me the chills. Still more rooms featured Belgian lace. Stopping at this museum was an afterthought and we were delighted that we chose to include it.

It was almost noon when we finished our tour. Wayne headed for the car park just a couple of blocks from our hotel and I went to our room to collect our luggage. When I had asked Wayne to lose the car during our stay in Bruges I hadn't expected him to take my advice literally. I waited for him in the lobby and then waited some more. Remember, this was years before cell phones. Meanwhile, back at the car park, Wayne had exited only to learn that Bruges had reversed the direction of one hundred of its one-way streets over the weekend. He encountered a new set of directions and twice he ended up on streets that dead-ended on canals. After backing up on each he tried other routes and after almost an hour he reached our hotel. So much for a place to park just two blocks from our hotel. Apparently, the city of Bruges reverses the direction of its streets twice a year and we picked one of these times to visit.

When he finally arrived, we headed across Belgium to Luxembourg for a two-day stay. We drove around the outskirts of Ghent and Brussels to the A4 motorway and the Ardennes, heading southeast toward Luxembourg. As I glanced at our map, not an activity that I often do since I am directionally dyslexic, I realized that if we had taken the E40 we could have gone through Liege and Bastogne. My father spent time in these areas during World War II and had talked about the Ardennes.

Just after passing Namur I spotted a road, the N97, that led to the N4 and Bastogne. Deciding to be adventuresome we gave it a try, enjoying the drive along the uncrowded road meandering through the rolling countryside. Quite by surprise, we spotted charming small villages and lush farms. We enjoyed the drive, even on a cold gloomy day.

Our bubble burst when we arrived in Bastogne. Filled with carloads of tourists, we had to move at a snail's pace. Parking was at a premium but we found a spot just off the main road. We then walked in a cold rain toward the town square hoping to find a monument to General "Nuts!" MacAuliffe. We discovered the monument in a parking lot well before we reached the town square. It consisted of a tank and plaque honoring MacAuliffe and we wondered how he would feel knowing that the location for his tribute was the far end of a parking lot. This wasn't much of a salute to the general who saved Bastogne and changed the course of the war.

We crossed the border into Luxembourg late in the afternoon and soon arrived in Luxembourg City. Our room in Hotel Le Royal was spacious and well appointed, and the hotel's service proved impeccable. We soon understood why Le Royal ranked as one of the world's leading hotels.

Although it remained cold, the rain had stopped enough to spur us on for a walk. With a map and a walking tour provided by the concierge we set out for an hour of sightseeing, strolling through several pedestrian malls filled with elegant shops. From there we walked to a park along the edge of a rocky bluff with a long drop to a river at the bottom. I had read that Luxembourg was referred to as the Gibraltar of the North. Nature provided near-perfect fortification.

We retraced our steps to meet Wayne's business associate Coen for dinner in the hotel's Le Relais Royal, conveniently open on a Sunday evening. We enjoyed one of the best meals of our two-week trip with exceptional food and service. I ordered a delicious mousse of bar, a soft yellow bass, wrapped in paper-thin black ravioli. Oh, the sauces! As in fine hotels in Paris, the dessert cart arrived with a variety of choices. We opted for floating islands and a slice of a rich dark chocolate gâteau. Even the coffee service was over the top, prepared at our table in a flame-heated apparatus that resembled a chemistry class bubble tube. The process fascinated us and the ensuing coffee was rich and delicious.

Once again, Wayne left our room quietly the next morning. I had arranged a private two-hour tour of Luxembourg starting at 11:00 a.m. and, with ample time for an in-room breakfast, I then packed for our flight to Paris.

My driver/guide met me in the hotel lobby. He spoke English, drove a Mercedes and promised a tour of the city and the World War II Museum on its outskirts. The first area we explored was the vast complex of buildings comprising the European Common Market. With the free trade agreement about to take effect throughout Europe, its mission would undoubtedly change. Luxembourg, according to my guide, ranked as the leading country for stashing money with no questions asked. Switzerland would no longer boast top ranking as it had bowed to international pressure to release information on questionable clients. Luxembourg, on the other hand, continued to guarantee nondisclosure. This may have changed in more recent times, but was the case in 1989.

We drove outside the city to the war memorial and tribute to General George Patton. Originally buried here, a prominent marker remains. More than five thousand American soldiers were interred here and I, as I had several years ago in the Netherlands, beheld an overwhelming sea of crosses and stars. Such vistas bring a startling reality to historical events. Memorial walls, one with a map of the routes taken during the Battle of the Bulge, framed either side of the entrance to the cemetery. Names of those missing in action were inscribed on them. We noticed several older American men who appeared to be World War II veterans standing in front of the walls in absolute silence. It was a profoundly moving moment.

As we headed for the old part of Luxembourg City we passed an excavation project. A fortification dating from 1742 AD—young according to European standards—was in process of being restored and turned into a museum. We then drove along narrow winding roads leading to one of the four gates to the ancient city of Luxembourg in the valley below us. A barrier had been placed across the entrance to the road but my driver ignored it. About halfway down the hillside we encountered a major road repair project and were forced to turn around and find an alternate route. My driver mentioned that the Tour de France would come through Luxembourg this year and many of the old roads were undergoing rehabilitation. I could not imagine cyclists riding up and down this cliff even on smooth winding roads.

We circled the valley and stopped at a vista point high above it. My driver pointed out a series of caves in the walls below and said that thirteen miles of ancient tunnels were still accessible throughout the cliffs. We could see the ruins of a 14th-century castle at the top of the ridge near us as well as two gates to the ancient city. Although its roots trace to Roman times, the city officially dates to 693 AD. Below us, a small river, the Alzette, flowed past a series of row houses dating from the late 1700s. When we later drove past them my driver mentioned that the houses were also under restoration so that this part of Luxembourg's history would be preserved. In stark contrast, a relatively new bridge painted bright orange-red spanned the far end of the valley.

The next section of the city we explored took us past the Royal Palace, now the headquarters of a steel company. Steel used to be Luxembourg's largest industry but in recent years banking moved to the number one spot. My guide told me that the Grand Duke now lives in a smaller residence on the outskirts of the city.

We crossed a bridge into another section of the city to a railroad station, modern Luxembourg's oldest building which opened in 1859. By now I had run out of film and we stopped at several shops in vain. We even stopped at a camera shop but—alas!—it only sold cameras. The rest of the tour would remain a mental memory.

I asked about the Villeroy & Boch factory that produced the charming sets of dishes so popular in the States. It wasn't far and we drove to it. We passed a shop but, with time in short supply, I decided to forego a look inside of it.

On our way back to the hotel my driver pointed out a restaurant of the edge of a cliff called Bouzonviller at 138 Albert Unden, which he recommended for its food and views. He also suggested that I take a day tour of the northern part of this small country on my next visit. He called the area Little Switzerland because of its charming small villages and he told me the best time to visit was in September when tourists are gone and the weather is still good.

When the two-hour tour ended, I had a much better concept of Luxembourg City and its surroundings. After a leisurely lunch in the hotel, I waited for Wayne's mid-afternoon return. We had talked about a quick trip to Trier, the oldest city in Germany, just across the border. We had a 5:45 p.m. flight from Luxembourg City to Paris, so at 3:15 p.m. with our luggage in the car we decided to give it a try. Our daughter Liz had visited Trier on a summer trip with friends and encouraged us to tour it.

Much to our dismay the good highway suddenly came to a standstill and a detour sign led us along narrow roads through small villages and farms. We forged ahead and crossed the border, continuing through the breathtaking countryside of the Mosel River Valley. We noted one sign to Trier indicating a turn and another pointing straight ahead. Totally confused, we drove straight on only to realize we'd made a mistake. Wayne made a U-turn and we soon entered the outskirts of Trier only to become mired in another massive traffic jam. Visions of missing our flight flashed through our minds.

All's well that ends well. After twenty minutes we reached the valley floor and maneuvered into a parking lot at the base of the Visitor Center near Porta Nigra, the ancient Roman gate to the city. We took the only available parking spot and, after a quick stop for a map, were on our way for the world's quickest tour of Trier. After passing through the Hauptmarkt at record speed we noted a cathedral in ruins.

Trier was a much larger town than we had envisioned and with only forty minutes to spend there we really had to keep moving. Our first stop was the Liebfrauenkirche, the oldest Gothic church in Germany built in the

13th century, with its massive pipe organ and elaborate marble altar. Our daughter Liz remembered the cathedral well. She and several friends rented a car and, as she later told us, also had difficulty entering the city. Finding no place to park, they left the car on a side street and then toured the cathedral. When they returned to their car it was gone. The area was posted no parking in German and they had to spend a considerable amount of time and money to retrieve the car.

We hurried on to the Kaiserthermen, or Imperial Baths, a two-block area of Roman ruins built in the 4th century AD and used as a castle, city wall and monastery. On our way we passed an enormous brick building called the Aula Palatina originally built in the 4th century and redesigned in the 17th century. With no more time we returned to the car park and, with a sigh, headed up the winding road to the top of the valley. Surprisingly, traffic going up the hill moved rapidly but the mass of cars heading downhill remained in a snarl. Our return trip took only thirty-five minutes and we reached the airport on the outskirts of Luxembourg City with time for a cappuccino before boarding our flight to Paris.

Arriving after dark we took a shuttle to the Sofitel at the edge of the Charles de Gaulle Airport. Following two weeks in elegant hotels and inns this was certainly plain vanilla. It was nevertheless quiet and clean and we were tired after a very long day.

On the flight to Los Angeles the next day I had ample time to reflect and give thanks for another opportunity to travel with Wayne through so much of Europe. Although Wayne's business kept us on the move, I thoroughly enjoyed the pace and its ensuing adventures. This trip offered me new travel experiences—Hamburg, the Ardennes, Bruges, Luxembourg City, and Trier. It brought me back to old friends—Paris and The Hague. In spite of cold weather and an abundance of drizzle, I would always treasure these memories.

EGYPT

with a Quick Stop in London

November 23–December 5, 1992

I HAD DREAMED OF a trip to Egypt for years and it was about to become a reality. In my next life I've always thought of myself as an archeologist. Our trip to the Yucatan in the early 1970s captivated my interest in the uncovered secrets of the Maya and their unique architecture. They, too, were fascinated by pyramids. When we received a brochure for a ten-day tour of Egypt, Wayne was reluctant but after I told him I was going with or without him, he acquiesced. It turned out to be his all-time favorite travel adventure.

On departure day we arrived at LAX with ample time to board our ten-hour flight to London where we would connect with a group of forty hardy travelers from the University of Michigan. With a five-hour layover in London followed by another five-hour flight to Cairo we wisely opted to arrive in London a day ahead of schedule to mitigate effects of at least eight of the ten-hour time difference.

After collecting our luggage, we joined a queue for a taxi ride into the city. To our delight we were directed to a new cherry red cab. Our friendly driver explained that he shared it with another man and together they had logged eight thousand miles in just over three weeks. At that rate it wouldn't be new for long.

The drive into London went smoothly and we arrived at our hotel, the Draycott, at 1:30 p.m. Wayne had stayed at this charming hotel on business trips and had talked of taking me to it. Comprising two bacon brick townhouses, the Draycott was located at 24-26 Cadogan Gardens in Chelsea. Our room had high ceilings with ornate moldings and was divided into two sections, one with a canopied bed and the other a sitting area. Looking out the window we noticed several trees in the inner courtyard that were bare of leaves but covered with delicate pink blossoms, an impressive sight on a chilly mid-November day.

What little sunshine we had en route to the hotel turned into grey skies and drizzle. Undaunted, we donned our woolies, opened our umbrellas and headed toward Sloane Square to the British Trading Company's café for a late lunch.

After a quick stop back at our hotel to book a dinner reservation—funny how eating in one spot cultivates more thoughts of eating—we walked to Harrods. Since the Brits do not celebrate Thanksgiving, their Christmas season was well under way. From a distance we could see lights and banners in Harrods' windows welcoming us to this year's holiday theme, *A New England Christmas*. After years of looking forward to seeing Harrods during the holiday season we chose 1992, the year with a touch of Americana. Picnic baskets and red and white gingham accents set the mood for what proved to be charming displays.

Once inside, a sign on the ground level announcing the Egyptian Room caught our attention. We couldn't resist a peek and were enchanted by Harrods' rendition of Egyptian art and décor. It had been four years since the luxury department store was purchased by Mohamed Al-Fayed, and the Egyptian Room, a new addition since our 1989 visit, provided an unexpected treat. Pillars covered with hieroglyphs, lotus flower motifs and lighting fixtures shaped like palm fronds set the mood. Fine Egyptian art and jewelry filled the display cases.

We cruised through Harrods' famous Food Hall, then headed to the third floor to look at Christmas decorations. What a treat for an ornament-aholic like me! Harrods during the holidays had become a mecca for American shoppers and it was an ideal time to visit. I purchased ornaments for our daughters and, of course, for me.

After dinner at Sambuca on Symons Street we returned to the Draycott and read newspapers in front of a cozy fire.

Sunshine greeted us as we opened our curtains the next morning. After a light breakfast in our room we walked to St. James's Palace, which is guarded by Gurkhas in austere khaki uniforms. Turning the corner toward Buckingham Palace we heard music and caught the end of the more colorful Changing of the Guards, an unplanned pleasure.

We returned to our hotel to collect our luggage and take a taxi to Heathrow for our flight to Egypt. As we were nearing our gate, we noticed another couple from Los Angeles wearing our tour group's U of M name tags and chatted with them until our 4:30 p.m. boarding.

Our flight to Cairo went smoothly and we arrived in four hours. Adding two more hours to the time-change mix, we entered the terminal just before 11:00 p.m. After collecting our bags and clearing customs, our tired group was met by our tour coordinator, John. He hailed from the Cotswold area of England and had lived in Cairo for the past three months. John had been working for the tour company for sixteen years and Egypt topped his list of favorite destinations. On our midnight ride to the Ramses Hilton, he shared as much information as our tired brains could absorb. After a stand-off between our bus and several vans in front of our hotel, we checked in at 12:30 a.m. and settled in for the night. Needless to say, we slept well.

After breakfast in the hotel's café we joined our group for a one-hour briefing session during which John told us about transportation, tipping and more. The Cairo underground system worked well, he said, but all the signs were in Arabic. There were three types of transportation available at hotels, each priced by the destination and not the number of passengers. Black and white taxis were the least expensive but few of the drivers spoke any English. John urged us to always confirm the destination and price before getting into a cab. Hotel taxis were also available, as were air-conditioned Mercedes, which could accommodate up to three people.

He continued with advice about tipping. Baksheesh, Egyptian for tipping, was to become one of the most common words in our Egyptian vocabulary. Bathroom attendants and guards at museums and antiquities expected piasters, or Egyptian pounds. At the time of our visit three pounds equaled one dollar. My first restroom experience had been at the Cairo airport. I was handed three or four squares of bathroom tissue as I entered the facility. The room was filthy and I zoomed in and out as quickly as possible. I hadn't taken any money with me and was yelled at by the attendant as I left. One of the tour coordinators gave me fifty piasters, half a pound, to appease the unhappy woman. John cautioned us to ignore children asking for handouts as the government was trying to discourage begging.

The next order of business focused on appropriate dress. Casual attire was advised. Sensible shorts were acceptable. Sometimes shoes must be removed. I made a mental note to tuck my airplane slippers into my shoulder bag to slip on, a trick I learned on a visit to Bangkok. Since we arrived at a relatively cool time of year, layers not unlike California dressing were recommended. Mornings and evenings dropped into the 50s but late November and early December days could reach the mid-to-high 70s in Cairo and the mid-80s from Aswan to Luxor. We had heard tales of the temperature reaching 120 degrees in the Valley of the Kings in early September and we rejoiced at the clever timing of our visit to Egypt.

John also suggested that when we tour Upper Egypt from Aswan to Luxor, we carry sunscreen, sunglasses, a hat, water, bug spray, a flashlight, plenty of Kleenex to double as bathroom tissue, and packaged hand wipes. Since we would always have a bus at our disposal, we could leave any or all of these items on it.

Following John's briefing we were introduced to Dr. Jocelyn Gohary. Having lived in Cairo for many years she shared some of her insights. She began by emphasizing that Egypt is a land of enormous contrasts, a concept that became the theme of my own personal observations. Once outside large cities like Cairo, she prepared us for the small villages we would encounter where the way of life had not changed significantly in three thousand years.

Dr. Gohary presented a number of interesting facts and statistics. Geographically, Egypt is ninety-six percent desert with the remaining four percent located primarily along the Nile. Much of the wildlife depicted in early art such as the lion, ostrich and gazelle are no longer found in Egypt. When camels and goats were brought in from the Arabian Peninsula in the last century BC they ate much of the vegetation along the Nile into extinction. This forced much of the wildlife that had been indigenous to the country to move further into Africa. As we later discovered there are no camels pictured on the walls of tombs and temples. Camels are relative newcomers to Egypt.

Although crocodiles often appear in ancient Egyptian art, they no longer are found in the Egyptian Nile. In modern times the dams built along the river forced the crocodiles further south and with the completion of the Aswan High Dam in 1970, these age-old creatures were virtually gone from Egypt. Their earlier importance was well documented in reliefs from Aswan to Luxor. A room filled with mummified crocs was discovered in one temple. Similarly, hippos no longer roamed these banks.

The Nile sustained Egyptian civilization in much the same way for thousands of years. Ancient writings etched into the walls of temples and tombs tell of annual summer floods called inundations. One of the highest festival days in ancient Aswan was July 19, a time of flooding. With each flood came a rich new layer of alluvial soil that rejuvenated the fertile Nile Valley. The ancient Egyptians designed series of dikes and irrigation channels to ensure a bountiful harvest.

Occasionally the floods would be too high or a drought would occur. Grain was stored for such emergencies and more than five thousand years ago an early system of taxation paid in excess grain was developed. It was even used to barter for goods from other countries.

The earliest recorded kings, or pharaohs, date back to 3100 BC, the beginning of Egyptian recorded history. It is widely believed that two

Egyptian kings ruled separately over Upper and Lower Egypt for five hundred years before King Narmer unified the two in 3100 BC, providing a relatively stable existence for the next three thousand years.

In 600 BC the Persians invaded Egypt. When Macedonian/Greek Alexander the Great conquered Egypt in 332 BC he was hailed as the liberator of the Egyptians from Persian rule. Alexander became pharaoh and his descendants, the Ptolemies, ruled until the suicide of Cleopatra in 30 BC. Modern rule includes the Roman Period from 30 to 395 AD, the Coptic and Byzantine Period from 395 to 540 AD and the Arab Conquest of 640 to 641 AD. In the 1500s the Ottoman Empire established itself and today's population remains largely Muslim.

The construction of the Aswan High Dam became both a blessing and a curse. Power generated from the dam supplied electricity to much of Egypt. The drought in Africa while we were visiting had little impact on Egypt because the 1970 opening of the dam flooded all of Nubia and created Lake Nassar, a vast water supply. Thus, conditions in Somalia, accompanied with massive starvation and war, did not happen in Egypt during those dry years.

However, because the water table along the Nile was now kept at a constant level, many of the treasured ancient monuments were endangered. With the dam now regulating water flow, salt water from the Mediterranean that flowed into the Nile could no longer be expelled after annual floods. Water seepage marks and white discoloration indicating harmful levels of corrosive salt flowing in from the Mediterranean were visible in ancient buildings all along the Nile. The corrosive effect of the salt may prove to be most damaging to the monuments and crops along the banks. Additionally, without the annual floods and accompanying deposits of fertile soil, nutrients were being depleted from farmlands along the river. With solutions came problems, it seemed.

A few other interesting tidbits:
- Royal rule ended in Egypt in 1952 and presidential elections were now held.
- Historically, Egyptians are very tolerant of other people. Even temples to foreign gods had been allowed and there were many discoveries in the decade preceding our arrival to support this.
- In 1992, sixty percent of all Egyptians were under five years of age and the population was increasing by one million every nine months. The average number of children in a family was seven, down from nine just a few years prior.

After our lecture we had some time for lunch on our own. Wayne and I chose the hotel's café, La Patisserie. The menu featured heavy choices, many with salads and raw vegetables. We opted for hamburgers and the taste distinctly differed from its American cousin. More about that later...

At 1:15 p.m. we met in front of the hotel and split into two groups of twenty. These groups stayed together for the duration of our twelve-day tour, each with its own bus and Egyptian guide. Our Cairo driver was Farid, and our guide Manal was a bright and beautiful Egyptian woman in her early thirties. She had a college education and three graduate degrees in Egyptology. Her English was impeccable and she had a deep love for her country and its people. She was a stickler for our staying together and for waiting until after her presentations to take photos. Some of those photo ops were awfully hard to resist.

Our first bus ride to the Egyptian Antiquities Museum was all of a block and a half from our hotel. We could see the building across a series of roadways but John had warned us that we would be taking our lives in our own hands by trying to cross the intersecting streets. As we soon discovered, a red traffic light in Cairo meant nothing. Cars, buses and trucks barrel on whether the lights were green, yellow or red. Though horns blared constantly, we saw no open hostility among drivers and surprisingly no collisions. Remarkably, we noticed donkey carts moving through the bustling traffic seemingly unaffected by modern motorized vehicles.

Once at the museum we made our way through masses of people in the courtyard. Inside, the crowds thinned and we suspected that our afternoon arrival time was intentional. As was the case at most of the museums and temples we visited, we needed to buy a permit to take photos. Although fees to take photos were reasonable at about US$3.50, they were astronomical for movie cameras. One member of our group religiously paid as much as US$25 to record our travels for posterity.

We began our tour on the ground floor with an introduction to Old Kingdom art, 2700–2200 BC. During this period, man was represented as a god and depicted in perfect proportion. We saw this in a 3rd-Dynasty life-sized statue of Djoser found in the Step Pyramid at Saqqara.

We also viewed an exquisitely carved stone statue of Mycerinus, the 4th-Dynasty pharaoh who built the smallest pyramid at Giza. This statue, one of four discovered by Harvard Professor Reisner in 1908, was indeed a treasure. Carved in triad form, Mycerinus was flanked by the district, or nome, deity and Hathor, best known as the fertility goddess, with horns encasing a disc sun. She would soon become one of my favorites. The triad, or concept of the trinity, has been adopted by modern religions and would appear in ancient

Egyptian art repeatedly throughout our tour.

We marveled at a grouping of foot-tall three-dimensional carvings with scenes of daily life. Small limestone statues depicted bakers, carpenters, potters, butchers, and even a woman making beer which, by the way, originated in Egypt. The well-preserved wood statue of a seated scribe dating from the time of Mycerinus haunted us with its piercing eyes of alabaster, rock crystal and black stone. The scribe's round body spoke of a good life in the inner circles of the court four thousand years ago.

The Old Kingdom ended after the building of the great pyramids of Giza. It is probable that a period of low flooding and resulting drought brought with it a time of famine and unrest. Unification and recovery did not occur until the 11th Dynasty at the time of Mentuhotep II in 1233 BC. The art of the Middle Kingdom lacked the quality of earlier times, both in the materials used and the workmanship. Sandstone was often employed instead of a firm stone. Eyes were no longer inlaid. Nevertheless, we were awed by a crudely painted sandstone statue of 11th-Dynasty Middle Kingdom Pharaoh Mentuhotep II discovered at Deir el-Bahari, and the art provided an invaluable record of life along the Nile.

We passed four large granite sphinxes dating from the Middle Kingdom's 12th Dynasty, 1991–1783 BC. From these it was evident that the concept of the pharaoh as a god, widely held in the Old Dynasty, had shifted to a more human conceptualization of the pharaoh. Realism replaced perfectionism in art. Faces bore serious expressions and even a wrinkle or two could be seen.

As we moved through the halls of this massive museum, Manal explained that ancient art was produced as art for eternity and not as art for pleasure. She pointed out several works that illustrated deformities in ancient man. In one a dwarf was realistically portrayed; in another a disfigured Queen Punt appeared to have had Elephant Man's Disease causing her to be short and squat.

One exception to reality, however, was a statue of Queen Hatshepsut depicting her as male. She ruled for twenty years from 1478 to 1458 BC and her stepson, King Tuthmosis III, did his best to obliterate her memory when he became pharaoh. The massive temple in the Valley of the Queens that we later visited gave sad evidence of this defacement.

Another interesting period occurred during the reign of King Amenhotep IV, also known as Akhenaten. He was in power around 1370 BC just prior to the now-famous Tutankhamun. Akhenaten attempted to establish a single deity to worship, Atum, the sun god. The exaggerated art of this period depicts humans with elongated heads, and much of the art was destroyed when this short-lived period of monotheism ended and King Tut's reign began.

On the second floor of the museum we encountered an overwhelming display of treasures from the tomb of King Tutankhamun who reigned from 1361 to 1352 BC from the age of ten to nineteen. Although an insignificant ruler, his tomb contained a legacy of artifacts that miraculously were never pillaged. The treasures were discovered by Howard Carter in 1922. To date every other tomb discovered in the Valley of the Kings had been looted and only etched reliefs and an occasional sarcophagus remained.

It is difficult to imagine the emotions that Carter and his team must have experienced when they entered Tut's chambers. From photos of the disarray of the artifacts in the tomb it is widely believed that some ancient grave robbers must have been caught in the act. Items were hastily tossed into the antechambers before the tomb entrance was resealed for what the ancient Egyptians had hoped would be eternity.

Wayne and I had been in the process of moving from Chicago to the Los Angeles area when select pieces from King Tut's tomb toured the United States in the late 1970s and we missed the exhibition in both cities. Many items that were not part of the traveling exhibit now lay at our fingertips, and today's opportunity to see this vast collection deeply moved us.

Case after case of jewelry and other funereal ornamentation encrusted with precious stones dazzled us. We noted necklaces in the shapes of falcons, cobras and scarabs. Tut's coffin weighing 242 pounds, primarily of gold, sat before us. If Tut was a minor king, we could only imagine the magnitude of items placed in tombs of more significant rulers.

Tut's gold burial mask rested in another display case. It was crowned with bands of blue lapis from Persia and had holes in the ears for earrings. Another case contained four exquisite miniature coffins for Tut's viscera—his liver, stomach, lungs, and intestines.

When the tomb was discovered it took seven years to catalogue and remove all the treasures. The mummy itself was fairly well preserved, particularly the face which had been covered with and protected by the burial mask. Since the mummy was now in danger of deterioration it was no longer on public display.

Other items from the tomb included two chariots, a throne, and among many other items of furniture, three beds in the shapes of a cheetah, a combination hippo/crocodile, and a cow. Clothing and sandals were recovered, as were three perfectly preserved dried floral arrangements and a collection of miniature statues and tools representing work to be done for the king in his afterlife.

A vast array of food and grains had been stored in the tomb. Musical instruments, a board game similar to chess and even boomerangs were unearthed. The art on one of the chairs depicted Tut and his wife with the sun-god Atum shining down on them. The exhibit simply must be seen to be believed and, as one of our fellow travelers noted, "It just goes to show that you can take it with you."

We returned to the hotel shortly after 4:00 p.m. and Wayne and I ventured into the workout center. It was well equipped and staffed by a muscular trainer who looked like Egypt's answer to Arnold Schwarzenegger. He helped both of us with the weight machines and floor exercises. Best of all he gave me a neck and shoulder massage that took away every kink I had accumulated during the past few travel days.

This particular day was Thanksgiving in the States and the Ramses Hilton featured a traditional Thanksgiving menu in its main dining room. We, however, celebrated with a Bedouin dinner in the hotel's Falafel restaurant. We all gathered for cocktails and brief introductions before being seated in a colorful tent-like dining room for the evening's food and entertainment.

John had ordered an assortment of hot and cold appetizers for each table to sample, including pita bread topped with baba ghanoush and sesame seed tahini. A favorite of mine was bessara, a paste made from mashed fava beans and topped with fried onions. Dishes of olives and pickled eggplant were coupled with warm tamiya fritters, deep-fried beans, coriander, and green onion balls. Boureke, a minced meat pie, and kobeba, a fritter of crushed wheat, meat and pine nuts completed the first course. We all avoided tabbouleh and other fresh vegetable dishes even though they looked enticing.

I selected moussaka for my entrée and Wayne had kofta kebob, ground meat formed into meatballs and then grilled on skewers. Desserts reflecting Middle Eastern influence included creamy puddings and honey-and-nut-laced pastries.

The entertainment was the climax of the evening. A show featuring a smattering of classical and a large dose of modern music, singing, dance, and comedy continued non-stop for well over an hour. The loosely choreographed show paid homage to Bedouin entertainment although it was largely a Hollywood-esque production. The highlights were a pole-dueling routine and a whirling dervish who performed so long that it made us dizzy just watching him. For the finale we were treated to a performance by a belly dancer. We all agreed that tonight would go down as one of our more unorthodox Thanksgivings.

Friday's wake-up came early with a 5:30 a.m. Muslim call to prayer. Just in case anyone was hard of hearing, the call was amplified by a loud speaker. This was a first for us and we would experience early morning calls to prayer on this and future trips. The words tell followers that God is the greatest, God is Allah, and Muhammad is Allah's last prophet. The caller can then ad lib at will. Some were quite beautiful, others abrasive, depending on the quality of the caller, or Imam. Manal told us that the government was considering a ban on the amplification of the calls since not everyone wanted to be bombarded by them from sunrise to sunset.

After breakfast, Group Two, as we had come to be known, boarded our bus with Manal for a city tour. The Arabic city of Cairo dates to 969 AD; its name means victorious. Cairo, however, has an even longer history and there remain three distinct parts to the city—the ancient settlement, the Coptic or Christian area and Islamic Cairo.

We drove along the Nile past the tower of the al-Manial Palace of Muhammad Ali Tewfik. Egypt's last royal line, established by Muhammad Ali in 1840, ended with the 1952 revolution. Another minaret-styled tower along the river commemorated the beginning of democratic rule in Egypt and visitors could ascend it for panoramic views.

Curving inland, we passed the ruins of a massive Roman aqueduct. This route gave us our first glimpse of the way of life in Cairo. Women in long black robes and covered heads cooked on small braziers along the roadway. Pushcarts and donkey carts loaded with fruits and vegetables lined the streets. The fertility of the Nile Valley was evidenced by the size of the produce. I had never seen such gigantic cauliflower.

Friday is the Muslim day of worship and most residents of Cairo consider Friday and Saturday their weekend. It was a good day for us to tour the city because the usual traffic congestion was at a minimum and we arrived at our first destination, the Citadel, in no time at all.

Resting on a rise, the Citadel encompassed an imposing view of the city. The centerpiece of the walled compound was an elaborate mosque built in the Ottoman style. Although a replica of the Sultan Ahmed mosque in Istanbul, it boasted two minarets. Wayne and I donned our trusty airplane slippers and entered the vast mosque with our group.

We sat in the center for some time as Manal told us more about the Muslim religion. The First Pillar of the faith was Belief that Muhammad is the last prophet after Jesus. The Second Pillar was Prayer five times each day after first cleansing the body. The Third Pillar was Fasting during the month of Ramadan. Exceptions were granted for illness, pregnancy, travel, or heavy work. Those who were exempted could make up for not fasting by feeding one poor person for each day missed. This could be done discreetly by donating food to a hospital or a mosque settlement. The Fourth Pillar was Alms Paying and the Fifth Pillar was the Pilgrimage to Mecca and Medina on specific days of the year. All five pillars applied to men and women, and all

Muslims were expected to make a pilgrimage at least once in their lifetime if they could afford the journey.

Manal then explained the three elements of design used in mosques—floral, geometric and calligraphic. Animals were considered pagan and never appeared. The Muslim calendar was lunar and the reason all minarets had a crescent moon at the top. Every mosque had a recess in a wall that pointed toward Mecca. In the Citadel mosque it pointed southeast.

She told us that Muhammad Ali loved this mosque. As a Turkish soldier fighting against Napoleon, he became a very powerful Ottoman leader. In 1840 his power was limited to Egypt and he became king. The last of his line, King Farouk, was defeated in the 1952 Civil War.

We boarded our bus and headed down the hill to the base of the Citadel for a tour of the Mosque of Sultan Hassan. Beautiful in its simplicity, this edifice offered an interesting contrast to the elaborate Citadel Mosque. Built in a more traditional form around a central courtyard, it was flanked by four large covered areas. Instead of an array of color on the walls there were etchings of floral and geometric patterns and calligraphy. Although we did not go inside, Manal told us that the Shah of Iran is buried in the mosque directly across the street.

Next we drove past the oldest section of Cairo, the City of the Dead. This vast burial area was covered by acres of tiny mausoleum-like buildings. We could see people wandering through the ruins and Manal told us that many of those left homeless in the recent October earthquake had taken up residence among the tombs.

We wound our way through the streets of Cairo to the Khan el-Khalili Bazaar. Manal led us through a series of narrow passageways lined with shop after shop selling brass, jewelry, rugs, traditional clothing, and trinkets of all sorts. It was crowded and touristy but the merchants, all men, were friendly and the area was relatively clean. Along the way we saw the first of many men smoking a water pipe of tobacco mixed with honey. Although alcohol is prohibited in the Muslim religion, most of the men are chain smokers and the smell of smoke is pervasive. Places like the bazaar felt claustrophobic to me and I gladly exited the maze, returning to the bus for the next phase of our city tour. Continuing through the streets of Cairo we were struck by the abject poverty in the older section of the city. The crumbling buildings had begun their process of decay long before the fall earthquake. In fact, we saw very little evidence of earthquake damage. An occasional fissure in a wall provided the only telltale signs.

The streets were crowded at noontime. We passed a flea market teeming with men and women in bright flowing traditional robes called galabeyas.

We also noticed that most rooftops were covered with old furniture and had laundry drying on clotheslines. Just before noon a call to prayer sounded and a group of men knelt on small prayer rugs along the side of the road.

Retracing part of our morning route along the Nile we headed for the Coptic area. On a side street that cut through the ancient aqueduct and followed along several blocks of open-air markets, vendors were roasting fish just inches from the dust stirred by passing buses and carts. There were so many people along the street that it seemed almost impossible for our bus to get through the kaleidoscope of people, donkeys and horses, carts and wagons, and piles of fruit, vegetables, meat, and fish. Unlike the people we saw along the streets near the bazaar in central Cairo, I noticed overweight people here. Judging from all the activity in the marketplace, eating was an important part of life in the Coptic area.

When we reached the center, we toured a small church. Manal explained that Christianity was introduced to Egypt by St. Mark in 61AD, and by the end of the century almost all of Alexandria had been converted. Christianity flourished because Egyptians saw it as a means of being rescued from the Roman gods and the Christian concept of the trinity fit with the centuries-old Egyptian belief in the triad. The early Egyptian Christians often felt persecuted and used the ankh, the hieroglyphic sign of life in the shape of a cross, to symbolize their belief. Today's Coptic cross looks quite different, however.

From the church, we wandered through an ancient walled area dating to the time of Christ. In fact, it is widely believed that Jesus, Mary and Joseph spent some time here. Tucked at one end of the small village was the Synagogue of Ben Ezra. Although it was undergoing extensive renovations, we were able to go inside for a quick peek. Judaism was introduced to Egypt by Moses, most likely between 1600 and 1200 BC. It is believed that the current synagogue, dating roughly to 1200 AD, was erected on the exact site of the oldest synagogue in the world, built around 400 BC.

Wandering back through the narrow dirt streets of this enclave was like stepping back two thousand years in time. The buildings were constructed as they had been for centuries and I felt as if we were walking into a painting from the time of Christ. Those who lived here still dressed in the age-old robes and used donkeys and horses as their means of transportation. It was truly awe-inspiring.

We returned to our hotel in traffic that had thickened significantly. Even on this holiday cars and buses whizzed along the main thoroughfares at a suicidal rate of speed. As John had warned us the day before, red traffic lights meant absolutely nothing to Cairo drivers and our coachman was no exception. The rule seemed to be he-who-got-there-first-could-go. Horns blared incessantly but for some unbelievable reason tempers never seemed to flare. During our days in Cairo we never saw an accident. Well, one. I'll tell you about that later.

All this in one morning! Wayne and I decided to have lunch at a different hotel and we bravely forged our way across the busy streets to a walkway along the Nile. John had warned us to be on the lookout for potholes in the sidewalks and this stretch had some gaps large enough to swallow an unsuspecting tourist. We kept one eye on the pavement and one on the Nile as we walked. After an unmemorable lunch at the InterContinental we returned to the hotel for a late afternoon flight to Aswan.

One of the marvels of traveling with a tour group was that when we touched down in Aswan at 7:00 p.m. we were met immediately, escorted to a waiting bus and, as if by some magic, our luggage appeared in our hotel room. This was Wayne's and my first organized tour and it was indeed a treat not to have to deal with all the travel basics. We simply showed up at the appointed hour and went with the flow.

We ferried across the Nile to our next hotel, the Aswan Oberoi, on Elephantine Island. Even in the dark we knew we were in for a treat. This relatively new luxury hotel could only have been built at this location since the opening of the 1970 dam. Without it the island would have been inundated by the annual Nile floods.

When we arrived at the hotel we were greeted by musicians and handed a drink called tamr hindi. To make this popular Egyptian drink, the seeds and bark of a tamarind tree were boiled in water, strained, sweetened with sugar and chilled. It was…interesting.

Our room overlooked a massive series of burial caves that had been carved into the cliffs along the river. The area was illuminated by a series of spotlights that created a spectacular night-time view. We absorbed the majestic scene from our balcony before joining our group for a buffet dinner in the Orangerie, the hotel's poolside restaurant. We politely refused a tempting array of fresh fruits and vegetables and had our fill of chicken, fish, lamb sausages, moussaka, and much more. Egyptians do believe in ample meals.

After dinner we took the ferry to the mainland with two fellow tourists. Other than the constant badgering by pony-cart drivers we had a pleasant walk along the bank of the Nile. On our return ferry trip, we encountered several others from our group who had ventured into the spice market, still thriving at this late hour. It had been a long but fascinating day and we were ready for a good night's sleep, hopefully one without an amplified 5:00 a.m. wake-up call summoning the faithful to morning prayer.

Sabah al Khair...*good morning* in Arabic. Khair is pronounced like the English word *here*. Today we had a relatively leisurely start and after breakfast we met our group for a felucca sail on the Nile. Although most of us assumed that we were in for a touristy time, we soon found it to be one of the highlights of our trip.

The boat's captain, a Nubian, guided our felucca back and forth across the river. The tranquility of the water and the silence of the boat lulled us all as we skirted between Elephantine Island and the rolling dunes of the Sahara on the western bank. The views were breathtaking and I would always carry a mental picture of the layers created by the Nile, a lush green belt at its edge and the vast Sahara stretching beyond it. With a clear blue sky above us, spectacular seemed too ordinary a word to describe the beauty of this morning.

NOTE: Sahara means *desert* in Arabic. The Sahara stretches from the banks of the Nile to the Atlantic Ocean. No wonder it is called vast!

Our boat docked on the west bank near the mausoleum of spiritual leader Aga Kahn and we walked up a steep incline to this impressive structure dominating the hillside. On the way up we saw what was to be the only scarab on our tour picking its way across the path in an attempt not to be trampled. In retrospect I wish I had taken a photo of it.

The Aga Khan was born in India and died in Pakistan. Because this area along the Nile held a special place in his heart, he built a home and mausoleum here. At the time of our visit, his younger widow still spent much of her year in the home. Ali Kahn, his son, married actress Rita Hayworth.

Manal told us the history of Nubia. Since the country was now under water, a result of the dam, Egypt had to absorb its population. The Nubians were easy to spot with their very dark skin and exquisite features. Our felucca captain, probably in his early twenties, was unbelievably handsome. He stood barefoot in a long flowing robe in the bow of our boat looking very much like one of the perfectly crafted Old Dynasty sculptures in the Egyptian Museum. Although there had been racial issues between the Egyptians and Nubians, tolerance now seemed to prevail. Most Nubians were fluent in Arabic as well as Nubian, a language that is only spoken.

After our tour we boarded the felucca and passed a small boat filled with young boys. Using the lids of large cans in their hands as paddles, they followed closely in hopes of baksheesh from us. They were persistent and one of the crew members used a long pole to push the boat away from us, accidentally hitting one of the boys. He was more humiliated than hurt and began to cry. The others gathered around him as we continued to glide across the Nile.

I noticed that the name of our felucca was Baraka, which Manal translated as *blessing*. Ironically, the bottled water we drank in Egypt was also called Baraka. Loosely translated, I guess we were drinking holy water.

We docked near our cruise ship, the *Nile Romance*, and checked into our cabin where, once again, our luggage had miraculously appeared. Our room was located on the upper deck just below the dining room. Most of the other top-deckers were under the ship's lounge and we gave a sigh of relief that we had drawn the quieter side of the ship. Wrong. I'll tell you more a bit later.

Following a plentiful if not wonderful lunch we boarded a bus with our group for a ride to the Aswan Quarry and its unfinished obelisk. Aswan comes from the Arabic word meaning *granite* and it is granite which gave the area its claim to fame for thousands of years. At the quarry we were greeted by vendors hawking their wares all along the walkway to the monolith still imbedded in the quarry. Wayne did his mountain goat routine and scaled the cliffs around the obelisk looking for the perfect spot for a photo. We were fascinated by the massive monument partially cut from the granite and then abandoned.

Our next destination was the Temple of Philae, built in the Ptolemaic era and located on an island in the Nile reservoir formed by a low twentieth-century dam. The temple dates from the third century BC to the third century AD, the Greco-Roman Period. When the dam was completed in 1970, the temple faced possible ruination because it would have been submerged under the waters of the reservoir for eight months each year. From 1973 to 1977, a team from Egypt, Italy and Germany moved the entire complex to higher grounds on the island in answer to a worldwide plea to save this magnificent treasure. I bought a postcard showing the temple nearly covered by water and marveled at the ingenuity of the relocation effort.

Construction of Philae took place during the rule of Alexander the Great at the end of Pharaonic Egypt and was dedicated to Isis, the Egyptian goddess of life and magic. After Christianity took hold in Egypt, Philae functioned as an active place of worship until the sixth century AD. At one point during our tour we noticed Coptic crosses etched into the temple walls. These would have been added after Egypt's conversion to Christianity in 315 AD.

We began our tour in an unfinished temple with only two completed panels. Next we looked at a piling with political propaganda etched into it depicting a Ptolemaic pharaoh grasping his enemies by the hair. As we would encounter many times during our tour, the face and body of the pharaoh had been disfigured to the knees by a later enemy.

We entered an open court featuring reliefs of the falcon-headed Horus— the sky and, later, war god—and my now-favorite goddess Hathor, patron of the sky, women, fertility, and love. Manal explained that in hieroglyphic drawings, paintings and carvings of the gods and pharaohs appear only in profile. This signified survival into eternity. Only a minor dignitary or an enemy could be etched into a temple wall full-faced.

At our next stop, a hypostyle room with a roof, we learned that the ancient Egyptians placed an extra block at the top of their columns to support the weight of the roof. Even though only a few had survived, one could tell if a roof was part of the original structure by noting whether or not the columns in an area were crowned with a support block. The Egyptians attempted to create architecture for eternity and they often succeeded.

Arriving at the innermost section of the temple we were struck by its small size. Manal explained that ancient Egyptians worshipped the idea that each god represented more than its replica. Therefore, any statue of a god was small and did not require a large space in which to be housed. In addition, since only the high priests were allowed to bring daily offerings into the inner sanctuary, the room's size did not have to be large enough to accommodate the greater populace.

While looking at some of the reliefs, Manal pointed out one of Isis breastfeeding an infant. This was political propaganda indicating the divine right of the child to become pharaoh. She explained how the early Christians were able to adapt these temple reliefs to their own beliefs. For example, Isis could represent the Virgin Mary with the Christ child. Isis protecting the mummy form of Osiris, god of the underworld, might symbolize death and resurrection. In fact, Isis was worshipped for two centuries after Christianity took hold in Egypt.

At the end of our tour, Manal showed us a deep, narrow opening in the ground with markings along one side. This, she explained, was a Nilometer. It was used by the ancient Egyptians to accurately measure the level of the yearly floods and, accordingly, to determine the taxes to be levied in a given year.

Our next stop was the High Dam completed in 1970. At 364 feet high and two miles wide, the dam did not command the majesty of the Glen Canyon Dam at Lake Powell in Arizona, but it had forever altered life along the Nile for all Egyptians. The area south of the dam where Nubia once stood was now Lake Nasser, stretching three hundred miles to the border of Sudan. It was difficult to fathom an entire country now under water.

The jury was still out on the overall benefits provided by the Aswan Dam. Flooding was no longer an unpredictable occurrence of nature, nor was drought. Electrical power was plentiful and irrigation of crops along the Nile was constant. Even tourism had benefited. As I mentioned earlier, the Oberoi Hotel on Elephantine Island could not have been built with the risk of high floods.

On our return trip some from our group hopped off the bus as we neared the famous turn-of-the-century Cataract Hotel in Aswan. Agatha Christie stayed here and the setting inspired her novel *Death on the Nile*. We skirted lush gardens as we walked up the road to the entrance. The good news was that we could all be seated in the Raffle-esque patio bar. The bad news was a fifteen-pound minimum per person. When it was all said and done, we agreed that it was worthwhile and provided a nice diversion after a long day of touring.

We decided to hire a pony cart for our return to the ship, foregoing the mile plus walk. As we neared the main road, we spotted a beautiful horse and cart that looked ready to go. After completing the usual price negotiation, the man we assumed was our carriage driver blew a whistle and we were ushered onto a dilapidated buggy. Talk about a bait and switch! Our driver puffed cigarettes the entire time but he got us back to the ship in good shape—no pun intended.

At 5:00 p.m. we gathered in the dining room for the first of four lectures presented by Lou Orlin, a University of Michigan professor traveling with our tour group. Describing the evolution of life along the Nile, he spoke of the physical, economic, administrative, political, psychological, and symbolic impacts the river had on Egypt and its people throughout its five thousand years of recorded history.

He expressed that Egypt was not urbanized. Rather, it consisted of a chain of people who had accumulated in small groups along the river. Time along the waterway was divided into four units—one for planting and harvesting and three for labor. It was believed that the ancient Egyptian monument builders were not slaves. They simply needed to work to earn their housing and food. Each class had a duty to perform and the higher classes were wealthy enough that they could buy out of their responsibilities.

Dr. Orlin claimed it was Egypt's economic destiny to produce tombs and pyramids. Ancient Egypt was an agricultural and mortuary state. From 3100 to 2200 BC the pharaoh equaled a god and all land belonged to him. As food became scarce and land for the many priests, scribes and other dignitaries began to diminish, the Old Kingdom with pharaoh as a god came to an abrupt end.

With the Nile as the main highway for all ancient Egyptians, Upper and Lower Egypt were unified by 3100 BC. Because the river's cycle was relatively predictable, life along its banks was unified and symphonic. Scribes recorded that from the earliest times Egyptian people had a positive, optimistic view of their destiny. Although it appeared that their focus was solely on death, the ancient Egyptians were at ease with the cosmic view of an afterlife and so they remained upbeat, sharing a sense of deterministic benevolence.

The Nile had a long history of attracting outsiders. Its waters made it accessible and its fertile banks made it desirable to invaders. Therefore, the ancient Egyptians were forced to form a strong military presence and be a part of a system of nations at war. Because Egypt needed wood, gold and precious stones, navigation expanded from the Nile to coastal areas in quest of these goods.

Dr. Orlin closed with the statement that religion in ancient times was the ultimate reality. Ancient Egyptians were religious societies; not societies with religions.

John received a collective chuckle from us when he took the microphone and advised us not to jump ship since our passports were being held by the crew until we checked out. That was followed by a chorus of sighs when he announced an extra-early wake-up call for our flight to Abu Simbel.

After dinner in the ship's dining room we all headed for our cabins in an attempt to maximize our sleeping hours. However, it was some time before we could turn off the memories of today's experiences. Wayne and I both felt as though we had passed through some magical time warp into ancient Egypt.

The next day we did the unthinkable and got up at 5:15 a.m. Wasn't this supposed to be a vacation? By 6:30 a.m. we had finished breakfast and I had jogged eight times up and down the long flight of steps from our ship to the street. If nothing else, it woke me up.

We boarded a bus for a short ride to the airport to catch an 8:00 a.m. flight to Abu Simbel located 168 miles south of Aswan. Abu Simbel is the most colossal temple in Egypt and one of the best-preserved. Built between 1300 and 1233 BC by Ramesses II, it was carved from the side of a sandstone cliff. The temple was dedicated to three gods: Ptah, god of the underworld in Memphis, the first capital of Egypt; Amen-Ra, the god of Thebes; and Re-Harakhte, a form of the sun god Horus, worshipped in Heliopolis. Ramesses II was in power for sixty-seven years and his empire extended from the Delta to Sudan. He built two temples at Abu Simbel; one for himself and one for his wife Nefertari.

With the opening of the High Dam, Abu Simbel was in grave danger of submersion and extinction. Once again, a world-wide plea resulted in a massive UNESCO effort to save it. All four hundred thousand tons of the structures, including the cliff wall, were cut into sections and then reassembled ninety feet above the old site. It was astonishing to see the near-perfect result of the four-year project.

At the entrance to the temple were four 565-foot colossal statues of Ramesses II in a seated position. On one of the walls was an inscription of a peace treaty between the Egyptians and the Hittites believed to be the first in recorded history. This inscription showed Egypt as the conqueror while one belonging to the Hittites declared them as victors. We may never know who won the battle but we can concede that a peaceful settlement must have been accepted by both nations.

Inside the great hypostyle hall, we were overwhelmed by the size and quality of the interior. The ceiling was supported by eight columns faced with statues of Ramesses II in the pose of the god Osiris, the protector of mummification. The ceilings and walls throughout were in excellent condition and we marveled at the quality of the painted reliefs. War and victory topped the list of themes.

After a brief tour of the Temple of Hathor, dedicated to Nefertari, we entered a passageway that took us inside a huge concrete dome forming the infrastructure of the Temple of Abu Simbel. It was upon this dome that the temple was reassembled, truly a feat that rivaled the construction of the original edifice. At a cost of US$35 million in the 1960s, the project received funding from fifty nations. Interestingly, the original site allowed the sun to shine into the inner sanctuary and light up the three statues seated on a bench, including one of Amun and one of the pharaoh, on February 21 and October 21, thought to correspond to the birthday and coronation of Ramesses II. After the edifice was moved, the sun hit the statues one day later.

Arriving in Aswan an hour before lunch, Wayne and I opted to tour the bustling spice market along the banks of the Nile. Several merchants tried to tempt us with their wares but we were more interested in simply absorbing the flavor of the local shops. This proved to be anything but a tourist area and it was teaming with Egyptians and Nubians doing their Sunday marketing. Wayne and I walked though several blocks of the marketplace people-watching and eyeing the merchandise they were offered.

Once back on the main street along the Nile we encountered the usual assemblage of street peddlers, felucca pilots and pony-cart drivers. We fended them off and walked to our ship for a quick shower before the beginning of our Nile cruise.

Lunch consisted of another overdose of overcooked rather ordinary food coupled with an ample assortment of no-no's—raw fruits and vegetables either standing alone or mixed with OP's—otherwise permissibles. We wondered at the logic of serving such fare to those of us on board who were obviously tourists. What was lacking in quality, however, was once again well compensated in quantity. After lunch we returned to our cabin to raid a plastic container I had packed with cookies and candy. M&M's never tasted so divine.

Our ship left port after lunch and we went to the top deck to watch the golden dunes of the Sahara and the lush verdant band of farmland beneath it pass by us. Wayne and I would never forget the breathtaking beauty of this afternoon and we sat for hours mesmerized by the scenery. Occasionally a group of men would appear as they plowed fields with oxen or herded their goats along the banks of the Nile. They wore long robes much like their ancestors had worn thousands of years before them. Groups of children in bright dress would sometimes wave from the shore. Women came to the river's edge to fill huge water jugs. Here and there fishermen worked in teams to gather their nets.

After an hour the dunes on the west faded and the east bank of the river became our focal point. We saw wide expanses of fertile land planted with sugar cane, bananas and date palms. The electrical lines that occasionally dotted the banks were the only indication that we were now in the 20th century.

Several hours later, our ship docked near the Temple of Kom Ombo. Divided into vertical sections, the temple was dedicated to two rival gods. The left side was the temple of Horus, the hawk-headed god of the sky while the right side honored Sobek, crocodile god of the Nile who brought fertility to the land. This double form of construction was unlike any other in ancient Egypt. Its hypostyle hall was roped off after a huge chunk of ornamentation had plunged to the ground during the October 1992 earthquake. Tourists were at the site during the quake and it was truly a miracle that no one was crushed by the sheer weight of the falling stonework.

Manal pointed out a series of hieroglyphs representing some of the world's first medical records. Ancient recipes for medicines listed ingredients that were part scientific and part superstition. The ancient Egyptians performed brain surgery, dentistry and set broken bones. I also noticed a figure of Hathor seated on a stool, the method used for childbirth in ancient times.

We passed a water well serving as a Nilometer that appeared to be approximately sixty or seventy feet deep. As we concluded our walking tour, Manal showed us a small sanctuary containing the mummified remains of several crocodiles. The room had been filled with croc mummies but on this day only a few remained for viewing.

Once back on board the Nile Romance we all gathered in the dining room for Dr. Orlin's second lecture. Today he spoke of the origins of religion. All religions, he said, distinguished between the holy and the non-holy, or demonic. Lessons were passed down from ancient times through fables, legends and history—that is, they were communicated through narrative.

From the earliest times, religious practices were perpetuated through imitative rituals that re-presented reality. The hyphen in re-presented is intentional. Continuance of religion is effected through repetition of core beliefs and practices. Other common threads were sacrifice, rights of acceptance such as baptism, and ecstasy. Practicing religion was therefore never an arbitrary act. Ancient religion was primarily involved with the group and not the individual. Thus, if one person violated the law it put the entire group in jeopardy.

Over time man transformed the forces of religion from the emotional to the analytical. In ancient times, however, the universe was seen as dramatic and religion was an emotional response to irregular occurrences. Religion could explain famine, floods and drought. It could explain the sun, moon and stars.

Most religions at some point tried to get rid of animal fetishes and adopt more human forms of worship. In early Egyptian religious beliefs, however, man and animal were intermixed. Also, concepts could be contradictory in early Egyptian religion without seeming to bother anyone. There simply was no uniformity of dogma in the ancient Egyptian religion—nor, for that matter, in most Eastern religions. In contrast, most Western religions have a set dogma.

Ancient religion was more a vast poem as poetry is essentially a mix of images, similes, hyperboles, and contradictions. To this day, Near-Eastern religious beliefs are an explosion of emotional images governing religion, politics and life.

Dr. Orlin posed the question: What is religion? The answer, he felt, was that it is simply the practice of cults. The ancient pharaoh was therefore the pontiff of a whole collection of beliefs. Ceremonies were created to celebrate the myth. It is important to note that a myth was not an attempt to evade for lack of scientific study but rather to affirm. Magic also played a role in ancient beliefs. Tomb art repeatedly depicted the human spirit moving from the invisible world of the dead back into the world of the living.

After Dr. Orlin's talk, John gave us the run-down on the next day's schedule. Fewer groans occurred this time when he announced another 5:30 a.m. wake-up call for an early morning visit to the temple in Edfu. Our group certainly believed in being the first to arrive at a site.

We had been asked to either purchase at one of the street markets or rent shipboard a galabeya for tonight's dinner. Wayne and I opted to rent knowing we would never wear them in California. Wayne's was operating room green and he commented that he looked more like a surgeon than an

Egyptian. Mine was black with colorful sequins scattered across it. Almost everyone was a good sport and wore a galabeya for the evening's festivities. Lou Orlin purchased a rustic string instrument called a rabab in one of the street markets and, much to everyone's delight, he played Michigan's *Hail to the Victors* on it. Just before dinner we all gathered for a group photo.

Tonight's shipboard dinner proved to be the best we were to have as we floated down the Nile. We were presented with an array of Egyptian dishes and all agreed that the kitchen staff earned rave reviews. I tried a variety of dishes including ground meat wrapped around a boiled egg, spicy spinach, an equally spicy green pepper puree, and moussaka.

After dinner we changed and went topside for a few minutes before retiring for our crack-of-dawn wake-up call. We had opted for an upper deck cabin assuming it would be quiet. Wrong! We were kept awake by a series of thumps and bumps in the dining room above us for nearly an hour. It sounded as if someone was off-loading supplies. Wayne finally dressed and decided to have a look for himself. He met John in the hall who assured him he would solve the problem. A few moments later the noise ceased. The next morning we learned that the staff was moving all the chairs and tables to shampoo the carpet.

Our early wake-up call was preceded by another amplified call to prayer shortly after 5:00 a.m. There was no rest for the weary with a window facing the speaker. We were up, dressed, coffee'd, and queued for our pony-cart ride to the temple in Edfu by 6:00 a.m., sharing the cart with two others from our group. As we rode through the streets, we noted that even at this early hour the village bustled with activity.

As had been promised, the Temple of Horus in Edfu was an impressive treasure. With its roof still intact one could feel the majesty of the ancient temple's architecture. Dating to the Ptolemaic Period, 237–57 BC, the temple was dedicated to Horus, the falcon-headed god of the sky and several large falcon statues remained on the grounds. Manal explained that when a temple falcon died, the populace would learn a replacement had been selected when a cloud of smoke rose from its roof. This method of releasing smoke to indicate the selection of a new Pope continues to this day at the Vatican in Rome.

Outer temple walls usually were decorated with sunken reliefs. When an interior wall had sunken reliefs, it indicated that it was once the exterior of the edifice. In the Temple of Horus, it was easy to spot such additions. Manal also told us that the art work in this temple was a step backward from what we would see in Karnak. The quality of stone in the buildings was inferior and the relief carvings were not as fine.

We walked through the hypostyle hall and courtyard to the inner chapel and sanctuary. Once again we were struck by the tiny sanctuary in contrast to the massive size of the temple complex. On the sanctuary walls were reliefs depicting the pharaoh entering the temple on the festival day that celebrated the new year. Every year on this day the statue of the god Horus was taken out of the sanctuary and paraded for all to view.

The outer walls of the temple depicted war scenes between Horus, the sky god, and Seth, god of war, chaos and storms. In an attempt to kill his brother and usurp his power the evil god Seth first tried to drown his powerful brother Osiris, god of the dead. When that failed Seth murdered Osiris, cut him into fourteen pieces and scattered them into the Nile. Isis, wife of Osiris, was able to collect thirteen of the pieces and reassemble her husband. Because of this ordeal Osiris became the god of mummification and is depicted in green, the color of rebirth.

As we walked back toward our pony cart we were struck by the beauty of the temple in the early morning light. We rejoined the couple from our tour and trotted back through the streets to our ship. The number of pony carts lining each block astounded us. There were hundreds of them in this small village and each had a driver dependent upon tourism for his livelihood.

After a shipboard breakfast we went topside and were again treated to the tranquil bucolic scenes of life along the Nile. We chatted with new friends as we took in the views. It is almost impossible to describe the beauty and serenity of life along the shores of the river.

We sailed for three hours, occasionally passing another tour ship traveling in the opposite direction. A traditional greeting of horn-honking was followed by waves from each ship's crew and passengers.

As we neared Esna, mountain ridges appeared in the distance on either side of the Nile. Reaching the town, our ship first had to pass through a lock. We had been forewarned that this was an unpredictable venture, taking anywhere from one to thirty-six hours. Ships had to queue in order of arrival for a turn through the lock and since only one lock accommodated ships traveling in this direction, delays could be monumental.

As we approached, we were delighted to discover that our ship was the only one in line. That was the good news. But something went haywire with the lock's mechanics just as we arrived, causing a four-hour delay. On the spur of the moment our guides decided to usher us off the ship for our tour of the Temple of Khnum, built between 180 and 45 BC, while our captain played the waiting game at the lock.

Having expected to remain on the ship, I wore Bermuda shorts while on deck and there was no time to change. Even though we were told that this was appropriate dress for touring, I was a bit uncomfortable. Egyptian women in small villages never had bare legs or arms and I usually wore slacks with a button-up shirt as a jacket over a lightweight T-shirt. I experienced some critical looks from women in the market area and I vowed that I would not venture beyond the ship with bare legs and arms in the future.

Pony carts were the mode of transportation in Esna and we hopped aboard one of them. As we started down the road along the river we saw a shrouded body being carried into a one-room building. With a hospital located directly across the street, we concluded that this was the local morgue.

As we rode through the streets toward the temple in the center of town we were astonished by the number of people and the level of activity along the roadway. We were also struck by the overwhelming stench of donkey and horse excrement, making it necessary for the locals to keep one eye on the ground while walking. We reached the street leading to the temple and, as usual, our drivers strategically deposited us at the beginning of yet another open-stall marketplace. We scurried past crowds of merchants waving their now-familiar array of trinkets in our direction.

Once at the temple we descended a long staircase to reach an imposing hypostyle hall with an intact roof. Now thirty feet below street level, the temple originally stood level with the Nile. Over time the floods completely covered the building with topsoil and much of the complex remained buried beneath the town of Esna.

The destruction caused by the rising salt level of the Nile waters was painfully evident along the outer walls. The temple honored the god Khnum, depicted as a ram, who created man on his potter's wheel. Manal pointed out the deterioration of the written form of language and showed us how the art work from this later period had less definition. We were growing more and more curious about what to expect over the coming days when we would reach Karnak and some of the earlier mastabas, or tombs, in Saqqara. The best was yet to come.

The ceiling panels in this temple were magnificent and Manal told us they had been restored in recent years. As they had done in other ancient temples, the Roman conquerors set up camp in the hall and the smoke from their fires had all but obliterated the reliefs. With layers of smoke painstakingly removed, the original splendor of the reliefs could once again be appreciated by visitors.

We had a few extra minutes after our tour of the temple and decided to walk further into the village with another couple. This was the first time any of us had ventured beyond the obvious tourist areas and we soon began to feel that we had crossed an invisible barrier. At one point we stopped to smile at a young boy of perhaps four who was carrying a tiny kid—baby goat—about the size of a cat. Other children waved and called out to us from the windows of their dilapidated houses.

At the end of the street, however, a group of men gave us disapproving looks and began to make some unwelcome sounds. We quickly decided to retrace our steps and head back toward the temple and shops. In retrospect, this was the only time we felt unwelcome and even then we did not feel that we were in any sort of danger.

Walking past the temple I thought of my own moment in time earlier in the day. As I crossed the gangplank my U of M name badge plopped into the river. I had worn it faithfully and so was sad to see it disappear into the murky water. Nevertheless, we had fun speculating on its discovery by some future generation when it resurfaced along the banks of the Nile. Barbara Smith and U of M would live on in Egypt.

Passing through the marketplace on the way to our pony cart I noticed people from our group gathered with Manal in one of the shops. Out of curiosity we entered the open stall and watched as a woman merchant—one of the few we encountered on our trip—showed us an assortment of long, colorful scarves. One with purple and green caught my eye and I purchased it for fifteen pounds—just under US$5. Manal later told me that it came from Akhmim, the home of silk weavers since the 3rd century AD. My scarf was a cotton blend woven in a time-honored pattern. I wore it over a silk jacket later in the day and received many compliments.

After returning to our ship for lunch, a group of us sat on the bow to take in the activities of the lock. We were struck by the number of men with rifles and machine guns posted along the banks of the river. Some were in uniform but many wore traditional long flowing robes. A few appeared to be teenagers. We were not sure whether to take comfort in the protective forces that surrounded us or be concerned for our safety.

Not long before we'd arrived, a British woman was killed and two British men were injured in Egypt. Wayne questioned whether we should cancel our trip and I assured him that the University of Michigan would cancel it if there were safety issues. Many tourists did in fact cancel their trips and we had Egypt almost to ourselves. I had read that extra security had recently been deployed along the Nile to ensure safe passage for tour boats and suspected we were now encountering it. No arbitrary potshots would be fired at us by fundamentalists today, at least not in Esna.

By the time we were finally ushered into the lock it was mid-afternoon and when the gates closed, we sat for another half hour before the water level began to change. I created my own Nilometer by counting a series of bricks along one of the walls. When more bricks began to appear, indicating a drop in the water level, it was only a matter of fifteen minutes before we were on our way. We never discovered the cause for the delay but were relieved to continue our journey after waiting four hours to go less than two hundred yards.

Due to the hang-up at the lock, we had the Nile virtually to ourselves. Only an occasional ship heading south obscured our vista. More farmers, goats and buffalos appeared from time to time and once in a while groups of children would run to the shore and wave.

It was so quiet that when we did pass a water pump at one point, the noise seemed almost deafening. We only spotted one or two factories along the 150-plus miles we cruised. Most of what we experienced was a step back in time. At one spot we noticed a young boy trying to hold on to a water buffalo. The animal slipped out of his grasp and from out of nowhere a second boy appeared. The two boys chased the water buffalo for quite a distance before cornering it. Later we watched a group of women in brightly colored robes gathered at the river's edge to do their laundry. At another point a chain of women filled water jugs, passing them up from one to another. The Nile functioned as an all-purpose life source for humans, livestock and crops.

We floated silently past bluffs with layers of topsoil deposited by centuries of flooding clearly visible. As we approached Luxor, our final shipboard destination, the countryside became more arid with vistas resembling the deep canyons of Utah and Arizona. The late afternoon sun cast a red glow over the rocky hills in the distance. Wayne and I would always cherish these images of life along the Nile. Actually, we would have no choice. When I picked up the twenty-plus rolls of film that we shot I knew we had much more than mental memories. I doubt that not many square miles of scenery went by uncaptured by our trusty cameras. We had this trip covered.

Late in the afternoon we gathered in the dining room for the third of Dr. Orlin's lectures. We were all touched by his sensitive portrayal of the ancient Egyptian people he introduced to us in today's talk. He began with an analogy comparing the study of ancient history to a brightly colored opera set. Over time the set begins to get hazy. The colors fade until only a grey palette with blotches of color remain. Like the set restorer, it is the job of historians to create a colorful vision of earlier societies. The picture cannot be complete without an understanding of the people who lived in ancient times. Dr. Orlin read some of the pieces used to entertain royalty along with some touching ancient love poems. We began to feel a strong link with the people who had lived, worked and worshipped in the villages and temples we were now exploring.

Dr. Orlin told us that Egypt's civilization predated Hebrew civilization by eighteen hundred years and so it had a much older literary tradition. He related a fable of a pharaoh's son who came back empty-handed from a hunting expedition and was afraid to report to his father. The story is supposedly narrated by a third party, an old man, who told of a shipwreck where the son of the pharaoh remained near death for three days before being rescued by a gilded cobra. The snake tells an enfolded story of the son's rescue. This charming tale has survived the test of time.

Our ship docked just north of Luxor at 6:15 p.m. and this evening our stateroom faced the river. With a two-day stay at this port we cheered our good fortune. Our euphoria did not last for long. Five minutes after we docked, a second ship anchored to our side and we discovered that we were just a few feet from our neighboring ship's dining room. With it came shouting, laughter and loud Egyptian music. So much for our peaceful two nights on the Nile.

Dinner at 8:00 p.m. featured a seafood buffet. After watching fish being chopped apart in the filthy streets of Aswan, we remained somewhat apprehensive. Assuming that cooking took care of any unwanted germs I sampled several unknowns and each was quite good. As usual, we passed on the array of fresh fruits and vegetables. With an abundance of rice and breads on the buffet we wouldn't go away hungry. We did wish the chef would stay with the Egyptian fare that he prepared so well and give up his attempts to create Western cooking. Something definitely lacked in the translation.

Our travel group meshed well and we sat with four fellow passengers. We had become a Group Two subgroup and shared many good times throughout our tour. Dr. Orlin and his wife also joined us and we had a lively discussion until the waiters flashed the dining room lights.

On impulse we left the ship with Ruth, a fun and funny woman from our group, and walked past the usual rows of stalls filled with tourist trinkets. We encountered the now usual, "Hello! You English? Want to buy?" The constant high-pressure selling was beginning to get to us and after wandering a couple of blocks we headed back to the ship, even though Wayne was tempted by a T-shirt featuring a cigarette-ad camel and the caption, "Nine out of ten men who try Camels prefer women." He quickly came to his senses knowing the T-shirt would never fly in the States.

Once on board, we spotted a wedge of rose-colored moon about to drop below the horizon. As we sat watching it disappear, we were joined by a Canadian woman I had met while jogging up and down the steps in Aswan. She was a doctor and had been in Cairo presenting a tuberculosis study to a medical group from third world countries. Since she was in Egypt, she decided to join our group. We chatted and sat under the stars while wrapped in our warmest coats until 11:45 p.m.

Returning to our stateroom we were disappointed that the music and shouting from our neighboring ship was still going strong. We finally figured out that the crew's quarters were not far from us and the crew went on well into the night. We finally resorted to earplugs in an attempt to block the late-night revelry.

To our delight the next morning's departure did not take place until 9:15 a.m. and even that was an optional visit to a local jewelry market. Tour guides work out a deal with shop owners and the inevitable stops for shopping crop up regularly. Wayne and I gave it a whirl and I purchased an 18-carat gold ankh, the ancient cross-like symbol of life. A number of our group ordered cartouches with their names in hieroglyphics. Since the symbols for Barbara were not particularly attractive, I decided to forego that memento.

Our next optional stop was a tour of the Luxor Museum with Manal. We shared a cab with several Group Twos and spent an hour in this small but mighty museum housing some of Egypt's finest sculptures. Many on display were discovered at the nearby Luxor Temple. The statues provided an almost mystical link to the past as we studied these three-dimensional figures. Horemheb, the last pharaoh of the 18th Dynasty, stood with the sun god Atum. Here, we learned that a statue with a figure sporting a straight beard represents life on earth while one with a curly beard represents life after death.

Hathor, my now favorite goddess, stood before us holding an ankh. She was carved during the reign of Amenhotep III, 1405–1367 BC. The last statue in the first room that we toured was of Amenhotep III himself. This statue had survived particularly well because the left hand was attached to the body, giving it more integrity. Many statues with outstretched hands had not withstood the test of time.

Manal explained that ancient artisans would divide a stone to be carved with a series of vertical and horizontal lines. Once a pattern of squares was overlaid on the stone the work could be produced to scale by using the spaces as proportional guides. The classical ideal was eighteen squares.

Moving through the museum we saw a headless statue of Ramesses II, the hippopotamus goddess Taweret, and the falcon god Horus. We also passed a small alabaster sphinx of King Tutankhamun. We could clearly see the difference between Old Kingdom art with an emphasis on perfection and Middle Kingdom art featuring more human aspects. Belly rolls and wrinkles replaced near-perfect forms as attested by the statue of a corpulent scribe.

By far my most favorite piece was a sculpture of Tutmosis III, 1482–1425 BC. As we approached it, tears came to my eyes. Carved from imposing black stone, the statue showed the king with a serious yet haunting smile, handsome yet strong. A sculpture of Akhenaten, the 18th-Dynasty pharaoh who promoted monotheism, fascinated us with its elongated face, heavy eyelids and dreamy expression reminiscent of works by Modigliani.

We hailed a taxi for our return to the ship and another round of ordinary lunch fare. Then we then boarded a large ferry boat and headed across the Nile to a dock near the Valley of the Kings and Queens, passing more than fifty other ferries docked along the east bank of the river. I had somehow envisioned only a few tour boats on the Nile yet even with tourism experiencing a dramatic drop there were many ships docked in Luxor.

During the Old and Middle Kingdoms, pharaohs were buried in mastabas or pyramids. Even the great pyramids at Giza did not prevent graves from being robbed and so the New Kingdom pharaohs opted for Plan B and had their tombs carved into the side of the rocky cliffs before us. Over time many of these well-concealed tombs were pillaged and what must have been vast treasures had long since been melted and divided. It was in the Valley of the Kings, however, that the treasure-filled tomb of young King Tutankhamun was discovered in 1922 by Englishman Howard Carter.

We boarded buses at the dock for a ten-minute ride to the extensive burial valley. As we drove through the desolate countryside, we were struck by the size of a large village along the roadway with buildings that appeared as though they were constructed two thousand years ago. The inhabitants also looked like relics from the past as they strolled along the dirt streets in long flowing robes. Donkeys were the only mode of transportation. Woman walked with baskets and water jugs atop their heads. It truly looked as if time had stood still.

When we reached the Valley of the Kings we were impressed by the enormity of the cliffs and the desolation of the area. Although it was comfortable this time of the year, I had read that temperatures can reach 120 degrees. The ancient pharaohs wanted a spot this desolate and if someone had told us that we were on a lunar surface we might have believed it.

It seemed to me that the only way a grave robber could possibly have discovered the tomb of an ancient pharaoh would have been by word of mouth from someone who had worked on the project. It is truly amazing that modern man has rediscovered so many of these well-concealed tombs, although all but one were pillaged. As of 1992, sixty-seven tombs in the Valley of the Kings had been located.

We first went along the passageway to the tomb of Ramesses IV who died in 1149 BC. Well-preserved reliefs told the story of the seventy-day funeral process. Manal pointed out a text depicting the weighing of the pharaoh's heart against a feather. If the heart was heavier than a feather, the pharaoh was denied an afterlife. Needless to say, the artisan etched a perfectly balanced scale.

As we moved along the corridor, we were astonished by the fine quality of the tomb art. At one point the sun god Ra was depicted with opened falcon-like wings to protect the body of the pharaoh. Since robbers sacked this tomb the magical protection apparently hadn't worked. Other figures representing a smooth twelve-hour transit to eternity lined the hallway.

At the end of the passage was a huge granite sarcophagus in which a casket had once rested. On the ceiling above it was an elaborate painting of the goddess Nut swallowing the sun at night and giving birth to it the next morning. A smaller Shu stood in the middle holding up the sky as a scarab pushed the sun into place. Boats lined the walls on their journey from death to eternity. The blue and gold details in the paintings were particularly striking.

The second tomb we toured was that of Ramesses IX who died in 1111 BC. Following the same principle, its walls documented the journey from death to afterlife. This tomb had recently been restored and cleaned so the colors of the reliefs were vivid. The inner section of the tomb was unfinished and had painted, rather than carved, walls. Most likely the pharaoh had died unexpectedly before the completion of his tomb.

Several other tombs were open to the public and we visited two. Manal delighted many of us when she announced that the tomb of King Tutankhamun, or King Tut as he was known to most of us, had reopened the previous day after a two-year renovation. Even though it was not rated as one of the more interesting tombs, Wayne and I couldn't resist a peek. We were not disappointed. The artwork on the inner chamber was beautiful and we envisioned the many artifacts that we had seen at the Cairo Museum as they might have been found in the tomb. What an incredible experience it must have been for Carter and his team!

Our final tomb was that of Horemheb, an 18th-Dynasty pharaoh who died in 1292 BC. Unlike the other tombs we entered we had to descend a series of steep steps to get to the inner sanctuary. As Manal had predicted, it was worth the effort. The colors that remained on the walls were the best we'd seen and the sarcophagus was extremely interesting. A set of elaborately carved wings wrapped around each of the four corners as if to give protection to the coffin within it. The detail was so precise that the wings seemed to fly away from the edges in three-dimensional detail.

On our way back to the bus we were accosted by a particularly forceful salesman carrying a scarab carved from green stone. It caught my eye—big mistake!—and there was no getting away from the persistent vendor. He asked for 150 Egyptian pounds, an outrageous price, and finally settled for 10 pounds—approximately US$3.30. Etched on the back of the scarab were a series of hieroglyphs. I haven't taken the time to decipher them but it wouldn't surprise me if it read, "Aha! You succumbed to tourist bait!"

As we continued on to the nearby Valley of the Queens, Manal told us that seventy tombs had been discovered to date. We visited that of Queen Tiye, wife of Ramesses III. She'd had a miscarriage and the mummified fetus was on display in the inner chamber. Since this was the only tomb open to the public in the Valley of the Queens, we continued on to the magnificent Temple of Queen Hatshepsut, also known as Djeser Djeseru, or Holy of Holies, built during the 18th Dynasty. She ruled from 1503 to 1482 BC and in order to maintain her power she sent her stepson Tutmosis III into exile. When Tutmosis later returned and took power, one of his first decrees was to remove all traces of his stepmother. Thus, much of the relief detail on the temple walls had been obliterated.

The magnificence of the temple, however, could not be erased and was a testament to its unique architecture. The structure was terraced and much remained to be uncovered and/or replaced. The Egyptians were working with a Polish restoration team and after fifty years of labor, only sections of the first and second levels were open to the public. Shattered pieces of pillars and walls lined the edge of the temple looking like giant jigsaw puzzle pieces waiting to be put into place.

The areas that had been restored were fascinating. Even though badly damaged by her stepson, the reliefs extolled the glories of Queen Hatshepsut. In some, she was depicted as a male to represent strength and leadership. Women's lib had a long way to go in her day. Reliefs—political propaganda, actually—told the story of Queen Hatshepsut as the daughter of the god Atum. As half god and half human, she could claim her rightful ascension to the throne of Egypt.

The temple's second level housed two chapels, one dedicated to Hathor and one to Anubis, the jackal god of mummification. The green color of mummification equaled the green color of the Nile which, in turn, symbolized the concept of resurrection or afterlife.

While driving back past the village we noticed several houses with elaborately painted scenes on the outer walls. Manal told us that these were pictorial representations of the dwellers' journey to Mecca. Later, on our return to Cairo, we noticed more travel scenes on houses. A trip to Mecca was a significant event in the lives of Egyptian Muslims.

Our bus played a game of chicken with a loaded tomato truck along the road. Fortunately, the truck driver swerved in time to avoid the Great Catsup Caper. We paused for a brief photo op near the Colossi of Memnon, two mammoth statues that once guarded a funerary temple but now rested in the middle of a farmer's field. We then boarded a much smaller ferry for our return trip to the Nile Romance. By the time we got on board the ferry there was standing room only and I sat on the steps at the front of it. The air was so close that it felt good to have a bit of a breeze. As usual, the crew puffed on cigarettes nonstop during the twenty-minute ride.

As soon as we returned to our ship, we gathered in the dining room for Dr. Orlin's final lecture. Today he tried something different and posed questions for us to consider. He first asked us what we would like today's civilization to be remembered for five thousand years from now. Answers ranged from the end of war, poverty and disease to advances in space exploration and communication. Dr. Orlin urged us to think about feelings as well as concrete achievements. This elicited responses such as better education and awareness of ecology.

His second question focused on what we thought would remain five thousand years from now that a future society could examine to understand who we were and what we had accomplished. Responses included photos, books and even garbage but we concluded that these probably would not survive. Certainly, our modern buildings could not compare with the lasting quality of the ancient pyramids. Someone mentioned that porcelain toilets, sinks and bathtubs might withstand the test of time. It appalled us, however, to realize just how little of substance we as a society create.

What will be remembered of our civilization is directly proportional to what can be preserved. Dr. Orlin concluded with an interesting premise. Like the ancient Egyptians, he contended, perhaps we should consider recording some of our legacy onto stone tablets. Interesting thought. We are certainly capable of being a lost society if we do not make some efforts to preserve our accomplishments for future generations.

Wayne and I returned to our stateroom to shower off the day's funereal dust and dress for our final shipboard dinner. Tonight we were plied with another huge buffet consisting of rice, curry, salads, and more. Candles lit each table and, for the grand finale, the full complement of waiters paraded in with a special three-tiered cake.

After dinner we bundled into sweatshirts and jackets and went topside for our last night on the Nile. Colder than usual, we only stayed for half an hour. As we walked toward the stairs to our stateroom, we heard the voices of several group members waving and calling to us from the shore. We assumed they were just being friendly and we waved back at them. Looking more closely we suddenly realized their dilemma. The gangplank had been removed and they were stranded. By the time we reached the entrance the gangplank had been replaced and everyone was safely on board. Apparently, the water level of the Nile shifted slightly and the gangplank had needed repositioning. The group on shore, however, had visions of the ship sailing without them.

While we sat on the deck, I again mentioned how disappointing it was to have our window facing directly into another ship. Just then our neighboring ship's engines fired up and it sailed off into the night. When we reached our stateroom and looked out the window, we had a magnificent nighttime view of twinkling lights surrounding the Valley of the Kings and Queens. No other ship tied up to ours and we sat for some time watching the moon set over the horizon before taking advantage of a quiet night's sleep.

In the morning we packed, had a light breakfast and checked out at the ship's front desk by 7:30 a.m. Buses were waiting to take us to the nearby Temple of Karnak, a vast complex built over seventeen centuries from 2000 to 300 BC. The temple and surrounding structures covered a hundred acres, a city in its own right. It was dedicated to three gods—Amun, god of sun and air; Mut, the mother goddess; and their son Khonsu, god of the moon. The three composed the Theban triad. As we approached, we were greeted by forty ram-shaped statues that lined both sides of the walkway to the pylon entrance.

Manal explained that ancient temples were built from the inside out. The sanctuary was the darkest area and it was flanked by dimly lit hypostyle halls. The outer pylon provided passage into the courtyard. As we entered, we noticed a series of window-like openings at the top of the pylon, used to hang flags. Reliefs on the temple walls depicted banners waving from the openings in ancient times.

The columns that once graced the courtyard were shattered in an earthquake that struck Thebes in 27 BC. One of the mammoth pillars had been pieced back together and since it had a square block at its top, we knew that it once supported a roof. The area appeared to be about the size of a football field so it must have been an awe-inspiring architectural achievement.

In the impressive hall, we encountered two more pylons with statues of Ramesses II and Nefertari. Huge pillars more than ten feet in circumference lined the area. Manal told us that 134 columns once had supported a vast ceiling. Because the center columns were shorter than those at the outer edge, the ceiling must have been constructed in two levels. This would have allowed sunlight to filter in to the inner area. The smaller columns were topped with lotus buds and the taller ones with opening blossoms. Legend had it the filtered sunlight supposedly caused the buds on the taller columns to open.

Manal told us more about the reasons behind the beautiful proportions of the Ptolemaic Period of art. First, as she had shown us at the Luxor Museum, squares were sketched as guides. In addition, a system of balanced measures was developed. The ideal height of a man was eighteen palms. A foot equaled two-thirds of a forearm. This method was later copied by the Greeks.

The problems caused by the rising salt level in the Nile were clearly evident at Karnak. Markings on the walls caused by the leaching salt rose as high as four or five feet. In time this might decay the structures to the point of collapse. It was tragic to think that the complex stood the test of time for thousands of years only to face destruction resulting from modern flood control provided by the High Dam in Aswan. It had not taken many years to cause what could be irreversible damage to these structures. The Temple of Karnak is too large to relocate but there is talk of moving the Temple of Luxor in order to save it. We appreciated touring at a time when the damage had not yet reached the point of devastation.

We next came to an area with two obelisks, only one of which still stood. They originally had been cut and then moved with the floods to Luxor from the Aswan quarry we had visited. Three of the sides were carved in Aswan and the fourth side was completed once the obelisk arrived at the site. They were set in place by first building a mud brick square and filling it with sand. Hundreds of workers lowered the obelisk into the sand and then slowly drained the sand through openings. In time the obelisk dropped onto a base already set beneath the sand.

Manal gave us some time to wander through the vast complex on our own and Wayne and I walked on a path that bordered the Sacred Lake. A large crane in the distance stood in modern contrast to the antiquities all around us. As we neared the crane it appeared that more excavation was in process.

When we reached an amphitheater, we were immediately approached by a guard who expected some baksheesh. Wayne had no more one-pound notes and so when he gave a five-pound note to the guard, he had made a friend for life. The guard took us up the steps and, seeing our camera, took us to the best location for photos. He even offered Wayne a cigarette which he politely refused. No one from our group ventured to this area and so we received the royal treatment from the guard thanks to Wayne's generous tip.

Having taken photos from every conceivable angle we began our walk back to the bus. It took us nearly fifteen minutes to reach the boarding area and we were again struck by the vast size of the Karnak complex. We chuckled over the many years we had enjoyed Johnny Carson's late-night routine called Karnak the Magnificent. As Karnak, Carson would hold a piece of paper to his forehead and recite an answer to an unread question. The punch line came when the question was read. Today's visit gave a new meaning to the phrase, Karnak the Magnificent.

Workers were all around the complex. Some were replacing blocks of stone along walkways while others were sweeping away the constantly blowing sands of the surrounding desert. As we approached the bus a pony cart laden with colorful fruits and vegetables passed by us. When one of our group raised his camera, the driver put out his hand for baksheesh. Once he had his tip he smiled and paraded his cart for all of our cameras.

Our bus headed for the Temple of Luxor situated in the heart of town along the banks of the Nile. Although it was not as large as the complex at Karnak, it was impressive in its own right. Luxor is an Arabic name meaning *City of the Palaces.* Thebes was the name given to the area by the ancient Greeks. The Luxor Temple was created by two pharaohs, Amenhotep III and Ramesses II. In front of the entrance pylon was an obelisk that was still standing. Its mate was taken to Paris in 1826 and now rests at the Place de la Concorde. A slight crack in the remaining obelisk saved it from a similar fate and so it still graces the temple.

Entering the open court, we noticed a small 11th-century mosque perched high above us on top of part of the temple complex. The original temple had been buried for so long by the desert sands that Muslims built their mosque on what appeared to them to be level ground. The ancient Egyptian temple below it was discovered later by means of excavation.

Manal pointed out the Opet Festival reliefs depicting the Battle of Kaddish. The faces of Africans and Asians were easily distinguishable in the works of art. Another relief portrayed the seventeen sons of Ramesses II. Because they were shown with long locks of hair, the boys were depicted as young princes. The elongated heads in some of the reliefs illustrated the influence of Akhenaten, who tried to instill the worship of a single god, Atum the sun god, during his reign. Still another series of reliefs told the story of a procession of musicians and priests traveling from Luxor to Karnak. Crowds marched and clapped as the procession passed by them. It was only during these ceremonies that the masses were allowed to participate first-hand.

Manal showed us the spot where twenty-eight statues, some of which we had seen at the Luxor Museum, had been unearthed. She also led us into Amenhotep III's hypostyle hall where she pointed out an area that had been plastered and painted by early Roman conquerors. The curators of antiquity in Egypt weare currently at odds as to whether the Roman workmanship should be preserved or the plaster overlay should be removed. It was generally agreed upon that the Roman art work would stay until a method to remove it intact was devised.

Moving closer to the inner sanctuary, Wayne pointed out a relief depicting a virile Egyptian, perhaps the god Bes, sporting an erection. The concept of proportion apparently did not apply in this instance as the gent was indeed well endowed. Several of us had some fun naming the panel, with *Homo Erectus* and *Erectus Envious* being the front-runners.

When we left the grounds of the temple to board our bus, we passed two of our group being interviewed by a Japanese television crew. The reporters wanted their reaction to the October earthquake and the recent shooting of British tourists. The couple assured the reporter that we all felt safe and welcome.

Today's lunch at the gracious Luxor Sheraton was a veritable feast after four days of ordinary food on board our cruise ship. The breads, olives and cheeses were outstanding. Our group was beginning to drop by the wayside with tourista and so Wayne and I continued to forego the tempting fruits and vegetables. John suggested a whitefish in a dill sauce which was delightful. We then indulged in an array of desserts, including a sweet coconut tart that was a favorite.

After buying a T-shirt in the hotel shop we boarded the bus for our drive to Luxor Airport. On the way we passed flourishing farmland made possible, I guessed, by the controlled flow of water provided by the High Dam. The airport terminal was very attractive, a new building done in the style of an ancient pylon. We boarded the crowded plane and enjoyed our flight to the north along the Nile. From time to time we spotted a cruise ship resembling a child's toy from our vantage point. A bank of fluffy white clouds obscured our view to the west, but to the east the vast desert stretched to the horizon. We spotted a number of natural pyramid-shaped sand formations and it was easy to understand how the ancient Egyptians were inspired to build their monuments in this time-honored wind-blown desert design.

Approaching Cairo, the clouds became thicker and thicker. By the time we landed we were in a deluge. Those in the front section of the plane were soaked as they disembarked. Since we were in the back, we had to wait quite a while to deplane and when we finally departed, the rain had miraculously stopped.

With a bit of a wait for our luggage, John herded us into a corner near an Egyptian shoe shine stand. Seeing a gold mine before him, the Egyptian encouraged us to let him remove the encrusted dirt on our shoes. One from our group couldn't resist getting a new lease on life for his leather shoes and it seemed a deal at one pound. Once one shoe was polished, however, the Egyptian smiled and asked if he wanted the mate polished for an additional pound. When our fellow traveler looked bewildered, the Egyptian just laughed and completed the job. We all chuckled at the shoe man's clever sense of humor and wondered how many customers actually rewarded him with an extra pound.

We soon boarded another inevitable bus and this time we were rewarded with a room at the Ramses Hilton that had a view of the Nile. Although the pyramids of Giza were twelve miles to the west, their immense size made them visible even from a distance. This was our first glimpse of these magnificent structures, the tallest as high as a forty-story skyscraper.

Nothing was scheduled for the evening, so a group of us met in the lobby at 7:30 p.m. for a short taxi ride to Arabesque, a popular Cairo restaurant. I had asked Manal for a recommendation and this was her pick. My travel brochure confirmed her suggestion, touting it as one of the local favorites. We had some suspicions when we were met by an armed guard at the entrance but, once inside, we received a warm welcome. Because of the size of our group of eighteen, two large seating areas were quickly set up for us.

At first glance the menu looked disappointingly French, not what we had hoped for in Egypt. Turning the pages a bit further I discovered the Egyptian fare. Wayne and I began with moussaka, the best I had ever tasted. Although meatless, it had a mouth-watering array of vegetables, raisins and seasonings. Wayne ordered the old Egyptian standby, kebab and kofta, and I decided to be brave and try melokhia. It was divine! First, a large bowl of a bright green puree flavored with garlic was set in front of me. The soup-like concoction was prepared from a vegetable similar to spinach. Next a plate of broiled chicken with steamed rice arrived. Condiments followed, one a spicy tomato sauce and the other a bowl of marinated onions. When eaten Egyptian-style, the procedure was to first cut a piece of chicken and then add a bit of rice, sauce and onion before dipping the entire concoction into the soup. In spite of the rather tedious process it was deliciously fabulous.

When I mentioned to our waiter that it was almost too much food he agreed and said that the Egyptians serve enormous portions at every meal. He chuckled when he told us that Egyptian women get wide but the men stay thin. With that in mind, I decided to do the Egyptian woman thing and ordered Om Ali, the national dessert that is a relative of bread pudding. It was outstanding and several of us enjoyed topping off our feast with this combination of bread, raisins, almonds, and coconut topped with a warm custard sauce. Tonight's unique dining experience was even more meaningful because of the special group of new friends who shared the evening with us.

Wayne's trusty alarm clock paid for itself the next morning. The hotel's computer system went down during the night and deleted the scheduled wake-up calls. Remember, this was well before cell phones with built-in alarms. Our group trickled into the breakfast room and word had it that hotel staff went from room to room to wake up guests the old-fashioned way—knocking on doors.

We eventually collected our group for a tour of the Great Pyramids. Once on our bus we boldly headed into the bustling streets of Cairo and were again struck by the absolute disregard for traffic signals as we barreled through red light after red light.

Our route took us past Cairo University. Manal explained that a university education was available for all Egyptians but because of the huge number of graduates there were not enough positions for all those with degrees. Although the government promised a job for every graduate, there was a backlog of six or seven years. She told us that one of the waiters on our ship had an engineering degree and could not find work in his field. In Egypt a plumber could make in a day what some college grads would earn in a month.

Manal pointed out the variety in the dress of female students. Some were in Western dress. Others wore Western-style skirts but covered their hair. Many wore traditional long robes and head coverings. We did observe that the faces of women were generally not covered in predominately Muslim Egypt.

I had watched a PBS program a couple of weeks before our trip that spoke of a resurgence of traditional dress for young female university students. When I asked Manal about this, she said it was not as strong a movement as the program had suggested. She added that many of the women liked to cover their heads and not wear makeup because of the convenience. She also pointed out that the women wearing galabeyas could cover up a multitude of excess poundage. It was sounding better all the time.

We passed a government school where hundreds of young boys stood shoulder to shoulder in a courtyard waiting to enter their classrooms. Looking at the overcrowded conditions we could understand how so many young children died during the October earthquake when panic prevailed and many were trampled.

Our route took us past apartment buildings that lined the main road almost to the base of the pyramids. This rapid encroachment of humanity coupled with the recent manipulation of the Nile had caused more damage to these monuments in recent times than what had occurred over thousands of years.

In spite of the contrast between modern Cairo and ancient Giza, the pyramids were simply awe-inspiring. Standing nearly 480 feet in height, the

Pyramid of Cheops emanates a majesty that has to be experienced to be fully appreciated. It was almost inconceivable that in just over twenty years, 2.3 million cut-limestone blocks, each weighing an average of two tons, could have been aligned by ancient man into the towering form before us.

Each of the pyramids contained an elaborate system of tunnels leading to the pharaoh's burial chamber. The assumption was that these interior chambers would remain undiscovered and therefore stay sealed for eternity. In fact, the pyramids were sacked by grave robbers soon after their completion.

Another program I had recently seen, entitled *This Old Pyramid*, came to mind. This Education Channel documentary chronicled a three-month pyramid-building project conducted by American scholars working with a team of Egyptians. Their goal was to construct a miniature pyramid with the same-sized blocks using what they assumed to be the same building techniques employed by the Egyptians in 2450 BC.

In order to keep pace with the ancient architects, the team calculated that twenty 2-ton blocks needed to be cut and placed each day. Several techniques were tried, and rollers, ramps and sleds proved to be the most effective. After numerous setbacks and differences of opinion the project reached its scheduled conclusion with little to show for their efforts.

We hopped off our bus at the foot of a rise leading to the pyramids and were given a choice of transportation to reach the top, either a camel or a pony cart. Wayne and I opted for camels and we were soon atop these massive animals. Jubilee, my beast, lurched up the hill just behind Wayne and my saddle, which came sans stirrups, gave new meaning to the word straddle.

The man leading Wayne soon realized that the two of us were a team and insisted on taking a photo with our camera. It took some doing to retrieve it but the inevitable request for baksheesh secured its return. We actually had fun taking this touristy ride to the pyramids and chuckled over the names of some of the camels. One of our group rode Austin and another, California.

John had forewarned us that the camel owners would do an Oscar-winning performance at the top of the hill as they pleaded for baksheesh. He told us to give them no more than one American dollar since they were already paid and tipped by him in advance. John laughingly told us that at the end of each day the camel owners hop into their Mercedes and drive to their luxurious homes. We needn't feel sorry for these men in their lowly galabeyas, he assured us. True to his prediction the camel drivers went to extremes to entice our generosity. Wayne and I said our thanks, handed them our one-dollar bills and rushed to our bus now conveniently parked at the top of the hill.

John's next words of caution were about the long tunnel into the Pyramid of Chephren. He told us there was not much to see once we reached the burial chamber. He added that the tunnel leading to the inner chamber was low, narrow, dark, and poorly ventilated. He concluded by telling us that people often panic with attacks of claustrophobia and he stressed that it was not easy to turn around for a quick retreat. I get claustrophobic. I abhor small, stuffy spaces filled with eau de body odor. And yet I couldn't resist going inside in spite of all the above and neither could Wayne.

Although this pyramid appeared to be as tall as or taller than that of Cheops, it was actually about ten feet shorter. Because it rested higher on the hillside and was better preserved, it seemed larger. As we began our descent into the bowels of the pyramid we were overwhelmed by its massiveness and amazed by the workmanship of men living forty-five hundred years ago.

We also trusted that this would not be the day that it all came crashing down as we inched our way closer to the inner chamber. No more earthquakes, please! After what seemed like an eternity, we reach the inner chamber. On our approach we heard an eerie humming that became increasingly louder as we neared the tomb entrance. The ethereal sound made me wonder if a recording was playing in the tomb to set a hypnotic mood for the brave souls making this trek.

Not so. We were greeted by a group of thirty or more entranced westerners in the midst of some sort of religious experience. Crystals had been placed in the open crypt by the participants who now stood in a tight circle that filled the entire room. The humming grew more and more intense as the trance-like state of the followers increased. Wayne theorized that they were channelers. After coming this far, I decided to go forward for a closer look at the crypt. No one seemed to notice my intrusion as they hummed away. It was, to put it mildly, just plain weird.

We inched our way back through the low, narrow tunnel and joined our group for a tour of the Giza Solar Boat Museum. Located adjacent to the Cheops Pyramid, the museum housed a magnificent 4,500-year-old boat that had been cut into twelve hundred pieces and buried next to the pharaoh's pyramid. Discovered in 1954 when the huge stones covering the boat's tomb were moved aside, the excavators could still smell the scents of cedar and incense. The area had been so completely sealed that the aromas were preserved for thousands of years. It must have been remarkable to experience them after all that time.

Just as remarkable was the task of reassembling the twelve hundred pieces into what was now referred to as the world's first jigsaw puzzle. It took twenty-eight years to complete the project. The boat, or barque, now rested in a museum just large enough to house the 130-foot ship. The best assumption was that it belonged to Cheops and the pieces were buried next to his tomb to provide transportation for his soul into the afterlife.

We donned huge fabric slippers that covered our dusty shoes before entering and we laughed at our duck-like feet. Once inside we viewed a number of artifacts which included bundles of papyrus and flax ropes recovered from the barque's crypt. As Wayne noted, the process of rope-making had virtually remained the same to this day. Pieces of papyrus reed baskets were displayed along with a series of photographs detailing the recovery and reconstruction of the boat. The actual tomb-like pit where the pieces were discovered was within the walls of the museum.

We all marveled at the construction of the boat. Put together with no nails, pieces of rope laced together the cedar planks fashioned from logs imported from Lebanon. When the ship was launched the water would cause the joints to swell together, forming a waterproof seal. The workmanship was so exact that some experts were not sure whether the ship actually sailed or was simply built to be disassembled and buried near Cheops' Pyramid.

As we climbed steps to a second level to another vantage point, Manal told us that we could learn more about the boat in an April 1988 article published in National Geographic. Looking at the bow with its unique Egyptian papyrus detailing was like seeing one of the reliefs from an ancient temple come to life. We rated the museum as a trip highlight and made mental notes to find the National Geographic article when we returned home.

Our next stop was the Sphinx located not far from the pyramids. Hundreds of school children in traditional dress queued with their instructors waiting for their turn to tour. We tried our Egyptian good morning greeting, Sabah al Khair, and got some smiles from the children as we passed them.

The Sphinx guarded the first valley temple built in the form of a mastaba, or bench. It was here that the mummification process took place for the ancient pharaohs of Giza. Manal explained that it took seventy days, thirty-five for drying the body and thirty-five for wrapping it. The brain was drawn out through the nostrils and the eyes were pushed back and removed. The viscera—intestines, lungs, liver and stomach—were mummified separately.

As we left the mastaba and approached the Sphinx, Manal told us that its nose had eroded as early as the 10th century AD. She then related the story of Tutmosis IV who supposedly fell asleep at the foot of the Sphinx after it had been buried by countless years of blowing desert sands. The Sphinx spoke to him in a dream and promised Tutmosis divine kingship if he would remove the sand. He did as he was told and became pharaoh.

We were saddened by the tremendous decay that had attacked the Sphinx.

Leaching salt from the Nile was causing further decay at an alarming rate. Nearly half of the Sphinx had been reconstructed from newly cut limestone blocks but the restoration had ceased. We were not sure whether this was temporary or, as we heard, the project had been abandoned because it caused more problems than it fixed. At any rate, we were glad that we could see the Sphinx in at least some of its original form. The lower part of the body and all four feet covered in newly cut stones seemed to make the Sphinx look like a modern-day reproduction.

Our next stop was at a papyrus institute, one of many in this area, for another buying opportunity. After a brief lesson on the making of paper from papyrus we were set free to wander through a series of rooms with numbered art on the walls. We soon realized we were being followed by a young Egyptian woman. When we moved, she followed. It became so unnerving that we were tempted to leave the studio. We eventually found several small art pieces that we decided to purchase and our shadow helped get the job done. For US$42 we bought paintings on papyrus of Ramesses IV, my pal Hathor with Nefertari and one of an ancient boat.

Our group was so plugged into schedules by now that we were like wind-up toys when it came to being on the bus on time. If John or Manal said to board at half past noon, we were there en masse. Not today, however. It took some of our group forever to complete their purchases in the papyrus shop. When they finally did board, we made our way to the Mena House Hotel for lunch.

Located at Giza, the Mena House stands graciously near the pyramids. It offers an imposing view from its impressive rooms and grounds. Originally built as a royal hunting lodge in 1886, the hotel with its exquisite arabesque detailing was expanded to its modern-day form in more recent years. We had a delicious buffet lunch in the Greenery at the far end of the complex before our afternoon excursion to Memphis and Saqqara.

Riding through the countryside on the twenty-minute trip to Memphis, Manal read questions that several of us had written and answered them. The first had to do with housing in Egypt. There was no mortgage system so one had to have the money up front in order to buy a home. Apartments were plentiful and no one had been homeless until the recent earthquake. Housing was rarely subsidized because the Egyptians believed that buying a house or an apartment building kept it from falling into disrepair.

I had asked about the rapid population increase and Manal told us there was a national campaign to curb it. There were clinics for birth control but abortion was not tolerated. In reality, Manal said, it was very difficult to change people's thinking about family size. "It is like committing suicide to try to talk to a man about limiting the size of his family," she added. As I mentioned earlier, Manal did say the average family size in the countryside had dropped from nine children to seven. Needless to say, there was still room for downsizing.

The Egyptian political system is a republic with a president as head of state. Since the revolution in 1952, there have been four presidents—Naguib, Nasser, Sadat, and Mubarak. As of our visit, there were five political parties represented in a Parliament consisting of an elected House with fifty percent of its body coming by law from farmers and workers, and an Assembly serving only for consultation.

Egypt had a free press and it was not unusual to find fiery articles attacking the president and other top officials. Manal told us of a series of articles that literally forced the removal of a corrupt politician who was suspected of being involved in the drug trade.

The social life of an Egyptian living in Cairo was not unlike that of an American. Cairo was called the Hollywood of the East and young people enjoyed going to movies and dance clubs. Even along the far reaches of the Nile people had television and it was not uncommon to find a satellite dish tucked inconspicuously along the banks. Wayne verified that he had, in fact, spotted one on our cruise.

We passed through miles of fertile farmland as we neared Memphis. At one point our bus stopped to allow us a photo op of a water buffalo tethered to a water wheel. Because the animal had to continuously walk in a tight circle, it was blindfolded to keep it from becoming dizzy.

I also was taken by the palm trees along the Nile. Even though we lived in an area of the States where palms thrived, the Egyptian variety had a symmetry unparalleled by their American counterparts. We passed groves of date palms that had recently been harvested. Their umbrella-like form was often represented in ancient reliefs.

We arrived at Memphis to view a Hatshepsut-era sphinx carved from an eighty-ton block of alabaster and a large statue of Ramesses II. The usual fee was required to take photos and Manal discouraged us from bothering with it. Wayne did sneak a snapshot of a sign on the outer fence reading, *Keep the Place Clean* in English and Arabic. The sign was so filthy that it was almost illegible and we chuckled over its paradoxical message.

We then boarded our bus for the short trip to Saqqara. Our first stop, another photo op, looked over the Step Pyramid with the two Pyramids of Sneferu, an Old Kingdom pharaoh who died in 2589 BC, in the distance. As we traveled, Manal told us that in one of the burial areas in Saqqara more than five hundred thousand mummified birds were discovered. Glancing in all directions, we could see that this must have been a happening place in ancient times.

On next stop was at a mastaba, the predecessor of step pyramid architecture. Designed as an ancient burial chamber, the mastaba we visited belonged to Ptahhotep, a nobleman who lived about five thousand years ago. This proved to be one of the highlights of our afternoon tour. On the inner chamber walls was a priceless record of life in ancient Egypt. Using one of our travel companion's movie cameras as a spotlight, we gazed upon a relief depicting the ancient nobleman getting a massage, manicure and pedicure. How civilized!

One panel showed a series of musicians with their instruments. In another, children were at play. Grape crushing was depicted in a third, while another illustrated the lassoing of cattle. The art was so captivating that we left feeling as if we had stepped back five thousand years in time.

Our last destination in Saqqara was the Temple of King Djoser, the second pharaoh of Egypt's 3rd Dynasty who ruled from 2668 to 2649 BC. Built by the architect Imhotep forty-five hundred years ago, the stone structure is the reproduction of an earlier mud brick palace. As we approached, I was struck by the similarity between the work of this ancient architect and that of Frank Lloyd Wright. It appears that Wright borrowed from these time-honored structures when he developed his own unique style.

Imhotep was known as the innovator of the pyramid. Utilizing the earlier principles of the mastaba, he built the Step Pyramid of Saqqara to house the burial tomb of Djoser. We spent some time wandering along the outer walls of this impressive structure consisting of seven uneven levels before returning to the bus.

Our final destination for the day was a stop at a rug factory. The draw was that it supposedly trained children in age-old weaving skills. Wayne and I were fairly certain that the children were being exploited and we were not willing to support this by making a purchase. We took a quick look through the rug gallery and then waited for our group near the bus.

Tonight featured our farewell cocktail party and dinner. Although it wasn't our last night, John felt that the following evening should be an early one because of our impending 4:45 a.m. wake-up call. The farewell gala provided our one opportunity to dress for dinner and the women in our group transformed from desert dust to an array of sparkles and ruffles by our 7:00 p.m. dinner. The men looked just as grand in jackets and ties. We were toasted by John and Dr. Orlin did his best to play *God Save the Queen* and *Hail to the Victors* on his rabab. We all enjoyed the festive evening with our newfound friends.

The next day was free for roaming. Through a banking contact, Wayne made a connection with a young couple stationed at the American Embassy in Cairo. Coincidentally, another couple in our group had also contacted the Embassy representative and the four of us made plans to meet him and his wife for lunch. But for starters...

The urge to explore ran in our blood by this stage of the tour so several of us decided to hire drivers and head just outside Cairo to the Friday morning camel auction. Eight of us gathered at 7:00 a.m. in the hotel lobby and hopped into taxis for this early-morning adventure.

Our driver was weak in English but strong in friendly. Like everyone behind the wheel of a vehicle in Cairo he slid through all colors of traffic lights. When one of us teased him about his rolling through reds, he smiled and gave us his best, "No problem!" We still had our doubts.

As we neared the outskirts of the city we were again struck by the contrasts between ancient and modern life. Donkey carts looking like a page torn from a history book blended into the raging traffic. Driven by men in galabeyas, the carts were laden with produce and bright green leafy fodder for livestock. A man on a bicycle rode past us carrying a mountain of pita bread in a wooden crate on his head. How he managed to balance the load and weave in and out of traffic remained a mystery to us.

At one point we came to train tracks and could hear a train approaching at a rapid pace. Our driver crossed the first track without flinching and stopped at a second track as the train flew by us. A rickety truck to our right had blocked the view of both tracks and we gave a sigh of relief that our driver guessed the approach correctly.

Within fifteen minutes we arrived at the auction grounds and persuaded our drivers to come with us. We walked up a dirt road bordered by stalls selling what looked like second-hand clothing and farming implements—not the usual tourist fare.

The second cab driver for our group spoke English well and explained that Egypt had an agreement with Sudan to import two hundred fifty thousand camels each year. It took forty days to drive camels to the weekly Cairo auction.

We noticed that the size and color of the animals varied and the cab driver explained that the rather mangy large camels are from Egypt and—alas!—are usually sold for their meat. When we looked stricken, he asked, "Haven't you tried Kebob and Kofta?" We all had, of course. Remembering our hamburgers in Cairo, we wondered just how much camel meat we had indeed sampled.

The Sudanese camel variety was smaller and lighter in color and these generally were used for transportation. The cab driver told us that the huge dark brown camels from Kenya often appeared large because their herders filled them with water to increase their weight just before the auction. Buyers had to devise ways to tell if they were buying flesh or a lot of excess liquid.

Off to one side was a small pen filled with goats. Two men methodically slaughtered and gutted them as we stood nearby. No sound came from the poor unsuspecting animals and so we assumed that they were not in pain during their final moments. Today's outing was definitely not for the faint of heart.

Two young boys hovered around us and seemed amused to find foreigners at the local auction. There were not many non-Egyptians present. We felt comfortable but were glad to have our cab drivers with us. A teen approached us and demonstrated how to use a whip made from the tail of a hippo. This wasn't a souvenir any of us wanted.

The auction itself fascinated us as groups of ten or twelve camels were purchased and led away from the stockyard. By the time we left, only a handful of camels remained. As we walked along the road to our cabs, we noticed a man beating the backside of a camel just as it passed an oncoming car. The camel instinctively kicked as the whip struck and we heard a loud thud. In two weeks of frenzied traffic we had just witnessed our first traffic accident. The camel kicked a huge dent into the passenger door of the car. As we left the scene the driver of the car and the camel owner were scratching their heads in an attempt to find a solution.

We arrived back at our hotel just before 9:00 a.m. and Wayne and I decided to pay one last visit to the Cairo Museum. Having now been to Tut's tomb in the Valley of the Kings we wanted to revisit his exhibit.

With our newly acquired knowledge of ancient Egyptian history we knew that the flexible gold collar with its jeweled falcon that covered Tut's mummified body symbolized Horus, the sky god. We stood for a long time before the golden casket inlaid with lapis, turquoise and other jewels. Acutely aware that we would soon be leaving Egypt we wanted to commit this exquisite work of art to memory. At the case filled with jeweled scarabs and other sacred symbols we read that the word ankh means mirror in Egyptian. Ankh = mirror = symbol of life. Before leaving the room we again marveled at the intricate solid gold mask that had rested over Tut's mummified head for thousands of years.

My favorite piece in the jewelry room was a beautiful statue of Hathor that could not have been more than two inches in height. Sculpted in gold, it was a perfect representation of the goddess. Hathor's crown of horns with a sun disc made her instantly recognizable. Her face and body were so exact in proportion that it was difficult to imagine how such detail could have been achieved in so small a figure. Even the tiny hands and feet had fingers and toes.

We revisited the section with the furnishings and artifacts recovered from Tut's tomb. I stood for a long time in front of a glass display case containing a large floral arrangement that someone had placed in the tomb at the time of the young pharaoh's burial. The bouquet had dried long ago but still its beauty remained.

Returning to the hotel, we showered off the early morning camel dust in preparation for lunch with the young couple from the American Embassy, the second largest in the world. We looked forward to an insider's view of life in Egypt. Our host had only been in Cairo for six months and he served as a political analyst with the State Department. We were told that the Embassy employed eighteen hundred Americans and twelve hundred Egyptians. In 1992, with the exception of Israel, Egypt held the largest number of Americans living in a foreign country. Because of its proximity to Iran, Iraq and Libya, much effort was made to maintain good diplomatic relations in Egypt. As a consequence, many aid programs focused on updating Egypt's infrastructure.

At 5:30 p.m. most of our group met in the hotel lobby and boarded our bus for a return trip to the pyramids, this time for the Sound and Light Show. Since it was a Friday and therefore a holiday, the streets were filled with activity. People crowded into small open markets and we noticed a goat carcass hanging in one of the butcher shops. Could it be one we had seen being slaughtered at this morning's camel auction?

We had good seats for the Sound and Light Show, a fifty-minute program narrated in a recording produced by members of Britain's Royal Theatre Company. Although the dialog bordered on the melodramatic, the spectacular lighting on the Sphinx and three pyramids filled us with awe. Some of the passages that Dr. Orlin had shared with us earlier were read and we felt the sensitivity of these ancient people. Absorbing the majesty of the show and our surroundings was indeed a grand finale for all of us.

We were up at 4:45 a.m. and placed our bags in the hallway five minutes later. After a quick breakfast we boarded our bus for a half hour ride to the airport. By 8:30 a.m. we had cleared passport control and were headed to London. Our flight took us over the Nile Delta with fertile farms as far as the eye could see. At one point we passed over the snow-capped mountains of Crete. Clouds then obscured the land below us for the rest of the flight. Once on the ground we said our farewells to many in our tour group and left knowing we had made lasting friendships during our time in Egypt.

As I reflected on our marvelous Egyptian adventure I was once again struck by a sense of stepping back in time to relive the history of ancient Egypt. We learned to appreciate the gods and pharaohs etched on so many walls throughout our travels. We connected with ancient Egyptians through their prose and poetry and gained a new respect for the age-old civilization and its accomplishments in art and architecture.

In contrast, we also enjoyed the present-day experiences of our travels through Egypt. Coupled with meeting so many interesting people in our University of Michigan group, we made Egyptian friends along the way. We were touched by a bit of magic from the present as well as the ancient past and would never be the same.

FROM MICHIGAN TO MILAN

Muskegon, Rome, Positano, Pompeii, and Milan

September 24–October 12, 1993

OUR TRIP TO EUROPE took a detour before we even left our home continent. Wayne, our daughter Liz and I met our other daughter Emily, who flew in from Boston, at O'Hare Airport where the four of us boarded a short connection to Muskegon, Michigan, just a few miles north of Grand Haven, my home town. My father was diagnosed with lung cancer just after Wayne and I visited him in July and we all felt a strong need to be with him.

Much to our surprise, Dad met us at the airport. He looked wonderful and had gained back some of the weight he had lost when we last saw him. Even his spunk had returned and we were all delighted to find him in such good spirits.

Stanley, Dad's first cousin and lifelong friend, also met us at the airport. He presented us with a key to his North Muskegon cottage on the shores of Lake Michigan. Dad drove his car and led us in our rental on the twenty-minute drive. We were soon settled in Stanley's beach home for the weekend.

The next day we entertained extended family for lunch and dinner. By my count we served twelve lunches and fourteen dinners. Not even a late afternoon rain could cramp our style and we grilled hamburgers and hot dogs under a tarp that my brother Charlie magically produced.

This reunion proved to be a bittersweet time. Dad's cancer took a strong hold shortly after our visit and he died the following April. We would always remember this poignant weekend, our daughters' last visit with their grandfather. We took many photos of him with his grandchildren and I still keep one of the four of us at the beach on my mantle as a reminder of this special weekend.

Taking advantage of frequent flyer miles, Wayne and I flew to Orly Airport in Paris. A forty-minute bus ride brought us to Charles de Gaulle Airport for our flight to Rome, the last leg of our journey. We were glad that each of the flights was relatively short and we had already acclimated to a few hours of the time change while in Michigan.

Once in Rome we checked into the Hotel Hassler located at the top of the Spanish Steps. The Hassler seemed old, tired and very upper class. We much preferred the Eden but it was closed for renovation. Next time...

After a short rest we hit the streets and wandered through some of our favorite parts of this magnificent city. We walked past the Forum and the Colosseum, then back to Piazza Navona and on to the Trevi Fountain. Stopping at a small trattoria in an alley just beyond it, we dined al fresco while enjoying a lovely, warm evening on this brief visit to Rome.

At noon the following day we boarded a train and headed to Naples. We spent most of the two-hour trip chatting with a law professor who commuted from his home in Naples to his teaching position in Rome. Having studied at Cambridge and the University of Wisconsin he spoke excellent English. He warned us that the Naples train station could be dangerous. Tourists often were targets of robbers and he advised us not to let anyone carry our suitcases for us. It might be the last time we would see them. He also gave us several suggestions for restaurants in Naples and Positano.

Our driver Antonio met us the second we stepped off the train and we scurried to his waiting car. True to our train mate's warnings we were swarmed by men offering their services. Antonio advised me to hide my purse as best I could. Once inside his car he locked the doors and told me to cover up any jewelry that might appeal to the gangs that surrounded his car. Needless to say, it wasn't the welcome we had hoped for and we were glad to begin our ride to Positano.

We drove by the bustling Naples harbor filled with ships and then along Mount Vesuvius before entering a tunnel that bypassed Sorrento. It took about an hour and a half to wind our way to Positano and reach our hotel, Le Sirenuse. This charming retreat overlooking the Mediterranean had originally been several elegant seaside villas perched high above the water. We were assigned a room with views extending almost vertically to the sea. From our perch at the uppermost level we looked across the way at small hotels and residences on the opposite side of the steep U-shaped village opening into the sea. Building these charming villas scattered along both sides must have taken determination and stamina. A single road laced everything together, eventually ending at the water's edge.

Our spectacular room had a large closet and bath near the entrance. A few steps led to the comfortably furnished sleeping and sitting area. It featured marble floors and elegant Italian décor. A large bouquet of freshly cut flowers added to the charm. Beyond this was a patio with chairs and a table surrounded by potted plants and flowers. It was restful and romantic. The sound of the waves, intensified as they hit the rocky cliffs below, mesmerized us.

With only one road running through Positano, stone and concrete stairways leading up and down the hillsides abounded. Even a walk on the steep roadway was a workout. We found ourselves wandering for hours along the almost-vertical terrain. The road was lined with shops, most of them filled with touristy trinkets we had no trouble resisting. In this stunning town dotted with expensive villas and filled with tourists, we were surprised that we did not find one high-end boutique.

As it had been three weeks earlier when I visited Cannes with a group of friends, Wayne and I were treated to sunny, balmy weather. In spite of recent weather reports promising cooler days, temperatures hovered in the high 70s and we wished we had packed more lightweight clothes. The continual trips up and down the steep hills made it seem even warmer.

We walked until 7:30 p.m. and came across a small family restaurant called La Vincenza that our friend from the train had suggested. The owners were delightful and brought us small plates filled with roasted peppers, deep-fried fritters and smoked fresh sardines in lemon herb olive oil. I don't care for the small, canned fish in the States but I couldn't get enough of the freshly caught variety in Positano. Following the antipasti we enjoyed pasta dishes, broiled fish and salads. We finished with divine chocolate tortes and cappuccinos—all for just over US$50.

Once back at Le Sirenuse we wandered through a myriad of sitting rooms, common areas and patios, each exquisitely furnished. The interior rooms featured fine art and antiques. We had originally planned to stay at Hotel San Pietro, a newer lodging tucked into the side of a cliff not far from the village, but Le Sirenuse did not disappoint us.

The next morning, we slept until 9:00 a.m. and enjoyed a leisurely breakfast on our patio overlooking the sea. What a life! As it often happens in Europe, breakfast featured an abundance of rolls, meats and cheeses with enough to make a Barbara's pack-your-own-lunch special. We opted to forego it today in order to try another of the small restaurants we had spotted on yesterday's walk.

Winding our way to the beach far below us took us past the small shops that lined the pathway. Wayne found a cotton golf shirt and I bought a swimsuit cover-up. My find of the day, however, was a pair of navy suede shoes with rubber soles. Now I had shoes that would properly grip the town's steep inclines and stairways.

We stopped for lunch at Covo dei Sareceni right at the water's edge. Once again, we enjoyed delicious pasta dishes at bargain prices. From there we wandered through a couple of art shops and found the paintings rather ordinary and very pricey, some as high as US$2,000. A pastry shop along the way offered a much better deal and we relaxed with a cappuccino before starting the uphill hike to our hotel.

After changing into our swimsuits, we headed back to the beach, this time descending the long winding steps from our hotel to the sea. My StairMaster could take a rest this week! The beach was filled with volcanic black rock, finely ground by wave action. We sat along the shore until the sun set behind the high cliffs at a little past 5:00 p.m. After hiking back to our hotel, we changed into our evening attire—slacks and cotton sweaters. Nothing is very formal here.

On impulse we decided to walk in the direction of Hotel San Pietro. We began our trek just before dusk and it never occurred to us to take a flashlight. As we exited the village it suddenly turned pitch dark. There wasn't a single street light to guide us along the narrow winding cliffside road with its precarious drop of hundreds of feet to the sea. Not realizing how far we needed to walk to reach our destination we continued onward. When headlights from approaching cars appeared, we hugged the short railing along the roadway for dear life. We were sure that the resort would magically appear around the next bend and after a two-mile trek it finally came into view. In retrospect, this was not one of our brighter stunts and we gave a sigh of relief when we finally approached the hotel.

Unique best defined this hotel. It stretched almost vertically down the edge of a steep cliff toward the sea. We followed a walkway into the hotel and then took an elevator down to the lobby level where we encountered a convention filled with cigar-smoking Americans. The noise and glitz made us grateful for our much smaller villa tucked into the hills of the village. We had already made a dinner reservation at San Pietro for the next night so we took the hotel's car back to Le Sirenuse and vowed never again to retrace this route on foot.

After dinner in town at another small family restaurant we walked to the far side of the village following a path that led to several small hotels and pensions. Although they were simpler by far than Le Sirenuse, some were quite charming. We returned to our room and sat for an hour on our balcony. Looking out over Positano from our hilltop perch, the night views were breathtaking.

We decided to have breakfast the next morning on the villa's patio and then headed back into the village in quest of an ATM, new batteries for our cameras and the opportunity to do some early Christmas shopping. Along the way Wayne couldn't resist a white Panama hat. It would be up to him to figure out how to get it back to the States in one piece.

Returning to the hotel just after noon we donned our swimsuits and sat poolside until 2:00 p.m. Then we changed clothes and headed down the pathway for a light lunch at the bakery we had discovered earlier. It featured baguettes filled with prosciutto and cheese, a welcome shift from our pasta-laced lunches. By the time we reached the beach the afternoon's haze turned into dark clouds and we retraced the steps to our villa for a rest before dinner.

We had made arrangements to drive to San Pietro with a delightful English couple we met at Le Sirenuse. Once there, Wayne and I were seated at a table along a covered patio overlooking the sea far below us. It would have been a charming location if we hadn't been right next to an enormous open brick oven filled with small pizzas. A couple from Indianapolis kindly moved their table so that we could maneuver further from the oven's intense heat.

After dinner, we regrouped with the English couple for coffee in the lounge before returning to our hotel. What had been a five-minute drive to San Pietro turned out to be a twenty-minute return trip. The one-way road through Positano meant that our driver had to circle the entire town to reach our hotel. We now understood why our driver dropped us off several blocks from Le Sirenuse yesterday and pointed us in its direction. He had opted not to take the entire loop to get us right to its doorstep.

Sometime during the night, we heard thunder and rain but we awoke to another glorious sunny day. After breakfast and another walk through the village we changed into our swimsuits and headed for lounge chairs along the hotel's pool. We spent the rest of the day lulled by the crashing waves far below us and lured by our lush surroundings. We capped off our day with another outstanding dinner at nearby La Vincenza.

We were up early the next day. After breakfast we walked into town to buy sandwiches and cannoli for a picnic lunch at Pompeii with our driver, Antonio. We said our farewells to Le Sirenuse and enjoyed Antonio's interesting tidbits as we drove. Pompeii is located between Positano and Naples so it made sense to visit it en route to the airport.

Once inside the entrance we arranged for a guide, a man named Andrea who claimed to be a retired professor. Guessing he was in his mid-sixties, he was well-dressed and articulate. Pompeii dates to the 6th to 7th century BC and was first colonized by the Greeks. The Etruscans arrived in 524 BC and the Romans came in the 2nd century BC. Pompeii developed as a business center and flourished until 79 AD, when Vesuvius erupted. It buried most of the city in a deep layer of ash, thus preserving its structures. Many of its twenty thousand residents escaped, but about two thousand were killed by the eruption. By 1993, fifteen hundred voids formed as bodies decayed while frozen in time under up to nine feet of pumice had been discovered. Plaster casts of the voids were on display and created a dramatic picture of the terror these people must have felt.

Extensive excavation began in 1924 and as of our visit, more than two thirds of Pompeii had been uncovered. The vast size of Pompeii overwhelmed both of us as we accompanied Andrea along the cobbled streets. Large, flat stones set strategically across the roadways allowed residents to traverse them during rainstorms. Centuries of wheeled cart traffic left deep ruts in the cobblestones on either side of the walkways.

Andrea took us to the courtyard of the Palace of Justice established in 200 BC. He pointed out the Temple of Apollo, one of ten pagan temples in the complex. We then toured the central marketplace, the town hall, Jupiter's temple and Augustus Caesar's temple. We passed an early water fountain and a bar/restaurant with built-in terra cotta pots to hold food and drink. We also saw a bakery with enormous grinding stones and a brick oven. Loaves of bread were discovered in them, petrified in the process of baking.

Next we toured villas with frescoes that remained vivid. Casa del Fauno had a stunning marble floor. Slaves were inexpensive and many of the villas had quarters for them. Of particular interest was the House of the Vietti, the home of two wealthy brothers. Just inside the entrance was the excitement room, a small enclosed area with erotic paintings on its walls. One depicted a man with a penis so large that it was suspended from a rope.

The central courtyard of this large villa featured a fountain tiled in vivid colors. It also had lead pipes with spigots. Lead pipes, a modern addition to Pompeii in its final days, caused the death of a number of unsuspecting inhabitants. Further on we passed public bath houses that actually had hot and cold running water. There were also public toilets for the residents of Pompeii.

After a forty-five-minute tour with Andrea he said goodbye and we headed toward the Colosseum. Walking at a fairly rapid pace, it took us nearly twenty minutes to reach it. Once more we were overwhelmed by the size of Pompeii with only two thirds of the buried city as yet excavated.

We exited Pompeii and met Antonio for our picnic. The cannoli we purchased earlier in the day were absolutely to die for and we rejoiced that we hadn't discovered them sooner. We would have gained ten pounds. Following lunch, we continued on to Naples for our flight to Milan. Unlike the train station, the airport seemed relatively safe. Our flight was delayed but once airborne we followed the spectacular coastline before turning inland and witnessing a stunning sunset. A brilliant band of scarlet tinged with orange created a light show unlike any we had ever seen.

We arrived in Milan in the dark and took a taxi to the Duomo Hotel just across from the Duomo Cathedral. As we had ten years earlier, we stayed in a room with a staircase and a two-story window overlooking the magnificent cathedral adorned with hundreds of statues. Our room's décor, however, had not fared well over the years and new carpets and fabrics were long overdue. We agreed that the view made up for the room's fading charm.

The next day it rained and, to make matters worse, most of Milan's glorious shops and boutiques did not open until late in the afternoon on Mondays. I did some window shopping before returning to the hotel to pack my bags. Wayne intended to stay in Italy for another week of business and I opted to return to the States. I took a taxi mid-afternoon to Milan's Linate Airport for a flight to Paris, where I would spend the night.

I had time at Linate to do some duty-free shopping and bought two designer ties for Wayne and a Valentino scarf for myself, all excellent and irresistible buys.

My seat on the plane from Milan to Paris was in the first row of tourist class with only a flimsy curtain separating it from the smoke-filled business section in front of me. The young woman in the seat next to me was equally turned off by the thick cloud of smoke that soon hovered over us and, although she only spoke Italian, we had no trouble communicating our mutual dissatisfaction. She spoke with an attendant who moved us back several rows. The anti-cigarette movement had not caught on in Europe as it had in the States and we found that planes, hotels and restaurants continued to exude smoke.

Once in Paris, I caught a bus for the forty-five-minute commute to Orly Airport. The connecting shuttle to my hotel for the night arrived just as I exited the bus and I was in my room by 7:00 p.m. I had plenty of time to hop in a taxi for the thirty-minute drive into Paris. However, a warm bath had an even stronger allure. With another long day of travel ahead it was a wise decision.

Strikes in Europe never cease to amaze me. There were no trains running from Paris to Orly the next day, making it necessary for those with a flight to find a taxi. People arrived at Orly in a frazzle and I rejoiced in Wayne's suggestion that I stay at the airport rather than a hotel in Paris for only a few hours.

Although the flight had a short delay, it made good time in the air. I had scheduled a two-hour layover in Chicago to allow plenty of time to catch my next flight to LA. A long travel day was a small price to pay and I gave thanks for the opportunity to have been in Europe for a second time in just over a month.

GREECE AND TURKEY

Athens, Istanbul, Cappadocia, Ankara, Kusadasi, Izmir, and Bodrum

September 29–October 15, 1995

WAYNE AND I had spent months planning an in-depth trip to Turkey with a quick peek at Athens en route. Through a local travel agent, we selected each of our destinations well in advance. Our agent had contacted a reputable overseas travel company to set up our connecting flights, accommodations, drivers, and guides. We allocated time for a three-day cruise on the Aegean Coast in a private sixty-five-foot Turkish gulet. With travel plans well scripted we flew from LA to Frankfurt for our connecting flight to Athens.

On this trip I achieved the impossible and embarked on a seventeen-day tour with two pieces of carry-on luggage. Against all odds I had limited my wardrobe to a few simple options. My greatest challenge was what not to pack. Khaki pants and T-shirts were the order of each day; blue and white striped pants went through several combinations and permutations to serve as my evening wear. Wayne had bet me that I couldn't make it happen and I never like to lose a wager. To go from an oversized suitcase to a carry-on that could be stored in the overhead bin was indeed a noteworthy feat. By the end of the trip I realized that even less would have sufficed.

When we landed in Athens our carry-on bags were ready to roll. Although our travel company had promised we would be met by a driver holding a sign, he was nowhere in sight. We waited… and looked… and waited some more. After a frustrating forty-five minutes we queued in a long taxi line. With no emergency phone number to call, we felt we didn't have a choice.

The next day we learned our travel company had sent the wrong flight information to its associate in Athens. As we were pacing the airport in search of our driver, he was preparing to meet us on a later flight. He did the same as we had and waited for almost an hour, not knowing that we had arrived earlier. This was the first of a series of glitches we encountered with this top-dollar travel company.

Our taxi ride from the airport turned into quite an adventure. The information from the travel agency was in English and Greeks use a Cyrillic alphabet. Our directions in English to our hotel made absolutely no sense to the taxi driver. In desperation we spoke the name of our hotel. As it turned out, the Andromeda, a small five-star hotel, was situated on a quiet one-block-long road and our driver had no clue where it was located. Puffing on cigarettes he finally pulled onto the narrow shoulder of the traffic-filled highway to make a call from a roadside phone booth. He returned to the taxi looking reassured and eventually got us to our hotel.

The day of disruptions continued. We were assigned to a room on the third floor that had not been cleaned since the last guest had departed. Returning to the front desk, we were led to a very nice room on the fifth floor. We enjoyed our stay at the Andromeda located near the American Embassy in a quiet part of this bustling city. With just thirty rooms, it had a bed-and-breakfast atmosphere. The only drawback was its distance from the Plaka and all the action of Athens.

For some unknown reason we both had a surge of energy and as avid walkers, took advantage of the distance and toured much of the city on foot. Wayne, our map man, charted a healthy hike to the Plaka and the Acropolis. On our way we passed the American Embassy, the remains of the 1896 Olympic Stadium and a bustling area of shops and hotels before arriving at the Plaka several miles later.

Athens' Plaka is a central grid of narrow alleys with numerous shops and restaurants tucked in along them. It is definitely where the action is. We wandered up and down block after block filled with shops featuring touristy merchandise. Restaurant hawkers tried their best to lure us into their establishments.

We stopped at an unimposing storefront restaurant with a charming courtyard on the periphery of the Plaka where I had noticed a spit roasting gyros as we passed and it looked too good to resist. The warm pita bread, crispy roasted lamb and freshly chopped tomatoes, onion and cilantro were inexpensive and delicious. We added a plate of feta cheese and olives to our fabulous first-night feast. Our guide the next day told us that we had chosen the best spot in town for gyros.

After dinner we headed toward the Acropolis, hoping to catch a glimpse of its collection of awe-inspiring architectural wonders lit at night by spotlights. We didn't have to go far before it came into view. As grand as it was the next morning in daylight, we would never forget the impression it made that night as we gazed at the brilliantly lit pillars of the Parthenon perched high above us.

We stopped at another café in the Plaka for coffee and baklava before walking back to our hotel. A pendant in a jewelry store window caught my eye. A replica of an ancient coin with a handcrafted gold band wrapped around it, I made a mental note to return the next day during business hours.

We took a slightly different route back to our hotel and passed a park-like area with monolithic remains of the ancient pillars of the Temple of Olympia erected in the 6th century BC. The sense of ancient history is indeed strong in Athens. We agreed that modern Athens was not particularly appealing; much of its architecture looked boxy and unimaginative. Apartment complexes and office buildings lined the busy streets. One sensed a third-world atmosphere juxtaposed with imposing historical points of interest.

After a six-mile hike through the streets of Athens we returned to our hotel ready for a good night's sleep. We slept so soundly that we never heard Wayne's trusty alarm clock the next morning. Fortunately, Wayne came to life in time for us to dress, grab a quick continental breakfast and meet Irene, our guide for the day, at 9:30. Accompanying her was a friendly driver named George who spoke English fairly well.

Our first stop was Philopappos Hill with its impressive birds-eye view of the Acropolis complex atop the next hill. We took some gorgeous photos from this perch. Heading to the Acropolis we passed the Odean of Herodes Atticus, built in 161 AD. Theater productions continued to be staged here as well as musical performances. Looking down on the ancient stage we noticed a group of actors rehearsing a tragedy. A Yanni concert that I had caught glimpses of on public television broadcasts was filmed in this Odeon, or music hall.

On the Acropolis, a hill that dominated the city of Athens, the most imposing structure was the Parthenon. The word Parthenon translates to House of the Virgin. Built between 447 and 438 BC of white marble, only the Doric pillars outlining the original structure remain today. It stood intact for twenty-two centuries until the Venetians attacked it with cannon fire from Philopappos Hill in 1687 AD. They did not realize that the Turks, then in power in Athens, had loaded the Parthenon with gunpowder. When the Venetians fired their cannons, the building exploded. By the time of our visit, most of the original pillars had been reconstructed and stood as reminders of this great era. Shards of the Parthenon strewn about its outer edges also hinted of this once-grand monument dedicated to the goddess Athena.

In the late 1800s a British archaeologist named Elgin was instrumental in the reconstruction of the Acropolis. Much to the dismay of contemporary Greeks, he was allowed to remove almost all the ancient frieze work that originally adorned the Parthenon. Elgin took them to England and they now were housed in a section of the British Museum.

Modern-day Greeks were attempting to lure these massive marble friezes depicting important historical moments back to their country of origin. The Brits, however, were perfectly content to keep the ancient treasures in London. They claimed, perhaps rightly so, that the marbles would have been destroyed if Elgin hadn't rescued them. The debate likely continues to this day and I have to confess that seeing the Elgin Marbles as they were displayed in the British Museum was an awe-inspiring experience.

Peering over the edge of the wall surrounding the Acropolis, we looked down on the imposing Theater of Hadrian built in the 2nd century AD. Greece was the birthplace of theater and dance and this grand arena could seat twenty thousand for a performance.

As we drove from the Acropolis, I mentioned my nighttime jewelry find to Irene. She agreed that it was in one of the better shops in Athens. Since it was on our way, our driver dropped us off for a peek at the coin pendant. The jeweler explained that it was a reproduction of a 3rd-century-BC coin depicting Alexander the Great wrapped in a band of gold. In less than five minutes I was able to negotiate a twenty percent price reduction resulting in a happy buyer and seller.

Our next stop, the Archeological Museum, housed works from the Stone and Bronze Ages to the Classical Period. The three major influences in early Greece were the Cycladic, from the 3rd to 2nd millennium BC; the Minoan, from Crete, from 1,500 to 200 BC; and the Mycenaean, from 1,500 to 1,000 BC. Relics from each of these ancient civilizations were displayed. From the Classical period, a bronze statue of Poseidon and another of a racing horse caught our attention. Both still existed because they had been underwater for many centuries until they were discovered by divers in modern times.

As we drove through Athens, Irene answered some of our questions. The city of Athens was approximately four square miles with a population of one million. There were twenty-five hundred Greek islands but only 170 were inhabited and, according to her, the best to visit were Crete and Santorini, so named by the Venetians in honor of Santa Irina.

We exited the city for an hour-and-a-half drive to Sounion, a small village at the eastern tip of the peninsula. Our route followed the coast and we passed through many charming resort villages. Irene explained that most of the homes were owned by Athenians and used for weekend getaways.

Although the day looked dreary earlier, the skies turned brilliant blue just as we arrived in Sounion. Against this picturesque background stood the ruins of the 5th-century Temple of Poseidon. Built in the Classical style, six columns outlined its width and thirteen its length. Before hiking up the hillside to this imposing site on a cliff high above the sea we sat on a patio overlooking the ruins while enjoying a late-afternoon lunch.

When we returned to Athens, I asked Irene for dinner suggestions. We later took a taxi to the Plaka and walked past both of her recommendations, the Daphne and the Diogenes. Since the Diogenes was located at the edge of the Plaka bordering the Acropolis, we selected it. Our patio table was surrounded by flowering bougainvillea and a bright half moon lit the area. In spite of the spectacular setting, the food did not match the ambience. Somehow it just didn't matter, and we enjoyed our final night in Athens.

After dinner we walked along the streets that sloped upward toward the Acropolis. As we wound our way along the narrow passages, we caught an occasional glimpse of the Parthenon's glowing silhouette. The vistas of the Acropolis at night would remain a highlight of our Athens visit.

For the next morning, we set our alarm clock and also requested a wake-up call. We weren't taking any chances. It afforded us plenty of time for a leisurely breakfast of cold meats and cheeses and delicious yogurt served with walnuts and honey. We then met our driver Vicky, the head of the Athens travel agency booked by our tour organizers. As we drove to the airport, she apologized for the mix-up at the airport when we arrived and personally escorted us through the check-in process. While waiting in the airline lounge, we nibbled on delicious pistachios. This was definitely not going to be a low-cal adventure.

The forty-five-minute flight to Istanbul went smoothly but we encountered long lines for our Turkish visa stamps. We had been asked to check our carry-on bags and then had to collect them. Not an easy entrance but, much to our delight, our driver held a sign with our names on it as we left the baggage claim area.

Exiting the airport, we drove along picturesque roadways bordering the sea. Passing through the old walls of Istanbul constructed fifteen hundred years ago, we had a clear view of the Bosphorus strait. Soon the impressive towers of St. Sophia and the Blue Mosque came into view. Bridges now spanning the Bosphorus connected the European and Asian sections of Istanbul. The bridges had promoted massive expansion into the Asian sector and now many lived in suburbs across from Old Istanbul.

As we entered the city we were stunned by its beauty. Although we noted third-world squalor, the breathtaking beauty of the city's setting on the Bosphorus captivated us immediately. An air of intrigue was ever-present.

We continued a short distance to the Ciragan Palace, pronounced Chir-on, part of the Kempinski hotel group. The hotel incorporated a 19th-century palace into its building scheme and housed restaurants, shops and a casino.

We were given a room on the third level of the main structure overlooking the Bosphorus Bridge. From our balcony we watched tour boats and ships traverse this important body of water connecting the Black Sea with the Sea of Marmara leading into the Aegean and Mediterranean Seas. The constant ship movement fascinated us. In the distance we could see the Blue Mosque.

As we stood on our balcony, we heard the late afternoon call to prayer amplified from a nearby minaret. Unlike the brazen calls we'd heard three years prior in Egypt, this was a softer and less piercing sound. With our windows closed we just might avoid another early morning wake-up.

Once settled in our room, we returned to the lobby and asked the concierge for suggestions for a walk. Taking his advice, we headed north and eventually turned into a narrow alleyway lined with small shops leading to the Bosphorus. This charming district called Ortakoy on a wharf along the water's edge was lined with coffee shops and outdoor tables. Several hundred people were either relaxing over their cups of coffee or sitting on benches in this popular gathering spot.

I ordered my first and last Turkish coffee in one of the shops. It arrived in a china demitasse cup and it looked and smelled appealing. One sip did it for me. As I stirred the steaming hot brew the spoon came out coated with what looked like thick brown mud. I later learned that Turkish coffee is prepared by mixing water, ground coffee and a slight bit of sugar together in a pot. It is then heated over a brazier of hot coals and poured unfiltered into cups. I'm sure my spoon would have stood up on its own in this thick murky concoction.

Palatable coffee was available throughout Turkey and was almost always simply called Nescafé. Occasionally we were served hot water and packets of instant Maxwell House coffee but we still had to ask for Nescafé. Just like Coke and Kleenex in the States, Nescafé meant any instant coffee mixed with hot water in Turkey.

We had our cameras with us and took some photos in this bustling area before heading down the alleyway to the main road. Directly across the street were stalls with goods from local markets and we decided to wander through a few of them. We always enjoyed doing this in foreign countries. When mingling with the townspeople we developed a clearer picture of how they lived.

Along the way we popped into several small markets. We bought some feta cheese, olives from a large barrel and crackers. Just beyond this market we watched a baker remove a ten-inch rectangular pizza from an oven and its delicious smell enticed us. We purchased one to share and carried it back to the waterfront for a mini picnic. Our pizza was actually a flatbread filled with a mixture of spicy lamb, tomatoes and an ample amount of olive oil. It was delicious and we dubbed it a Turkish calzone.

Before dressing for dinner, we toured the palace connected to our hotel and then the state-of-the-art health club. We returned to our room and sat on the patio enjoying our olives, cheese and crackers while watching the continuous activity on the Bosphorus until nightfall. At 8:30 p.m. we taxied to a restaurant named 29 Ulus. The food was B+ but the ambience and views ranked high. We made a reservation on short notice and even though our table was at the back of the restaurant we still had majestic views of this intriguing city on the water. It was a memorable first evening in Istanbul.

The next morning, we enjoyed a sumptuous breakfast at the Ciragan. Much to my delight, the yogurt in Turkey was just as outstanding as it was in Greece. Dishes of roasted walnuts and thick rich honey accompanied it. An astonishing array of fresh and dried fruits, olives, cheeses, and meats graced the buffet table and we found the baskets of fresh breads irresistible.

We met our Turkish guide Arda and our driver Halil after breakfast and we were ushered into a roomy Mercedes for our day tour of Istanbul. We first stopped at the Dolmabahçe Palace not far from our hotel. Since only a limited number of tickets were sold each day at the entrance, our admission was ensured by arriving early.

Arda told us that the Topkapi Palace, which sits across the finger of water called the Golden Horn dividing the European and Asian parts of Istanbul, had been the official residence of Sultans from 1455 to 1855 AD. At the end of that period, Dolmabahçe Palace became the Sultan's home. This grand palace, now a museum, consisted of 280 elaborately decorated rooms. The few we viewed were filled with a profusion of tiles, carpets, fabrics, furnishings, art, crystal, and gold. A crystal chandelier weighing four and a half tons, a gift from Queen Victoria, was but one of the hundreds of spectacular artifacts housed in this museum. It was difficult to comprehend the vast amount of wealth that the last of the Sultans commanded.

Revolt was in the air by the turn of the 20th century. The Young Turks forced change and a Parliament formed in 1908 ended centuries of Ottoman rule. Its accompanying lavish lifestyle ended with it.

The great Turkish leader Ataturk used the palace to entertain heads of state and foreign dignitaries. I can only imagine what they thought when they encountered the opulence of the Dolmabahçe. In deference to Turkey's great leader, all clocks in the palace were set to 9:05 a.m., the precise moment that

Ataturk died on November 10, 1938. It was interesting to note that Ataturk, a Muslim, was a heavy drinker and died of cirrhosis.

Following our tour of the Dolmabahçe, we drove north out of the city along the sea coast. Arda pointed out the tomb of the pirate Barbarossa, dated 1525 AD. He terrorized the seas during the reign of Suleyman the Magnificent, undoubtedly adding to the riches of this powerful Ottoman Sultan.

Arda mentioned that at the time of our visit, ninety-five percent of Turks were Muslim. A smattering of Jews, Christians and Catholics practiced their religions without interference. He told us that although most of the Muslims in the larger cities were quite liberal, a small minority living in the eastern part of Turkey near the Iranian border were radical fundamentalists and they continued to cause disruptions.

He also pointed out that ninety-seven percent of Turkey was in Asia. Some of the countries bordering it were Syria, Iraq, Iran, Georgia, and Russia. Turkey was indeed strategically located. Its total population, estimated between 63 and 65 million, was rapidly increasing. In Istanbul, the 1965 census totaled 1.6 million. By 1990, Istanbul was home to 8.5 million and now, just five years later, the estimated range was between 12 and 14 million. As in Egypt, birth control remained an unspeakable topic. Even though it is illegal, men in the countryside often had an official wife and a concubine.

There were numerous political parties in Turkey, not always in the country's best interest. Because of this fragmentation, candidates from the Fundamentalist Labor Party had recently won mayoral races in both Ankara and Istanbul. This resulted in the closure of tea rooms in parks and valuable art works risked removal from their permanent locations. The last election had taken everyone by surprise and caused turmoil. Since each of the mayors received less than twenty-five percent of the popular vote there was a movement underway to create run-off elections, thus guaranteeing that no candidate without a majority vote could serve.

During our visit, Prime Minister Tansu Ciller held on to her coalition by a thread. On the Sunday of our return to the States her government fell. Turkey was governed by a single Parliament made up of elected representatives. Provinces with dense population bases had more representatives than their more sparsely populated neighbors. The President was largely a figurehead, as the Prime Minister held the power.

People were delighted when Ciller was elected PM. However, she continually courted more radical elements to garner support and had lost favor with the general population. Additionally, her husband was involved in some business scandals. It was of interest, nevertheless, that a woman could and did rise to power in a country where outside of large cities they remain repressed.

We soon arrived at the Sadberk Hanim Museum in the seaside village of Sariyer. The front section of this small museum once served as the beach home of a powerful Turkish family. The inside now featured period furnishings, art and clothing. The newer building added at the back fascinated us with its impressive collection of pottery, metalwork, jewelry, coins, and artifacts from the Assyrian and Hittite Period, 2000–1200 BC, to the Byzantine Period, 330–1450 AD. Ancient Phrygian, Urartian, Mycenaean, Lydian, and Hellenistic artifacts were also on display.

The beach house and its collections were donated to the museum by the wealthiest businessman in Turkey, a man named Koc, pronounced Kah-ch. Now in his 90s, he was befriended by Ataturk and given authority to bring foreign business opportunities into Turkey. He also developed a number of industries internally. Fortunately for the Turks, he shared his wealth and this was one of two Koc museums we would tour.

Our next stop was the Sirene, a seaside restaurant also in the village of Sariyer. We sat at one of only a few tables taken, usually reflecting a poor choice in the States. Not so in Turkey. We enjoyed a multi-course seafood feast selected by Arda that lasted well over an hour. As we were about to discover, this was the first of many lengthy and large lunches we would encounter over the next two weeks.

After lunch we drove a bit further to the north for a view of the Bosphorus as it connected to the Black Sea. With an abundance of fish in this area, we counted at least fifteen small boats with nets circling large areas of the sea.

Arda booked us on a late afternoon cruise along the Bosphorus and as we boarded the boat designed to hold a hundred passengers, discovered that we had it all to ourselves. We sat on the upper level in bright sunshine as Arda pointed out the significant sights slowly floating by us on our hour-long cruise. Much to our delight, the tour boat collected us from and returned us to a dock along our hotel. Talk about door-to-door service!

We said goodbye to Arda for the day and decided to walk back to the waterfront area of Ortakoy. This time we opted for Beltas, the outdoor café closest to one of the bridges, and tried our first narrow glass cup of *bartak çay*, or Turkish tea. Watching tour boats like ours filled with passengers silently slip by, we sipped the bitter strong brew. I made a decision that Nescafé and an occasional apple tea would be my drinks of choice for the duration of our stay in Turkey.

Smoking seemed to be a national pastime and the cafés were no exception. The odor pervaded our space even in outdoor settings. We gave thanks that

Arda was a non-smoker and made every attempt to keep us away from it. When we were on our own, we would request a table on the fringe to get a slight break from the tobacco-laden air. As Californians we were spoiled by laws prohibiting smoking in restaurants.

Having booked 7:00 p.m. massages in the Ciragan's spa, we headed back to the hotel. My masseuse, a gal, and Wayne's, a guy, spoke no English. No words were needed. It was all business. We were led into adjacent rooms separated by swinging doors. Five minutes into his massage I heard a lengthy series of slapping sounds emanating from Wayne's room. Knowing that he was the recipient of chops, I had all I could do to keep from laughing out loud. It was a good thing I didn't because a minute or two later I got the same treatment. Expect chops with a Turkish massage.

Wayne's skimpy towel remained over his privates during his session, but my gal gave new meaning to a full massage. This was definitely not designed for shy types. I decided to just go with the flow as my travel-tight muscles were chopped and massaged into relax mode. Our team left us feeling wonderfully refreshed.

Meanwhile, back in the States.... After months of front-page news, the O.J. Simpson murder trial reached a verdict in short order and Judge Ito postponed its reading until today. We were so tired of hearing details on the news all day and night and we were glad to leave the trial behind us during our two weeks in Turkey. We knew that the verdict would be announced today and assumed it would be of little interest to the people in Turkey. While dressing after my massage, a young Irish woman entered and announced that O.J.'s jury found him innocent on all charges. The American justice system took a giant step backward that day.

We returned to our room and broke out our booty of cheese and olives. After relaxing on our patio we dressed for this evening's dinner at Hanedan, just a few blocks from our hotel. This restaurant offered meat dishes on the first floor and seafood on the second. Having enjoyed fish for lunch, we opted for shish kebob on the lower level. Once seated, we were offered selections from a large platter of Turkish mezes. These dishes were almost always presented at lunch and dinner. We chose an eggplant salad, fiery-hot red rice and hummus. They were accompanied by huge discs of freshly baked pita bread.

Next came our main course, a delicious kebob featuring lamb, chicken and beef served over a bed of hot spiced yogurt. It was so rich that I couldn't finish it but I'll never forget how good it tasted. After dinner we topped it off with a milky rice pudding and, you guessed it by now, Nescafé. Truly wonderful!

The next morning we met Arda, who told us that instead of being met by local guides in each area we visited, he would be our guide for our entire two-week stay in Turkey. We enjoyed him and admired his deep appreciation of his country's people, culture and history.

Arda was forty-one years old and single, although he hoped to marry someday. He was a very liberal Muslim and, much to our surprise, he always ordered beer with his lunch and a concoction called lion's milk with his dinner. The latter is a healthy shot of anisette served with soda water on the side. As the soda water pours over the liquor it forms a frothy, milk-colored drink—thus, the name lion's milk. Our assumption that all Muslims were forbidden to drink alcohol proved not to be the case in Turkey. For religious reasons, Arda never touched wine but beer and alcohol were permissible.

He hailed from Çatalca, about twenty miles from Istanbul. After graduating from the University of Istanbul with a degree in English language and literature, Arda spent some time living in England, Spain and Germany. His German had slipped so he preferred to lead tours in English and Spanish. He was easy-going and we always felt he had everything under control. We also enjoyed his sense of humor.

As we drove through Istanbul, Arda shared bits of history with us. We learned that Ataturk, the great reformer of Turkey, selected Ankara as the country's capital in 1922 because it was centrally located. At that time, it was a city of forty thousand. As of our visit, it was home to 4 million.

Driving on, he pointed out miles of aqueducts built by the Romans in 370 AD. We also passed parts of the ancient city walls dating to the 2nd century AD. We continued on through a congested area of small hotels and shops. Arda explained that many Russians, Romanians, Bulgarians, and Polish came to this area. They arrived by the busload on a regular basis and bought massive quantities of goods to take back for resale in their respective countries. We would see some of these shoppers in action the following week.

Halil stopped for a few minutes at a large fish market situated along the ancient Roman aqueduct. We were impressed by the large quantities of fresh fish that were available. We then continued on to the oldest section of the city. With traffic at a crawl we finally arrived at our destination, the Turkish and Islamic Art Museum, housed in a 1525 AD building.

The history of the Turkish conquest was well-documented in this museum. The Turks arrived in 1071 AD and a string of sultans ruled the land until the beginning of the 20th century. From the 11th to 14th centuries AD the Seljuk tribe remained in power. After that, the Ottomans ruled the empire. We enjoyed seeing displays of how various tribes lived and worked and also had our first introduction to elaborate Turkish rugs and tiles.

From there we drove a short distance to the entrance of Topkapi Palace, home of the Ottoman Sultans from 1458 AD to 1855 AD. As we walked through one of the massive courtyards, Arda mentioned that three more also graced the palace grounds. Our first stop was the kitchen where meals had been prepared each day for as many as twelve thousand people. As we walked through, Arda taught us a few Turkish words. Tamam means *okay*, şerefe (pronounced sheriff-ey) means *cheers*, and sagol (pronounced saa-ool) means *thank you*. The letter "g" in Turkish seemed to just sit there and do nothing. Our hotel's name was a good example of that.

Next we visited the newest part of the palace complex which now housed the Konyali restaurant. While the three men found a table, I queued in a long line for a WC stop. It took twenty minutes to reach my destination. This restaurant that easily seats 300 guests offered only one four-stall WC. Time for another modern addition...

We were served a multi-course meal, this one just so-so. Wayne and I could easily have done without it. Arda, however, didn't like to miss a bite and didn't stop until every morsel had been devoured. This would continue throughout our time with him in Turkey.

After passing on the fruit course and dodging the occasional bee that landed on one of our plates, we continued our tour. We visited several rooms filled with opulent china and jewels. The highlights were a magnificent jewel-encrusted dagger, the eighty-six-carat Spoonmaker's Diamond that belonged to 17th-century Sultan Mehmed IV, and two solid gold candlesticks made in the mid-1800s weighing 110 pounds each.

Mid-afternoon we visited the palace's Harem, pronounced har-eem. Dating from 1582 AD, this inner sanctum was home to each Sultan's four official wives, his eight favorites, the queen mother, and as many as a few hundred concubines. The only males allowed to enter were 100 black eunuch slaves, and even they could venture no further than the outer periphery. The eunuchs would porter food and drink to an area where they were met by concubines who then completed the deliveries to the inner sanctuaries. We toured the queen mother's quarters, the Imperial Hall, the baths, and several other areas of the vast 400-room harem.

Our next destination for the day was St. Sophia, a Christian church commissioned by Constantine I in 326 AD. Until St. Peter's Basilica was constructed between 1506 AD and 1626 AD, it stood as the largest cathedral in the world. St. Sophia's dome soars 190 feet skyward and the massive structure is supported by 107 columns. It remains an impressive architectural wonder.

Some 9th-century mosaics that had only recently been restored dazzled us. After the Ottoman Conquest in 1453 AD, St. Sophia became a mosque and most of the Christian mosaics were plastered and whitewashed. In retrospect this probably helped to preserve them over the centuries.

We made our way to a corridor leading to circular steps that rose to the upper level of this enormous structure. From our bird's-eye perch we could make out the intricate details of the mosaics covering the dome and main apse, all restored within the previous four years.

Our final stop was Istanbul's famed Covered Bazaar housing more than thirty-five hundred small shops. As we entered without Arda, we soon had thousands of shopkeepers clamoring for our business. We quickly walked past stall after stall filled with jewelry and made a turn down rug alley where the heat for our dollars was turned up to high. Deciding we had seen enough, we made our way back to the main street filled with small shops that suddenly seemed like Madison Avenue boutiques following our experience in the bazaar.

After a Nescafé at one of the sidewalk cafés we reconnected with Arda and our driver to return to our hotel. What should have been a fifteen-minute ride took more than an hour in Istanbul's rush hour traffic. We crawled along at a snail's pace.

Since we were tired after a long day of touring and still full from our too-large lunch we decided to walk back to the market area we'd visited earlier for a fast-food run. We ordered a stuffed pita bread and opted to eat it at one of the small Formica tables in the shop. The owner seemed surprised and pleased that we made this choice. When we finished it, we bought an assortment of small honey-glazed pastries and carried them back to our hotel room. After our in-room dessert we packed for the next day's flight to Cappadocia.

Arda met us at 7:30 a.m. in the hotel lobby and we left to catch our flight. The morning rush hour traffic crawled along but we finally reached the terminal. With little time to spare, we still needed to pass through three security checks before we could board the plane. Arda later explained that there had been a terrorist attack the day before, resulting in extra security measures.

The flight into Turkey's interior passed over desolate, uninhabited plains. An occasional narrow road snaked across the landscape. As we neared our destination, a monolithic snow-covered mountain rose from the flat plains, peaking at thirteen hundred feet. Plots of cultivated farms dotted the landscape as we approached the city of Kayseri and the landing strip on a military base.

We met our driver Hikmet who had arrived from Ankara early that morning. He loaded our bags into the trunk of his car and we waited while

Arda made some phone calls. He later told us that he called his mother every morning and evening and checked in with his office in Istanbul every day.

Wanting a photo of the snow-capped volcanic mountain rising up from the desert floor, I focused my camera for a perfect shot. As I was about to take my photo, two armed soldiers from the military base ran toward me waving their arms in protest. Deciding not to argue with men carrying machine guns, I lowered my camera and returned to the car. The photo of the mountain would just have to wait.

What had looked like barren land below us on our flight was actually some of the most fertile in the world. We would pass hundreds of miles of small farms growing everything from fruits and vegetables to vast fields of sunflowers, cotton and tobacco during our two-hour drive to Cappadocia. Arda told us that Turkey is one of seven self-sufficient countries and could therefore feed itself.

As we drove out of Kayseri, he filled us in on more about the city. It was currently home to half a million people, approximately 800 km from Istanbul, and 300 km from Ankara. In ancient times it served as the capital of Assyria. At the time of our visit, one could find many small industries in Kayseri and its businessmen had a reputation throughout Turkey for being wheeler-dealers. There was also a medical university here. Kayseri's size and importance made us wonder why it utilized a military base for plane traffic.

After passing through the city we came to a park with a 12th-century *kumbet*, a small round guard tower. We stopped for a photo and noticed two older women seated at the edge of the tower with heads covered and wearing traditional dress. Instead of protesting when I raised my camera the women smiled and waved cheerfully. As we moved further into the interior of Turkey this was not always the case.

Once out of culturally forward Istanbul we noticed a distinct difference in how women were treated in this male-dominated Islamic society. In larger cities like Kayseri, women were on the streets dressed in dark, drab clothing that covered their bodies. Although most did not cover their faces, they did wear large scarves over their heads.

Moving away from populated areas into rural farmland, the plight of women became apparent. While men sat in large groups along the streets drinking coffee, playing backgammon or simply chatting, the women filled the fields doing backbreaking farming with hand tools. They labored from dawn until dark. Returning home, they assisted their oldest daughters with dinner and catered to their husbands. It was a time-honored way of life for women and the Islamic Fundamentalist men in the eastern part of Turkey battled to preserve it. To a Western observer it bordered on criminal and this archaic division of labor deeply disturbed us.

As we approached Cappadocia the landscape reminded us of parts of the western United States. We passed hilly flat-topped plateaus sprinkled with scrub brush. Orange and green gourds hanging from vines dotted miles of fertile farmland. We noted white lean-to tents that Arda explained provided shelter for field workers.

We asked about irrigation for these seemingly barren plains and were told that the rainy season lasts from November to April. Snow melt from the volcanic mountain in the distance supplied water to the Halys River, known as the Red River in English. Water, it seemed, was abundant.

Traveling along a smooth two-lane highway, small trucks, or lorries, posed our only obstacles but Hikmet was able to pass them with ease. As we would later discover, the lorries did create havoc on roadways with more traffic. Most were overloaded, often piled twice as high as the vehicle itself while carrying as much as twenty tons of goods. These overloaded lorries had extreme difficulty making it up the most gradual grades and posed continual danger to cars that traveled at fast speeds or attempted to pass. Accidents, Arda told us, were frequent and disastrous.

We soon spotted herds of sheep along the now-hilly landscape. Occasionally we saw cattle. Twice we passed cow carcasses along the roadway. With no fences to keep them at bay, livestock created road hazards as well.

As we drove for mile after mile, I thought of earlier travelers who traversed this parched landscape without the aid of modern transportation. Travel by camel caravan was the norm for many centuries. The camels refueled with water at strategic points along the way, much as today's auto traveler does with stops at gas stations.

Suddenly and dramatically we reached Cappadocia. We seemed to transcend from the desert to a magical wonderland in an instant. Before us rose high weather-beaten cliffs. In the foreground, formations called fairy chimneys stood like sentinels rising from the barren ground.

Photos of Cappadocia simply cannot capture its grandeur. It must be experienced in its entirety in order to make the lasting impression it did on us. This magical valley featuring spectacular windblown rock formations and cliffs dotted with man-made caves would remain one of our favorite memories.

As we approached a village at the outer edge of the valley, I noticed row after row of three-story buildings that seemed like empty shells. Similar structures stood along our route to the Istanbul airport. When I questioned Arda he told us that in the early 1900s the Turkish government mandated a US$100 exit fee for all travelers leaving the country. This money was earmarked for low-income housing and, to cash in on this bonanza, thousands of building projects were launched. Sadly, the cash flow did not keep up with the demand. Consequently, thousands of projects remained unfinished throughout Turkey.

Arda told us that Cappadocia meant *The Land of Beautiful Horses*. We mentioned that we had not seen a single horse other than those attached to carts in Istanbul. He said we would see some donkeys in this area but no longer many horses.

Tourism in Cappadocia took firm root in the 1950s when a team of French archaeologists came to search for reported hidden churches in the valley. Only a few hotels were available at that time, but the hotel industry had since flourished.

We pulled into Urgup, a small village of eleven thousand, early in the afternoon. Our first stop entailed another huge but unremarkable lunch at a local tourist restaurant, a part of which was incorporated into an ancient cave. We then drove a few blocks to our hotel for the next two nights, the Esbelli Evi. This unique seven-room hotel combined a newly built native-stone block structure constructed over a lower level of rooms, each a cave dating to the 3rd century AD. It was one of a few hotels permitted to incorporate these ancient caves. Our room had been transformed into a structurally sound space with the addition of large support blocks cut from the surrounding cliffs. In general, cave dwellings were now considered dangerous and living in them was prohibited.

We totally enjoyed our stay at this charming bed and breakfast. Each morning the owner, a businessman from Ankara with a passion for Cappadocia, served a simple breakfast to guests. His enormous friendly cat was ever-present. In the main house were the breakfast room, a music room and a patio that overlooked the village. Clay pots filled with flowers and greenery stood in contrast to the stark sandy stones used for the building and patio. It was a first-class act.

Upon our afternoon arrival, we gave ourselves an hour to get situated before regrouping for the rest of the afternoon's activities. With only our carry-ons to unpack we were ready to roll in ten minutes and decided to take a short walk through the upper village. Looking down from the roadway along the ridge we saw literally hundreds of carved cave dwellings created during the 2nd and 3rd centuries AD by Christians fleeing Roman persecution. In the Cappadocia valley there must have been thousands of similar dwellings.

Until the early 1950s, the caves remained inhabited. Although modern residents were Muslim rather than Christian, they desired the dwellings for their natural insulation that kept them cool during the hot, dry summers and warm in the winters. They were also easy to maintain. Over the centuries many of the cave dwellings became structurally unsafe, most likely the result of numerous earthquakes. Finally, the government condemned the caves and provided alternative housing in the valleys below. It took a great deal of persuasion to move the cave dwellers into modern living quarters.

Hikmet returned to Esbelli Evi after checking into a nearby hotel and Arda, Wayne and I joined him for our late afternoon tour of the Goreme Open Air Museum, which comprised nearly two hundred small churches carved into rock formations in a three-square-mile area. A number of them either had been or were in the process of being restored and all were open to the public.

We began with a tour of Tokali Church, best known as Buckle Church. Carved in the 4th century AD, most of its artwork was added during the Byzantine era of the 11th and 12th centuries AD. The museum grouping consisted of twelve churches with only the Buckle Church having been completely restored. Paintings of Jesus, Mary and many of the saints adorned its walls, now in their original splendor.

Crossing the street, we passed a monolithic refectory that rose several stories. It was dotted with small doorways and windows that gave it the appearance of a giant sandcastle. It had once served as the residence of the village nuns.

Seven additional churches dotted the cliffs in this area and all but one could be toured. One was dedicated to Saint Barbara. Another featured a wizened and naked old man holding a small branch over his privates, his long white hair flowing unkempt almost to his feet. Interestingly, he was drawn with swirls representing breasts. Many folk tales accompanied this bizarre painting.

Just as the sun set, we drove to Pasabag, or Valley of the Monks, an area not far away which had a scattering of narrow chimney-shaped rock formations capped with mushroom-like tops. Arda encouraged us to use our imaginations as we viewed these unique natural works of art. Sculpted by centuries of wind, we imagined birds and a lion as we gazed at them.

When we departed this area, Arda asked if we would like to stop for tea. We agreed and soon pulled up in front of a large building topped with a sign advertising pottery. As soon as we entered, we knew we had been had. Our invitation for tea was in fact a ploy for us to do some pottery shopping.

Arda and the owner led us to a back room and invited us to have seats on a bench. The owner's assistant offered us tea and we accepted. Then the owner/potter demonstrated how to throw a tea pot. Using clay from the Red River he formed a perfect pot. With Arda translating, he invited Wayne to try his hand at the potter's wheel. Wayne had worked with clay as a teen and agreed to give it a whirl.

We had made it very clear to our travel agent that shopping was of no interest to us. We'd been on overseas group tours and knew how many hours were wasted in tourist-oriented shops. With just the two of us traveling with a guide, we made it abundantly clear that we would not even consider it. In fact, one of the reasons we opted for a private tour of Turkey was to avoid these time-wasting stops.

With no intention of buying a piece of pottery, I mentioned this to Arda and offered to give the owner a tip. Arda assured me that it wasn't necessary and after a quick perusal of pots on display we left the shop. It was awkward and I told Arda firmly that shopping was not our focus on this trip.

After returning to Esbelli Evi to remove the dust we again joined Arda and Hikmet for a short drive to Kapadokya Lodge and Country Club, an ultra-modern hotel designed to reflect the architecture of the ancient caves. It was spectacular. Even more spectacular was the opulent dinner buffet it offered. We enjoyed a large selection of mezes, Turkish cold appetizers, and an array of hot starters. Then we feasted on fish, chicken, lamb, and beef dishes. Completely doing us in, we indulged in an array of desserts. The sumptuous table was laden with honey cakes, pies, puddings, and more. After an hour and a half of eating we joined a group of Arda's tour-guide friends and chatted until the 10:00 p.m. closing time.

We began the next day with a tour of Cappadocia. While driving to our first destination we passed a number of women riding in open wagons drawn by donkeys. Although each was a photograph waiting to happen, I decided not to risk offending the women by pointing my camera in their direction. More mental memories...

We drove along the narrow Pigeon Valley to Uchisar Castle, the fortress that dominated much of the countryside. Climbing three hundred feet to the top we had an impressive panoramic view of Cappadocia. We easily understood why this enormous formation was chosen for the area's defense. Little could go undetected in the valley below from this bird's-eye view.

Although we had made it very clear to Arda the day before that shopping wasn't on our agenda, the next stop was a shop operated by the local onyx cutter. As we pulled into the parking lot, I told Arda that we had no interest in buying anything. He told us the cutter was a good friend and we were under no obligation to make a purchase. With a "let's make it quick" from me, we entered the shop.

Once again, we were offered tea and this time we politely refused as we stood for the obligatory onyx-cutting demonstration. The owner spoke enough

English to ask if we knew any Turkish words. When Wayne responded with *sagol*, the carver presented him with the onyx egg that he had just carved. We did a quick tour of the shop and saw virtually nothing of interest to us. As we left, we told Arda more forcefully that we had no interest in shopping.

Whether with a tour group or just two individuals, the accompanying tour guide always wanted to earn a bit of extra pocket money by showcasing local businesses. Arda was no exception. We were beginning to understand that not all his phone calls were to his mother. He was intent on bringing us to these venues in hopes of claiming his commission on our purchases.

We continued south toward Derinkuyu, a massive underground village excavated to an eight-story depth by early Christians during the 2nd and 3rd centuries AD. A team of road builders happened upon the site in 1964. The vast underground city provided an escape for early Christians from the Romans. Derinkuyu means *deep well*, aptly named since a well rests at its base.

The early Christians sealed themselves into their underground town by rolling enormous millstones into place at various points throughout the connecting tunnels. Many of the stones had remained intact and were rolled aside for modern-day tourists to pass through the tunnels to the lower levels.

The village had schools, churches, kitchens, living quarters, and much more. Our visit covered only about fifteen percent of the vast underground complex. Air channels were ingeniously cut into the rocks and even at the lowest depths we breathed an ample supply of fresh air. Although electricity lit our way through the tunnels, Arda brought a flashlight to point out the intricacies. It was difficult to imagine as many as fifteen thousand Christians huddled in these dark depths as they hid from their persecutors.

Continuing on through the valley at ground level, we made a number of stops to capture on film the beauty and majesty of this unique corner of the world. The day was crystal clear and the deep blue sky provided the perfect backdrop for the cave-riddled cliffs that greeted us at every turn.

Arda mentioned that tulips were native to Turkey and were exported by the Dutch centuries ago. Not only was I raised in Western Michigan, an area with a large Dutch population, and which holds a colorful tulip festival every spring, but I had also visited vast tulip fields in The Netherlands and never knew they were not a native plant.

We stopped for lunch at a restaurant adjacent to the Ataman Hotel in Goreme. Although the hotel remained under construction, its restaurant was open for business. We sat in a small side room with no smokers, a rare treat in Turkey. Another substantial but very ordinary meal was served and we dutifully sat with Arda and Hikmet until they had consumed every morsel.

We dubbed Arda the Human Garbage Disposal. This man could pack away more food than anyone I'd ever known!

While at lunch, Arda mentioned that he would like to take us to a place that would show us how Turkish rugs were woven. Having been lured to a similar spot in Egypt on an earlier trip, red flags went up for us. Even though I had told Arda we had no interest in buying a rug, he insisted he only wanted us to learn how they are made. He made another phone call and we again suspected it wasn't to his mother. We then headed for Avanos, the largest city in the region, situated on the Halys River. The town had no redeeming value that we could see.

The reason for our drive to Avanos soon became apparent. We turned onto a dusty road that bordered the river and parked outside an enormous modern building flanked by tour buses. We were greeted by a swarm of bees and a slick Turkish carpet salesman. Batting away bees, we followed him into the building. The game plan consisted of a quick look at the weavers and then a full-on sales pitch on the second level. By now I was furious. When asked what size and color carpet I would select, I responded that I was not looking for a rug. Mr. Slick suggested I pretend.

Asking us what colors we used in our home, he hailed two bulky assistants who unrolled eight or ten rugs for us to view. After fifteen minutes at this game, Mr. Slick suggested we walk through the vast display area and see if we spotted any rugs to our liking. We walked. Nothing appealed to us. We left.

It was interesting to note that the carpet market in Avanos sold twenty thousand carpets every year. If the store was open seven days a week, which we suspected it was, then the store sold 55 carpets each day. The rugs appeared to be of good quality and the prices were relatively reasonable. For the avid carpet buyer who knew his merchandise, this was probably not a bad place to make a purchase. We simply were not in the market.

On our way back to Esbelli Evi we paid a fee to enter an area on high ground for a late afternoon look at the sculpted rock formations in an isolated part of the valley. No matter where one goes in Cappadocia, the striking beauty of the landscape is breathtaking. The cave-filled cliffs and the giant sandcastle-like formations on the valley floor would forever be with us in our memories.

When we returned to the hotel, Wayne and I decided to walk into the lower village before sunset which, at this time of year, was by 6:00 p.m. We passed several groups of people who ignored us, but two young village boys tagged along near us. In their limited English they asked us for our names and then asked where we lived. After a short time with us they waved goodbye.

The major money maker in this village appeared to be the wine industry.

Vineyards were prolific in Cappadocia and judging from the barrels of sludge from pressed grapes that we passed, most of the crop made its way to the wine presses in Urgup. Arda had told us earlier that the Koran forbids Muslims from drinking wine and we were surprised to see its production here. Perhaps it was made for export.

Meanwhile, back at our cave, I brewed a batch of Nescafé in the main kitchen and we took our cups into the music room. We were joined by two men and three women, all from England. They were not guests but one of the men had stayed here a year ago and brought his friends for a late afternoon drink. The hotel owner also joined us and we chatted for almost an hour. One of the men was with the British Embassy in Ankara. We had a delightful discussion about travels all over the world.

An hour later we met Arda and Hikmet for a drive back to Avedon and dinner in a modern-day cave carved to create a restaurant named Altimocak, *Gold Kitchen* in English. It featured a set menu accompanied by folk dancing with musicians performing on native instruments. After our mezes and hot appetizers, we were served slices of lamb from the large roasted carcass that was paraded around the room by the waiters.

The evening's program lasted an hour and a half and showcased a variety of dances and costumes from different regions of Turkey. We were introduced to music played on an oud, a cross between a guitar and a mandolin. Drums, tambourines, an accordion, and a high-pitched horn completed the musical repertoire. Our handsome driver Hikmet had nothing but smiles for the pretty female dancers. We all had a delightful evening.

Nights in Cappadocia were almost more beautiful than the days. We could not have timed our visit more perfectly and were treated to a nearly full moon view each evening. As we drove across the valley late at night, it cast a warm glow on the chimney spires of rock formations lining the roadway.

The next morning, we said goodbye to Suha, the owner of Esbelli Evi, his assistant Ersoz and, of course, the resident cat. Soon we found ourselves on a two-lane roadway leading to Ankara located approximately 225 miles further east. We passed a 16th-century *caravanserai*, or roadside inn, in ruins and I thought of the early traders who traveled for weeks along this route. As if reading my mind, it was at this moment that Arda pointed out that the first leg of our drive followed the ancient Silk Road.

After an hour's drive we stopped near the village of Agzikarahan for a quick tour of a restored caravanserai built by the Seljuk Turks in the 12th century. The Seljuk tribe ruled for three hundred years before the Ottoman rule. Huge cut-stone blocks formed this rest stop for men and their camels as they traversed the Silk Road. Since camels could only travel about thirteen miles each day, ruins of caravanserai appear at approximately these intervals.

Most of the ride from Cappadocia to Ankara was relatively flat with an occasional rolling hill to break the monotony. Saturday was not a day of rest in this part of Turkey and we encountered donkey carts, tractors and hundreds of dangerously overloaded lorries. Nearing Ankara, we came to a standstill before we could safely pass the multitude of slow-moving vehicles.

Arda mentioned that drunk driving is a big problem on Turkey's roadways. He told us of an incident when a drunk bus driver in Istanbul turned into the wrong lane and hit two taxis, killing two and injuring three. Each year, ten thousand were killed and one hundred thousand injured. He then assured us that our travel agency was extremely careful about the drivers it hired.

When we reached the periphery of Ankara, we made a right-hand turn and stopped at a small modern-day caravanserai, a gas station with a much-needed WC. At this point we left the Silk Road and followed an alternate route toward Ankara. Arda mentioned that this region was known for its sunflowers; their seeds and oil were harvested. As the growing season had already ended, we noticed piles of discarded sunflowers along the way.

A little later we spotted an imposing lake bordering the roadway. Arda told us that this salt lake was the second largest inland body of water in Turkey. The largest is close to the Iranian border far to the east.

I asked Arda about the relations between Turkey and Iran. He confided they are cordial on the surface but some deep rifts exist. Iranians do not recognize Ataturk, the national hero of Turkey who westernized the country and brought it into the 20th century. The Iranians are also pro-fundamentalist, which is not a belief shared by the majority of Turkey's Muslim population.

As we approached Ankara, we passed another small lake. Hikmet jokingly told Arda that he and his friends called it the Sea of Ankara. Entering the outskirts, we were impressed by the evergreen-lined roadway leading into the city. Arda explained that in the late 1970s, Ankara had a terrible air pollution problem. Much was done to correct the situation in the capital and that included massive plantings of trees and evergreens and, at the time of our visit, the air was relatively clean.

We followed a scenic route into the heart of Ankara and were impressed by the mix of modern buildings with well-preserved turn-of-the-20th-century structures. The city was vital and bustling, filled with landscaped parks and fine sculptures. The new fundamentalist mayor had started a campaign to remove the works of art in the city, much to the chagrin of the majority of the population.

Driving up a steep grade we soon came to the ancient fortress of the city where the Museum of Anatolian Civilization was located. I had read a book about its impressive collection of artifacts dating to 6000 BC and it was to be one of the highlights of our trip for me. Since it was already 1:00 p.m. and we needed to leave for the airport at 3:00, I asked Arda if we could just grab a sandwich or something light so we would have ample time to visit the museum. Wayne agreed and said that we did not want another hour-long lunch.

Arda assured us that today's prearranged lunch at Zenger Pasha, located in a restored 1595 AD wooden house, would not take much time. In reality, he simply ignored our request for a light lunch and ushered us into another gimmicky tourist spot for a lengthy multi-course meal. His idea of a quick lunch was to eliminate one of the starter courses. When we finished the main course, we passed on the fruit and coffee. Even though they knew we wanted to get to the museum, Arda and Hikmet continued with all the courses.

Frustrated, I asked if we could go ahead of them and meet them at the museum. Arda assured us that they would be finished in no time and we went outside to wait. And wait. It was another ten or fifteen minutes before we were underway and, with an hour spent over lunch, we now had less than an hour to see Ankara's world-class museum. We were not happy campers. Neither Wayne nor I enjoy long, heavy lunches but it seemed to be the highlight of the day for Arda and we expected there would be more to come.

By the time we reached the museum, housed in a 15th-century restored covered bazaar, we found ourselves touring with a sense of urgency. It had one of the richest collections of antiquities in the world and I had hoped to have at least two hours to peruse its artifacts. Although we were able to catch the highlights, it would have been wonderful to see this powerful collection in a more relaxed mode.

We joined Hikmet for our ride to the airport where we said goodbye to this capable and friendly driver. Even though we did not speak each other's language, we developed a special friendship with this young man.

Although our interior flights were short hops, we did wonder why we were always seated in tourist class. With the top dollar price we paid for our private tour we expected business class seats. Three soldiers smelling as though they had spent the past week in the same uniform sat directly in front of us. Thank goodness for short flights!

Landing in Izmir late in the afternoon we were met by our third driver, Ibrahim. He led us to a fairly new but very small Toyota Corolla. There was not enough room in the sparse trunk for our compact carry-on luggage and Arda's suitcase, so he straddled one of the bags during the hour-long drive to Kusadasi. There was very little leg room in the back of the car and we soon felt cramped.

On a positive note, we enjoyed the scenic beauty we encountered on the late afternoon drive to our seacoast destination. The golden hills dotted with emerald green foliage reminded us of similar areas along the Central Coast of California. This was indeed a varied and beautiful country!

As we approached our newest destination, Arda explained that Kusadasi translates to *Bird Island*, as the island has the shape of a bird's head. After a bit of a search for tonight's remote hotel, the Ephesus Princess, we checked into a villa room in this massive complex. Arda's room was a hike up the hillside and we arranged to meet for a four-mile drive into town after we unpacked.

Our room looked more like an operating room than what I'd expected of a five-star hotel. It was white. Stark white. White plastered walls with white kitchen-style tiles on the floor. No rugs. An occasional dash of hot pink attempted to break up the monotony. When I looked into the bathroom, I was sure the housekeeper had left us a used bar of soap. Then I discovered a wafer-thin twin in the mildewed shower. No tourist would pocket one of these bars for a souvenir! On the back of the bathroom door, a literally translated German sign read, "We have to emphasize that all the room inventory, as towels, sheets, etc.; the maids are responsible. Please consider in case of getting lost these things they have to pay." Verbatim. I kid you not. And, rest assured, the towels were not about to go into either of our suitcases.

We chuckled over the hotel, perched so high above the water that we could not even see it from our waterfront room. Although we could live for three nights in this less-than-wonderful room, we were disappointed that our original hotel, the Kismet, had pulled our reservations at the last minute.

Arda asked Ibrahim to drive into the village to the Kismet Hotel. It was situated on an isolated point with a commanding view of the entire Kusadasi Bay. Although the building housing its thirty rooms appeared rather stark, the ambience of the lobby, grounds and outdoor eating area was elegant.

Having seen the Kismet, we were even more disappointed that we had been bumped. From what we'd heard, the Turkish government had taken over the hotel for a political meeting. When we asked the concierge if a room might be available, he rather haughtily waved what looked like a reservation book at us and shook his head. No room at the inn for the Smiths.

Since the Kismet was fully booked for dinner, we drove into the village to a seafood restaurant. We found an outdoor table away from the ever-present smoke and Arda helped us select some of the freshest and best fish we had ever tasted.

We returned to the Ephesus Princess at 11:00 p.m. ready for a good night's sleep. It had been a full day of touring and travel and we were tired.

As we headed up the path, we heard disco music coming from the pool area below us. Even with our doors and windows shut we still heard the loud music. Adding insult to injury, it was freezing in our room. Wayne followed the directions on the thermostat but no heat came from the register. He called the front desk to ask about the heat and request an end to the noise from the pool. He was told that the heat was only on in winter months and the music would continue until 2:00 a.m. At 1:15 a.m. I called again and let fly with an earful to the person at the front desk. It made no significant difference.

The next morning, I suggested to Wayne that we either change rooms or move to the Izmir Hilton. Wayne called Arda and he agreed to the move. Although we were packed and ready to go, Arda asked for some extra time to make a couple of phone calls and pack his bag. He appeared almost an hour later. We wandered around the hotel grounds while we waited until Wayne was somewhat mollified after strolling past a gorgeous young blond sunbathing topless along the pool.

By the time we reached the ancient city of Ephesus, a highlight of our visit to Turkey, tour buses had arrived en masse. Since the Ephesus site is vast, we were able to reach each point of interest without too may delays. We spent several hours taking in each magnificent aspect of this once-grand city, built in the 10th century BC by the Greeks and still flourishing when it came under Roman control in 129 BC. The Goths destroyed Ephesus in 262 AD. Some restoration took place, but it never regained its splendor. Earthquakes during the 6th and 7th centuries AD left Ephesus in shambles.

We found the scattered fragments littering the ground as interesting as the reconstructed buildings. Of particular interest were the Celsus Library façade, the multi-seat public toilet flushed by running water, the baths, and the massive amphitheater. The pillar-lined streets of marble must have been grand in their time. Arda was touched by our love of Ephesus and took us for a side tour of the ruins of a massive Christian Church dedicated to Mary, the mother of Jesus.

Since it was now the famous lunch hour, we stopped at another tourist spot simply named the Special Restaurant. We had one of many versions of what Arda called imam bayildi, an eggplant, tomato, and onion dish reminiscent of ratatouille. Literally translated, the dish means *the imam fainted*. According to legend, a Muslim religious leader ate so much of this delicious concoction that he fell to the floor in a heap.

After lunch we visited the Ephesus Museum. This small but mighty museum included the original multi-breasted statue of Artemis that I knew so well from photographs. We then drove to St. John's Hill for an overview of the ruins of the Temple of Artemis. Of the fragments outlining this once-massive structure, only one reconstructed pillar stood today. It was burned by a madman in the year 356 BC, the same year that Alexander the Great was born.

Atop St. John's Hill we noticed the substantial ruins of the Church of St. John the Baptist. St. John himself was actually buried near the main altar, the exact spot signified by a marker. A Seljuk citadel built in the 13th century AD now dominates the highest point on St. John's Hill.

Our last stop for the day was a visit to the area where Mary supposedly lived after Jesus was crucified in Jerusalem. Not far from the ruins of Ephesus, we reached the location after a five-minute drive up a steep hill high above the ancient city. A small chapel was all that remained.

We headed for Izmir, a city of 2.5 million, late in the afternoon. Ibrahim rejoiced that he could now stay in his own home for the next two days rather than a hotel in Kusadasi. An hour later we checked into our room with a commanding view of the Izmir harbor.

After a couple hours' rest, we met Arda in the lobby for a short walk to Deniz, a seafood restaurant that had been recommended by a stateside friend of ours. Arda knew it well and agreed that it was an excellent choice. We were even more delighted when we discovered it had a non-smoking dining room. True to our friend's word, the food was outstanding. We all finished with a baked quince dessert served with a slab of soft, creamy cheese. Arda told us that quince has a very short growing season and we felt fortunate to sample this highly touted delicacy.

We had a good night's sleep in our new quiet hotel and joined Ibrahim for our early morning drive to one of Arda's favorites, the ruins of Aphrodisias. Traffic was a nightmare and it took half an hour to make our way to the countryside, all the while dodging astounding numbers of pedestrians darting through the streets. Arda confirmed that many accidents did occur.

Having left the city and its congestion, we soon encountered donkey carts, tractors and the usual excess of overloaded lorries. Today's lorries were often stacked with bags of raw cotton just picked from the surrounding fields. Laborers came here every fall to harvest the cotton by hand. Families made the annual trek together and we actually saw a few men working side by side in the fields with the women. We would pass hundreds of miles of cotton fields over the next two days.

Just past Ephesus we turned eastward for our long journey to Aphrodisias. We were struck by the beauty of the countryside as we passed fields of cotton, figs, olives, peaches, and plums. In the distance a range of hills reaching into rugged peaks flanked the farmland. The Meander River flowing two hundred miles from Pamukkale to the Aegean irrigated the fertile valley.

With today's lengthy drive, occasional WC stops were in order. Arda usually selected Shell stations because they had a reputation for being the cleanest. I still found that BYOTP was a necessity throughout the interior of Turkey. It was scarce to nonexistent at most pit stops.

It took nearly three hours to reach Aphrodisias. As Arda had promised, it was well worth the drive. We could have gone to Pergamon but we took Arda's advice based on his fondness for this site. He was particularly impressed by the method of excavation used at Aphrodisias. Unlike earlier European teams that pillaged the ruins they'd uncovered, this site remained intact. Only a few objects and some statuary had been moved to a museum on the premises.

To our delight we had the site almost to ourselves, a phenomenal experience after yesterday's crowds at Ephesus. Like most of these ancient sites, Aphrodisias was finally toppled by a massive earthquake and we marveled at the thousands of fragments covering the landscape. As we wandered through vast areas of broken pillars and façades, we spent quite a bit of time photographing interesting details.

Passing through the ruins of Aphrodisias was a spiritual experience. We tried to picture life as it must have been when the city stood in its splendor. Hadrian had added his touch with a massive bath named in his own honor. As in Ephesus, there was an Odeon for music and plays. We were struck by the size and grandeur of the vast stadium at the edge of the complex. Its elliptical shape had benches that could seat thousands of spectators. The three of us tried to envision a chariot race in progress while we sat by ourselves in the vast amphitheater.

As we drove on to our restaurant du jour, Arda told us that tobacco grew in this area. Since the plants had been harvested, we only saw plowed fields ready for next season's crop. The Marlboro Man had a large presence in Turkey.

After one more unmemorable and too-long lunch we headed further east to Pamukkale, a unique geological area where calcium dioxide deposits spewing from hot springs had covered a two-mile stretch of the hillside with a chalk-like glaze. In English, its name translates to Cotton Castle. Tucked into it are pools of warm spring water and visitors can wade or soak in any number of hot springs. In one area the ruins of an ancient Roman bath lay in shards at the bottom of a pool and people swam over them as they enjoyed a warm mineral bath.

Although Pamukkale was not in our original plan, Arda recommended the detour as it was fairly close to Aphrodisias. It took us at least another hour to reach the area after brief stops to look at the necropolis of Hierapolis, the ancient Hellenistic cemetery with a variety of burial chambers. Since the sun was beginning to set, we urged Arda to move on to Pamukkale so we could see it with a bit of remaining daylight. Once again, we wished that our rather ordinary but extremely lengthy lunch could have been shortened and we had had more time to enjoy this unique natural wonder. We scurried around throngs of tourists pouring out of rows of buses and then took off our shoes for a quick wade across the surface of the smooth calcified white rock. After shooting a few photos in the late afternoon sun, we departed for a return to Izmir.

Ibrahim drove like a madman through Denizli, a fairly large city in the Meander Valley. I closed my eyes so I would not have to witness his well-timed but often-frightening maneuvers. He sped along country roads and we arrived in Izmir in just under three hours, a miracle considering the number of trucks on this two-lane roadway.

Although we had made reservations in the Hilton's scenic top-floor restaurant, we asked Arda to cancel them. By the time we reached the hotel we were too tired to even consider a late-night dinner. We said goodnight to Arda and Ibrahim and ordered sandwiches and a salad from room service. To tell the truth, a little light eating was just the ticket.

The next morning, we met Ibrahim for our drive to Bodrum. Arda told us that we would beat the rush hour traffic by leaving early, but you could have fooled us. It was crazy! Once outside the city we headed south toward the seacoast resort town of Bodrum where we would board a sailboat, a sixty-five-foot Turkish gullet, later in the day.

As I mentioned earlier, this cruise was always intended to be a private adventure for Wayne and me. Even though Arda had accompanied us throughout Turkey, it never occurred to us that he planned to join us on the boat. When I casually asked Arda if he would be flying back to Istanbul while we sailed, he said that his marching orders were to accompany us through the entire trip, including our cruise.

Most awkward of all was having to explain to Arda that we envisioned the cruise as our own private time. We had not planned to share the staterooms with Arda nor were we ready to share breakfast, lunch and dinner with him for the next three days. At age 51, I was not the picture of beauty in my two-piece bathing suit and I wanted some privacy. We thought we had made it abundantly clear to our travel company that this cruise was just for the two of us. I still cringe when I think about uninviting Arda on our voyage.

As we drove toward Bodrum we put the awkward situation on the back burner and enjoyed the spectacular scenery. We began our drive along the road leading to Ephesus and soon headed south through the Soke Valley for another hundred miles. Ibraham once again flew his Toyota over the bumpy roads. We came to a standstill outside of a raw-cotton-processing factory while dozens of lorries loaded with sacks jockeyed into position to deliver their goods. Wayne had time to hop out of the car for photos.

We passed Priene, another Roman site in ruins. Shortly afterward we passed through the village of Didim with more ancient remains. Those Roman Guys, as Wayne referred to them, were certainly busy along this route. Next we came to Lake Bafa, a stunningly beautiful natural lake surrounded by rugged peaks on the eastern side and sloping hills covered with wild olive trees on the western side. It was surprising to see this vast lake in its natural state with no signs, shops or vacation homes built around it. Arda told us the lake belonged to a private owner until the 1950s and, under government auspices, now was designated as park land.

A bit further on we entered the Turkish province of Muğla, home of the seacoast villages of Bodrum, Marmara and Fethiye. We passed a hilly area scarred by a recent fire and I asked Arda how it had started. He said that many of the forest fires in Turkey were the work of fundamentalist arsonists. They hurt themselves with these acts as much as anyone else.

Truck traffic diminished and we made good time reaching the large town of Milas, just thirty miles from Bodrum, by mid-morning. Arda told us that two more ancient sites are located here. Turkey was indeed an archaeologist's treasure trove.

Shortly afterward we reached the edge of the Bay of Bodrum. Although it appeared to be undeveloped, occasional pockets of condo complexes appeared along the hills overlooking the water. Since all sported white paint, we assumed the province mandated that color.

Soon we arrived at the bustling resort town of Bodrum. We made our way to the southern edge of the village and followed a road along the coast to the MTM Hotel where we were to meet our ship's coordinator to discuss provisioning the yacht for our onboard dining before taking a midday tour of the Museum of Underwater Archaeology housed in a dramatic castle on a promontory above the harbor.

The woman who met us at the hotel told us that she had already stocked the boat because she had not been able to reach us. We were not exactly sure why. I asked her to add yogurt and fresh fruit. Since it was a perfect day to sail, our coordinator suggested we save the museum for later. She was expecting Arda to join us and we had to undergo several more awkward minutes explaining the misunderstanding.

Wayne then asked where we would sail. The woman was vague, explaining that there wasn't much time in three days to go far from port. Wayne was upset and replied, "Now wait a minute. That is not what we were told by our travel company." He made it clear that we expected to sail all day and drop anchor in tranquil ports. She did a quick turn-around and assured us that this would be the case. Wrong.

Over a period of several weeks, Wayne had requested information from our travel company about where we would sail. He was told that the boat was at our disposal and the captain and crew of two would take us wherever we wanted to go. Of course they would speak English. We had been *assured* they spoke English. This could not have been further from the truth. In reality, the ship was a floating hotel and the crew had no intention of going more than a few miles from Bodrum.

We were impressed by the stunning gulet, *Sheikha*, moored to the hotel's dock. It seemed much larger than its sixty-five feet. We were whisked aboard and the yacht motored away from the dock. Waving to Arda we began what we hoped would be a highlight of our adventure in Turkey.

We selected our stateroom and then returned to the deck as we motored out of Bodrum's harbor. After anchoring in a cove on a small island, the captain and his crew served us a delicious lunch with stuffed grape leaves, a fresh tomato and cucumber salad and more. We had anticipated simple food on this cruise and if our lunch was any indication of things to come, we would be well fed.

After lunch we sat on the deck for a bit of Aegean sunshine. We sat. And we sat. Now realizing that none of the crew spoke a word of English, Wayne conversed with the captain using hand motions indicating that we sail out of our luncheon cove. The crew raised the jib and we rejoiced. As it turned out, this was one of two very short times the captain would employ the sails on our cruise.

In less than forty-five minutes we entered another inland cove and dropped anchor next to an empty fishing boat and two other gulets loaded to the hilt with partying German tourists out for a good time. They blared music and shouted back and forth, disrupting what we had hoped would be a tranquil bay. We rejoiced when the gulets sailed away. Today's mostly motor sailing had taken us only a few miles from Bodrum and we were indeed disappointed.

Tranquility was a fleeting luxury during our non-cruise. Shortly after the boats left with their noisy crowds several fishing boats anchored not fifty feet from us. We listened to blaring Turkish music along with a constant stream of conversation and joking well into the night.

There were some positive, memorable moments. I had noticed the crew looking over the side of the boat and when I joined them the sea was covered with pencil-thin foot long needle fish. Because they were a transparent blue, it would have been easy to miss them as they skimmed the surface.

We stayed on deck and were treated to the most spectacular moonrise we had ever witnessed. It ascended over the eastern hills surrounding our small cove looking like a giant red-orange disc and seemed to be lifted into the night sky by some invisible force. It was magnificent. We then enjoyed lying on our backs and gazing at the multitude of stars in the night sky.

By 10:00 a.m. the next day we were still nestled in our overnight bay. The fishermen had quietly disappeared before we awoke but our captain and crew made no moves to set sail. With his trusty map of the Bodrum coastline in hand, Wayne pointed to areas along the coast that we hoped to see. He also drew a sail with his hands in the air in hopes that we might finally get underway. The crew reluctantly pulled up the anchor and once again we motored forward.

After half an hour our captain pulled into another bay and his crew prepared to drop anchor. We rejoiced at not seeing another gulet but our joy soon turned to terror. As we came to a stop, swarms of bees descended. Wayne had mentioned to the coordinator at the hotel that he was deathly allergic to bees and she seemed alarmed. She handed us a gadget that extracted the stingers and venom from a bee sting and told us that bees were a big problem this time of year. We should have been advised well in advance. Knowing Wayne's medical history and his near-death experience years earlier from a sting, we probably would have foregone the gulet trip.

I was terrified when the swarm of bees surrounded the boat and did my best imitation of a sting and then dying. Signaling that we had to leave, the captain started the engine and took us right back to the cove we had left earlier in the day. We had lunch, jumped into the water for a swim and then Wayne did his now-famous pantomime of *Let's Get the Show on the Road*.

Reluctantly, our captain headed out of the bay. Unbelievably, he turned in the direction of Bodrum, not far from our current position. Wayne got out his map and pointed in the opposite direction. The captain made buzzing noises, indicating that any other port would be filled with bees. We found that hard to believe, but we were at our captain's mercy.

Back in our cove for a second night we found ourselves in the midst of nine other gulets filled with more partying Germans on holiday. We were amazed by how many bodies could be packed onto one sixty-five-foot boat. Radios were blaring. Children were screaming. Adults were drinking, singing and shouting. The tour boats didn't leave until 6:00 p.m. and the commotion was so bad that Wayne and I sat in our suite with the doors and windows closed.

By now we had figured out that we were captives on a floating hotel that never intended to set sail on the Aegean. We had paid a premium for what we had hoped would be a simple gulet that would set sail and take us along the coast for miles. Our luxurious gulet with its equally luxurious staterooms was not designed for the open seas. Its purpose was to motor to a safe nearby cove and drop anchor. That night we shared our port with three other boats that pulled in beside us. Fortunately, the passengers were relatively quiet and we slept well.

Remaining anchored in the harbor seemed to be *de rigueur* and there we lingered into the next morning. Wayne gave the high sign to get underway and we no longer even expected to see the sails. Motoring for fifteen or twenty minutes, the captain turned into the next bay. Hundreds of condos dotted the hillside above us, some still under construction. We were greeted by the not-so-friendly sound of a jackhammer. Wayne had had enough by now and shook his head when the anchor was about to be lowered. Reluctantly, the captain motored to the next cove and dropped anchor near a small farm.

We decided we could live with the crowing of a few roosters. With no one in this cove we actually enjoyed a couple hours of tranquility, but by late morning the day sailboats overloaded with passengers began to appear. The one right next to us was filled with children who dove from their boat with accompanying shouts and squeals. After too much of this, Wayne signaled a move and we ventured all the way to the other side of the otherwise charming cove. Later in the day we returned to Bodrum, not soon enough for us.

As we headed to port to meet Arda for our museum tour, the crew actually raised the jib for the second time. Yesterday the sail never went up. Today, with very little wind, we soon heard the now-familiar hum of the motor. We soon docked in a slip at the Bodrum Yacht Basin. End of cruise. Not that we really ever had one to begin with...

We had planned to meet Arda for our tour of the Bodrum Underwater Maritime Museum but he was nowhere in sight. We knew that the museum closed its doors at 4:00 p.m. and it was already after 3:00 so time was of the essence. As it turned out, Arda had been given the wrong docking directions and, after searching for us, he went to the museum in hopes that we would do the same. We finally took a taxi to the museum and there stood Arda. We slipped into the museum just before closing time but one of the two exhibit rooms had already locked its doors for the day.

We invited Arda to select a restaurant of his choice and be our guest for dinner. Still feeling uncomfortable about dumping him in Bodrum and knowing his propensity for food, we figured this would be a good peace offering. He picked a winner, a family-run restaurant called Kocadon, pronounced Koja-don, meaning *baggy bloomers*. Although the most expensive meal we had in all of Turkey, it was a delightful experience.

We dined on the patio which looked like something out of *Architectural Digest*, bordered on either side by vine-covered walls. Pots filled with palms and flowers were scattered about and lit with soft outdoor lighting. At the end of our meal we were delighted to find another sampling of baked quince.

Before returning to the yacht basin for our final night on the gulet, nestled in its Bodrum berth, we said goodnight to Arda and then packed our bags for our return trip to Istanbul the next day.

When I looked out my porthole the next morning, the face of a sleeping man was pointed in my direction not four feet away from the gulet. This gave new meaning to up close and personal. I rigged a towel over the porthole so I could dress with some semblance of privacy.

Reminiscing about our non-sailing experience on the Aegean, we noted that we never traveled more than a few miles. The ship was beautiful and the two main staterooms were exquisitely decorated. One even had a bathtub. The captain and his crew were gracious and our meals on board were very good. For someone wanting a floating vacation, it was perfect. Not so for the two of us who specifically asked for a sailing experience. As beautiful as the *Sheikha* was, we were terribly disappointed. This was not the trip we had anticipated.

After an uneventful flight to Istanbul we were delighted to see Halil, our first driver, at the exit gate. He drove us to the Ciragan Palace where we checked into room 547, which we had requested when we checked out the previous week. We had done a reconnaissance run through the hotel to determine which room had the best view of the old city and we picked a winner. From our balcony we could see Topkapi Palace and St. Sophia's as well as the bustling ship traffic along the water.

It was another beautiful day and, on Arda's advice, we took a taxi to the Akmerkez, Istanbul's newest shopping mall. It turned out to be just that—a shopping mall. We were surprised to find a security check at the entrance which everyone had to pass through before entering. Not finding anything but Western style clothing shops, we did a quick walk-through and hailed a taxi for a ride home.

We hadn't said much to Arda about how upset we were over our non-sail but he got the picture. Just as we entered our room the phone rang and it was the owner of the travel agency contracted by the high-end travel company we had paid dearly to plan our trip. She asked us if she could come to the hotel to talk with us and Wayne agreed. When she arrived she was defensive. She claimed that the ship was not rigged for sailing and was meant to be a floating hotel. We had taken photos of the ship's rigging and knew this wasn't true. She finally conceded that the ship did not go far enough but made no apologies. Wayne opted to end the conversation and take it up with our stateside travel agent when we returned.

Putting that behind us, we had breakfast with more fabulous yogurt, then met Arda and Halil for our final day's tour. Our first destination was the mosque of Suleyman the Magnificent designed by the architect Sinan and completed in 1557 AD after eight years of construction. As its name suggests, it is truly magnificent. We then visited the Blue Mosque built between 1609 and 1616 AD by Sultan Ahmed I. It is the only known mosque with six minarets and, in contrast to the simplicity of Suleyman's, the interior is bejeweled with 21,600 painted blue tiles.

As we traveled from the first to the second mosque, we became mired in traffic that barely moved. Escaping the busy thoroughfare, we entered an area bustling with Eastern European shoppers. We watched a group of them attempting to stuff huge bundles of goods into the already filled storage area of a bus. This frenzy went on for several more blocks. The shoppers planned to re-sell their wares in their home countries.

Our next stop, a highlight, was Justinian's Basilica Cistern located not far from St. Sophia's. We vaguely remembered that there was an ancient underground cistern in Istanbul but we hadn't given much thought to it. We were most grateful that Arda brought us to it on our final day. Entering through a rather obscure building we descended into what could have been the set for *Phantom of the Opera*. Built in 532 AD, more than one hundred pillars supported the arched ceilings of this cavernous water storage area. Classical oud music piped in, creating a theatrical atmosphere. The cistern covered an area larger than a football field and not to be missed was the face of Medusa at the far end.

After a quick peek at Istanbul's spice bazaar we entered a restaurant located just inside its entrance. An obscure staircase led to the second floor family-owned Pandeli Restaurant. We decided to go with the flow and take as long as Arda wanted for our final lunch in Turkey, enjoying a multi-course extravaganza selected by him. Our entrée was sea bass with tomatoes steamed in paper, a real winner.

As we headed for Chora, a small 5th-century-AD Byzantine church with mosaics that had been restored in recent years, Wayne and Arda did their after-lunch nod-off-to-sleep routine. Both of them could cat nap and come back to life as soon as I asked them a question. Big lunches did these guys in almost every day.

The area surrounding the church proved to be another highlight. We were impressed by rows of wooden houses that had been lovingly restored.

Some were shops; others had been converted into small hotels. Most impressive, however, was the Chora. The original structure had fallen in a 9th-century-AD earthquake and was rebuilt by the Byzantines in 1324 AD. Its pale paintings and mosaics were some of the best in the world. Like those in St. Sophia, most were plastered and painted over by the Ottoman Turks, thus preserving them. Beautifully executed by the Byzantine artists, they had been restored and the scenes were awe-inspiring.

We said goodbye to Arda and Halil when we returned to the Ciragan. Arda was scheduled to begin a new tour that evening and Halil's new driving assignment took him to Izmir. We will miss Arda. He became a good friend during our two weeks in Turkey and we appreciated his kindness, his openness about the good and the not-so-good in his country and particularly his extensive knowledge of his country's history and culture. Although we had some low points with Arda over long lunches and shopping stops, we never could have connected with Turkey without him.

SOUTH AMERICA

Buenos Aires, Iguazu Falls, Rio de Janeiro, Santiago, Lima, Cusco,
and Machu Picchu

February 15–28, 1997

SOMETIMES YOU MEET the most exceptional people on group tours and Ruth was one of those souls. While on a trip to Egypt sponsored by the University of Michigan, she won our hearts with her wit and wisdom. When I read about a tour of South America offered by the same university, I contacted Ruth in Bloomfield Hills, Michigan, and she agreed to accompany me. Wayne, still working at the time, was content to stay at home since he had traveled through South America on business, but it would be a first for both Ruth and me.

On the designated departure day, I flew to Miami International Airport where I planned to connect with thirty-six fellow travelers for our thirteen-day tour. Just by chance I arrived at the check-in line at the same time as Ruth. Two years ago, we traveled to Switzerland and southern France so this would be our third shared adventure. All went smoothly and we picked up our boarding cards from Doug and Peggy, our travel representatives. Once at the gate we met a few of our fellow travelers.

Our scheduled 8:45 p.m. departure for Buenos Aires was delayed for three hours. With a full plane I rejoiced at having an aisle seat. We arrived after an eight-hour flight and Victoria, our local guide, whisked us through customs and baggage claim. Our group boarded a waiting bus and Victoria filled us in on some interesting history and statistics en route to our lodging. She told us that in a country of 33 million people, 13 million resided in Buenos Aires.

Soon we arrived at the InterContinental Hotel in the heart of the business district. To our delight the hotel was new and attractive and had a friendly staff. However, some travelers in our group were greeted with an unpleasant surprise when they opened their suitcases. A downpour had hit Miami just as our luggage was being loaded onto the plane and some of the bags were direct targets. Mine escaped damage but Ruth unpacked soggy, wrinkled clothing, some so badly stained from the lining in her suitcase that they were ruined. What could be salvaged she ended up sending out to be cleaned and pressed.

After lunch in the hotel's bar, with very slow service but good food, Ruth checked out the hotel's H. Stern shop. As we would discover, almost every hotel during our visit had an H. Stern and each offered a small silver charm depicting a significant aspect of its location. The Buenos Aires shop gifted us a small silver lasso typical of those used by Argentine gauchos.

Early that afternoon we boarded a bus with Victoria for a city tour. As we passed the main square, she explained that Buenos Aires, founded in 1580, means *Good Wings*. She then pointed out the Pink House, or president's office, with its famed balcony where Evita and, more recently Madonna, who played her in a film role, stood to wave to the crowds in the square.

Since ninety percent of Argentines were Catholic, churches and cathedrals abounded. We passed a number of them along our route, the Avenida de Mayo. The once-lovely boulevard looked weary but one could still detect its original elegance as we drove along it toward the oldest part of the city. Known as San Telmo, its oldest *barrio*, or neighborhood, was first settled by the Spaniards and was now an area with a bohemian vibe. Victoria mentioned that Argentina's war for independence from Spain began in 1810 and ended successfully in 1818, and the city was now a mixture of nationalities with approximately forty percent Spanish and forty percent Italian. After World War II many Germans came to Argentina, ironically both Nazis and Jews. The president at the time of our visit, Carlos Menon, was of Syrian descent.

We stopped for half an hour at a Sunday flea market. Compared to the one I had scoured two weeks before in Pasadena it was quite small yet we enjoyed seeing what each merchant had to offer. Ruth and I chuckled over a small plaque for a WC that read, *Pipi Room*.

After passing a massive soccer stadium, we paused for a stroll along a small street lined with two-story frame houses, all painted in bright primary colors. The mix of canary yellow, bright blue, kelly green, and red buildings offered the camera bugs in our group a golden opportunity for spectacular photos. Victoria explained that the entire area used to have brightly colored buildings and this small section showcased the few remnants of this festive tradition.

Our next destination, the waterfront, took us along the vast port first developed in 1884. By the 1940s it had become obsolete. Miles of old brick warehouses had stood vacant for decades until some entrepreneurs turned them into apartments, businesses and restaurants. It was once again thriving.

Continuing on, Victoria pointed out a beautiful customs building, a steak house called Las Nazarenas, the English Tower, the Fine Arts Museum, and an area called Palermo Chico which was filled with elegant turn-of-the-century mansions. A small replica of national hero San Martin's Paris home stood prominently on one corner. We skirted the 400-acre Palermo Park with its striking bronze and Carrara marble monument that celebrates Brazil's independence, a gift from Spain. A zoo and the American Embassy were also on our route as were a few ombu, the only tree native to the *Pampas*, or plains.

Our final stop, the Recoleta Cemetery, served as the final resting place for many wealthy and famous Buenos Aires residents. Row after row of elaborate above-ground crypts stretched as far as the eye could see. As we wandered through the ornate burial vaults it was easy to become disoriented. Victoria scurried us along to the crypt that housed the family Duarte where Evita was now interred after having been buried for decades in Italy. She was so beautifully embalmed that her face and hair were still intact when her grave was opened for the journey back to Argentina. She had died in 1952 and was returned to her beloved country in 1976. It should be noted that Argentines either loved Evita passionately or absolutely despised her. She remained a saint or a sinner depending on one's point of view.

We returned to our hotel late in the afternoon with a leisurely hour and a half to primp for a welcoming cocktail party. Little did Ruth and I know that our party plans were about to become history. While I was in the lobby with the concierge designing an on-our-own tour for the next day, Ruth went to our room and discovered that our key no longer opened the door. Several bellboys attempted to resolve the problem to no avail. We waited in the hall for almost an hour while a string of employees tried unsuccessfully to open it. The lock finally worked at which point Ruth and I decided that we would move to another room. We had no desire to go through this charade again any time soon.

It was at this point that Ruth decided to give up trying to dry her clothing on hangers and called housekeeping for some assistance. I concluded that after two days of travel sans sufficient sleep, the lure of a bubble bath was irresistible. Alas, the tub's stopper was missing. I improvised with a piece of cardboard from the soap's box and weighted it with an ash tray. After a quick relaxing soak, we dressed and scurried to the U of M party, now almost a *fête accompli*.

Taking Victoria's advice, we hailed a taxi for a short ride to Las Nazarenas, the steak house she had recommended. Although it catered to the tourist trade, the ambience was appealing and we sampled our first taste of lean, tender Pampas beef. Near the entrance were pigs, goats and lord only knew what else skewered and slowly roasting over hot coals. This was not a place for a vegetarian. Our waiter was friendly and, with my thirty-something-years-ago Spanish, we managed to communicate. Well fed, we returned to our hotel and discovered that the keys to our new room worked like a charm.

The next day the majority of our group boarded a bus for a daylong tour of the delta area and lunch on an island. Ruth and I opted to spend a full day enjoying Buenos Aires. We arrived for our leisurely breakfast just as the tour departed.

Mid-February in Buenos Aires is comparable to mid-August in the States and so our days were hot and humid. We guessed that the temperature ranged in the mid-eighties during the day and dropped to the low seventies at night. Flowering jacarandas and other colorful trees lined the parkway along the taxi route to our 11:00 a.m. tour of Teatro Colón, Buenos Aires' spectacular opera house.

Teatro Colón ranks near the top of the world's best opera houses with its world-class performances and near-perfect acoustics. Our guide encouraged us to sing a few notes to test them. We sat overlooking the stage for several minutes taking in its grandeur. Its elaborate closed curtain was made in England from embroidered velvet and weighed six thousand pounds.

Interesting displays abounded in the hallways. There were at least a dozen miniature sets from famous performances encased in glass as well as mannequins dressed in actual costumes worn by world-renowned opera singers. Because of the reversal of seasons in Buenos Aires, many famous singers were able to perform here when they were not singing in the U.S. or Europe. Toscanini conducted, Maria Callas sang in *Turandot* and Enrico Caruso performed in *Rigoletto.* It must have been grand. Our tour concluded with a look at the Golden Hall, a reception area with plastered walls covered in 24-karat gold, and the Gallery of Mirrors copied from Versailles.

We exited at noon and I attempted to take a photo of the opera house, only to discover that the battery in my brand-new camera had expired. I soon learned, much to my dismay, that my state-of-the-art Pentax and its accompanying batteries had not yet reached South America in great numbers. Ruth and I visited several camera shops along the Avenida Nuevo de Julio as we crossed this expansive boulevard time and again in search of the elusive battery. With no luck, I began to query passers-by in my rusty Spanish and we soon found ourselves in an underground bazaar beneath the bustling street. Still no luck. Another man led us to a side street filled with shops and after several more stops and many blocks of walking I actually found the right battery. I bought two just to be on the safe side.

Ruth was a good sport and agreed to return to the Recoleta for a more leisurely stroll through this famous cemetery. It is a magnet for the people of Buenos Aires and its surrounding parks are usually filled with people. The Monday afternoon crowds were minimal, offering a perfect opportunity for a more detailed tour. We enjoyed ourselves even more the second time around although, as Ruth pointed out, "We don't want to get too comfortable here." I led the way right to Evita's crypt and took a few more photos without Sunday's mob surrounding it.

While there we met a delightful journalist from Equador. She was fascinated by my Pentax and offered to take a photo of Ruth and me. We then wandered through row after row of crypts for another half hour before hailing a taxi for a shopping fix at Plaza San Marco.

After checking out two jewelry shops, we stopped for a late lunch at the Plaza Hotel. This once-elegant but now rather timeworn hotel had maintained its air of gentility and we enjoyed a delightful lunch in one of the dining rooms before hitting the streets in quest of the ultimate Inca Rose, rhodochrosite, a rose-red semiprecious stone mined in Argentina. Ruth adores jewelry but finding none that appealed to her, we returned to the InterContinental late in the afternoon to prepare for another Argentine beef extravaganza.

On the recommendation from a South American business contact of my husband's we had booked a reservation at Cabaña Las Lilas. This lively spot, located in one of the rehabilitated warehouses along the harbor, offered great food. *When in Argentina, eat beef,* seemed to be the rule and we went for it. My Spanish failed me slightly and we ordered skewered chunks of beef rather than a filet. Nevertheless, our choice could not have been more delicious. After dinner we walked along the waterfront and then hailed a taxi for a return trip to our hotel.

The next morning began with the first of several lectures presented by Santiago, a young U of M Professor of Romance Languages with a specialty in South American Literature. Over the next two weeks he would intertwine South America's history with its literary heritage. He began by suggesting that the wide mix of racial and ethnic groups and the great disparity between wealth and poverty impacted the legacy of South America's history.

Today's lecture focused on the continent's unifying threads:

1959-1997: The Cuban Revolution
1929-1957: ISI/Populism

1870-1929: Modernization
1826-1870: Colonial Period
Before 1500: Pre-Columbian Period

Santiago talked about the massive movement toward privatization in Buenos Aires and the resulting loss of jobs. He mentioned that in the mid-seventies the Ford Falcon was known as the Death Squad car. The agents of death during the Dirty War usually drove Ford Falcons and thirty thousand residents suspected of being political dissidents and anyone believed to be associated with socialism, left-wing Peronism or the Montoneros guerilla movement were either killed or went missing.

A 1973 revolution in Chile led to a military dictatorship. It succeeded because people wanted to stop subversion and desperately sought economic stability. However, it took enormous state budgets to fund the military and, in the end, the movement failed. History repeats itself: dictatorships never succeed.

Focusing on the period from 1929-1959, Santiago talked about ISI, Import Substitution Industrialization. During this period Argentina attempted to move from an agrarian to an industry-based economy. A populist form of government typified by Juan Peron swept the country. Nationalized railroads purchased from England were installed. Massive amounts of gold were stockpiled. Argentina, an import-export nation before World War II, became isolationist. Middle-and lower-class fear and rage typified this period and eventually Peron's military dictatorship was replaced with a democratic government.

A focus on Modernization characterized the period from 1870-1929. Absentee landowners had huge incomes based on shipments of beef and leather. Lawyers, importers, exporters, and city shop owners abounded. Buenos Aires' residential areas boomed. Many poor and often radical Italians immigrated to Argentina. Gauchos were required to carry ID cards categorizing them as either ranch hands or soldiers. A massive expulsion of natives resulted in the development of huge estancias, or cattle ranches.

After the lecture we checked out of the hotel and boarded a bus to the airport for our two- hour flight to Iguazu Falls. As we flew to the north, we passed over the delta area of the Parana River with its multitude of tributaries fanning out over verdant farmland. Approaching our destination, Ruth and I had a spectacular view of the falls and the surrounding forest. It far exceeded my expectations. I had considered the stopover at Iguazu a frivolous break in our series of city visits. It now appeared from my perch high above the falls that we were in for a very pleasant surprise.

Once on the ground we boarded another bus for a short ride to the Argentine side of the falls. We learned that the word iguazu translated to *y*, meaning water, and *ûasú*, meaning high. It certainly made sense to me as we began our quarter-mile hike along the upper edge to the spectacular Devil's Throat. The combination of tropical rain forest, breathtaking vistas, misty spray, and the roar of the falls created an almost spiritual experience.

On the bus ride to the border crossing into Brazil, we learned that the falls were the sole possession of Paraguay until 150 years prior when both Brazil and Argentina fought for and acquired this natural wonder. At this point, eighty percent belonged to Argentina and the remainder to Brazil. The view was best from the Brazilian side as it looked back onto the lion's share of the falls.

Our new guide explained the origins of some of the names. Paraguay, with a population of one hundred fifty thousand, meant *river of the parrot*. Parana, the river we followed on our flight and upon which the falls are located, meant *brother of the ocean* and originated under the city of Parana some seven hundred miles from the falls. Argentina comes from argentum, meaning *silver*, while Brazil means *red wood*.

A few more Iguazu Falls factoids: the falls were discovered in 1541 by the Spanish explorer Alvar Nunez Cabeza de Vaca. In a stretch of nearly two miles there were 175 separate falls. The canyon they formed was 1.8 miles deep. Iguazu was created 125 million years ago by a volcanic explosion. Originally there were only eight falls, but now numbered nearly three hundred. Jaguars, pumas, tapirs, iguanas, and many other species inhabited the surrounding forest which showcased more than two thousand varieties of trees. Iguazu was one of the three greatest falls in the world and the longest. Victoria Falls in Africa was the tallest, reaching 110 meters. Iguazu reached 80 meters while Niagra Falls measured a mere 51 meters. The surrounding tree-filled areas were actually sub-tropical rain forests.

We were ushered off the bus at the border crossing at 6:00 p.m. Ruth had a bit of a scare when the border agent looked at her paperwork and rejected it. One of the travel reps came to the rescue and fixed whatever had been the problem. Ruth rejoined our queue and we were soon on our way to our hotel in Brazil.

Our guide cautioned us not to wander at night because of the wild animals. He promised us that in daylight we would be treated to some friendlier creatures including the coatimundi, which resembled a thin raccoon with a long snout and tail.

A sprawling hotel complex we had viewed from the Argentine side of the falls turned out to be our home for the evening. Built in 1939, the Hotel das

Cataratas proved to be as gracious as it was confusing. We followed a maze of hallways and navigated a series of stairways up and down to reach our room. With my dyslexia I became hopelessly turned around on my first attempt to find our room on my own. I could have used a large ball of string to retrace my route.

Our room was sparse but it worked for us. We soon discovered, however, that we were not alone. A very frightened chameleon scampered up the curtain and parked semi-permanently on the ceiling. While I felt he added a bit of local charm, Ruth decided that a call to the front desk was in order. Soon afterward a hotel employee with a rickety ladder played tag with the chameleon until he captured the frightened critter in a handkerchief. A myriad of flying and crawling insects continued to parade on our walls and I silently wished the chameleon had remained to feast on them.

The next day began with an 8:00 a.m. hike led by local guide Donello to the bottom of the falls. He offered an elevator ride to any in our group who could not make the trek but most of us opted to be ambulatory. We followed a series of switchback trails that were easy to traverse. Many photo ops later we reached the river's edge and viewed the falls from a new perspective as we looked up at them. Incredible! A few of us braved a walking bridge that stretched out into the river and were drenched by the time we reached the end of it by the tumultuous spray of the falls. It was an awesome experience.

After ascending to the upper level, I walked back to the hotel with Nancy and Jim, a couple from Midland, Michigan. Jim was an avid bird watcher and he talked about some of the species he had observed. As we walked along the road a young boy gestured across the street and pointed to a large tree. We soon spotted a toucan family perched just outside a nest in the trunk of the tree. What a treat it was to see these beautiful birds in their own habitat!

As we neared our hotel we spotted coatimundi, furry elongated animals with long tails comparable in size to a large domestic cat. Although wild, these fellows were used to tourists and came right up to many of us in search of handouts. Some young children offered food to the furry beggars and many of us grabbed our cameras to capture these whimsical creatures on film.

Six of our group then boarded a bus with our local guide for an optional US$35 river-raft cruise to the edge of the falls. After a Jeep ride through the forest we donned lifejackets and boarded our bouncing rubber pontoon for a wild ten-minute jaunt to the base of the falls in the Devil's Throat area. It was a thrilling experience and, after pausing for photos, we made our return trip. The ride was relatively smooth but the current was so strong that we all knew our life jackets were virtually useless. Surprisingly, I did not get nearly as wet as I had on the footbridge earlier that morning.

We returned to the hotel at 11:45 a.m. to pack and check out. I discovered that a fairly healthy drink tab had erroneously been added to my bill. I was asked to write a note of explanation for the hotel's bookkeeper, which I did, and the charges were removed from my bill. A little bizarre. Ruth and I then sat by the pool for an hour and did a quick change in the ladies' room before our flight to Rio. We sadly learned that several in our group were suffering from *la tourista*. Not a fun way to fly.

Just before we left the hotel, I heard that a video of our early morning hike to the border of the falls had been shown in the lobby and copies were sold for US$25. While Ruth and I were poolside, I missed the opportunity to see the video and purchase a copy. One woman in our group said I had a starring role at the base of the falls and offered to have a copy made for me. I promised her a copy of my trip notes in return.

The flight to Rio was diverted to São Paulo, adding two hours to our travel time. Our perfect record of no rain looked threatened as we watched brilliant flashes of lightening pierce dark clouds. The rain held off until later that night and never caused us to miss a beat.

It was easy to see why early settlers selected Rio de Janeiro as the ideal location to inhabit. As we approached, the city looked magnificent. From towering monolithic slopes to a myriad of bays, harbors and waterways, this was paradise. Once on the ground we drove along the Red Line Highway from the airport to the beach area in a crush of traffic that actually moved smoothly.

As we drove through the city our newest guide Fernando pointed out Sugarloaf Mountain and Corcovado and its massive statue of Christ with outstretched arms. He told us it had been made in the same factory in France that produced the Statue of Liberty. Fernando also explained that the modern art on the posters and banners scattered throughout the city were the proposed logo for the 2004 Summer Olympics that Rio would use if selected to host the games. Rio was one of the final five cities under consideration.

After a very long day Ruth and I checked into our hotel, the InterContinental at São Conrado Beach and said an early goodnight to our group. We had a corner room on an upper floor of the hotel but, as luck would have it, the two men in the adjacent room talked loudly well into the night. With very little sleep we did our best to rev up for the next day's tour of Rio, meeting Fernando and our group in the hotel lobby at 8:45 a.m.

On our way to Corcovado, we passed Rio's largest shantytown, home to forty-seven thousand,, but could see very little of it. Fernando mentioned fully sixty percent of its residents worked in resort hotels. Rumor had it that preying on tourists accounted for a sizeable amount of shantytown income.

Robbing tourists was a considerable problem in Rio and we were advised many times to carry nothing of value and lock all jewelry in our hotel safe. It was a sad paradox that we could not safely stroll through this magnificent city and the majority of our sightseeing would be confined to buses.

As we arrived, we saw for ourselves why the mountain was so named. Corcovado was a granite peak meaning *hunchback* in Portuguese. Located in central Rio, it stretched upward 710 meters—2,329 feet—and was the city's focal point. We boarded a tram that took us upward to the park's entrance. One of the best parts of being with our U of M fellow tourists was that we never had to think about tickets for planes, buses, trams, parks, or museums. In a flash we were magically ushered into the right place at the right time. And so it was today.

Rio's monument to Christ, created by Polish-French sculptor Paul Landowski, officially opened on October 12, 1931. Getúlio Vargas, the dictator of Brazil at the time, chose the work of the second-place winner, overriding the Madonna and Child prototype that had taken top honors. Today, Rio's Art Deco statue of Christ the Redeemer is considered one of the seven New Wonders of the World. Constructed of reinforced concrete, it is covered with bits of light green Brazilian sandstone in the manner of a mosaic. It stood ninety-eight feet high with a ninety-two-foot span between its outstretched hands and weighed seven hundred tons.

The view of Rio from atop Corcovado Mountain was as enticing as the close-up of its famous statue. It was another postcard-perfect day and the coastal views were particularly gorgeous. I hadn't expected so much of Rio to be this spectacular. Geographically, it is one of the most beautiful locations on earth. Not even the shantytowns hidden at street level by high walls deterred from the city's grandeur.

Fernando spoke of the children in Brazil. Before 1990, ten year olds were on the streets begging and selling dope. A strict law was passed requiring parents to keep their children in school. If children were truant, parents got one warning. The next time they were sent to jail. It seemed to be working and children were now seldom seen on the streets.

We toured a good part of the city before driving to the Barra district for a Brazilian barbecue buffet. Then we re-boarded the bus for a beach tour. We drove along the coast past our hotel and on to Leblon and Ipanema, comparable in atmosphere to New York's Soho. Ironically, Ipanema meant *bad water*. Then we skirted Copacabana. Dense population coupled with an abundance of tourists had diminished the area's once-fashionable image, and high-rise apartments lined the entire Copacabana beach.

Because of the nighttime safety concerns in Rio, I decided to organize a group dinner at Satyricon, a restaurant in Ipanema highly recommended by our local guide. I circulated a list on the bus and made a reservation for ten at 8:30 p.m. Ruth and I met the diners in the lobby and we all hopped into three hotel cars for the fifteen-minute ride to the restaurant.

I had assumed the restaurant would be in the beach area, but it was a good distance inland. The décor in the crowded spot was unmistakably nautical and not good nautical at that. We had a surly waiter who made our meal miserable and was terribly upset when we requested separate checks. Food, service and ambience rated somewhere between a C- and a D+. This was not repeat-worthy. We all wondered what our tour guide received for our reservations. Despite the poor food and service, it was great fun to be with our new U of M friends.

The next morning was one of leisure and Ruth, always in search of the ultimate jewelry find, opted to take a car to the H. Stern shop in Ipanema. While at breakfast, I noticed that travel agency guides Doug and Peggy seemed animated and I asked them what they had planned for their morning. They said they had arranged to go hang-gliding over Rio. I mentioned that I would like to give it a try and they invited me to accompany them to the launching area high above the city. In retrospect, they never should have allowed me to go but it all happened so quickly that they overlooked any legal issues that might have arisen.

Santiago wanted to go but declined because of the cost. When I offered to cover his fee, he happily accepted and opted to wait until the afternoon to give it a try with Doug. Peggy and I headed up the mountainside for our adrenaline rush of a jump. Winding our way up to one of the prominent peaks above Rio, we arrived at the launch site at an elevation of twelve hundred feet. I was charged with anticipation, but Peggy suddenly felt a bit queasy as she looked over the sheer drop and suggested I go first.

My pilot and I made a couple of four-count practice runs to the edge of the cliff before wiring ourselves into the hang glider and donning helmets. At his request I removed my tennis shoes and tied the strings together. He hooked our shoes to a metal strip on the glider before we took our final four counts at full speed and disappeared beneath the launch platform.

If I had known more about hang gliding, I might have been frightened. Instead, as the wind whooshed beneath our wing and we stabilized, I experienced an incredible sense of exhilaration. I asked my pilot if I could extend my arms to fly and he laughed and said, "Of course!" We sailed over a tropical forest and then over a series of high rises and hotels. The city of Rio and one of its largest shantytowns appeared below us in one direction and the island-dotted water sparkled in the other as we circled back and forth.

The volume of the wind under the wing was surprisingly loud. I had expected absolute silence and the noise surprised me.

As we sailed high above Rio, I mentioned to my pilot that I hadn't even asked his name. "It's Eelton," he replied. "Eelton? That's an unusual name," I said. "How do you spell it?" "H-i-l-t-o-n," he answered. "Just like the hotels." Conrad Hilton played a major role in the development of Rio and many of the locals named their children after him. I asked Hilton how many hang-gliding flights he had logged. He said he had completed more than two thousand. He was a pro and sometimes did as many as six flights in a single day.

Time literally flew by and we landed after ten or twelve minutes on São Conrado Beach. As we circled over the water to prepare for our landing, I looked down at our multi-storied hotel and could not believe how tiny it looked from our vantage point. Hilton eventually glided us to a relatively smooth landing on the beach about a quarter of a mile from the InterContinental.

Unbeknownst to me, Hilton had installed a camera at the end of the passenger side of the wing. As we flew through the air, he steered with one hand and squeezed a rubber ball connected to the camera with the other. When we landed, he opened the camera and handed me a roll of film ready to be developed. To my surprise and delight I now had a pictorial record of my maiden voyage.

With our hotel in clear sight I opted to walk back to it rather than return to the mountaintop to watch Peggy's flight. At mid-morning only natives sat along the beach and I quickly realized that I stood out like the tourist I happened to be. I had left most of my jewelry in the hotel safe but wore a pair of gold earrings. The sand was burning hot but I decided not to stop to put on my tennis shoes and walked toward the InterContinental at record speed. The gate to the hotel's pool entrance was a welcome sight and I delighted at returning to the land of tourists.

Spotting Santiago at the pool and still on an adrenaline high, I stopped to share details of my recent experience. He was having some serious thoughts about not going in the afternoon and my enthusiasm seemed to put him at ease. When we all met poolside later in the afternoon, he, Peggy, Doug, and I swapped war stories. We formed a special bond as the only ones who dared to take the leap that day.

After my flight I met Ruth at the hotel and oohed and ahhed over her H. Stern purchase, a charm with semi-precious stones. She thought I was certifiable for hang gliding and assured me that jewelry shopping was a far safer endeavor. After a quick lunch we joined a number of the U of M group for a bus trip to Petropolis, a resort city high above Rio. Pedro II, the Portuguese prince who proclaimed Brazil's independence from his native country, commissioned a palace in the mountains to escape a yellow fever outbreak in 1843 that killed forty-five percent of the population in Rio. Today it stood as a thriving weekend resort community for the city's wealthy. Bus lines offered express rides to and from Rio, an hour away, so it was possible to live full-time in Petropolis and work in the city.

We stopped to tour the picturesque palace-turned-national-museum and its beautifully furnished rooms filled with art and portraiture. The well-maintained gardens surrounding the palace were noteworthy. After a look at a nearby cathedral, our tour of the city continued. We noticed several prominent pink buildings and our local guide told us the color represented nobility.

Our downhill ride through tropical forests along a toll road heading back toward Rio offered scenic panoramic views. Although misty and grey at times, the mountain region enhanced the beauty of the vistas. Contrasting with the verdant slopes, occasional splashes of purple and bright yellow flowering trees added a dash of color to the mix.

Ruth and I enjoyed a quiet dinner at Alfredo's in the InterContinental before calling it a day. The next morning Santiago gave a lecture to our group. He discussed the works of Spanish writer Julio Cortazar who was born in Belgium in 1914 and immigrated with his family to Buenos Aires in 1918. In 1951 he moved to Paris where he remained until his death. Cortazar wrote short stories and novels including the well-known *Blow-Up*. This tale was released as a film in 1966 and remains one of my all-time favorites. He then wrote *Hopscotch*. Its 155 chapters begin with a table of instructions inviting the reader to proceed in various ways through the novel. One can stop reading after chapter 56, concluding that the story has ended. Another suggestion was for the reader to begin with chapter 73 before reading chapter 1. This concept of disposable chapters was certainly unique.

We boarded a plane mid-afternoon for our flight to Santiago, Chile. My seatmates, two young women from Santiago, were returning from a month's vacation. They began in Florida and ended in Rio with a few intermittent stops. Both were of Indian descent and well educated. They spoke excellent English along with French and their native Spanish.

We talked about points of interest in Santiago and they also outlined an impressive weeklong driving trip to the southern tip of Chile for future reference. As we neared the airport, they plastered themselves against their seats so I could have a clear view of the surrounding mountains and the extremely narrow pass into Santiago. The woman closest to the window asked for my camera and took photos of the mountaintops.

Navigating the narrow passage into Santiago ranked right up there with my hang-gliding ride. I felt I could almost reach out and touch the mountainside and was convinced the plane's wing was in for a too-close encounter. It didn't surprise me when I later learned of a long history of air tragedies in this area. I wouldn't want to fly through this pass on a cloudy day. Actually, not seeing the peaks at such close range might be a blessing as long as the plane's radar did its job.

Our newest guide, Domingo, asked us to pile our reclaimed luggage in a special area and we sailed through customs. Ah, the perks of traveling en masse. In no time at all we boarded a bus for the half-hour ride to our next hotel. Passing through the outskirts of Santiago, the effects of a three-year drought were evident. The landscape was parched and withered, and we passed a number of orchards filled with dead trees. The topography resembled California's high desert area near Palm Springs. The contrast between the lush tropical forests surrounding Rio and the arid conditions in this part of Chile was dramatic.

As we drove through a pass and descended into Santiago we were immediately impressed by the city. It was clean, obviously well off and quite beautiful. I hadn't expected such opulence. Our hotel, the new Santiago Hilton, was magnificent. Ruth and I couldn't believe the size and quality of our room. It had a step-down sitting area and a roomy bathroom. Just as impressive were the common areas in the lobby, the restaurants and the large pool. After a light dinner and a walk through the hotel's landscaped grounds we called it a night.

The next morning, we boarded a bus for a tour of the city. We drove through a stunning residential area and then past the rather stark American Embassy before passing block after block of attractive high-rise apartment buildings. Chileans are hard-working people who make things happen in their cities.

Domingo told us that when the early Spanish arrived in Chile on horseback the Mapuche Indians thought they were gods. They soon realized that these supposed gods were intent on killing them and taking over their land. Three hundred years of war ensued.

More factoids: chile was indeed the Indian word for *cold*. People from Germany, France, England, and Croatia as well as India and Spain settled Chile. The country had a large middle class and only five percent could not read. Until 1970, the inflation rate averaged thirty percent annually; in 1997 it was a much lower six-and-a-half percent. Chile was known as a developing country and not a third-world country. Bribery was not permitted. In the old days, Chileans had as many children as God would give them, and often God was overly generous. Today, a two-child family was considered a good size.

Chile's government consisted of a coalition with a president and two houses of Parliament. Elected for a six-year term, he or she could be re-elected but had to wait six years before running for a second term. Pablo Neruda's Santiago home was now a museum honoring one of the two Chileans awarded a Nobel Prize in Literature.

Our first stop was at the base of an enormous statue of the Virgin Mary perched on a peak high above the city. On this Sunday we spotted pockets of hazy smog lingering below us. Heading down the hillside we paused to look at two araucaria araucana, the symmetrical pine-like national tree of Chile. Once on flat ground we followed the gracious Avenida Bernardo O'Higgins leading from the residential to the business area. We then turned onto a roadway leading to the elegant Club Hipico de Santiago, a private racetrack and jockey club, where we noticed several horses getting a morning workout.

Next we drove past the Presidential Palace, now offices rather than a residence, en route to the Plaza de Armas and the Archaeological Museum for a tour of its fascinating pre-Columbian artifacts. As we headed back to the hotel, Domingo asked if anyone was interested a stop at a lapis shop. Among the takers were Ruth, another woman and her husband. In no time at all, the gentleman returned and said, "If you've seen one lapis lazuli, you've seen them all!" When someone asked where his wife was, he replied, "I left her in a lapis frenzy." His wife and Ruth made some purchases before returning to the hotel.

Nothing had been scheduled for that Sunday afternoon and most in our group opted for a bit of R&R at the hotel on this beautiful day. I took a short walk to have my hang-gliding photos developed at a one-hour shop in a nearby mall. After wandering through a number of other shops I collected my prints and returned to the hotel.

Donning our swimsuits, Ruth and I headed poolside late in the afternoon only to discover that every deck chair was occupied. We finally snagged a couple of vacated seats and enjoyed the remaining daylight. When the sun disappeared, I went to the spa and sat in the sauna before adding a brief workout in the exercise room.

Ruth and I met some of our fellow travelers for dinner in the hotel's main dining room. The food was delicious but the ambience created by four young American businessmen seated near us left something to be desired. They finished their meals well before us and proceeded to light cigars. It became so intolerable that I suggested moving to another table. Since we had almost finished, we paid our bills with a recommendation to our waiter that cigar smokers be invited to an outdoor patio while others were dining.

Our wake-up call came at a very early 4:45 a.m. and we all groggily gathered for breakfast before checking out of the hotel and boarding the ever-present bus. Ruth and I were served breakfast by the drop-dead gorgeous Sebastian, a Chilean hunk who had waited on our table yesterday. He made the early morning hour a bit more tolerable.

Luck was with us and Ruth and I had exit row seats with extra leg room on our hour-long flight to Lima, Peru. Kika, our newest local guide, and Julio, our bus driver, met us as we landed. Kika told us that from April through November the weather is usually grey, caused by the Humboldt Current that originates in Chile. However, it only rains an average of six inches per year in Lima so the grey skies are all show and no go. Lima is, in fact, a semi-desert.

The miles of slums from the airport to the city that we passed were appalling. Kika explained that multitudes came from mountain villages in search of a better life and ended up in this squalor. The government was actually giving incentives to Peruvians who remained in their native villages. What we witnessed on our way to Lima was a far cry from a better life.

Kika delivered a history of Peru as we continued into the city. Lima was founded as the City of Kings on January 18, 1535. From 1569 to 1820, Peru remained under the control of Spain. José de San Martín led the crusade for independence in the south along with Simón Bolivar in the north, succeeding in 1821. For many years, Peru's power remained in the hands of a few wealthy landowners but that ended in the early 1970s.

The government in Peru had been based on terrorism. Under President Alan García, the country experienced seventy percent inflation in just one month. Many were convinced that Peru would not survive. In the last election Alberto Fujimori was one of two candidates for president and to everyone's surprise he won. The inflation in 1997 was now about one percent per month.

The minimum monthly salary in 1997 was US$70 and the average monthly salary, US$200. Therefore, it was necessary for three or four family members to work in order to support a household. At any given time, Lima's unemployment rate was fifteen percent. There were eighteen universities in the city and sixty in the country. The population primarily consisted of Mestizos, a mixture of native Indian and Spanish as well as Creole, a mixture of Spanish, African, Indian, and Chinese. Like Santiago, Lima wa subject to earthquakes and the only remnants of 17th-and 18th-century buildings were those constructed with a type of flexible cane incorporated within the walls.

Compared with Santiago, Lima was a bit of a shock. Much of it looked like poor areas in Mexican cities. The town square, Plaza de Armas, came as a welcome respite. Many of the buildings had recently been restored and the results were spectacular. Bright banners floated above the central park, ringed by a cathedral, several military buildings, and the President's Palace, now housing government offices. Some fine examples of Lima's unique hand-carved wooden balconies graced the buildings in the plaza.

After a lengthy tour of the cathedral, several of us zipped across the street to snap some photos. As the clock struck noon, we noticed a Changing of the Guard ceremony taking place in front of the palace. We tried to take photos but the crowds were too deep around the iron gates. What we could see of the ceremony would have to remain a mental memory.

Our next stop was a Jesuit monastery. Originally there were eight active cloisters; today there were three. The most fascinating aspect of the monastery was its underground catacombs where the bones of dozens were systematically sorted and arranged in stylized piles. At the very end of a large circular pit stood a decorative spiral of skulls.

More Peruvian factoids: the native Indians of Peru belong to the Quechua tribe. Peru was the center of the Inca Empire and Quechua, the ancient Incan language, was still spoken in remote villages. Metropolitan Lima was divided into forty-two suburbs and was home to a population of 6 million. Only six years of schooling were required in Peru.

We passed a mere two blocks from the Japanese Embassy in the San Isidro district. For the previous two months a group of dissidents held hostage a large group of international delegates attending a holiday party at the embassy and no end to the siege was in the foreseeable future. We noticed a strong police presence in the surrounding area and traffic in the streets leading to the embassy was blocked. Journalists and reporters gathered at every intersection as they waited for a breaking story. Our hotel was located not far from this hotbed of international turmoil.

Continuing on toward the coast we entered the fashionable Miraflores district. The surrounding land appeared dry and desolate with steep cliffs showing signs of erosion, and expensive homes and apartments perched precariously at the top of the unstable hillside. The beaches below were dotted with surfers and Kika told us that this was indeed considered a surfer's paradise.

We stopped for lunch at a seaside restaurant called Rosa Nautica. To enter it, we walked along a pier that extended into the ocean leading to a platform housing this charming spot. We were ushered into the gazebo room where tables had been set for our group. Ruth and I invited two others to join us and we enjoyed a delicious lunch accentuated with interesting conversation. Once back on the bus, group member Doug announced that the lunch was just what we needed. "I was really dragging," he said. "Instead of dragging, now we're staggering," added Lena, another member of our group. She was referring to the potent *pisco* sours served with lunch.

Our next stop was the Oro Verde in the San Isidro district, another relatively new hotel with a stunning reception area. For the most part, our hotels ranked very high on the accommodations scale and this was no exception. Ruth and I took the elevator to the eleventh floor and, although only Ruth's suitcase had arrived, we decided to head out for some retail therapy at a mall not far away.

A Peruvian shop offering handknit sweaters and small items made from colorful cotton prints caught our eye. After checking out the merchandise, Ruth decided that a nap was in order and returned to the hotel. I continued on and bought a few items for myself and small gift items for friends and family.

When we first got off the elevator at the eleventh floor of the hotel we noticed a small satellite dish with a camera wired to its base aimed out the window at the end of the hallway. Heavy cords were strapped to the floor with electrical tape and they disappeared under an emergency exit door. Upon closer inspection we noted that the equipment belonged to the Turner Broadcasting Network and the camera, pointed at the Japanese Embassy not far away, operated round the clock. We felt a bit too close for comfort even though the embassy was several blocks from our location. Our hotel was filled to capacity and the majority of guests were journalists. Interesting times...

The next morning, we met our group for a bus ride to Lima's National Archaeological Museum. We passed more streets leading to the Japanese Embassy and again found the police and military presence staggering. Groups of young men stood with machine guns casually slung over their shoulders. Just outside our posh hotel several uniformed men armed with machine guns stood at the ready. I wondered if this practice continued when there was no hostage crisis.

Today's bus ride took us through the residential area of San Isidro and we noted an array of brightly colored houses. Varying shades of coral, gold, grey-blue, and burgundy seemed most prevalent. This was one of the more prominent suburbs and yet it didn't compare to the elegance of Santiago. Shards of broken glass were embedded into the walls that surrounded many of the homes. Lima and Santiago were geographically close but worlds apart economically and politically.

I was surprised by the multitude of American billboards touting fast-food choices for chicken, burgers, soft drinks, beer, and even cigarettes. Pizza Hut, McDonald's and Kentucky Fried Chicken had a strong presence in Lima.

We soon entered the Pueblo Libre district showcasing some 19th-century buildings. Then we arrived at Lima's impressive National Archaeological

Museum arranged around two colonial-style courtyards. Its extensive collection of pre-Columbian artifacts was the best I had ever seen and this was a not-to-be-missed excursion.

Our next stop at the private Larco Museum housed one of the world's finest collections of pre-Columbian tapestries and ceramics. Mummified remains also were exhibited at each of today's museums. The Larco literally had stockpiles of ceramic artifacts shelved behind glass and categorized by design. For example, one case held only pitchers with squirrel motifs. Before leaving we popped into another smaller building that housed an extensive erotica collection. The Incas left nothing to the imagination as they depicted a wide variety of sexual activities. I suspect this collection might even embarrass *Hustler's* Larry Flynt.

After lunch at the hotel a smaller group gathered for another bus ride to the third museum of the day. We drove a fair distance to the outer periphery of Lima and entered the grounds of the privately owned Gold Museum. Here we encountered a staggering collection of Inca artifacts, many of which were cast in gold. As our travel material pointed out, it was sobering to see this magnificent collection and then realize that these were only a small part of what was originally produced. The Spanish conquerors looted and melted down most of the fine pieces. From intricately woven fabrics to jewels and funerary decorations, the Gold Museum's stunning collection of Quechua and Moche artifacts merited the price of admission.

We were offered an additional half hour to wander through the museum's armament collection or look through a series of shops on the grounds. Most of us opted for the latter. There was an H. Stern shop among them and several in our group made purchases. Ruth and I collected our H. Stern charms, this one depicting a llama. I secretly wondered what would become of the charms once I returned to LA. Long may they live hidden in the back of one of my jewelry drawers!

As soon as we reached the hotel we raced up to the second level for another of Santiago's lectures. Today he focused on two South American authors, Jose Maria Arguedas from Peru and Pablo Neruda from Chile. The former committed suicide at age fifty-eight while writing *El Zorro de Arriba y el Zorro Abajo*, a combination of fiction combined with his own personal diary. It ends with his admission that he had nothing more to offer. Santiago concluded with a reading of *The Heights of Machu Picchu*, a poem by Neruda, a prolific writer of history and fiction.

Somehow our expected 3:45 a.m. wake-up call never came the next day but for some reason Ruth woke up just after 4:00 a.m. We raced to dress and grab a roll and coffee before our early morning bus ride to the airport for our flight to Cusco, Peru. We boarded a packed plane and noted that another difference between Chile and Peru was the quality—or lack of it—of its airplanes.

When we landed an hour later, our local guide Wilbert was there to greet us. We took a bus to the Don Carlos Holiday Inn and were delighted that our rooms were ready for us at the early hour of 8:00 a.m. The first order of business, however, required spending a few minutes in the hotel's restaurant where we were served hot coca tea. Handed a cup of this tried and true remedy for altitude sickness, we were assured that it was a must. Wilbert suggested we drink our tea and then rest for two hours before beginning our tour.

Ruth was under the weather from her bout with a cold and she had no trouble following these directions to the letter. Unfortunately, my new Pentax landed on the stone floor of the Cusco airport as I took a photo of an intricate Inca motif and it no longer worked. The telephoto lens zoomed to its full extension when I opened it following my fumble-fingered fiasco but the shutter was inoperable. After planning for years to reach the heights of Machu Picchu, I no longer had a working camera to preserve the memories.

As soon as we reached the hotel I had asked Wilbert if it was possible to get the camera repaired quickly. He thought it could be done and asked me to meet him immediately after the coca tea fest. While the others rested, Wilbert and I toured Cusco in quest of a bit of camera repair magic. After three or four unsuccessful stops by foot and by taxi, I decided to do the next best thing and buy a few disposable cameras. However, the extremely high price of the disposables made the purchase of a plain vanilla camera an option. I bought a very basic camera and some film, only to ruin the first roll as I attempted to load it. The new camera didn't work well and I finally gave up on it. I'll have to rely on mental memories.

In spite of the missed rest I managed to keep it all together stomach-wise and was ready to go for the afternoon tour of the nearby Sacsayhuaman Fortress. Perched at an elevation of 11,907 feet high above Cusco, it is believed that this fine example of stonework dating to 1100 AD and stretching a thousand feet in length once had a religious significance. It may have been a monastery for virgins. Huge boulders were quarried and then moved great distances to form near-perfect fits into this puzzle-like structure. Since some weighed as much as thirty tons; that was no small task. The magnificence of this architectural wonder, pronounced *sexy wo-man*, had to be seen to be appreciated.

The evening's main event was a meal at La Retama, Cusco's answer to a dinner club. A short bus ride away, we were ushered to seats along both sides of two long tables at which the ever-present *pisco* sours were served along with *agua con gas* and an eggnog concoction. The food was very good with choices of soup or a cooked vegetable salad as a starter and either lime-marinated skewered chicken or red fish in a garlic sauce as an entrée. Entertainment was provided by a group of musicians playing typical Peruvian folk music. Dancers in native costume accompanied them from time to time. We all had a delightful evening.

The next morning came with another early wake-up call and we boarded a narrow-gauge train for our three-hour-and-twenty-minute ride through the Andes to the base of Machu Picchu. This adventure was at the top of my list of reasons for visiting South America and it made our crack-of-dawn departure worthwhile.

Our train passed through a series of five switchbacks to a height of twelve thousand feet as it rose above the city of Cusco. The early morning vistas from our lofty perch were spectacular. As we sped along the tracks, we passed miles of farms and small villages with mud brick houses. Families worked together to mix the red soil from the hillsides with straw and water in this age-old home building process.

As was the case throughout the journey we were blessed with another glorious day. A group from Dartmouth accompanied us and their travel guide said that this clear morning offered her the first glimpse of the Andean peaks in more than four months. She told us that last week's torrential rains caused a mudslide that buried six hundred people not far from today's route. What a difference a week can make! The only evidence of that powerful rainfall was the raging water in the Urubamba River bordering our train tracks. We saw no boats or rafts in this popular river and surmised that its rapid flow spelled danger.

We witnessed mile after mile of Andean splendor as we left any hint of civilization behind us and began our train trek through narrow mountain passes. The rugged snow-capped peaks were juxtaposed against a background that varied from high desert to semi-tropical. I will never forget the majesty of this mountain range glistening against the backdrop of a clear blue sky on this picture-perfect morning.

As the train arrived at the Sacred Valley station en route to Machu Picchu, hordes of men, women and children surrounded it armed with T-shirts, woven bags, postcards, and more. One woman in our group bartered with a salesperson through the train window and pulled a stunning woven bag into the train. When someone asked what she had paid, she replied, "Twenty." I noticed a man holding an attractive green woven bag and handed him a twenty-dollar bill as he slipped the bag into my outstretched hands. I soon learned that my friend had paid for her purchase with Peruvian money, the equivalent of US$8. Oh, well. I made my merchant's day a bit brighter and, in truth, the bag was well worth US$20.

Wilbert pointed out a faint trail high in the Andes and explained that it was the ancient Inca trail. He told us that from May through October it was possible to hire guides for a five-day/four-night trek from a starting point outside of Cuzco to Machu Picchu. For about US$260 per person, groups of eight or ten would follow the trail while guides carried their packs. A cook also accompanied the trekkers as they hiked about six miles a day, reaching a maximum of height of nine thousand feet. Robbers who occasionally raided the trekkers along the trail presented the only drawback.

Nearing Machu Picchu, more lush semi-tropical vegetation appeared. Thick foliage sprouted from every crevice in the rocky cliffs with the raging river at its edge. Wilbert pointed out a terraced hillside with the remnants of an important Inca site called Winay Wayna, which appeared to have been virtually inaccessible to ancient invaders.

When we arrived at our final train stop, we boarded buses that climbed the steep rise to Machu Picchu. As we switched back and forth on the narrow dirt roadway, evidence of last week's destructive rain was apparent. At one point we had to stop while a repair crew moved equipment to the side of the badly damaged road, but we managed to make the twenty-minute trip to the top without incident.

At the summit the vistas were breathtakingly beautiful. As remote and isolated a location as this was, it was easy to see why it proved irresistible to the Incas. Nature formed a near-perfect bowl nestled in the midst of the spectacular peaks of the Andes. At a mere 9,000-foot elevation, far lower than Cuzco, I felt a sudden burst of energy.

Although it was not as vast a complex as I had envisioned, Machu Picchu ranked right up there as one of the most spectacular archeological sites in the world. Even though the temple complex of Egypt's Karnak and Italy's Pompeii are grander in size and stature, the magic of Machu Picchu is incomparable. Yale's Hiram Bingham discovered it in 1911 after it had been abandoned for centuries. Since there is no recorded history of Machu Picchu, the reason why the Incas developed it has remained a mystery.

The fortified complex had only one entrance and it was a self-sustaining city. Terraced areas prepared for farming fed the thousands of inhabitants who once lived here. We spent two and a half hours touring the steep terrain and saw houses, barracks for soldiers, temples, a cemetery, and even what appeared to be a prison. Surprisingly, the Incas only lived in Machu Picchu for a hundred-year period between 1400 and 1500 AD.

A man in our group took pity on my camera fiascos and lent me one of his, complete with a fresh roll of film. I tucked away the not-so-trusty camera I'd purchased in Cusco and rejoiced at having one that worked well. As luck would have it, the camera jinx followed me to Machu Picchu and all my photos were overexposed. Today's cell phones would have been such a blessing!

As we boarded the buses for the long ride down the steep cliffs to the train station, we noticed a young boy in native dress waving at us with a big smile. When we waved back, he let out a loud hoot. Winding our way around each of the fourteen switchbacks, he magically appeared ahead of us at each, flashing his infectious smile and a wave. We were all enthralled by his daring antics as he raced down the mountain to greet us at every turn. When he boarded our bus at the end of our descent, he was amply rewarded by most of us. We later learned that a young boy typically followed each bus in hopes of collecting a monetary reward.

A few clouds had appeared during our tour and it began to sprinkle as we boarded the narrow-gauge train for our return trip. The usual throng of merchants hovered outside our windows hoping to tempt us with one last purchase.

The return trip seemed a bit longer, partly because it was difficult to recapture the magic of this morning's ride and partly due to a twenty-minute delay along the way to repair one of the connecting switches on the car directly behind us. We all heard a loud whoosh and then a clank followed by the smell of either burned rubber or scorched metal. When Ruth asked why we had stopped, our steward replied, "We're uncoupled." As only Ruth, a widow, could do, she quickly responded, "I've been uncoupled for years so what's the big deal?"

We were soon underway and passed miles of cactus, vivid yellow wild mustard and tall, willowy stalks of Pampas grass grouped together in clusters along the bank of the river. As we approached signs of civilization we saw men, women and children working the farms. We chuckled when we noticed two young children taking a ride on a low wooden plow pulled by oxen. As dusk approached, cattle and sheep were herded back to their pens after a day of grazing.

Not far from Cusco, a woman in our group pointed out a striking cloud formation above a snow-capped mountain behind us. The sun was about to set and a wisp of cloud in front of a peak appeared to be on fire. None of us had ever witnessed anything like it and we all agreed that it offered the perfect final image to a memorable day.

One last treat awaited us. The twenty-minute delay brought us close to

Cusco in semi-darkness and by the time we completed the series of switchbacks above the city it was in total darkness. Looking down on the twinkling lights from our vantage point created a lasting memory.

Ruth and I opted for dinner at the hotel before returning to our room to pack for the next day's trip back to Miami. After all the recent early morning departures, our 5:30 a.m. wake-up call was a breeze. We had ample time for breakfast before backtracking to Lima for our group flight. Although the plane out of Cusco was delayed for forty-five minutes, Doug assured us that Aero Peru would hold the Miami flight since we were such a large group.

As we touched down on the landing strip in Lima only the right tire hit the runway. The pilot accelerated and lifted the plane briefly before he literally dropped it back onto the runway. We were stunned, to say the least, as we were first tossed forward and then jerked back into our seats. Not one word of explanation from the pilot or crew followed.

We boarded the plane to Miami in good stead and arrived with plenty of time for my connection to Los Angeles. I said good-bye to Ruth and the rest of our new U of M friends and then headed toward my departure gate. What a glorious two weeks of touring South America with my dear friend Ruth! I will always treasure the experiences we shared.

ENGLAND AND WALES

London, Gravetye, Chewton Glen, Gidleigh Park, Dartmoor,
Tinturn Abbey, Bodysgallen/Llandudno, Conwy Castle, Portmeirion,
Snowdonia, Betws y Coed, Snowdonia, Caernarfon, and Cliveden Manor

May 25–June 7, 1997

ALTHOUGH this would not be my first time in England, I nevertheless
looked forward to a return visit. It was almost like reconnecting with a
treasured friend. We added Wales to our itinerary, a first for Wayne and me,
making this trip even more special.

Arriving at Heathrow just before noon with carry-on luggage, we sailed
through customs. Because it was a bank-holiday Monday, traffic was light and
we registered at the Cliveden Town House located at 26 Cadogan Gardens
in Chelsea by 1:00 p.m. Formerly the Draycott, this series of connected
townhouses was nestled in a prime residential area. Under either name it was
one of our London favorites.

Wayne, a seasoned overseas traveler, had mastered the art of sleeping on
planes, a skill I never managed to acquire. While the birthday boy hiked up
and down King's Road, I opted for a two-hour nap. The late May weather
couldn't have been better and I joined Wayne after my rest for a stroll in
Knightsbridge and then back to the hotel via Sloane Square before dressing
for dinner at the Ivy. We enjoyed the food and service at this popular spot
near the theatre district and it proved to be the perfect place to celebrate
Wayne's fifty-sixth birthday.

Our taxi driver dropped us off at Kensington High Street so we could do
some late-night window shopping in this well-known antiques area. The shop
windows were indeed enticing and I promised myself a return trip during
business hours. A pair of small Staffordshire lions unquestionably spoke to me.

It was such a spectacular night that we decided to walk the almost two
miles to our hotel. We arrived at 10:30 p.m. and headed to our room, the

Galsworthy. Like all the rooms we had experienced in this charming hotel, ours had a sitting area with a fireplace. A pair of Staffordshire lions just like the ones I admired in the shop window sat at attention on the mantle.

Wayne departed early the next morning for a day of work in Marlowe. I slept late and enjoyed breakfast in our room, doing my best imitation of the lady of the manor. As I looked out the window, I noticed a group of uniformed children queuing for photographs. The process continued by class from youngest to oldest as the students marched from a nearby school with their hands clasped behind their backs.

On a beautiful day filled with blue skies and plenty of sunshine, it was a perfect time to explore London. I took a taxi to Kensington High Street to revisit the antiques in daylight and was struck by how much more charming the shops had looked in the evening's glow. Lewis and Lloyd on Kensington Church Road carried some lovely period pieces. An early 18th-century Duncan Phyfe piece caught my eye, a supposed bargain at US$14,500. Next time, perhaps…

I went into the shop where I had spotted the two Staffordshire lions and discovered that they were priced at 5,000 pounds—US$8,500. I patted myself on the back for picking these pricey items and decided to be on the lookout for replicas like the pair in our hotel room.

My taxi ride to the area cost 8 pounds, about US$13, so I opted for the tube to New Bond Street at a mere 1.2 pounds to visit Grey's Antique Centre. This complex featured the collections of dealers specializing in a myriad of old and not-so-old items. At a stall featuring Majolica I met a couple from Los Angeles. They collected Wedgwood Majolica and amassed enough pieces over time to exhibit them at the Huntington Art Gallery. I bought a small Majolica plate to add to my collection.

I then walked the length of New Bond Street filled with elegant shops. Reaching Green Park, I took the tube to Sloane Square. After purchasing a book on Wales, I went to Peter Jones, a department store, to purchase a coffee maker and two mugs. I made a quick stop at a gourmet market for freshly ground coffee beans. The English know how to brew tea but coffee, even in the best of hotels, tastes like warm water. Now we'll brew our own at our leisure.

We shared dinner with business friends at Le Soufflé in the InterContinental in Hyde Park. Although rather plain vanilla in appearance, the dining room served excellent food. My choices of an asparagus soufflé followed by veal scallops and sweetbreads served on a bed of spinach were outstanding.

The next morning promised another beautiful day in London. Since Wayne had one more day of business, I walked to the Reject China Shop on

Beauchamp Place where I bought six Portmeirion floral bowls and shipped them home. My next stop was Harrods for a one-hour *what's new* tour. I purchased more coffee beans in the Food Court, asking for a blend with a punch. We later discovered that it lacked much depth. There was a definite niche for a Starbucks or a Peet's in Merry Old England.

After dropping the coffee off at our hotel, I headed for King's Road and popped into Antiquarius, the shop where I bought a Pinchbeck necklace a year earlier. Much to my dismay I later saw an exact duplicate in the antique jewelry section of Bergdorf's for considerably less.

I returned to Harrods to look at its incredible fine china department and then continued on to the Harvey Nichols home furnishings floor. While there I found a tole cachepot in rusty red embellished with hand-painted gold leaves. Knowing it would fit our newly decorated living room's décor, I arranged to have it sent home.

Returning to our hotel, I met Wayne for coffee and a bit of Stilton cheese and crackers for a pre-theatre snack. Tonight's tickets were for *Art*, an award-winning three-man play at the Wyndham Theatre. Performed without an intermission, this powerful one-and-a-half-hour play presented an intriguing study of what constitutes art and friendship. Opting to forgo another restaurant dinner, we decided to walk to our hotel and munch on more crackers and cheese in our room.

Now that Wayne was officially on vacation, we began our day with another walk along Sloane Square in quest of antique print shops. Our first stop, Sotheran's Rare Books and Prints, offered an eclectic array of English and Continental prints. We looked at a number of original David Roberts drawings of the Holy Land and Egypt. One of Karnak particularly appealed to us and was priced at US$3,300, not an unreasonable amount. We spotted a promising 18th-century architectural print of a canal and surrounding buildings in The Hague. It was paired with another 18th-century print of Piazza San Marco in Venice.

We stopped for lunch nearby and checked out a few more print and antique shops. The two architectural prints we liked at Sotheran's continued to call to us and we returned to the gallery. After assuring us that we could reframe the Venice print to better match its Dutch mate, we made arrangements to ship the two prints stateside.

I had visited the shop some time ago with my friend Karen who had studied antique botanicals while living in London and was particularly fond of those by Basilius Besler. The shop owner remembered her and mentioned that Besler prints, although scarce these days, did come in from time to time. She brought out a set of eight Haarlem floral prints that were exquisite.

Although two were on hold, I selected four of the mid-18th-century hand-colored prints by a Dutch artist and we added them to our shipment. All six prints remain in our home to this day.

We returned to our hotel to collect our luggage and meet our driver, not wanting our vacation to begin with Wayne tackling an hour-long drive through London's traffic. We relaxed while our driver maneuvered through the busy streets to a car rental on the outskirts of the city. Once Wayne was behind the wheel of our rental, our route took us along the A23 south on narrow roads to the more modern M23 to East Grinstead in west Sussex. In no time at all we were on the road leading to Gravetye Manor, a gracious country estate.

After registering, we were led to a top-floor room, the Lime, in a relatively new addition. Any disappointment in our assignment to the new section was quickly dismissed when we looked out our expansive windows with views of both the main house and gardens. The architect who designed the addition did a near-perfect job of duplicating the style of the original house built in 1598 AD, making it difficult to tell where one ended and the other began. Unlike the original manor house, however, we had a modern bathroom and all the amenities of a luxury hotel.

William Robinson, known as the father of English gardening, lived at Gravetye until the turn of the 19th century. His landscaping techniques, reflecting his aversion to straight-laced gardens, were showcased throughout the manor grounds. On this bright spring afternoon, tea was served on small tables scattered throughout the rear garden. In late May the rhododendron were at their peak and vibrant splashes of violet, rose, pink, and white abounded. At the far end of the garden white wisteria covered an arbor. More color from an abundance of meticulously tended flower beds added to the beauty of the grounds.

The manor was situated on a thousand-acre estate with an abundance of walking paths. We followed one around the perimeter of a three-acre lake, passing a large herd of dairy cattle grazing in a fenced pasture. On the lake, two swans paddled near the shore toward us, hoping for a handout. Finding us empty-handed they soon moved back into deeper water. We strolled for almost an hour before returning to our room.

Dining at Gravetye was an experience not to be missed. It had quite possibly one of the best kitchens in all of England. We began the evening seated in the garden for drinks. After making our dinner selections we were escorted into the main dining room. Everything was perfect—the setting, the service and, to our joy, no smoking was permitted. With a mere eighteen guestrooms and no off-premises diners, it was an intimate experience. Our exquisitely presented meals were exceptional.

After breakfast in our room we strolled through the manor gardens one more time before checking out and heading south to Chewton Glen Hotel in New Milton, Dorset, on the edge of the New Forest. We came to the village of Linfield with its excellent examples of Tudor architecture and noticed one home with a sign dated 1390 AD. From there we passed through Cuckfield, Cowfold, Crossbush, and Arundel along the A27. Most of the route took us along two-lane roads and we endured near-crawls whenever we encountered farm equipment. Coupled with a myriad of roundabouts, the trip progressed at a snail's pace. At Chichester Harbour we never got above three miles per hour, a new record for slow.

Following the A337 to Lyndhurst and then the A35 to Christchurch, our first impression of the New Forest was less than favorable. Flat land covered with sparse growth bore little relation to the tree-lined area we'd hoped to find. The landscape actually reminded us of a semi-arid southwestern desert with any remnants of a forest long gone. We finally arrived at Chewton Glen and, after the intimacy of Gravetye Manor, were struck by the number of vehicles in the hotel's car park.

Once again we were led to a room in the new addition and once again we were not disappointed. We had a two-floor suite with a charming sitting room on the first level that had its own private patio. A bedroom filled the second floor and from its balcony we spotted a castle on the horizon. English chintzes and wallpaper lent their usual charm to the décor.

After unpacking we followed a maze of connecting halls to the spa and then to the main lobby. On impulse, Wayne decided to buy a golf shirt and hat and rented clubs to play the nine-hole course on the grounds. I did the next best thing and relaxed with a massage and sauna—my kind of sport. A somewhat underwhelming dinner at 8:00 p.m. concluded our day.

Today marked my fifty-third birthday. For some reason I awoke at 6:00 a.m. It was so bright outside that even our heavy curtains couldn't block the sun. At this time of year, the sun is high enough by 6:30 a.m. that one could actually sunbathe.

Wayne slept soundly until 8:30 a.m. and after breakfast we drove to the nearby Salisbury Cathedral. With stop-and-go traffic for most of the way it took us an hour to drive the thirty miles. Despite the gridlock, luck was with us and we found a spot in a car park just a short distance from the city's center. As we entered the outer gates and approached the massive cathedral, we noticed a number of people stacking what appeared to be concrete blocks in the courtyard. What looked like a restoration project from a distance was in fact a set constructed with Styrofoam blocks for an outdoor opera scheduled for that evening.

The cathedral itself was an imposing but rather austere structure. After years of visiting John Constable's painting of Salisbury Cathedral at the Huntington Library and Art Gallery in San Marino, California, it was fascinating to see the structure in person. Once inside we took a forty-five-minute docent tour. Our guide pointed out that the most important feature of the edifice was its tower. Begun as an addition years after the cathedral was constructed between 1220 and 1258 AD, it soared 404 feet upward since its 1549 AD completion and remained the tallest in England. A century later the famed architect Christopher Wren discovered that the tower was twenty-nine inches out of sync and added the mechanism to stabilize it.

After walking through much of the surrounding cathedral grounds we went into town to find a market for picnic fare. We discovered a charcuterie with fresh baguettes and good white English cheddar. With our lunch in hand we headed back to collect our car. About halfway to Chewton Glen we pulled off the road for our picnic in, of all places, a parking lot.

Once back in the village closest to Chewton Glen we decided to find a shop where we could purchase my take-out birthday dinner. Since last night's meal was less than exciting, we opted for light fare in our suite. We bought fresh strawberries in a produce market and added a quiche and apple turnovers from a nearby bakery.

Later in the afternoon we walked along the golf course and through the estate gate to a wooded path leading to the sea. It was a pleasant walk and we were soon treated to a spectacular view of the Isle of Wight with its chalky bluffs. Even though it continued to be a warm, sunny late afternoon, the wind picked up considerably. After an hour-and-a-half walk along the bluffs we returned to our suite for our own version of in-room dining. This was a birthday to remember.

The pampering continued! After a breakfast of bakery scones and coffee *au* Wayne, I returned to the spa for a manicure and pedicure before we checked out and began our three-hour drive to Gidleigh Park in Chagford, Devon, tucked into the Dartmoor National Park. Our route took us through the rolling East Devon countryside with lush farms cascading down to the sea. As we continued on our drive the wind picked up and the fields of grain undulated in rippling waves. This was the England we preferred as opposed to the flat barren land of the New Forest region.

Eventually we parted company with a string of caravans when our directions took us off the beaten track and onto a series of narrow hedge-lined roads leading to Chagford. At one point we had to back up a hill to avoid an oncoming car. We continued to snake along to Gidleigh Park, the manor house we first discovered in 1981 on a day trip from Bath. An enticing article in *Gourmet* magazine inspired that earlier visit and we promised ourselves to return someday. We clearly remembered seeing an Englishman dressed in tweeds and waders fly fishing in the stream leading to the inn. It only took us sixteen years to return.

Often a second visit does not live up to one's expectations. Gidleigh Park was all that we'd remembered and more. Only the English gent casting in the stream was missing from the picture. We were led to room #1 overlooking the front garden and stream. The room had a table in the bay framed by leaded glass windows, a sitting area with a couch and club chair and an ample dose of charming English chintz.

We enjoyed tea in the drawing room before changing into jeans for a four-mile hike through the surrounding forest and into the moors. After half an hour we cleared the forest and discovered the first of many butt circles, prehistoric gathering places formed by large rocks set in rounds. In the distance we could see an enormous natural monolithic outcropping called Kester Rock. We hiked on toward it in the late afternoon, passing more butt circles and herd after herd of sheep grazing along the moors. With the exception of a vocal ram or two the sheep seemed oblivious to our crossing their pasture. Young lambs scurried after their mothers and dodging droppings became an art as we continued onward.

When we finally reached Kester Rock, the wind was so ferocious that we could barely hear each other. Wayne began the climb up the side of the monolith with me in close pursuit. Upon reaching the top we both shouted over the wind that the view was worth the difficult climb. I stayed on top to shoot a few pictures and Wayne started down the opposite side. I shouted to Wayne that I was about to follow him but he couldn't hear me above the roar of the wind. As I started my descent, I lost my balance, bruising my left leg and right hand and hitting my head solidly against a stone ledge. Fortunately, my sunglasses took the brunt of the blow from the rock which was sharp enough to crack the frame. I had a first-class headache but no need for stitches.

We returned to prepare for dinner. Gidleigh was known for its dining and we were not dissatisfied. I began with a chicken mousse with asparagus and morels followed by wild salmon over a bed of spring vegetables. Wayne opted for a squab pâté followed by pigeon in a red wine sauce. As simple as these dishes sound, they were exquisite. Selections from a knock-your-socks-off cheese trolley were followed by a chocolate tart topped with coffee crème anglaise. Perfection!

A much cooler, greyer day, more like the England we had come to know, greeted us the next morning. In the dining room for our full English breakfast we met Cindy and John, two lawyers from Pasadena, California. They shared a wealth of information about the area, having stayed at Gidleigh many times. One suggestion was a drive into the moors through Chagford to Postbridge and then back through Moretonhamstead. They had also been to North Wales and shared their favorite route with us.

We left in a light rain and headed for Chagford. Our first stop was a general store where I bought a new pair of sunglasses and batteries for my camera, another victim in yesterday's tumble. Then we followed a series of narrow one-lane roads to Dartmoor Forest. The vistas even on this drizzly day were spectacular. We marveled at the vast number of sheep and wild ponies that covered the equally vast expanse of moors. At Postbridge we stopped at a visitors' center and chatted at length with the woman at the desk. She told us that she was also involved in lambing each spring and explained how ewes could only raise two offspring. If triplets were born, she would find a ewe with a single lamb and pair one of the triplets with her.

We stopped at one of the highest points in Dartmoor Forest, a.k.a. the moors, for our picnic. Because of the rain and wind, we opted for lunch in the car. Sheep surrounded us, some of the thousands grazing in every direction. The ponies, we later learned, were owned by farmers who let them graze along the moors before they were rounded up in the fall. We continued to tour the surrounding moors and took a hike late in the day not far from Gidleigh. Of course, we returned in time for another fabulous meal.

After enjoying another full English breakfast and a chat with our new friends from Pasadena we said our good-byes to Gidleigh with a promise that we would return soon.

On our way to the A30 we stopped at the historic Fingle Bridge. Our waitress last night suggested it as a perfect spot to fly fish. She did say it was a little out of our way and indeed it was—a twenty-mile detour. We questioned our wisdom until we arrived at the picturesque stone bridge set against steep forested hills in the background. The swift river below it did indeed look like the perfect place to fish.

Driving along the A30 toward Exeter, we then took the M5 north to Bristol. Now back on four-and six-lane highways, Wayne practically flew. We crossed into Wales at Severn Bridge in Chepstow and drove toward Tintern Abbey. The day turned warm and sunny and we paused after a few miles along a river gorge in the Wye Valley at a wooded picnic area. En route we bought fresh bread and cheese and added treacle tarts, a brown-sugar pie topped with pecans.

We next stopped at the ruins of Tintern Abbey, subject of a poem by

William Wordsworth that I remembered so well from my English literature studies. Even in decay it possessed an aura of dignity. I was touched by the sight and felt some sort of connection to it. We continued on, re-entering England as we approached Monmouth via the A40 on our way to the A49. On impulse, we stopped in Hereford on the Welsh border at a small antique shop, noting that it had some of the best pieces we had seen outside of London.

We drove north into Wales through a lush green valley, but our view was soon obliterated by a large lorry that was impossible to pass on the narrow two-lane road. The super highway of earlier today was a mere memory since we were now in the land of country lanes. The new road signs used the Welsh language and we soon came to Betws y Coed, or Betsy Coed, as Wayne called it. The literal pronunciation is Bet-uhss-uh-Coyd. Try that one on for size.

Entering Conwy County, our destination, we were struck by the patchwork of lush green farmland covering the hillsides in all directions. The names of villages printed on road signs continued to baffle us. Some of the spellings were so lengthy that they barely fit on the signs at all. Just try to pronounce Gwyddelwern & Rhydlydan. How about a roadwork sign reading Pan welwch olau goch sefwch yma? Translated, it meant *stop here on red.* Diwedd meant *end.* Un rhes o draffig meant *single file traffic.* Fortunately, most of the directional signs included both Welsh and English.

The atmosphere in Wales was undeniably different from England. In the north most of the homes were constructed from blocks of stone quarried from the local mountains. An endless supply must have existed since countless miles of roadside walls were constructed from the same material. About ten miles south of Bodysgallen the hazy peaks of the Cambrian Mountains of Snowdonia appeared and we later saw a number of mining and stone-cutting facilities in this region.

After a late afternoon visit to Betws y Coed, a charming village nestled along a road bordering riverside parks on one side and quaint quarry stone shops and B&Bs on the other, we backtracked to the A5. We followed it to the A470 and headed toward Llandudno, our final destination. The roads through Wales proved more than adequate. Even though most were only two lanes wide they often offered enough extra space to improvise a center passing lane. We only hoped that someone coming from the opposite direction didn't have the same idea at the same time.

We arrived at Bodysgallen Hall in Llandudno just before 6:00 p.m. A group of four young tourists pulled in behind us with what looked like enough luggage to travel for months. One of the couples was given room #17 and we were led to room #4 right below them. We soon discovered that as charming as it may be to stay in a 17th-century manor house, the floors did indeed creak. After listening to the floors groan and luggage bang above us for half an hour, we decided it was time for Plan B.

We were ushered to the only other room available, a tiny two-room suite in the fourth-floor attic. The ceilings were so low that we tied ribbons on them to remind us to duck. With a promise of a quiet third-floor room tomorrow for the remainder of our stay, we settled into our loft. In spite of the doll-sized space we enjoyed our private hideaway with spectacular views of the garden below and the Cambrian Mountains in the distance. And it was indeed quiet!

Although our dinner was good, the coffee left a lot to be desired, so we opted for scones in our room and some of Wayne's home brewed coffee to start the next day. Afterwards, we headed to the nearby Conwy Castle built between 1283 and 1289 AD by Edward I, Conqueror of Wales. A narrow suspension bridge built by Thomas Telford between 1821 and 1826 offered the only modern way onto the castle grounds and the village of Conwy until another bridge opened in 1938. At the time of our visit the Conwy Bridge, an architectural gem, handled foot traffic only.

Conwy village remains one of the best examples of a walled city. We walked along its charming streets to the spectacular Conwy Bay. The vistas were breathtaking, with ships in the bay in one direction and the imposing castle in the other. We found a local bakery to re-supply our stash of bread and cheeses, adding carrot cake along with some scones for tomorrow's breakfast.

After touring Conwy Castle, we drove on A55 toward Bangor and the Irish Sea coast. A smooth four-lane highway took us along the beautiful coastline on the northwestern edge of Wales. The vistas were idyllic on this sunny day. Wayne reminded me that the average rainfall along the coast was two hundred inches per year.

Our next destination was Caernarfon with its 13th-century castle, another commissioned by Edward I and considered one of the most beautiful in all of Great Britain. It was here that the investiture of Prince Charles took place in 1969 just as it had for other English princes through the centuries. We wound our way through the congested town center to a car park near the castle. As impressive as the structure was, we felt that Conwy Castle had more charm. A highlight was a man playing a Celtic harp in the courtyard whose music was so stirring that we bought a CD.

We headed back to the A487 through the Lleyn Peninsula of Snowdonia National Park to Porthmadog en route to the small fishing village of Portmeirion. As we passed more rolling farmland, we noted that there were virtually no crops, just sheep pastures. The individual grazing areas were separated by walls of piled rocks, giving the landscape its patchwork quilt appearance.

Arriving at Portmeirion, an Italianate seaside village, we paid the three-pound admission, nearly US$7. Reading our tour notes we learned that the village was founded in 1925 as a cluster of Mediterranean-style stucco resort homes. Although charming, it was certainly not Welsh in appearance and therefore a bit of a disappointment. We walked to the bay which, at low tide, was a vast stretch of wet sand. Finding a bench, we broke out our bread and cheese and had a seaside picnic. We then bought a few Christmas gifts in the Portmeirion shop before continuing our day's trek.

Winding eastward we turned back toward Snowdonia National Park, at one point stopping to allow two sheep to meander across the road. Slate mining covered a vast area and we marveled at one series of switchback trails used by miners to get up and down the sheer mountainside. We would never forget the stark beauty of Snowdonia. Grey slate slabs covered the mountainside for miles broken only by an occasional burst of color from wildflowers blossoming from the crevices.

Our drive back to Bodysgallen was extremely slow. First we encountered roadwork and then a string of tour buses too large for the narrow slate-lined roadway, one that nearly hit us. A large truck then held a string of cars hostage, moving at a painfully slow thirty-five mph. To add to the mix, more sheep in the road provided another delay. We looked forward to the his-and-her massages we had booked at our inn earlier in the day.

Tonight's dinner, tender slices of lamb served on a bed of fresh mushrooms, was simple and delicious. The apple tart that followed was also quite good. After dinner we strolled through the garden in the moonlight before returning to our spacious new room on the third floor. After last night's tiny turret room, it seemed like a palace.

Coffee and scones in our room started our day. This had become a habit. We then drove on the A470 to Llandudno, the village just north of us. Ll in Welsh is pronounced as cl so the town is actually pronounced Clandudno. On this overcast day the possibility of rain caught up with us. Although our trip notes proclaimed Llandudno a quaint little Victorian town with turn-of-the-century charm, we found it a bit tired. Tourism seemed its major claim to fame and hotels lined the streets near the harbor.

Our next stop took us seven miles south to Bodnant Garden, a multi-acre estate developed in 1874 by a wealthy landowner. He began by planting specimen trees and his descendants carried on the tradition. Although we missed the peak of the rhododendron season by a week, blooms remained on almost every bush. We wandered along numerous paths throughout the expansive park and thoroughly enjoyed our visit.

We consulted our guidebook for an interesting dining experience, which suggested that we watch for a sign on a large rock advertising Tan Y Foel Country Home Hotel in Capel Garmon. Its name meant *house under the hillside*, which perfectly described this award-winning Snowdonian hideaway. Missing it on our first pass, we backtracked and found its name on a small boulder with an even smaller sign nearly obliterated by tall grass.

Undaunted, we turned up the narrow road that led us to a slate farmhouse-turned-inn. The nine-room family-run inn had a small dining room with only eight tables. Unlike so many restaurants in Great Britain, we were delighted it did not permit smoking—our kind of place! We made a reservation for that evening and a mental note of the rock and sign.

We continued on to Betws y Coed and found a market for today's bread, cheese and cakes, adding banana muffins for tomorrow's breakfast. Then we drove along the A5 and into Snowdonia National Park on the A4086. Our route took us through incredible upland moors with stunning vistas of the peaks of the Cambrian Mountains in the background. As in Dartmoor, sheep were plentiful. On this hazy day the mountains in the foreground stood out clearly while those in the background remained shrouded in mist, creating an ethereal portrait.

We turned upland at the picturesque village of Beddgelert on A4085 and encountered more moors. Eventually the road followed a wide river that flowed along the base of sheer slate cliffs. We knew that Sir Edmund Hillary practiced for his historic Mount Everest climb in the Cambrian Mountains and now understood why he chose this challenging spot.

To avoid another drive through the bustling city of Caernarfon we took a detour to Savant and then hooked up with the A4086 to the southwest of Snowdonia. Along the way we made another short detour to Bryn Bras Castle which turned out to be privately owned. When we reached the A4086, breathtaking panoramic vistas of the Cambrian Mountains greeted us and we stopped at a park along the river for our picnic lunch. All went well until we realized we didn't have a knife and couldn't cut through the hard cheese.

Driving on to the next village, we stopped at a café for take-out coffees and plastic utensils. As we waited, the shop owner, a delightful fellow, told us about the area's history and a few interesting facts. Bryn, he told us, meant *hill*. Llan meant *church*. He also told us that Wales has a TV station devoted to the Welsh language, which is Celtic in origin but spoken with a French accent. We had noticed a cog railway and he told us it was a one-hundred-year-old Swiss system. The five-mile ride up the side of the slate cliffs and the return trip took two hours to complete.

Leaving the village, we stopped at a turnout for a second attempt at our picnic. Across the roadway we spotted an enormous cliff strewn with fragments of grey slate, sentinels of bygone mining days. At its base, narrow strips of pasture held more sheep. Snowdonia would always be associated in our minds with two "s" words: sheep and slate.

As we returned to the roadway a light rain began to fall. It didn't last long and we decided to take a longer route to Bodysgallen via the A5 heading northwest to Bangor. Driving through a valley with spectacular mountain ridges, we spotted several groups of hardy rock climbers. Two rappelers dangled precariously halfway up a vertical cliff just as the rain began to fall once more.

We soon reached the village of Bethesda. I had not realized how many American cities borrowed their names from the Welsh. Bryn Mawr, Bangor and even Yale have their origins in Wales. After many hours on the road we returned to our hotel.

Our 8:00 p.m. dinner at Tan Y Foel proved both delightful and delicious. While the owner's wife served as chef, her husband and an assistant took orders and chatted with the guests in this intimate setting. Roast lamb followed by a superb apricot tart with clotted cream provided a perfect finale for our visit to Wales.

After dinner the owner gave us a tour of some of the inn's rooms. The bright, playful and even theatrical décors astonished us. Each room had its own character and charm while the bathrooms were relatively new and quite modern. We concluded our evening with coffee in the sitting room.

After breakfast the next morning we took the four-lane A55 toward Chester, England. By now driver Wayne had had his fill of narrow roads. As we passed through more rolling countryside with our mystical harp music from Caernarfon Castle playing, we reflected on our incredible visit to Wales.

Re-entering Merry Old England at Chester, we drove to Manchester and continued almost 250 miles to Birmingham. We stopped for twenty minutes in Stafford, hoping to find a Staffordshire China shop. Alas, there were none. Driving on, we looked forward to our final destination, Cliveden House in Taplow.

Arriving mid-afternoon, we checked into our room, the Gilson, located on the top floor overlooking the front courtyard. It was large, graciously furnished and filled with charming details. Elaborate high ceilings added to the elegance. We were sure the rooms at the back of the manor overlooking the gardens were even more desirable—and priced accordingly.

This grand home constructed in the late 1800s by John Jacob Astor on a 375-acre tract sat on a bluff overlooking the Thames. Located just a few miles from Windsor, Cliveden made history in the 1960s as the site where Lord John Profumo had his little affair with nineteen-year-old Christine Keeler.

We met a business acquaintance and her husband at 8:00 p.m. for a leisurely three-and-a-half-hour dinner in the Cliveden dining room. Her husband was a professor of economics at Eton and we had stimulating conversations throughout our incredible meal.

One interesting note. Today was the anniversary of D-Day and we found no mention of it in the *London Times*.

Our final day in Great Britain began with an elegant breakfast buffet in the manor's dining room. We sat at the same table we had the previous evening and were treated to a spectacular view of the rolling gardens leading to the Thames River Valley.

Before checking out we took a walk through the estate to the bank of the Thames. Following a steep hillside trail, we made our way back to Cliveden. After showering and packing our bags, we stored them and had a light lunch before meeting our driver for the ride to Heathrow and our flight home. As the Brits would say, "Lovely!"

NEW ZEALAND & AUSTRALIA

Christchurch, Lake Rotoroa, Franz Josef Glacier, Queenstown, Wellington, Wharekauhau, Auckland, Lizard Island, and Sydney

November 5–23, 1998

THE IDEA OF EXPLORING New Zealand and Australia always intrigued us and we decided to finally turn this dream into reality. Having amassed a multitude of frequent flyer points, we treated ourselves to first-class seats for our twelve-hour flight to Auckland, New Zealand. An airline representative met us curbside at LAX to collect our luggage, escort us to passport verification and then led us to the first-class lounge. When it was time to board, we were ushered through a private entrance. Alas, the glory days of travel no longer exist and we treasure the memories of true first-class service.

Our seats reclined comfortably enough for five or six hours of sleep on our flight to the North Island. We had departed LAX on a Thursday and, having lost a day in transit with the time change, arrived at 7:30 a.m. on Saturday.

On our connecting flight to Christchurch, our final destination, we sat next to a delightful young man named James who hailed from Blenheim on the South Island. During the one-and-a-half-hour flight he answered many of our questions about his country and gave us travel tips. We planned to pass through Blenheim the following day and I asked James for a lunch suggestion. He drew a map and said, "Here is the best place." On the paper was a map to his family's home. We were unable to meet with him but this kind of New Zealand hospitality continued throughout our stay.

Our seatmate informed us that the northern part of the South Island had experienced record amounts of rainfall in recent days, but we were welcomed by bright sunshine as we arrived at Christchurch. After claiming our baggage, we headed to the rental car park and located our Ford Explorer. The name of the rental agency was emblazoned all over the exterior and we concluded that we were an easy mark as tourists. Its saving grace was an abundance of room for us and our luggage.

We arrived at the George Hotel just before 1:00 p.m. and since our room was not ready, opted for a quick tour of central Christchurch. Following a map from the front desk, we headed for the Botanic Gardens set along a small meandering river. We noticed several couples in boats skippered by punters dressed in whites and wearing straw hats. Since November in New Zealand is the equivalent of May in the U.S., we passed by gardens filled with pansies, zinnias and other spring flowers. Rhododendrons in full bloom added spectacular splashes of color throughout the park.

Heading toward the city center we came upon a square filled with vendors displaying a variety of handicrafts. Out of curiosity we strolled through and I bought a small carving of a pear to add to a bowl of wooden fruit in our family room. We added a few bars of goat's milk and honey soap and enjoyed chatting with the merchants.

Having transported an ample supply of Peet's coffee beans with us, we looked for a local department store to purchase a coffee maker and grinder wired for New Zealand and Australia. We're particular about our coffee and we've discovered from past travels that a coffee pot and grinder pay for themselves during our overseas visits. Following the advice of a street merchant we walked for a couple more blocks and found exactly what we needed.

Since it was well past lunchtime we stopped at a small, rather ordinary looking bakery-café. Signs proclaimed it the winner of the best bakery award in New Zealand for the past year. We ordered sausage rolls and a small quiche and quickly agreed that the shop's award was well deserved. Our lunch, including a latte and a cappuccino, cost only US$4.75. What a bargain!

Having scoped out the city center we walked to the town's cathedral square and stepped inside for a quick look before returning to the George to check into our room for a one-night stay. Once settled, we hopped into our trusty Explorer and drove to the outskirts of the city for a gondola ride to a viewing area high above Christchurch. The late afternoon sunshine made it difficult to see the city below us; however, the shipping port of Lyttleton, the original English settlement of the bay leading to Christchurch, glittered in the distance. We thoroughly enjoyed the ride up and down the hillside.

After returning to the hotel we walked back along the Avon River, hoping to find the location of the punters. By the time we reached the small wooden building that housed the boats we were too late to book a ride. It would have to go on our to-do list for a future visit.

Dinner at Pescatore on the second floor of the George did not disappoint us. The small restaurant featured some of the best seafood we'd ever tasted. My oysters, a variety only found in New Zealand and not exported, earned raves. Bluenose, a new fish in my vocabulary, proved equally delicious served over barley with a rich demiglace. Wayne's crab and scallop starter followed by local salmon also earned high marks.

Although we lost a full day in transit, our internal clocks only registered a three-hour time change so we were up and ready at 9:00 a.m. the next day for a seven-hour drive from Christchurch along the coast and then inland to Lake Rotoroa. Narrow two-lane highways with little room for error wound us through rolling hills covered with sheep. We had no problem believing that the ratio of sheep to people in New Zealand was indeed twenty to one.

A brilliant blue sky created the perfect backdrop for the rich green pastureland. Very few trees remained on the eastern edge of the center of the South Island and the only contrast to the blue-green hues came from dots of white sheep and occasional clusters of yellow gorse. As we traveled further north the hills became steeper and more forested. To our delight but to the dismay of most New Zealanders who regard it as a repugnant weed, golden flowers on the shrub-like broom plants blanketed much of the countryside. On a sunny day like this the effect was magical and we stopped along the way to take photographs.

Wayne drove with skill and apparent ease along the narrow winding roadways. As in England, one drives on the left-hand side. In our favor there was very little traffic. Although passing an occasional slow vehicle added challenges, he waited until the curving roadways straightened, allowing better visibility. On this day, as would be the case throughout our New Zealand drives, road kill far outnumbered other vehicles on the highways. New Zealand was not the place to be a small animal with friends on the other side of the road.

James, the young man who sat next to us on our Auckland to Christchurch flight, had mentioned how good the crawfish were in the resort/fishing village of Kaikoura. Since it was just before noon, we decided to take his advice and give it a whirl. Driving into the town we soon realized that (a) fishermen did not work on Sundays, and (b) in early November, the equivalent of early May in the U.S., the town hadn't yet geared up for tourists. At the very edge of town we found a small restaurant offering freshly cooked crawfish and we treated ourselves to a grand lunch.

Driving on we skirted the ocean for a good twenty miles. The color palate for today now included the brilliant turquoise of the water. We soon turned inland and drove another half hour before reaching the bustling town of

Blenheim. After a quick stop for gas we continued westward on Highway 63 in the direction of St. Arnaud. Blenheim's well-known vineyards bordered the road for many miles.

We were beginning to understand why New Zealand had so few people. Except for a few port cities and a rare valley like Blenheim, the land truly seemed best fit for grazing sheep. The beautiful rolling hills and higher, more rugged peaks allowed little space for towns or villages to develop. As a scenic paradise, however, New Zealand was unequaled.

Leaving the Blenheim valley, the road bordered gravel-covered dry river beds. Eventually small rivulets appeared. By the time we reached our destination, Lake Rotoroa, the Buller River had become a torrent. More broom added bright touches of color along its banks and on the distant hillsides. We noticed mile after mile of reforestation in the north central section of New Zealand, a testimony to a strong environmental commitment.

In late afternoon we arrived at Lake Rotoroa Lodge situated on the large lake at the mouth of the Gowen River running at an angle into the Buller. Bob Haswell, the owner-manager, met us as we parked the now-trusted Explorer and gave us a tour of the lodge's main floor. We were then taken to a corner suite facing the lake for our two-night stay. Popular for fly-fishing, this lodge ranked right up there in my book as a gracious resort. With only seven guest rooms, it offered an abundance of personal service and camaraderie.

Bob told us that we brought the sunshine after forty straight days of rain. Any more would have meant road closures due to imminent flooding. He cautioned us to stay on paths and pointed out that the front lawn had been under water until the morning of our arrival. We ventured into the surrounding woods hopping over puddles along the way. Native tree ferns, the first of many we would encounter, grew in profusion in the forest along with New Zealand podocarps and beech trees. The path we followed led us toward the lake nestled artistically into the surrounding mountains.

Dinner was served at 7:30 p.m. in the dining room. Since the building originated as a fishing lodge, one had the feeling of being at a sophisticated camp for grown-ups. Aside from two women who each dined alone by the window, the remaining guests sat family-style around a large central table. We chatted with two English couples who return every year, a couple from Boston and a man from Perth. After dinner we all gathered in the sitting room for coffee and Wayne and I picked up some interesting tips on Sydney and Lizard Island from the Boston couple.

What a day! We began with a full breakfast at 7:30 a.m. before meeting Peter, our guide from the nearby village of Murchison, for a day of fly fishing for New Zealand's challenging—and on this day, elusive—brown trout. We had expected to be fitted in wading boots that reached up to our hips. Instead we were asked to wear our own nylon pants and a pair of wool socks. The lodge furnished short lace-up boots. Wayne's were leather; mine were nylon mesh. No waders and tweeds in this country!

Peter drove about forty-five minutes to a river where he and the fellow from Boston had caught five brown trout the previous day. Stopping downstream a mile from yesterday's hot spot—he never fished the same location twice in a row—Peter explained that New Zealand rivers average only thirty fish per mile. Although there were fewer fish to catch, those that hit were big. We were about to learn the art of fly fishing from an expert in some of the world's best rivers.

Before stepping in, Peter taught us how to cast along the rock-strewn shore. Then he began to stalk the waters for calmer pools along the edge of the river where fish might lurk. Our new friend from Boston had marveled at Peter's ability to locate fish and we hoped that he would find his target again today. Although no rain ever fell, the sky was overcast and spotting fish was not an easy task. We waded for two hours practicing our casting and hoping that a wayward trout might meander by. No such luck.

Before leaving this stretch of the river, we sat along the rocky shore and enjoyed the lunch packed for us by the lodge. Then we hiked back to Peter's truck which we left in a neighboring cow pasture. Our next stop was a deeper and much swifter stretch of the river near Murchison. Just maneuvering down the steep, slippery bank was a challenge. The three of us then linked arms to keep our balance in the raging river as we crossed to the opposite bank. Interestingly enough, our soaked nylon pants shed the water and dried quickly. Our shoes stayed wet all day but the wool socks kept us warm in the frigid water. Keeping our balance as we straddled large rocks in the rapid current presented the biggest challenge.

By mid-afternoon with only one trout spotted in a shallow pool that was impossible to fish, Peter opted for the Gowen River not far from the lodge. It was almost 4:00 p.m. by the time we arrived. New Zealand's infamous sandflies attacked and this river was bitter cold and very swift. Determined that one of us catch a trout before sundown, Peter forged ahead. Wayne had a mighty hit and began to reel in a beauty that jumped out of the water twice. Then the clever fish swam under submerged logs and snapped the line. Ah, the one that got away…

Peter walked us to a tree-lined area with perfect, calm pools for trout. He cast once or twice and had a hit. Immediately he handed his rod to Wayne and let him reel in a nice three-pound brown trout. After a quick photo op, the trout was released. Sport fishing is the rule here and few catches are kept. In fact, when I later asked Bob if trout would be on the lodge's dinner menu, he told me it was illegal for him to catch or buy brown trout to serve his guests.

If a visitor wanted to keep a fish, he or she could bring it to the kitchen and the chef would then prepare it. Both Peter and Bob showed such respect for the brown trout that we never considered keeping any we might have caught. Even though we didn't have a good day of fishing, our reward was a sense of accomplishment for having mastered the technique of casting. The long day flew by and we both loved every minute of our introduction to the sport of fly fishing. We returned to the lodge at 6:30 p.m. exhilarated and eager to share our adventures with staff and guests.

After breakfast the next morning we said goodbye to the lodge and turned our faithful Explorer westward along New Zealand's roller-coastering Route 6 bordering the Buller River gorge. The drive twisted and turned through majestically scenic countryside. Flora became thick and dense, almost rainforest in appearance. Now-familiar tree ferns grew in clusters creating a tall umbrella-like canopy along the roadway. Touches of gold from the ever-present broom plants added bright color.

Often the road became so narrow that it seemed impossible for more than one vehicle to pass along it. At one point we took a chance and drove into a one-lane section chiseled out of a granite cliff. To add to the adrenaline rush the road curved sharply, making it impossible to see oncoming traffic. Just a few miles beyond it we passed a bus heading in the opposite direction, and didn't even want to contemplate what could have happened if it had been on our stretch of the road just minutes earlier.

There literally were no towns, no traffic, and not even sheep along the rugged Buller River gorge. After two hours we finally reached the west coast and came to the tiny village of Punakaiki, home of the famous Pancake Rocks. Not wanting to spend the half hour to walk to and from the rocks, we continued south along the Tasman Sea. This rugged stretch with huge monolithic rock formations rising from the sea reminded us of the Oregon coastline. Fog and a light mist hovered over us.

We drove into the port city of Greymouth in search of a restaurant and stopped at a small freshly painted hotel. Not a garden spot on the tour list! Served cafeteria-style, the food was barely edible and the average age of the handful of diners must have been eighty.

Road kill continued to outnumber passing cars at the rate of at least two to one. We later learned that most of the dead animals were what the New Zealanders called possums, although the shape and fur differed greatly from the American version. With traffic as light as it had been it seemed impossible for so many animals to perish on the roadways. The odds were definitely not in favor of possums. At one point along our way we had the unusual opportunity to stop while a duck crossed the road.

We soon headed inland and wound our way upward to Franz Josef. Upon entering the village, a large sign announced the Franz Josef Glacier Hotel. We pulled in to register, only to discover there were two Franz Josef Glacier Hotels and this one was not ours. We traveled just a few miles further to the correct location and registered for a two-day stay. The rooms in this tourist hotel were clean but sparse. Our view was of an enormous parking lot and by that evening we looked over rows of tour buses parked just outside our window. In its favor, the hotel was quiet and well located.

After walking through the village and booking a helicopter tour for the next morning we drove to an area with hiking trails near the foot of the glacier. We took a forty-five-minute trek along the Douglas Walk leading to the Waiho River spanned by a suspension bridge strung high above it. The area was sprinkled with more tree ferns and clusters of tropical plants. Juxtaposed with the icy background of the glacier it was a most unusual sight. After stopping back at the hotel for quick showers, we returned to the small village of Franz Josef and popped into the Blue Ice Café for pizza.

It rained during the night and a heavy fog obliterated the glacier as we headed for our scheduled helicopter tour. Just as we feared, the pilots were grounded until conditions improved. The only other option was a thirty-minute drive to Fox Glacier where the weather appeared to be more favorable. Not wanting to miss an opportunity for a bird's eye view of the two glaciers and Mount Cook, we scurried up the mountain road. To our delight the skies improved with each mile and by the time we took off in the chopper we enjoyed crystal clear vistas.

Wayne and I sat in front with the pilot for most of the forty-five-minute flight. In no time at all we skimmed across the face of Franz Josef with an awesome view of this mighty glacier. Then we turned back to Fox Glacier where the young pilot landed for a few minutes. Along with an Englishman in our chopper, we hopped out for a quick walk on the glacier surface. Mount Cook glittered in the background. This ride was a must for all visitors.

Returning to our little town by noon, we bought cheeses and crackers and some citrus bars, our new favorite treat, and drove to the hiking trailheads for a picnic lunch. We sat on a ledge high above the valley with a panoramic view. Then we raced back to the hotel to change into shorts and grab heavy jackets for our three-and-a-half-hour glacier walk.

The glacier climb ranked right up there on our all-time list of challenging experiences and proved to be a definite E-ticket hike. About twenty-five hikers gathered in the village where we were given thick wool socks, heavy boots and crampons to navigate the ice. Since the first part of our hike would have us cross a river of rocks, about a half mile walk to the start of the glacier, we tucked the crampons into our knapsacks for later use.

What looked beautiful from a distance became rather ominous at close range. However, we were in good physical condition and assumed that we could meet the challenge. When our head guide asked us to divide into three groups based on ability, in a moment of bravado Wayne and I opted for the most difficult climb. We would later question our sanity. The A Team, as we called ourselves, included nine or ten young travelers, all of whom could most likely complete the Boston Marathon. One young man was sailing around the world. Another had trekked through Australia and the South Pole. A couple from England were bicycling and camping all across New Zealand. And then there were Barbara and Wayne, two middle-aged glacier climbers.

Our copy of the New Zealand Handbook, which we read after the climb, best described the precarious trek. "If ice is stable," it stated, "the outfit supplies you with special boots and poles—and before you fully comprehend what's going on, you're in a line of courageous people scrambling up and down the pinnacles and jumping crevasses, a guaranteed adrenaline rush not recommended for chickens, with no turning back." Well said.

Mike, our absolutely fearless and, I might add, gorgeous leader, began the ascent via steps chiseled into the face of the ice that looked like they were carved for a giant. It was tough going right from the start. It soon became apparent why shorts were a must. As long pants would have been too confining on the ice floes, shorts truly were required to maneuver the steep, icy terrain. At some of the steepest points, ropes had been anchored to the ice wall so we could grab on and pull ourselves up the inclines.

Suddenly I felt like a character in the IMAX movie, *Everest*. There were ladders to scale and narrow wooden planks crossing deep crevasses to navigate. We had read signs stating the Franz Josef Glacier was one of the few in the world where amateurs were permitted. Nevertheless, this was no ordinary trek. I now knew that I was out of my league and offered to turn back and join a less rigorous group. The young climbers in our group encouraged me to continue with a "Come on, Mom! Go for it! We'll help you!" By now my hands and knees were bleeding but I again felt empowered and moved forward. Wayne, in macho fashion, seemed to be handling the challenges with ease.

After the first and steepest part of the ascent, we came to a box filled with wooden poles with pick axes at one end. We each took one for stability as we began to crisscross the huge waves of ice. Mike led us up and down the sides of the floe and taught us the Franz Josef shuffle, a tricky but essential method of cross-stepping while scaling steep ice cliffs. The object of this maneuver was to keep our posture erect so we remained parallel to the ice walls as we stepped into foot-sized indentations which Mike chiseled for us. A slight tilt forward might mean losing one's balance and some of the drops were indeed hazardous.

At times we cross-stepped along narrow bands at the tops of the ice ridges. Several of Mike's trails *du jour* had us straddling between two narrow ridges. He even took us below the surface of the glacier through a tunnel so narrow I was not sure I could negotiate the passage. To add to the challenge the tunnel floor consisted of blue ice and freezing water. Each of us had to hunker down and straddle the two sides of the cave in order to stay dry.

After almost two hours of our ascent, the descent seemed like a piece of cake. Well, almost. Some of the steeper declines presented a whole new set of challenges. I cut two fingers grabbing onto a piece of ice along the walls to keep from sliding into the climber in front of me. It was like a game of human bowling balls on ice.

We reached the bottom of the glacier with incredible feelings of exhilaration and accomplishment. Wayne was very proud that I was able to keep up with our young group of super athletes. I must confess that I, too, felt an unparalleled sense of pride. Age is relative and the two of us at fifty-four and fifty-seven did a first-rate job of keeping up with the twenty-somethings. We formed a bond with everyone in our group and we earned their respect for choosing the toughest route.

After stopping for coffee with the English cyclists who called me mom during the climb, we returned to our hotel to book a dinner. When we explained where we had been the receptionist handed us a key to a private Jacuzzi room and told us that it was ours for the next half hour. After our adventure-filled afternoon, nothing sounded better!

The sound of a bus revving its engines just outside our room at 7:00 a.m. worked like a charm to wake us the next day. With a healthy driving day ahead of us we wanted to get going early. We did our in-room coffee and yogurt routine and headed south along Route 6 on another overcast morning. From Franz Josef to Haast, a distance of nearly eighty miles, we passed only one small cluster of buildings.

For an hour or two we drove through rain, the first that we had experienced since our arrival. We never counted rain at night. Haast, for all the signs posted to announce it, proved to be another sleepy little village with a gas station, a few tattered buildings and a sprawling tourist hotel surrounded by buses on the outskirts.

As we drove through a spectacular national forest just beyond Haast, heavy rain began to fall. Along these steep, narrow roads we also encountered several groups of soggy cyclists. Wayne and I summed up this activity in three little words—not a vacation.

We had to admit that the forest was beautiful even in the rain. Rugged peaks bordered both sides of the road that paralleled the Haast River. We were treated to spectacular waterfalls at almost every turn. The river flowed rapidly on a downward course over huge boulders creating even more white-water vistas. As scenic as it was, we had difficulty accepting the fact that Route 6 is the main north-south highway through New Zealand.

The rain ceased at the crest of the Haast Pass and by the time we reached the Lake Wanaka Valley the sun had reappeared. We followed the lake on our right for miles and commented on its remarkable beauty and clarity. Soon a second lake, Hawea, appeared on our left. Both were a bright turquoise in the mid-morning sunshine. At the end of the lakes we came to the town of Hawea, the first real town since Greymouth.

Deciding not to stop for anything but a quick refill on gas, we drove through a large farming valley en route to Queenstown. We did a quick picnic-in-the-car with our remaining cheese and crackers and Wayne cruised along with virtually no traffic until he noticed a flashing blue light in the rear-view mirror. One of New Zealand's finest clocked him at twenty-five percent above the speed limit of one hundred km, or about sixty-five miles per hour in U.S. terms. Seeing that we were tourists with our well-marked rental car, he took heart and simply gave Wayne a warning.

Continuing on we soon came to the Kawarau Gorge, the pass leading into Queenstown. It is in this area that the world-famous bungee-jumping bridge spans the gorge high above the Kawarau River. I had contemplated taking the big plunge for several weeks and, as we neared the bridge, decided to go for it. We pulled into a parking area that was packed with cars and buses. Most of the saner people lingered along the wall of the gorge watching the crazies who paid big money to jump fifteen stories into thin air with nothing but a cord wrapped around their ankles. There I was, wanting to be one of those crazies.

I had heard that November 12 marked the tenth anniversary of the first bungee jump at the Kawarau Bridge, so it seemed the perfect day to do the deed. What I didn't know was that A.J. Hackett, the wild man who initiated the sport, wanted to break a world record for the number of bungee jumps in one day. All the tried-and-true locals were booked one after another and, by the end of the day, 330 had bungeed over the edge. A normal day, I guess, would be well under a hundred. After watching a few take the leap, I signed up as a novice for a 10:15 a.m. plunge the following day.

We reached Queenstown in fifteen minutes and were overwhelmed by this spectacular town. Nestled at the end of a large picturesque lake bordered by towering mountains on either side, it appeared to be the perfect resort spot. We later learned that it is called the adventure capital of the world with bungee jumping just one of many exciting opportunities. A visitor can water ski or parasail, tandem paraglide from the top of a mountain, go for a parachute jump, take a highspeed raft ride on the Shotover River, trek on numerous trails, and much, much more. For the less physically inclined, Queenstown is a place to shop or simply enjoy a walk along the lake.

We located our hotel, Nugget Point, on the outskirts of town above the Shotover River. After our last two nights in a large tourist hotel, this seemed like a palace. Each unit was a suite with a kitchen/living room. Although we were unable to get one with a river view, it really didn't matter. We found the staff attentive and friendly, the restaurant quite good and we particularly enjoyed the other guests we met. A feeling of family developed during our three-night stay and many of us gathered in the sitting rooms after dinner.

We were tired after a long day's drive and opted for dinner at the hotel. With tomorrow's bungee jump on both of our minds, Wayne referred to it as my Last Supper.

I awoke at 5:00 a.m. the next day contemplating the Big Jump—and wished that I could have done it yesterday on the spur of the moment. Having all this time to consider it left me a bit apprehensive. I reassured myself with the thought that I didn't have to go through with the jump once I returned to the bridge.

With that in mind, we headed back to the Kawarau Gorge. Yesterday's group of holdover novices all seemed to show up at the same time and there was quite a crowd ahead of me. Wayne paid the fee for the jump and an additional fee for photos and a video and then walked with me onto the bridge.

Watching jumpers from the outer wall yesterday was quite different from actually standing near the platform on the bridge perched 143 feet above the river. While waiting nearly twenty minutes for my turn to launch, Wayne and I chatted with a young man from South Africa who now lived in England. It made the time pass quickly.

Wayne returned to the viewing area along the wall to serve as resident photographer and I sat on the platform while a pony-tailed, ear-pierced macho man wrapped a towel around my ankles and wound a blue nylon strap around it. He attached the bungee cord to a clip on the strap and then helped me stand and hop on tethered feet to the starting point.

Talk about a reality check! I looked down and thought, "Oh, my God! What am I doing here?" Getting a grip—literally, with one hand on the rail and the other on the shoulder of macho man—I took a deep breath and said to myself, "You can do this!" I let go of the rail and my helper, waved and smiled at the cameras, focused on a bridge downriver and waited as macho man called out, "Five, four, three, two, one!" I then did a quasi swan dive into thin air.

Time almost stood still. It probably didn't take more than five seconds to drop to a point just inches above the river. At the end of the first drop I was surprised by how smooth the jump felt—not a jolt but a springing sensation. I was equally surprised by how high I shot back up as I flew past the trees alongside the river. By my third spring someone in the recovery boat below called out for me to grab the end of a long pole. Before I knew it, I was on my back in the rubber boat with the cheerful crew busily detaching the bungee cord.

Still flying high, I started up the winding steps to the top of the gorge. Wayne met me with lots of praise for my daring deed. We stayed to watch another couple of jumpers, including the young man we had met on the platform. Then we returned to the registration building to collect my video and commemorative T-shirt. My photo would be available at the Queenstown A.J. Hackett office the next day. Only later in the day did it dawn on me that I had taken my plunge on Friday the 13th.

We booked a four-hour helicopter tour of Milford Sound and surrounding areas for the next day before donning our hiking shoes for an afternoon trek. Mulling over several suggestions, we drove to the quaint but very touristy village of Arrowtown. A hike from this point did not appeal to us so we hopped back into our trusty Explorer for Plan B.

Once in Queenstown, we rode the gondola to the observation deck halfway up the mountain bordering the village. From there we took the Ben Lomond Trail, walking uphill in bright sunshine for nearly two hours. It was a hot, dry climb, but I was still fully charged with adrenaline after the bungee jump and walked at full speed. We climbed to the saddle and then followed a goat path to the crest, offering us a panoramic view of Queenstown far below us and the mountain range on the far side called the Remarkables. Needless to say, our joke was, "That's remarkable!"

From our lofty perch we could even see Arrowtown, many miles in the distance. After a ten-minute rest and many photos, we started the downhill leg. We passed only two groups of two all afternoon on this arduous trail and congratulated ourselves for accomplishing the climb.

A soak in the hotel's outdoor Jacuzzi was next on our to-do list, offering spectacular views of the Shotover River. We then dressed for dinner at the Bath House, a quaint circular waterside pavilion in Queenstown topped with a regal gold crown. We later learned that the charming building's official name is King George V Coronation Bath House and that just recently a capable chef had taken it over as a restaurant. Our meal was first-rate and we enjoyed watching the late sunset as we dined.

The next day offered us our first leisurely start in a week. After breakfast we fulfilled one of my New Zealand wishes, a visit to the Kiwi Birdlife Park to see these flightless birds. Since they are nocturnal the center reversed day and night in their dwelling. After waiting a few moments for our eyes to adjust to the darkness we spotted two of the North Island birds pecking at the soil in search of insects. These un-birdlike creatures were the size of a chicken and looked furry rather than feathered. They had small inoperative wings but we could not detect them.

Next we walked around the end of the lake and onto a shopping street. We ended up at the A.J. Hackett booking office at 11:00 a.m. to collect my bungee jump photo. Unfortunately, I had left the claim ticket at the hotel. After a forty-minute round trip to our hotel and back to the booking office, I had my unique souvenir.

Returning to the hotel, we had just enough time to get to the Nugget Point helicopter pad for our aerial tour of the Milford Track and surrounding areas. The wispy pilot with cropped blond hair, no makeup, and wearing jeans, a work shirt and boots shook our hands and introduced herself as Louisa in a husky voice that belied her stature.

Our raspy-voiced New Zealander turned out to be a hoot. She handled the Hughes 500 expertly and gave us a four-hour tour we would never forget. Joining us were a grandmother from northern California and her twenty-something granddaughter who lived in Hawaii. Louisa started out with a bang, skimming over rugged mountain peaks leading to the coast at such a close range that we were sure she would scrape the bottom of the chopper. After gliding over the razor-sharp peaks, she dropped into the valleys below, giving us the sensation of a roller-coaster ride. This was definitely an E-ticket trip.

When we reached the Milford Track she skimmed over it and pointed out its significant features. As appealing as it looked, it is home to the dreaded west coast sandflies. Wayne did not react to these pests but I had a few bites from several days earlier that were still driving me wild. The helicopter tour of Milford gave us a birds-eye view of the trek without encountering a single stinging bite.

We passed over spectacular waterfalls along the trail en route to Milford

Sound and landed for a brief look at the picturesque fiord leading into the ocean surrounded by mountains shrouded in fog. After refueling, Louisa—Choppy, as she was known in the Queenstown area—followed the length of the Milford Sound to the ocean. Along the way she pointed out steep waterfalls that seemed to stop at midpoint. She explained that strong winds literally reversed the direction of the flowing water.

Following the coast to the south, Louisa landed the chopper in the midst of a seal rookery. We were quite taken by the young pups frolicking in the shallow pools like miniature porpoises. They shot out of the water in graceful arches and then slid under the surface without a hint of fear. Those more curious came close enough for us to look into their dark eyes. A group of pregnant seals gathered in shallow pools waiting to give birth to the next generation. Unlike the pups, they were visibly unhappy with our visit and we stayed together in a group to prevent them from attacking us.

Choppy then flew us back into the mountains where we landed on a pristine glacier, one of three thousand in New Zealand. We hopped around, sometimes sinking up to our knees in the melting snow cap, and tossed a few snowballs before re-boarding the helicopter.

Our final stop was a deserted sheep farm dating back to the turn of the twentieth century. Louisa knew the owner who seldom came to the log cabin dwelling on the property. She set up lunch for us on a weathered picnic table overlooking mountains on one side and rolling foothills on the other. She occasionally flew the owner gratis and in return was allowed to bring guests to his property. We appreciated his generosity and enjoyed this unique experience.

Our helicopter traveled at a hundred miles per hour and maneuvered in a straight line over the terrain. Our ten-minute ride to Milford Sound would have taken two-and-a-half hours by car or bus. Likewise, our few minutes' tour of the Sound provided us with a spectacular view that would have taken two hours to see by boat. We also did the Milford Trek in a few short minutes. In just four hours we were given the tour of a lifetime.

Louisa returned us to Nugget Point at 4:30 p.m. and Wayne and I drove to Queenstown for one final walk through the village. As touristy as it was, we were captivated by its attractive streets filled with high quality shops and restaurants. When we reached the lake, we returned to the Bath House for cappuccinos, then strolled through the public gardens on a peninsula just beyond. The old coal-driven steam ship that had been a mere speck in the water from yesterday's mountaintop perch sailed by us in all its majesty.

We returned to the hotel to soak in the Jacuzzi before our dinner at Gantley's, a historic farmhouse-turned-restaurant just a short walk from

Nugget Point. Although the ambience was warm and inviting, the food did not measure up to our expectations. As we walked the short block back to our hotel at 10:00 p.m. not a single car passed us. LA this definitely wasn't.

The next morning, we said farewell to Queenstown after filling a large box with a week's worth of warm clothing to ship back to the States. In spite of the purging, my suitcase still weighed a ton. We then drove the short distance to the Queenstown airport and turned in the Explorer. It had served as a good companion during the 950 miles we put on it.

The first leg of today's journey took us back to Christchurch where we boarded a flight to Wellington. On this clear day the vistas from the plane's windows were breathtaking. Wayne looked out over the Kaikoura mountain range and I tried unsuccessfully to spot a whale or two in the turquoise coastal waters.

As we approached Wellington on the southern tip of the north island, its idyllic setting charmed us. The city was situated on a large bay with homes tucked into the rolling hills surrounding it. Sailboats dotted the water on this breezy, clear afternoon. We later learned that it often rained in Wellington and that it was nicknamed the Windy City. On our arrival day, conditions made it picture perfect.

Wayne had arranged for a helicopter ride to complete our journey from Wellington to Wharekauhau, our sheep farm destination. The drive over less-than-ideal roads could have taken up to two hours but we arrived in a bright red Squirrel in just under twelve minutes. Andy, our pilot, met us when we landed in Wellington and drove us to a wharf in the harbor to board the chopper. In no time at all he set us down on the gracious lawn of Wharekauhau.

Victoria, the daughter of owners Bill and Annette Shaw, greeted us in front of the main lodge as we stepped down from the helicopter. A charming young mid-twenties gal, she remembered our next-door neighbors in San Marino who had stayed there and recommended the resort to us. Our friends Judy and John had been the second international guests to visit the farm seventeen years earlier. At dinner that evening Annette brought out the first guest book and shared Judy's glowing comments with us.

After checking in at the lodge we were escorted to Room #3, a bungalow overlooking a grassy sheep pasture bordering the bay. An overwhelming feeling of tranquility settled over us. The Shaws listened to their guests over the years and combined the results with their own good taste, creating a near-perfect environment. We felt as though we were in a seaside cottage with every comfort we needed.

The original four-guestroom farmhouse had been moved to another section of the farm and an architectural gem of a Georgian lodge now occupied its location. Officially opening along with ten guest bungalows the previous January, it was perfection. The lodge served as the central gathering place for breakfast, lunch and dinner and each night we met in the cozy living room for cocktails and camaraderie.

After unpacking for our three-night stay we took an hour's walk on a road through pastures leading to the beach. The shore of Palliser Bay consisted of black gravel and sand. Tucked at the base of a steep bluff were a considerable number of small austere dwellings. We later learned that Wellington families had built these simple cottages. Ironically, as placid as the area seemed, the water had such a strong riptide that it prohibited swimming. Shoreline casting and walks along the beach had to suffice.

Returning to the lodge for dinner we met two charming Wellington couples who had spent the weekend participating in the local food and wine festival. This accounted for the more-than-full house of twenty-two guests this Sunday evening. Another sixty-something couple from Pennsylvania joined our table for dinner and told us they often come to Wharekauhau. Over our five-course dinner we had ample time to discover much more about New Zealand.

As we walked to our bungalow after dinner we marveled at the vast number of stars in the sky. With no other lights to obscure the view, the Southern Cross twinkled above us along with a myriad of unfamiliar south-of-the-equator constellations.

After breakfast the next morning we met James Shaw at the lodge for a half-day tour of the farm. The Shaws have three children: James, the oldest who concentrates on guest activities, John, who manages the farm and Victoria, a trained chef who interfaces with guests and helps in the office.

James' love of Wharehauhau immediately became apparent. A bright, handsome young man, he talked with passion and conviction about sheep and cattle farming in New Zealand. His family's farm consisted of seven thousand acres. After driving us along pastures and explaining the history of the farm's Romney sheep and Hereford cattle, he took us to a native forest now protected by the government. James spent well over an hour leading us through and pointing out the names of each plant and tree, some with exotic Maori names such as ti, manuka and kanuka. We wandered past an 800-year-old rimu tree, black and silver tree ferns and thick vines called Super Jack used by the Maori for furniture and baskets. James' admiration for the forest was contagious and his knowledge, enlightening.

As we continued through the farm, James told us more about the famous Wharekauhau Romney sheep and how they were bred. Romney are large, gentle animals with an abundance of white fleece. At this time of year lambs surrounded the ewes. Through selective breeding most ewes had two offspring. Only rams that were a twin or, more rarely, triplet, were kept as studs. The rest were destined to become chops. The lambs in the pasture, now three months old, would soon be weaned from their mothers. This was not an ideal time to be a guest because the ewes wandered for days calling out for their missing lambs. Afterwards, they would simply forget and go on with life on the farm until the next breeding season.

We concluded our three-hour tour with a drive through the family's latest land acquisition, Wharepapa. This 2,000-acre farm lay directly to the north and was home to both pastureland and more protected forest. For our finale James took us on a wild shoreline tour, maneuvering his Toyota Land Cruiser with skill over the rocky terrain.

After returning to the lodge for a late lunch in the family-style kitchen, Wayne rejoined James at 2:45 p.m. for a few hours of ocean surf-casting along Palliser Bay. I opted to relax in our luxurious room, catch up on my postcards and trip notes and simply reflect on our New Zealand adventure. To date the trip had surpassed all expectations. There simply was not enough time to experience all this enchanting country had to offer. We often found ourselves saying, "We'll do that when we come back." New Zealand was meant to be experienced, not merely visited. Not to diminish its abundance of natural beauty, it was nevertheless an adventurer's paradise.

Wayne returned from his surf-casting expedition without so much as a nibble from a sea trout. We decided to take advantage of the beautiful late afternoon with a walk through some of the grazing pastures. The sheep seemed oblivious to our presence and only scurried away when we approached a bit too close for their comfort.

At dinner that evening we discovered that we were one of only two couples now at Wharekauhau—quite a change from yesterday's full house! Joining us and the Seattle couple were Bill and Annette and Suzanne Turley, a premiere New Zealand landscape architect. Bill, my seatmate, kept me spellbound with tales of how he and Annette developed the sheep farm into a premiere tourist venue. They did it well enough for Andrew Harper to rate Wharekauhau as the number one small resort in the world.

Nevertheless, Bill told me, both farming and operating a resort were difficult businesses, and he had the toughness and savvy to make anything work. Before buying Wharekauhau he played rugby until age twenty-eight. Although rather short in stature he exuded strength. When he married Annette, a nurse, they pursued his dream to become a sheep farmer and hers to operate a small inn. No one did it better than the two of them. Wayne sat near Annette and after dinner we both commented on the lovely, intimate evening we had shared with the Shaws.

We joined the two other guests for breakfast in the country kitchen before collecting a picnic for today's coastal tour. Retracing our first day's beach walk, James drove his Land Cruiser expertly onto the rocky shore. We then forged the Mukamuka, or Big Lizard, a stream that flowed to the bay from a 3,000-foot peak, the highest point on the farm property. Stopping to unlatch a series of gates across the treacherously narrow path that sometimes seemed to balance on the edge of the cliffs bordering the bay, we rode for nearly an hour through Wharekauhau and then through land leased by the Shaws for extended grazing.

The vistas were spectacular. Winding up and down along the coast, we traveled for miles along Palliser Bay. To the west, rolling hillsides reached toward the more rugged peaks. In this region, cattle roamed and grazed in some of the most idyllic pastureland we had ever encountered. On our return route, James detoured to a steep hillside bluff for our panoramic picnic.

Once back at the farm center, James took us to the shearing shed for a demonstration. Just then Bill drove past us in a dune buggy with a toy poodle sitting on his lap. In retrospect we wish we had captured this macho man and his fluffy little dog on film. We saw James' brother John from a distance as he herded a group of sheep into the enclosure with his sheepdog, but he disappeared before we had an opportunity to meet this elusive Shaw.

We watched as fifteen or twenty ewes and lambs were herded into a pen. As he sharpened his tools, James explained the shearing process. Then he selected a ewe with a thick coat and brought her into the shearing area through a small door in the pen. In less than five minutes her coat was expertly removed in one large piece. James then repeated the process on a second ewe.

We had an opportunity to feel the fleece before the flock of corralled sheep returned to the pasture. James told us that the price for wool was down so there was not much of a profit in the then-current market. When we asked how many sheep could be sheared in one day, he said that professionals could handle about three hundred. His own record of 218 left him exhausted.

We returned to the lodge just after 3:00 p.m. for cappuccinos on the patio. As we sat in the garden at the back of the lodge we were joined by Bill and his poodle along with Annette and Victoria. We took photos of the Shaws to share with our San Marino neighbors.

Returning to our cottage we packed another box to ship to the States, lightening our suitcases sans the hiking boots and jeans. We then sat for nearly two hours on our cottage patio while we read and watched the sheep meander across the meadows.

Tonight's guests numbered six with the addition of a couple from Sydney on assignment from *Small Hotels of the World*. A spunky gal named Susie served drinks and appetizers to the guests. She was James' girlfriend of five years and the two of them lived in a small house on the farm. Bill and Victoria joined us but Annette bowed out for the evening. Bill's captivating smile and impish twinkle charmed us and Wayne and I agreed that James had inherited much the same personality.

Surprisingly, we never were served lamb or beef during our three-day visit. Instead we dined on salmon, venison and duck, each accompanied by delicious embellishments. Every meal was superb.

On a dare from Bill, we set our alarm for 4:00 a.m. to watch the Leonid meteor shower which occurred only once every thirty years. We sat outside gazing upward and did see a shooting streak or two in a fifteen-minute time span. Deciding that the meteor shower was a bit of a fizzle, we went inside for a few more hours' sleep. When we met Bill the next morning, he agreed that it was less than thrilling and later learned that the real show had occurred closer to 3:00 a.m. I don't think we'll return in another thirty years to catch the next one.

After another anything-you-want breakfast in the lodge kitchen we hopped into the helicopter for our return trip to the Wellington Airport. Suzanne Turley and Bill came out to bid us farewell, Annette had given us a hug a bit earlier, and Victoria and James were taking a few well-deserved days of rest.

I later learned that twenty years after our visit, US investor Bill Foley wanted to expand his growing wine business in New Zealand. While enjoying some down time, he and his wife Carol fell in love with Wharekauhau and became the proud owners of the lodge and farm six months later.

Our quick flight in the now-familiar red chopper took us directly to the airport. We were able to change our 2:00 p.m. scheduled flight to an earlier one departing at 12:30 p.m., giving us more time to explore Auckland, our next destination. We were thrilled to have been able to change our schedule as we looked out over the rolling hills of the North Island on our one-hour flight.

On a recommendation from Bill and Suzanne, we changed our hotel reservations from the Stanford Plaza to the Carlton Hotel. Apparently, smoking was still permitted at the Stanford but not at the Carlton. Another option was the Key West, an apartment hotel, but it was fully booked.

Suzanne had been a prominent fashion designer in Auckland before switching gears to landscaping, her real passion, and gave us shopping tips as well as the name of her favorite Auckland restaurant, where we booked a reservation before leaving Wharekauhau.

The drive from the airport to our hotel was extremely slow due to traffic snarls. After two weeks on nearly deserted country roads we had almost forgotten about urban gridlock. Once registered and shown our suite for this evening's stay, we ventured out to do a bit of exploring. We took a taxi ride to Auckland's Newmarket area which reminded us of LA's Melrose Avenue. The shops leaned toward slightly funky with an appeal to the younger crowd. I was in desperate need of a manicure and found a place to get one. It was now 4:00 p.m. and we scurried to the end of the shopping district to the Trelise Cooper Boutique recommended by Wharekauhau guests from Wellington.

Although still borderline funky, the designer knew how to make clothes that worked for twenty-somethings as well as fifty-somethings. I put together an outfit with soft black pants and a sheer flowing asymmetrical jacket, adding a black lace blouse and a bright green stretch top to complement the ensemble.

We continued on toward Parnell, an upscale suburb near Auckland's famed harbor. By the time we reached it the shops were closed for the day, but window shopping worked for me after my earlier spending spree. We enjoyed browsing in this vibrant area of boutiques, specialty shops, cafés, and restaurants and looked forward to returning that evening for dinner.

Dressing somewhat formally for the first time in many days, I donned my new ensemble and we retraced our earlier route to Parnell for our 7:30 p.m. dinner at Antoine's. This was one of Suzanne Turley's Auckland favorites and we soon learned why. We were led into a small dining area with one other table set for a group of ten or twelve. At first I was disappointed to be in an area with a large party but it turned out to be a sophisticated group of yachting representatives from New Zealand, the States and Canada discussing the next year's America's Cup Race.

Suzanne had called the restaurant owners, Tony and Beth Astel, and asked them to take special care of us. Beth introduced herself and welcomed us to Antoine's. She was charming and chatted with us at length. Hailing from Christchurch, the couple opened their Auckland restaurant in 1979. Tony closes the doors for a month or two each year and travels around the world in search of new cuisine. Tonight's menu offered a variety of tempting choices. Wayne's lamb and my venison provided a perfect grand finale for our New Zealand tour. Passing the open kitchen as we exited, we thanked Tony for an incredible dinner.

The next day's wake-up call came at 4:30 a.m. and we met our driver a half hour later for our flight to Cairns, Australia. With a three-hour time change from New Zealand to Australia, we departed at 7:00 a.m. for our flight and also arrived at 7:00 a.m. Our connection to Lizard Island was delayed from 11:00 a.m. to 2:30 p.m. and by the time we reached our hotel we had chalked up a fourteen-hour day of travel.

The views from the window on our flight taking us over the Great Barrier Reef made us acutely aware that our long travel day would be worthwhile. An abundance of pale green reefs looked like submerged islands tinged with a band of brilliant turquoise. Unlike anything we had ever seen, the reefs exuded natural beauty.

We finally arrived at Lizard Island, about eighty miles north of Cairns. It was so named by Captain Cook when he passed it in 1770 and saw no other animals but lizards, and plenty of them. The resort had been highly recommended because it was well out of the range of the many Cairns day cruises. Landing on this tiny speck in the ocean proved to be an adventure in itself. As we circled for our landing Wayne noticed a submarine just off shore. We later learned that the Australian Navy conducts training missions nearby. Judging from the myriad reefs just below the surface, it must have been risky business.

A small bus met us at the landing strip and shuttled us to the Lizard Island Resort. We registered for Room #2, a deluxe cottage at the edge of the property on Sunset Beach. Intentionally sparse, the large room had a Zen-like feel and the front patio overlooked the ocean through a veil of tropical plants. The hazy sunsets that followed each day were sensational. Serene proved to be the operative word on Lizard Island.

We wound our way back to the main lodge for drinks on the patio with the other new arrivals, and chatted with a couple from Bonn, Germany, and another from Australia, all of our vintage. Then we returned to our room to change into swimsuits for a late afternoon dip and a peek at a reef or two close to shore. With snorkels and fins rented from the lodge we followed the steep path to Sunset Beach. Choppy water and late afternoon sun obscured the reefs but the warm salt water refreshed us after a long day of travel.

Dinner was served on the lodge veranda overlooking the bay. In spite of being a long way from anywhere, our meals were very good. The winner was ocean trout and Wayne gallantly swapped his for my lackluster veal chop. We decided that fish would be our choice for the duration of our stay. After dinner we strolled along the beach and watched brilliant flashes of lightening in the distance.

Although a healthy electrical storm roused Wayne in the middle of the night, I slept right through it. To our delight we awoke to a clear sunny morning. We had been told the night before that our dive/snorkel trip was iffy at best given the weather conditions, but learned at breakfast on the veranda that it was a go. The group for the day trip to Cod Hole soon congregated at the bay and we were ferried to a forty-foot fishing boat for our next adventure.

Our first stop, called No-Name Cove by our guides, was located about forty-five minutes from Lizard Island. We spent nearly two hours on this spectacular reef. Although it was a hazy day, we marveled at the colors of the coral—rose, pink, salmon, green, blue, and gold. Small fish in brilliant colors swam over the shallow reefs and deep purple-blue starfish added to the natural beauty. Giant clams with undulating aqua lips appeared from time to time. The setting was simply breathtaking and we snorkelers were convinced that the divers were missing great sights.

Our companions for the day were an Estonian woman, a couple from Montreal, a spunky English woman and her German husband, a couple from Germany, newlyweds from New York City, a couple from Belgium, and another from Massachusetts who kayaked from Cairns to Lizard Island. We all became acquainted over an incredible shipboard lunch.

After lunch our captain weighed anchor and headed for the world-famous Cod Hole. We waited while the divers made their way to the bottom and sat still in their underwater theater. Then we snorkelers floated above them for a show that we will long remember. One of the diving guides carried a container of fish to the bottom and soon a swarm of 200-pound potato cod, so called because of the large brown potato-like spots on their white bodies, approached.

The guide began to chum the cod with an occasional fish pulled from the container and the other divers gathered around her. We had been told that the fish were friendly and, with caution, could be stroked. Several of the divers did just that. Pulling fish from the container, the guide began to lead one or two of the huge fish toward the snorkelers at the surface. Five or six of us encircled her and reached out to pet these incredible creatures. I managed to make contact with one of the fish and it felt almost like velvet.

When the guide finished with the chum and the potato cod swam away, we followed the edge of the reef for some distance and swam directly above a number of five-foot white-tipped sharks. They appeared beneath us singly or in twos and we trusted our guides' advice that these creatures presented no danger to us. As we glided above them, it was nevertheless an eerie sensation. I also spotted a sea turtle and then the head of the largest eel I had ever seen. I later learned that an enormous eel did indeed reside on the edge of the reef.

The boat returned to the hotel at 3:30 p.m. with our new group of friends reveling in our adventures. A small dinghy came out to transport us to shore. Not all of us could fit in it, so Wayne and I waited with another couple and watched one of the crew toss the seafood shells from our lunch overboard. In an instant, two 500-pound grouper appeared for the handouts. Amazing!

Wayne and I sat on the beach in the late afternoon sun and ventured out to some of the reefs along the bay. Nothing, however, could match the absolute beauty of No-Name Cove and Cod Hole.

That evening we met Angie, the English woman, and her German husband Gerrit for drinks and decided to share a table for dinner. We were the last guests to leave and we talked of other memorable travels and of our new vacation homes—theirs in the Cotswolds and ours on Rincon Beach near Santa Barbara. It was a lovely end to a perfect Lizard Island day.

Another nighttime storm resulted in a clear but very windy morning. We had hoped to arrange for a dinghy to do a bit of exploring around some of the small islands not far from shore. This was still possible but we had to take a bus to the Blue Lagoon on the opposite side of the island near the airstrip. We soon learned that this remote airstrip doubled as the road to the beach.

After a healthy twenty-minute walk along a path to the lagoon we boarded our dinghy, an aluminum three-seater with a tiny outboard motor. Moving at a snail's pace we headed out to sea toward two small islands. Our destination was an inviting strip of beach but as we approached, we noticed two other dinghies were already anchored on it. One of the guests took advantage of the semi-private beach and opted to sunbathe in the nude. We continued on in search of our own private beach.

We soon realized that the best beach was just around the bend from the Blue Lagoon right on Lizard Island. Putt-putting to a pristine stretch of sand, we set up the picnic lunch the resort provided. After lunch we cruised along the reefs in search of a good spot to snorkel. In this part of the world it didn't take long and we spent some time in the water looking down on a rainbow of coral formations along with some brilliantly colored tropical fish.

Deciding that we'd had enough sun for the day we returned to the lagoon at 3:00 p.m. for a bus ride back to the resort. However, we were in for a slight delay. Because an incoming flight was due within the hour the bus could not use the runway-turned-roadway until it had landed. We had to wait an hour for our short ride home.

Every Saturday evening the resort hosts a cocktail hour for guests and we joined in the festivities. While talking with Angie and Gerrit we noticed a group of six new guests who had been at our hotel in Franz Josef. We compared notes on our doings since parting ten days earlier and chatted so long that Wayne and I ended up being seated at the last available table, which was on the edge of the veranda. Halfway through dinner it began to sprinkle. I had a section of the roof above me to serve as an umbrella but Wayne did not and he scooted to the inner edge of the table. Fortunately, the rain was short-lived.

We awoke to another beautiful day in paradise. As I peered out of our front window, a large boat cruised by towing a string of dinghies. That meant that the water had calmed enough for guests to board the dinghies from the resort. No waiting for plane delays today.

The standard fourteen-seat plane didn't leave Lizard Island until mid-afternoon so we chartered a plane leaving at 9:30 a.m. After saying our good-byes we arrived at the airport in time to watch our pilot land on the narrow runway. We boarded the small Italian four-seater flown by a pilot from Cape York. Wayne sat with him in the cockpit, and a suitcase and I shared the two seats in back for the one-hour flight. It was a treat to fly relatively low in our prop plane—eight thousand feet at 155 miles per hour—and the pilot took us directly over the string of reefs for the entire route.

Once at the Cairns airfield we taxied right to the departure terminal for our next flight. While Wayne waited for our luggage, I went to get our boarding passes. Since the plane would be boarding in five minutes we were on a tight schedule. I joked for a bit with the man behind the first-class check-in counter, then asked for an exit row for my extra-long legs. As he handed me the boarding passes, he said, "I think you'll have plenty of leg room," with a grin. Indeed we did with upgrades to row two in first class for the three-hour flight to Sydney.

We touched down in Sydney at 3:00 p.m. after the leisurely flight and met our driver for a comfortable ride into the city and the Park Hyatt Hotel. Within an hour we were checked into our room with a view of the harbor overlooking Sydney's world-famous Opera House.

We began a magnificent walk along the waterfront past a row of restaurants, sidewalk cafés, shops, cruise and ferry boat docks, and finally the Sydney Opera House. To our dismay, late on a Sunday was not the time for a tour. The doors were locked. Before leaving the States, we attempted to book an opera but there were no Sunday performances. Next time…

We spent quite a bit of time wandering around the circumference of the building inspired by sailing ships in the harbor. Danish architect Jorn Utzon won a design contest in 1956 and it took fourteen years to complete the structure. We then walked to an area called The Rocks and picked up a few gifts.

We returned to The Rocks for dinner that evening at a hot new restaurant called Bel Mondo. Finding the out-of-the-way spot was no easy task, even with directions from our concierge. After asking several people en route, we finally found a series of exterior steps that led us to the newly constructed rooftop eatery. It didn't take long for us to applaud the effort we had made to get here. The ambience, service and food were excellent. I ordered bugs, my new favorite Australian cuisine, a cross between lobster and crawfish. Best of all were the fried zucchini flowers with Tasmanian cheese. What a perfect finale for our days in Australia!

As luck would have it, we awoke to a drizzly overcast day. Assuming that the weather would hold for a few more hours we walked to the cruise ship dock for a Cook Harbor Cruise tour. As two of only a handful of passengers we had our pick of the upper deck seats and never felt a drop of rain. Yesterday's afternoon cruises had been packed and we agreed that a morning tour on a weekday was the only way to go.

When the tour ended, we raced back to the hotel to collect our luggage and meet our driver for our ride to the airport. While driving we talked about how much this trip had meant to us. We not only saw, we experienced. Our New Zealand and Australian adventures included so much—fly fishing in freezing rivers, glacier hiking, trekking, E-ticket helicopter rides, a bungee jump for me, life on a luxurious sheep farm, and snorkeling on the Great Barrier Reef. It was truly amazing for anyone but even more so for these two mid- to late-fifty-somethings.

Adding to the most interactive vacation that we had ever experienced was the friendliness of the people we met in both countries. We would long remember the spectacular scenery, the charisma of the Kiwis and Aussies and the unending list of exciting activities both countries had to offer.

CHINA

Beijing, Badaling, Great Wall of China, Xian,
Terra Cotta Warrior Pits, Wuhan, Yueyang, Yichang, Three Gorges Dam,
Wushan, Three Lesser Gorges, Wanzian, Chongqing, and Shanghai

September 21–October 10, 1999

MY ONLY TIME IN CHINA consisted of a quick two-day visit to Hong Kong in 1986 and I wanted to experience the Yangtze River and its treasures before the completion of the Three Gorges Dam and the first inundation. When I read about a tour sponsored by the University of Michigan that included a river trip, my husband Wayne encouraged me to go. Cashing in a multitude of frequent flyer miles, I booked a first-class ticket to Hong Kong and embarked on a nineteen-day tour. My thirteen-hour flight departed on Tuesday at 11:55 p.m. LA time and I settled in for a long night in the air. At some point we crossed the International Date Line and the plane touched down in Hong Kong's sparkling new airport at 5:20 a.m. on Thursday morning. Wednesday had simply disappeared.

Opened less than twelve months earlier, the airport was indeed impressive. However, it seemed someone must have decided that luggage carts would meddle with its feng shui. Carrying my weighty bags, I trudged for what seemed like a mile to my connecting flight to Beijing. Once at the gate I met several fellow U of M travelers and we soon completed the last leg of our long journey. A spectacular view of the Hong Kong Harbor appeared below us upon takeoff. As the last high rise disappeared, the terrain turned into rugged low mountains with a river flowing through it. Spotting an occasional small village from my 35,000-foot perch, I wondered where China's billions lived. It certainly wasn't in this picturesque region.

Since Beijing lies at the northern end of China, those of us who landed in Hong Kong had to do a bit of backtracking to get there. Most of our group traveled from Detroit on a nonstop flight and were scheduled to arrive later in the day. Those of us who traveled from LA arrived in Beijing six hours earlier with ample time to settle into our hotel, the Shangri-La.

Fred, our Chinese in-country guide, met us at the airport. As we bused into the city, he shared some interesting facts with us. In 1999, there were thirteen million people living in greater Beijing, an area approximately the size of Belgium. The residents owned nine million bicycles. China's currency was the yuan and at the time one U.S. dollar equaled 8.27 yuan. It was easier for me to multiply the cost in yuan by twelve; ten yuan equaled US$1.20.

The Shangri-La sat on one of Beijing's outer rings. After unpacking I ventured out along the bustling roadway in search of bottled water. The hotel did not offer it and Tom, our American tour director, assured me it was safe to walk in the area. Fred recommended a small market a few blocks from the hotel. I walked along a sidewalk bordered by a sea of autos and buses mixed with nonstop bicycle traffic. A formidable-looking guard stood stiffly at the gate of a construction site not far from the hotel and I scurried past him. I finally reached the market which proved to be a small roadside stand. With no English spoken here I did my best pantomime of swimming and then of drinking. In no time at all a bottle of water appeared from behind the counter. I held up six fingers and soon had a bagful of purified water. Or so I hoped…

That evening I joined the two couples I had met on our connecting flight out of Hong Kong for dinner in the hotel. A large bowl of noodles and broth did the job for each of us after a long day (or was it two?) of travel.

Sometime during night the rest of our group of twenty-five arrived and we all gathered for breakfast. Tom, Fred, and a couple representing the University of Michigan introduced themselves. We also met Dr. Mei-yu Yu, who was born in the city of Chongqing and studied medicine in China before emigrating to the States. She was currently with Michigan's School of Nursing. We then boarded buses to visit the Temple of Heaven.

I have to confess the Temple of Heaven blurs a bit as I attempt to pull it out of my memory bank. The evil jet lag god did its best to obliterate most of the morning. I do recall groups of locals practicing tai chi, playing hacky sack with shuttlecocks, walking birds in cages, families with children, and tour groups in abundance. A profusion of flowers set in concentric circles around monuments created a festive mood. On closer inspection of one of the colorful flower circles I noticed that each remained in its own pot. We would see carefully placed clusters of potted flowers throughout our visit to

China. In some locations these arrangements appeared to grow out of cement.

As we drove to the infamous Tiananmen Square, we passed a large vacant area filled with military-looking floats. Fred told us they were to be part of next week's fiftieth anniversary celebration of the People's Republic of China. When we signed on months ago for our tour, none of us realized the significance of the October 1st celebration and it later turned out we could not have chosen a better time to be here. The festive mood continued throughout our journey.

In preparation for the anniversary, Beijing residents were ordered to shut down factories and restrict driving in the city in an effort to clear the usual layers of thick smog. Braziers, all too common in the streets of China, were currently forbidden in Beijing. The Chinese leaders knew their country would get media coverage for this significant event and they wanted the world to see it at its finest. That meant clean air. Consequently, we saw Beijing at its best.

My mind and body began to function about the time we reached Tiananmen Square, the largest public gathering space in the world. I vividly recalled the student rebellion ten years earlier that turned into a killing field as the world watched in horror. In contrast, today's jubilant activity quickly erased those memories. The square was filled to overflowing with Chinese chatting and strolling at leisure. Fred allowed us half an hour to wander and I used the time to take photos and simply feel the festive vibes emanating all around me.

We regrouped and darted across six lanes of seemingly nonstop traffic to the Great Hall of the People where lunch was served in a private second-floor dining room. The significance of this hit home as we stepped off the elevator and peered through a window into the Great Hall just below us. It was awe inspiring to be the only guests in this elegant private room. I felt that I should have dressed for the occasion. Somehow khaki pants and white tennis shoes seemed terribly out of place but no one seemed to mind. Where were the Chinese Fashion Police?

After a multi-course lunch served with Fred's favorite Yanjing beer we returned to the hotel. New tour friend Janet and I opted for a walk. Janet's Aunt Irene had traveled with me on a U of M trip through South America. It was indeed a small world. Janet liked to pound the sidewalks as much as I did and we chose a recreation area several blocks from the hotel called Purple Bamboo Park. We made our way through pedestrians and cyclists and almost missed the entrance tucked at the side of a curio shop.

Once inside we were amazed by the acres of tranquility nestled in the midst of the bustling city just outside the entrance. We walked up a hill and discovered a lovely small lake filled with tiny four-man pedal boats shaped like swans. Young and old alike sat on benches along the lake or strolled leisurely. We felt fortunate to have discovered this beautiful oasis.

On our way back to the hotel we encountered two wizened old women in drab traditional Chinese dress standing beside a pedicab. I used my best sign language to ask if I could take their photograph. One gave me a toothless smile and they posed for a snapshot. The day ended with a cocktail party in the hotel where our group continued to become acquainted and form friendships. It was the perfect end to our full day in Beijing.

Day two began with the first of accompanying professor Mei-yu's lectures, this one focusing on China's economic policies. From 1949 to 1978, China worked to transform into a modern, powerful socialized nation. However, this centrally planned economy failed to produce the desired economic growth. It simply did not work. The populace experienced a standard of living that barely provided food, clothing and housing. The death of Mao ushered in an era of economic reform, intended to increase market economy without eliminating central control. This resulted in more self-control of industry and agriculture and also opened doors to foreign businesses and investors. Whenever dramatic changes took place, they resulted in mixed consequences. Serious social problems created by widening income disparities occurred along with crime, corruption and unemployment.

Mei-yu pointed out the vast changes that occurred within the span of twenty years. When she was married in the 1960s, each bride expected her husband to provide "forty legs". This meant ten pieces of furniture. By the 1980s, the rule of thumb became "six big stuff": washer, dryer, TV, stove, refrigerator, and video camera. In just two short decades a vastly new and different set of expectations replaced generations of tradition.

Next on our agenda was one of the highlights of the trip—a tour of Beijing's famed Forbidden City, the world's largest imperial palace. Although I knew the complex covered a vast area, experiencing this elite city staggered me. We covered only a fraction of the structures in the compound, even though we spent nearly four hours at the site. Forty percent of the Forbidden City is still not open to the public. Built between 1406 and 1420 AD, the complex was central to Beijing. It served as the political and ritual center for more than five hundred years and was home to twenty-four emperors, their families and servants. A masterpiece of Chinese architecture, it featured ninety palace quarters, nine hundred buildings and more than eighty-seven hundred rooms.

Most of us popped into the palace museum and gift shop and I spotted a stunning round red lacquered box the size of a large cookie tin. Its scalloped edges and whimsical array of round Chinese men painted on the lid and sides captivated me and I simply couldn't leave without it. Priced at US$500, it supposedly dated from the Qing Dynasty spanning the years from 1644 to 1912 AD. Employing my best bargaining skills I got it down to an affordable US$150. As I soon discovered, this bulky souvenir presented a challenge as I lugged it all over China for the remainder of our journey.

On our way to lunch we passed a mangled bicycle in the street next to a car with a smashed windshield. It did not bode well for the cyclist. Fred told us that five thousand Chinese died each day in bicycle accidents. It seemed a high number but as we watched cyclists zoom through traffic we weren't surprised.

After lunch at Fang Zi Xuan, Temple of the Earth in English, we visited Beijing's Llama Temple where worshippers practiced a Chinese style of Indian Buddhism and offered prayers before an imposing eighty-foot wooden Buddha carved from a single tree.

When we returned to the hotel late in the afternoon, Janet and I walked for forty-five minutes through the bustling streets. Going in the opposite direction of the park we encountered families out strolling and shopping at various markets along our route. Although modern construction bordered the busy thoroughfare, occasional glimpses down side alleyways revealed decaying low structures that had not given way to modernization.

At 6:30 p.m. we met in the hotel lobby for a bus ride back to the Tiananmen Square area. Many of us had asked for Peking duck followed by a nighttime walk through the world-famous square. Dinner at a nearby restaurant, served family style in a large room, included our first taste of this city's famed duck served in pancakes with plum sauce. Afterward, Fred led us across six lanes of incessant traffic into the square. Teeming with Chinese of all ages, an air of pre-anniversary festivity prevailed and we soon found ourselves caught up in the nighttime celebration. Children scampered and colorful kites sailed toward a full moon. Laser beams crisscrossed the square as families and friends grouped together in conversation and laughter. Just finding a spot to stand proved a challenge. Even though we were obvious foreigners, we felt welcome. I would never forget the electricity in Tiananmen Square on this evening.

The next morning, we departed on our bus for the much-anticipated tour of the Great Wall at Badaling, about an hour's drive from Beijing. En route, Fred—now officially known to us as Chairman Fu—filled us in on some of the Great Wall's history. As early as 700 BC separate walls were constructed. By 200 BC the powerful Qin (Chin) Dynasty controlled all of China and, in an effort to keep out the Mongols to the north, eighteen hundred miles of separate walls were connected. This incredible feat was accomplished within ten years utilizing a work force of one-third of China's male population.

From 200 BC to 100 AD the Han Dynasty expanded the wall from the border of Korea and China to Pakistan and Afghanistan. Wide enough at its top to serve as a passageway, it was used for transportation as well as protection. The wall also served as a message center across northern China. Construction continued in piecemeal fashion through the 16th century AD.

The following is a list of China's great dynasties:

Zhou - 1046 BC–2216 BC
Qin - 221 BC–207 BC
Han - 206 BC–9 AD
Shu - 221 AD–263 AD
Wu - 222 AD–280 AD
Wei - 368 AD–534 AD
Sui - 581 AD–618 AD
Tang - 618 AD–907 AD
Song - 960 AD–1125 AD
Jin - 1125 AD–1234 AD
Yuan - 1271 AD–1368 AD
Ming - 1368 AD–1644 AD
Qing - 1644 AD–1912 AD
Republic - 1912 AD–1949 AD
People's Republic - 1949 AD–present

Some interesting tidbits: In 500 AD, feudal art and culture were at their best. The Japanese came to China and learned calligraphy, dress styles and the tea culture. The Song Dynasty was famous for its paintings and its gardening.

The Great Wall was breached by the Mongols during the Yuan Dynasty. They conquered every part of China and Beijing became their capital. Since the Great Wall had kept them out for centuries, the Mongols let it deteriorate. The Ming Dynasty drove out the Mongols, reconstructed the wall over a period of three centuries and was best known for its fine porcelain. Late in the Ming Dynasty the peasants staged an uprising. The Manchurians defeated the peasants and established the Qing Dynasty. Enough history; back to our adventure…

We arrived at the Valley of the Great Wall in mist-shrouded Badaling. As we queued for a cable car ride up the mountainside toward the wall, the skies opened and a deluge began to fall. Fortunately, the rain didn't last long. Fog drifted in and out creating an ethereal mood.

The rain could not dampen the overwhelming thrill of actually being on part of the Great Wall. From our stance at the top, the wall stretched in a seemingly endless line until it faded from view in the distance. Steep steps meandered up and down the mountaintop serving as access points. The width of the passageways on top of the wall surprised me, even though I knew of its use as a roadway. It easily handled six to eight visitors abreast.

Gazing across a mere few miles of the structure, I could not imagine how this impressive wall could have been built to extend more than four thousand miles across northern China. It truly ranks as one of the wonders of the world. Someone in our group mentioned that astronauts can identify China from space by locating the pattern made by the Great Wall. It is the only manmade structure visible from space.

We spent two hours wandering from point to point along the wall and stopped often to take photos. At one point our tour coordinator Tom caught up with a group of us and took snapshots as we held up the University of Michigan banner. When the time came to descend the mountainside and return to our bus, we did so with regret.

Fred directed our bus driver to the Beijing International Golf Club for our lunch stop. The modern facility would have been a treat were it not filled with a group of Japanese who smoked incessantly. A big hit with the gals was the ultra-clean Western style bathroom. No holes in the ground here...

Our final destination for the day took us to an area of Ming tombs. As the rain intensified, we donned our raincoats and entered a courtyard with a series of structures honoring those buried here. Returning to the bus we drove for a short distance to a half-mile-long outdoor mall lined with enormous sculptures of domestic and exotic animals. We strolled along under our umbrellas and admired horses, elephants, camels, dragons, and more. Our bus met us at the opposite end for our return to Beijing.

We arrived after dark and the beauty of Beijing at night struck me. The sparkling lights and lanterns in the city rivaled Disneyland. Buildings outlined with strings of lights looked like something out of a fairy tale. Magical best described the look of Beijing after hours.

The next morning's tour took us to the relatively new Sackler Museum of Art and Archaeology on the campus of Beijing University. Fred revealed more history en route. May 4, 1919 marked the beginning of the Revolutionary Movement in China. The Chinese Communist Party formed in 1921. United farmers took control and the revolution that began in the countryside soon moved into the cities. The People's Republic took hold in 1949 and Chairman Mao remained a major figure until his death.

In the ten years since the uprising at Tiananmen Square, great strides toward democracy and freedom had been made in China. Fred told us that today he could say anything to us without fear of censure. Even jokes about the Republic's leaders were tolerated. Indeed, Fred spoke to us with candor—and with humor. Friends who had traveled to China ten to fifteen years prior had a far different experience with their in-country guides.

The Sackler Museum, small but mighty, housed a wide range of burial objects, pottery and other ancient treasures. In the entrance hall stood two massive terra cotta warriors. Assuming they were replicas, I asked someone in our group to take a photo of me with an arm around the shoulder of one of the formidable soldiers. Just as the flash on my camera went off, Fred cautioned me not to touch the statue since it was an original. Oops…

We next visited the Summer Palace complex and, after enduring a dreadful WC experience, we walked under a charming painted wooden arcade that stretched for blocks. At the far end a marble ship extended into a lake. This faux vessel served as an entertainment center during the palace's days of grandeur. Our group boarded a large swan boat for a cruise back to the Summer Palace entrance. It was easy to understand why this location had been a favorite of the last Qing Dynasty Empress.

After a family-style lunch at the Friendship Hotel we returned to our home base for a free afternoon. Three of us chose a cross-town adventure and hailed a taxi for a forty-minute drive through a maze of traffic to a seedy-looking pearl market. We let the taxi go and then questioned whether we were in the right location. Once we entered the massive structure's first floor our doubts quadrupled.

On impulse we walked to the third floor and made our way to the back of the cavernous space. To our delight we discovered two others from our group buying irresistible bargains. They introduced us to a pearl salesperson and I bought two necklaces for my daughters.

During the last few days, I had struck up a friendship with two couples and they invited me to join them for dinner. Chairman Fu, a.k.a. Fred, suggested we try one of Beijing's Mongolian hot pot restaurants. Located near Beijing's Modern Shopping Center, this bustling establishment brimmed with locals. The two couples had been friends for years and the men were the gourmets of the group. They ordered an array of meat, shrimp and vegetables that we cooked in the two vats of bubbling oil at the center of our table. We all agreed that it was very good.

We hailed a taxi and returned to our hotel. Neither of the men would let me pay for the taxi rides or my dinner so I offered to buy after dinner drinks at the Shangri La. My bill totaled twice as much as the dinner and taxi rides.

I knew what day it was because the floor mat in the Shangri-La said Tuesday. It changed every day. We began with a lengthy transit to the Beijing airport followed by an hour-and-a-half flight to Xian. Once on our tour bus our new guide Ping shared some highlights on Xian. The city's name meant *peace*. Six million people resided here. Xian was the burial site for many Chinese emperors and their treasures. The excavation of the fourth emperor of the Han Dynasty was now underway and many artifacts had been recovered. While not life-sized like the famed terra cotta soldiers, among the unearthed treasures were statues of men, women and eunuchs. Although dressed at the time of the emperor's burial, the fabrics had deteriorated and now revealed their anatomically correct—or altered, as the case may have been—bodies.

As we drove past many miles of farmland, the major crop of the region appeared to be corn. Ping told us that farmland was still owned by the state and farmers had been given the option to leave their plots and move to the cities. Villagers shared the land and the rule of thumb was 1/3 acre per person in each family. Until recently many farmers had lived in caves dug into the clay mounds that dotted the landscape. Those were then vacated by law and farmers and their families lived in simple adobe homes or two-story brick homes built in the 1980s and 1990s.

Xian was home to forty universities and ranked third in all of China for higher education. An imposing city wall dating from the Ming Dynasty ringed the old city. The vast 600-year-old structure proudly stood as the only complete city wall in all of China. Four massive gates along the eight-mile ring allowed passage to and from the city center. As our bus entered through one, its counterpoint at the opposite wall loomed in the distance.

Our first stop was the Orient Hotel for a late lunch. The food proved to be an unexpected treat. We feasted on eggplant, beef and onions, and thin crispy pork. We then crawled through a snarl of traffic to the Muslim district where we wandered past several blocks of street venders. Eventually we reached a mosque set in a peaceful garden. I was struck by the contrast between the noise of the street vendors and the solitude of the mosque. Ping told us that sixty thousand Muslims lived in Xian. In the 12th century, Kublai Kahn introduced the religion during the Yuan Dynasty. Muslim men married Chinese women and one could see the influence of each nationality in today's descendants.

Like Beijing, Xian looked its best in anticipation of the fiftieth anniversary of the People's Republic of China. The now-familiar pots of flowers graced department stores and parks. We wound our way through the never-ending streets filled with cars, buses and bicycles to the Hyatt Hotel. While waiting for room assignments and keys I chatted with a young man from Holland who worked in hotel management. Once settled in my Zen-inspired room I ventured back to the lobby to meet new friends for dinner in the hotel café.

At 9:00 a.m. the next day we boarded our bus for the much-anticipated tour of the famous Terra Cotta Warrior Pits. As we slowly entered the center of Xian, I was once more struck by the vast numbers of buses, trucks, taxis, cars, bikes, and pedicabs loaded with food and other goods. Traffic lanes meant virtually nothing and electronic traffic signals were nonexistent. Instead, at several frenzied intersections, women sat on stools and placidly waved either a yellow or red flag. Cyclists heeded these signals and stayed out of harm's way.

As in Beijing, bright red lanterns hung everywhere in anticipation of China's upcoming celebration. Leaving the city, we encountered pastoral farm country and Ping shared more Xian history. The terra cotta warriors dated from the Qin Dynasty and were not rediscovered until 1974. Farmers digging for water discovered this great treasure and six of the farmers were now employed at the site.

Emperor Qin built the beginnings of the Great Wall in 221 BC and had his elaborate burial tomb in Xian constructed over a forty-year period. Immediately following his death, the peasants staged an uprising and destroyed every one of the thousands of terra cotta soldiers before setting the vast tomb on fire. The underground structure burned and collapsed, forming a protective shield over the remains of the soldiers. Soon afterward a flood filled the spaces around the fragments with a thick layer of clay. This saved them from further destruction for more than two thousand years. Teams of archaeologists were now painstakingly piecing each of the life-sized soldiers together. Although tedious, the results were impressive. Each of the soldiers had his own distinct personality and no two were alike. Originally each had been painted but the color faded in just three to six minutes when unearthed. A new method utilizing a spray applied immediately upon excavation was now used to preserve color.

Some pieces had been stamped with the name of the artist along with where and when the statue was made. To make each soldier, feet and arms were constructed separately. These were fired and placed into the hollow bodies. Each head was individually crafted and then fired at 1,000 Celsius, or 1,832 degrees Fahrenheit. After an application of mineral pigments, the soldiers were transported to the burial site and placed in seemingly endless rows to serve as eternal guards for the dead emperor.

The first pit, unearthed after its 1974 discovery, covered an area of twelve thousand meters, or 39,370 feet. The size of the dig almost defied description. It equaled two regulation football fields side by side. To protect it from the elements, a massive structure covered the site. Once inside, no photography was permitted. I did sneak one irresistible photo and felt guilty for doing so. Postcards would have to convey my pictorial images. The dust from the dig overwhelmed many of us and I thanked a woman in our group for sharing her extra face mask with me.

Until 1974, no records of the terra cotta soldiers had existed. Some of the elders in surrounding villages had heard tales of their ancestors discovering bits and pieces of the shattered warriors. However, fear and superstition kept them quiet. In 1979, the site opened to the public with eight thousand warriors in pit #1, six thousand in pit #2 and sixty-eight cavalrymen and their horses in pit #3. The third pit miraculously escaped destruction and fire but the process of stabilizing the color did not surface in time to preserve it on these artifacts. Larger pits also contained gold and silver, clay horses and a magnificent bronze chariot. These pits, set up much like the palace grounds, enabled Qin to figuratively take all of his soldiers and animals with him in death. The Chinese call this find the Eighth Wonder of the World and I agree.

Several of the doctors in our group asked Ping about ancient Chinese medicines and on our return trip Ping made an unscheduled stop at a local medicine market. We wandered through stalls of all kinds of unimaginable dried creatures as well as animal parts, horns and a vast array of herbs and spices. Dried lizards stretched out and lashed to a foot-long wooden cross attracted the attention of my walking buddy Janet. On impulse we decided to buy it as a gift for one of the women in our group celebrating her birthday that day. With Mei-yu as our negotiator we completed the deal, carried our find back to the now-filled bus, and presented the birthday girl with her lizard-on-a-stick. It won the award for her all-time most unusual gift.

After a rather ordinary Cantonese lunch at a local hotel we visited the Big Wild Goose Pagoda built one thousand years ago. Buddhism came into China during the first century AD when Indian traders traveled along the Silk Road. Because it was a merciful religion it was quickly accepted in China.

As we walked through the impressive grounds of the compound, two young Chinese girls from a village along the Yellow River tagged along with us. We soon discovered they were studying English at a school in Xian and they were absolutely charming. We told them where we were from and listened as they described their homes. They posed for photos before saying goodbye.

At the far end of the pagoda complex we toured a museum with replicas of tomb paintings. Many detailed elegant women in flowing gowns. One reminded me of John Singer Sargent's Portrait of *Madame X* that hung in NYC's Metropolitan Museum. It was always interesting to see how art transcends time and place. We were turned loose to visit two galleries with art for sale. Thus, our museum tour morphed into a shopping opportunity, one of many…

Tonight's dinner, theater-style at tables overlooking a stage, preceded what was billed as a Chinese folk performance. In fact, it resembled Las Vegas in China complete with all the glitz and glamour. Having seen row after row of tour buses in the parking lot as we entered, I suspected as much. We actually enjoyed the food and a cake was presented to our birthday girl in front of the hundreds of people in the theater. With her lizard-on-a-stick and everyone in the audience singing happy birthday, this was one she would always remember.

Today's bus departed at 8:30 a.m. for our half-day tour. Roy, our resident songster, led us in a couple of Michigan tunes while en route. Not far from our hotel we encountered another lady in the middle of a traffic mess waving a red flag attached to a long stick. Cyclists waited for the flag to drop before continuing through the pudding-thick traffic.

We had been told we were on our way to a shopping area and we soon found ourselves in a government store filled with overzealous sales personnel. After gazing at ordinary jade and silk carpets, I entered the clothing department. I bought three inexpensive scarves with machine-sewn rather than rolled edges.

At our next stop, the Shanxi Province Museum, we saw an excellent collection of artifacts from the Qin, Han and Tang Dynasties. The hour-and-a-half tour put much of China's history into perspective. The museum's buildings, designed by a contemporary female architect, replicated the spirit of the Tang Dynasty. I liked the powerful simplicity of the structures.

We returned to the hotel for lunch and then several of us ventured into the bustling streets of Xian. Unlike the clean air we had experienced in Beijing in anticipation of the fiftieth anniversary celebrations, thick smog cast a dark pall over the city. Every breath felt like standing in front of the exhaust of a large truck. Following the lead of many locals on the streets I declined putting on my face mask, still conveniently tucked in my purse. China had a long way to go in air quality control. Someone mentioned that a measurement of ninety particulates per square meter constitutes a major smog alert in the US. A reading of five hundred particulates is an everyday occurrence in Xian.

People literally packed the sidewalks along the mile of shops we passed on our way to the Muslim open-air market near Xian's famed Drum Tower. Families with their one child, usually a boy, were everywhere. Vendors sold Chinese flags for one yuan, about 12 cents US. We bought a few as souvenirs before making an attempt to cross the busy street without getting hit. In this country, pedestrians must respond to traffic rather than traffic to pedestrians. We played the ultimate game of chicken and dodged the cars, buses and bicycles hurtling toward us.

As we walked, we met a young girl from Xian's art school near the Drum Tower. She spoke English well and followed along with us through the square. When we reached the gate to the Muslim area, she invited us for a tour of her small school and art studio. While there I spotted a charming painting of a young man and woman with a donkey and asked if it was for sale. Our young friend found the artist and I bought the painting for US$42.

Once we reached the bazaar, Janet bargained for some incredible deals as we wandered through the area. John and Judy found adorable appliquéd clothing for their grandchild. I bought a couple of inexpensive primitive paintings and two carved jade necklaces. Returning to the hotel we passed a woman with triplet daughters about three years old, then another with twin boys. If a woman had multiple births she was allowed to keep all of her children. I must confess that the woman with three little girls looked stressed to the max as she tried to herd them along the street.

Dinner took us back near the Drum Tower to a touristy dumpling restaurant. We had great fun at our table and managed to eat when we weren't laughing. With a convincing straight face, John cajoled me into trying a fire-hot sauce on a dumpling. After recovering from a too-large bite and the ensuing laughter, I vowed to retaliate. For the rest of the tour John was on alert for the smallest hot pepper that I promised to slip into one of his meals.

Today marked the official fiftieth anniversary of the People's Republic of China. Tom gave us an extra half hour before our departure to watch the Tiananmen Square celebration headed by Chairman Jiang Zemin. Watching the show of strength and military force in the square where we had stood just days earlier moved each one of us. A goose-stepping military unit marched in absolute precision into the square and saluted Jiang and his accompanying dignitaries. Jiang called out over a loud speaker, "Hello, Comrades!" and the troops responded with "Hello, Chairman!" It was a chilling display of force and power.

We were struck by the lack of bystanders along the parade route. Although half a million people taking part in the celebratory pageant filled the square, the absence of Beijing citizens was noteworthy. It seemed all too staged and contrived which, in fact, it was. Even press representatives from around the world who booked rooms overlooking the parade route months in advance were forced to black out all windows facing the square. Manhole covers were locked into place. Vagrants and the mentally ill were locked up for the day. No uninvited participants were allowed in the vicinity of the square. It appeared that in spite of exponential leaps forward, China still had a long way to go to achieve real democracy.

After a short flight to Wuhan, we met our new city guide, Toby. Now the fourth largest city in China, greater Wuhan had a population of seven million. Textiles and metallurgy were the major industries and a large production plant manufactured Citroens.

Like the other cities we visited, traffic moved at a crawl in the late afternoon as we headed to a bonsai garden along the river. Toby told us that a fireworks extravaganza was to take place that evening and it seemed that all seven million residents intended to stake out their own prime viewing spot. Better air quality was mandated in Wuhan for the anniversary and we delighted in the breathable air.

Another shopping opportunity followed a disappointingly brief garden tour. After far too much time in the garden's shop we boarded our bus for an early dinner at the Holiday Inn. It was imperative that we board our ship, the *Victoria*, by 6:00 p.m. for our Yangtze cruise so that we could be underway by 6:30 p.m. and avoid the fireworks along the river. We rushed through dinner and arrived at our ship's dock on time. However, one of the three tour groups sharing our river boat did not make it and that meant we were stuck at the dock until the fireworks ended. It proved to be a blessing in disguise.

My cabin, located on the second deck, more than qualified for a shoebox award. Fortunately, I didn't have to share the minute space with anyone. All the couples were squeezed into rooms that barely accommodated one person. Our bathrooms housed a toilet, sink and shower in one small space. When the shower was turned on it soaked the entire floor and everything around it. I convinced myself that I could do this for five days.

I unpacked very little since the closet's depth measured about eight inches. Only then did I realize that I left my small jewelry box well concealed in the back of a drawer in the Xian hotel. I relayed my plight to Tom and then joined a group on the upper deck awaiting the fireworks gala. Deciding that I would probably not see my jewelry again, I put it out of my mind and readied for the celebration about to unfold along the river.

As the sun set the fireworks began and they simply dazzled us. At three different points along the river bright bursts of color sparkled in the evening sky. Just when we were sure we had seen the finale another incredible display appeared. After half an hour the show ended and immediately thereafter our ship motored out of port.

The night was balmy and several of us stayed topside watching Wuhan's lights fade as we moved upstream. Our Yangtze River cruise had begun! Returning to my room, the boat's motion and the engine's faint whir lulled me to sleep almost immediately.

After a shipboard breakfast the next morning we boarded a bus for a short ride to the village of Yueyang in the Hunan Province. Home of Dongting Lake, the second largest in the province, the area was called the land of fish and rice. Although the rice had been harvested a month earlier, we passed numerous marshy fields with new shoots as we headed for the famed Yeuyang Tower. This 1,700-year-old Buddhist-style pagoda proved to be my favorite. Built without nails and virtually freestanding, our guide told us that it could be lifted straight up by a large-enough helicopter. Hardly likely.... The structure, built from interlocking pieces much like a giant puzzle, sat in a park overlooking the lake. Its gently sloping roof and colorfully painted surfaces charmed us.

After the now-inevitable shopping op, this time for foul-tasting silver leaf tea, we returned to the *Victoria* and immediately motored upstream. I sat on one of the tiny twin beds in my room and admired the passing scenery for an hour before lunch. At this juncture of the river, flat farmland seemed to stretch forever and watching it glide past created a hypnotic effect.

Mid-afternoon, Mei-yu gave a shipboard lecture on China's population-control program. We had noted that the majority of children seemed to be boys in the single-child families we passed on the streets. If families terminated female pregnancies in favor of bearing a son, it stood to reason that these boys would have difficulty finding a wife when they reached adulthood. Mei-yu said that the Chinese accepted the one child program. Signs everywhere proclaimed, "One house, one family, one child." Although the population explosion of the 1950s and 1960s desperately needed to be reversed, the ramifications of this family planning by law remained to be seen.

Late in the afternoon I treated myself to a massage. Given by the ship's female medical doctor, the technique differed from any I had previously experienced. It felt wonderful to work out the travel kinks and at 200 yuan, about US$24, it was a bargain. One of the women in our tour group was also in the salon having her hair washed and dried. As she sat under a hair dryer, she discovered that only half of it worked. She hadn't bargained for half a hairdo, but emerged with dry hair on one side and wet hair on the other. Ah, the perils of travel!

Following the captain's reception and a Chinese dinner with a touch of Sichuan flair, we regrouped in the lounge for a fashion show presented by some of the young staff. The show featured many elaborate pieces representative of the Qin, Han and Ming Dynasties for both men and women. Not missing a shopping op, the finale featured modern fashions for sale in the ship's boutique.

Once again, we all were later rocked to sleep as the ship cruised through the night.

The next morning luck was with us as we neared the Gezhouba Dam. Only one lock was in operation and, fortunately for us, it was empty. There could have been a wait of up to six hours to pass through it. Placing wagers on how long it would take to exit the lock, one of the men in our group guessed the time within forty seconds. The cagey staff kept half of our wagers and awarded the other half to the winner.

Soon afterward we arrived at the first of the famed Three Gorges. Peering through the mist in the river valley, the soaring cliffs with majestic mountains in the background painted a lasting picture for me. Seeing the Yangtze River in its original form before the opening of the Three Gorges Dam had prompted my visit to China. Just a partial loss of this geological treasure saddened me. The new dam would forever change the Yangtze's gorges and river valleys and displace 1.28 million people as the water level eventually rose 165 meters, or 541 feet. The entirety of the spectacular geological formations of the gorges had to be seen now or never.

I wanted to despise the dam and did not anticipate the impact that it would make on me. In a word, it was awe-inspiring. How else could one have described the magnitude of the Three Gorges Dam project, now well into its final stages of construction. When completed, it would rank as the world's largest, measuring 7,661 feet long by 600 feet high. Construction began in 1994 and costs were estimated to be somewhere between US$25 and US$37 billion. A crew of twenty-five thousand worked seven days a week to meet the 2008 completion date. Following the three phases of inundation, China would lose 140 small towns, thirteen cities and numerous historic sites in its effort to control flooding and harness power. Much more can be said about the negative effects of the dam but at this moment we were overwhelmed by its size and grandeur.

We docked at Yichang and boarded a bus for our tour of the dam construction site. Our local guide explained that this location had been selected because it lay in a broad valley lined with stable granite rock and earthquakes were rare here. As we approached the dam we stopped to watch a set of locks being carved out of clay. This six-step series would move commercial traffic up and down the river quickly and its size was simply mind-boggling.

When the bus reached the top of the dam, we were told that what was now the summit would eventually be surrounded by water and become an observation island. We stood there in awe as we surveyed the vast project from our lofty perch. I shot four rolls of film here, a marvel for this traveler at a technical site. I simply felt compelled to capture the immensity of the project.

On our return drive to the ship our guide pointed out the pros and cons of the dam.

Pros:
- Cleaner water (now debatable)
- Flood control
- Environmental protection (also now debatable)
- Massive clean-air powered generator
- Ability to divert water to areas with shortages

Cons:
- War and subsequent destruction of the dam would result in a devastating flood
- Centuries of alluvial soil along the banks would wash away with the inundations
- The rise in the river's level would raise the temperature along the Yangtze by 2 degrees, changing the ecology and altering the ability to grow certain crops
- Much of the natural beauty of the river and its gorges would be destroyed when the river eventually rose. Fish would no longer be able to follow an age-old migratory path upstream, although the redirected flow would add more nutrients.
- 1.28 million people would be displaced; homes would be bombed to clear them and only the graves of the last three generations would be moved

Both sets of arguments held their own merit and the world would have to wait to see whether the dam succeeded or failed.

When we reached our ship's dock, I fumbled for my plastic re-entry card and couldn't find it. "I guess I'll have to become a dam(n) worker. Just my dam(n) luck," I quipped to friends Ruth Ann and Bill. Fortunately, my pass materialized at the bottom of my purse.

After lunch we headed for the open air at the bow to watch the second half of the Xiling Gorge float majestically by us. While our Chinese guides Jonathan and Davis pointed out significant features, we stood for nearly two hours entranced by the sights. We felt fortunate to view these magnificent works of nature just before the first inundation. Both man and nature would suffer the consequences of the dam. Extinction awaited entire villages along with every terraced farm situated below the series of three inundations.

At 5:30 p.m. the ship entered the second of China's famed Three Gorges. Once again many of us gathered topside in drizzle, hoping to catch a view of this imposing gorge. The light drizzle turned into honest rain and darkness fell before we could see all the peaks. Just a smattering of breathtaking pinnacles reaching almost vertically upward came into view. My attempt to photograph them did not work in the semi-darkness so it would have to remain a splendid mental memory.

Tonight, the ship's dining room offered spaghetti along with traditional Chinese dishes. In a moment of weakness, I bypassed the local fare and went for the pasta. After all, didn't Marco Polo bring pasta from China to Italy all those centuries ago?

The ship anchored in Wushan for the evening. I lamented having a floating grocery ship and restaurant that catered to ferry traffic anchored just outside my window. The chatter went on well into the night and resumed at 5:00 a.m. However, those on the other side of the ship fared even worse. Not only did they look directly into a ship filled with boisterous Chinese, they were greeted with a 4:00 a.m. wake-up call from a nearby rooster.

Although tired from our noisy overnight docking experience, we nevertheless gathered enthusiastically for a much-anticipated sampan cruise on the Daning River to view the Lesser Three Gorges. We walked en masse to a nearby dock filled with tour boats and quickly boarded. I sat in the back row until Tom invited a few of us to take the empty front seats. This proved to be both good news and bad news. More about this later...

Many of us had envisioned spending a morning in a quaint, small sampan much like those we had passed on our river cruise. Instead we landed in boat #34, a clunker of a motorized and oversized sampan. At times the river became so congested that we literally collided with other boats, much like carnival bumper cars. It seemed to be standard operational procedure and our two strong helmsmen used bamboo poles to propel us away from one collision after another.

As other boats streamed past us it soon became apparent that our sampan wasn't cutting it. We barely managed to stay ahead of the onrushing current. Not only did we have an underpowered boat, we had a captain who seemed incapable of keeping us out of harm's way. We disembarked at a passage in the rapids where it was too dangerous for tourists to stay on board and watched in horror and a bit of amusement as underpowered #34 missed the narrow channel and grounded itself on a rocky sandbar that every other boat had navigated without problems. After several unsuccessful attempts to free itself, #34 got a much-needed tow from another sampan.

We re-boarded somewhat apprehensively and, as we soon discovered, for good reason. Boat #34 ran its engine full steam and could not make any progress heading upstream in the swift current. Our boat blocked the passageway for other boats and we played another round of bumper boats as we crashed into a series of other sampans. Having been advised to bring our life jackets from our ship, we all donned them in unison just as we crashed onto the rocky shore. The captain, our tour guide for the day and the two helmsmen hopped onto the ground and a heated discussion ensued. We U of M'ers protested that enough was enough and demanded another boat. To our dismay, the crew pushed off and headed back into the turbulent stream. As we shook our heads in disbelief the boat lurched across the river to dock and we soon boarded a boat that worked. Enough of *The Little Engine That Couldn't*! So long #34!

With our misadventure behind us we traveled on in sync with the other boats. The river widened and we cruised past miles of terraced farms that meandered far up the mountainsides. Usually two or three family members worked the plots with hand tools. Some carried poles across their shoulders with water buckets for irrigation hanging from either end. Men in traditional sampans cast huge fishing nets into the river. Children played along the river's edge and a few dangled bamboo fishing poles in the water. We all waved at a group of children and one young boy decided to run along the shore in step with our boat's progress. A few on board tried to toss coins in his direction but none reached the shore. After ten minutes of pursuit the boy called it quits.

Given the delays caused by the now-infamous boat #34 and the ride upstream against the flow of the river, it was indeed time for a pit stop. The boat docked and, with limited facilities, I led the way up the hill to an outcrop of rocks. I'm tall; the rocks were not. After a moment's hesitation I decided it was now or never and the others followed suit. Friends claimed they photographed my head bobbing up and down behind the rocks. That was a photo I could definitely live without seeing.

Although it had taken us nearly three hours to make our way upstream it took less than fifty minutes for the return trip. Janet and I sat with two other women at the front of the sampan as we splashed our way downstream. Each time a wave approached the boat the two helmsmen quickly shut a set of doors to block the water. Poor Joan, who sat halfway back in the boat, unexpectedly caught the brunt of a wave that crashed through an open window. She got a mouthful of the river in the process.

I was grateful for the set of doors but noticed that a triangle of the plexiglass had broken and was lashed back in place with a piece of wire. It kept opening and I declared myself the keeper of the dike, proclaiming it my job to close the flap when a large wave appeared. This I did faithfully—

except for once. A soaker hit us and, not wanting a mouthful of dirty river water, I managed to turn in time for it to hit the back of my head. I matched Joan for the drenched look, however. We looked like drowned rats.

I later discovered that the force of the water knocked off one of my earrings. Unfortunately, I didn't notice it was missing until we returned to the *Victoria*. Iris, one of my new travel friends, loaned me a pair of stunning earrings she had purchased in Greece. I was touched by her generosity and, given my track record, her trust.

Joan and I decided that lunch could wait and headed immediately for our showers. We joined the group in time to grab a bite. Today's selections included a Chinese version of a hamburger. The buzz was A+ for the bun; D- for the meat patty. I opted for the traditional Chinese veggies, convinced that I would have to go through bok choy withdrawal upon my return to the States.

After lunch, as I had promised, I led a scarf-tying demonstration in the library. I brought a number of scarves to serve as jewelry during the trip and our two handsome Chinese river guides asked if I would be willing show others the techniques. They said they wanted to learn so they could teach their girlfriends. The room filled with fellow travelers, much to my surprise. I had asked Jane, a model-esque fellow traveler, to serve as a mannequin during the half-hour demonstration. She wore a black sweater which made the scarves pop. She always dressed to perfection and I later learned that she won the award for having the heaviest luggage in our group. No problem for Jane to pull out just the right thing to wear!

At 3:00 p.m. we gathered at the bow for the last of the Three Gorges, this one the shortest but nevertheless magnificent. Having shot a dozen rolls of film at this point I hoped that some of my attempts to capture the magic of these natural wonders would be successful, but the mist, combined with the distance, proved too great a challenge. In retrospect, I should have brought a telephoto lens to capture the immense glory of the gorges.

Later in the afternoon I returned to my cabin and watched the scenery roll by. What a peaceful respite after this morning's excitement! Mile after mile of gentle family plots covered terraced hillsides and the impending devastation from the Three Gorges Dam hit home. So many lives would be forever altered. Markings along the rock walls adjacent to the river indicated the levels that the water from the dam would consume in three separate stages as it was released in the impending inundations. I felt an overwhelming sadness for the people I watched tending their farms as their ancestors had done for centuries. Life would never be the same.

I joined Janet, Mei-yu and three others for dinner in the ship's dining room. Afterward we all went to the lounge for a crew and passenger talent show. Roy, our resident musician, surprised us with his talent on the piano, playing two jazz pieces to perfection. We muddled through a few old alum tunes before belting out the Michigan fight song. What we lacked in skill we more than made up for in volume.

Many of the young crew demonstrated Chinese dances while wearing costumes during their well-rehearsed and most charming performances. A member from the Cambridge group, wearing a costume borrowed from the cruise director, recited several poems translated from Chinese.

Tonight the *Victoria* dropped anchor along the banks of the river far from the sounds and lights of any villages. No other ships did the same and the gentle rocking rewarded us with a good night's sleep.

Just before 5:00 a.m. the captain fired up the engines and motored upstream before docking at Wanxian. After an early breakfast we climbed a steep staircase to a waiting bus and met our tour guide for the morning. Making our way back and forth on an incredibly narrow switchback road we passed block after block of homes and small businesses that we knew would simply disappear once the dam's floodgates were opened. Judging from the 167-meter marker far up the hillside, it appeared that half of this bustling town was targeted for destruction by 2001.

We wound our way further uphill to a series of streets serving as a wholesale food market. Set up much like a farmers' market in the States, the similarity ended there. We popped our umbrellas in the heavy drizzle and spent half an hour walking along the stalls. The ubiquitous bok choy graced each produce stand along with baskets of melons and other exotic fruits and vegetables. Of interest were the open-air stalls featuring gutted animal carcasses. The remaining body parts graced the countertops. Nothing was wasted in China.

Fishmongers grouped at the end of the street displayed fish, eels and other assorted river creatures. A variety of live fish swam in washtub-sized containers set on the ground. Most disturbing, albeit interesting, were a series of tables literally covered with live chickens, ducks, pigeons, and other small birds with their legs shackled. The birds, seemingly oblivious to their fate, remained stationary as women and their children selected their live entrée for the evening's dinner. Ruth Ann and I took photos of a young girl holding a piece of string with two live pigeons dangling from it.

Once back on the bus I noticed Fred holding several floral nosegays. With a smile he told us that they were gifts for some of the ship's female crew members. Looking out the window I noticed the flower lady standing nearby and, with Fred as my interpreter, I bought two small bouquets of tea roses. One graced my room for the rest of the river trip and I gave the other to tour mate Diane who was down and out with Montezuma's Revenge—or perhaps I should say Mao's Revenge. Along with the flowers, I gave her a care package of food that I had lugged all over China, hoping that she would like the instant mashed potatoes, macaroni and oatmeal. Surprisingly, I hadn't used any of these emergency provisions.

After our jaunt through the food market we rode the bus a short distance to a local theater for an acrobatic show. Extremely limber and flexible, the young female star of the show literally sat on her head. When a magician asked for a volunteer from the audience, Ted, a member of our tour group, bounced onto the stage and served as the shill for several tricks. One trick involved the magician handing large fans, one at a time, to Ted. When the magician opened a fan it was in perfect condition. Each time Ted opened one, it was in shreds. They passed fans back and forth, always with the same results. We all howled when Ted pulled out his wallet and offered the magician a few yuan for the damaged fan.

We returned to the ship for lunch and steamed onward toward Chongqing. Today's buffet offered pizza and, in a moment of American food nostalgia, I tried it and found it quite good. I added a bit of egg drop soup and bok choy to my tray for good measure. After lunch Mei-yu spoke to us about the contrasts between Chinese and Western medicines.

Late in the afternoon we drifted past the famed Shibaozhai Pagoda swathed in mist. Soaring twelve stories skyward as if attached to a steep jagged cliff, this towering red pagoda had graced the river since the 1700s. Fortunately, it was positioned high enough above the river to survive the inundations. Once the waters rose, the pagoda's resting spot would become an island.

When I returned to my room, I discovered a very special note under my door. The captain's dinner was scheduled for this evening and I was invited to sit at his table along with Mei-yu. As it turned out, the captain asked his first mate to fill in for him. Since he spoke no English, Mei-yu and he sat together. I found my place card between Juliette, our French cruise director, and the poetry-reading scholar from Cambridge. I talked with Juliette about her transition from her home in northern France to China and with the scholar about his teaching position in Wales. All in all, it was a delightful evening.

We cruised the remainder of our 840 miles along the Yangtze that night and reached the bustling city of Chongqing at 9:30 a.m. the next day. As we left the ship and headed up another steep set of stairs to our tour bus du jour with our luggage in tow, we were surrounded by men offering to carry our bags—for a fee, of course. One grabbed at my shoulder bag and it took my firmest "No!" for him to let go. I scurried up the steps with my two heavy bags and quickly hopped on the bus. Some members of our group couldn't get away from the would-be porters and had their luggage held as ransom until they produced enough yuan. Not a pleasant experience...

Chongqing is situated high above the Yangtze at the junction of the Jialing River, its second-longest tributary. Because the river was already at the 160-meter level at Chongqing and because of the city's altitude, the rising water would not affect it. With its steep roads, there were no bicycles to be found. In fact, there were very few private cars, as residents preferred to take buses and taxis.

We stopped at the square of a large government building erected in the early 1930s. Today it served as a theater with a hotel in one wing and an art museum in the other. The museum proved to be—you guessed it!—another shopping op. This time I dropped quite a few yuan for a small multi-colored glazed pot from the Qing period. It had my name all over it and I couldn't resist. Once again, Mei-yu acted as my interpreter and we bargained the US$800 asking price down to US$250. This charming memento merited a prominent resting place in our home.

Chongqing is enormous with a population of four million, another thirty million living in the outlying areas that continued to grow as the result of the dam project. We learned this as we drove through the city on our way to a local hotel for lunch. Much to my delight we were served Peking duck. Unlike the fare served in the too-large hall in Beijing, we were presented with delicate pancakes, rich plum sauce, slivers of green onion and a platter of perfectly crisp duck skin with just a hint of meat attached.

Our next stop was the airport, and on our way, we passed fields of rice and bananas, which flourished in Chongqing's subtropical climate. Once at the airport we again did our hurry-up-and-wait routine before boarding a flight to Shanghai.

An attractive young woman met us at the airport and, once situated on our bus, gave us some statistics about the city. In 1999, Shanghai boasted a population of thirteen million. With tourists and job seekers, another two to three million were added to this mix on any given day. The longest tributary of the Yangtze divided the city into two distinct parts. As we approached our hotel, the Portman Ritz Carlton, we passed numerous new high rises, all built within the last seven years. Shanghai, once called the Paris of the Orient, had faded during the latter part of the twentieth century but redevelopment of the city was being fueled by foreign investment. We also learned that a new city, Pudong, sprang up after the first of several bridges and tunnels spanning the river were constructed in the 1990s. We would later see Pudong's striking new buildings from the historic Bund, an Indian word meaning waterfront. One final factoid. Shang means *going to*; Hai means *ocean*. Thus, Shanghai translates to Going to the Ocean.

My husband Wayne had cautioned me that the trip from the airport to the hotel could take up to an hour and a half. However, since his last business trip to Shanghai two years prior, a new expressway from the airport to the city center had opened and we zoomed into the city. He had also mentioned that most of the world's largest cranes used to build high rises were now in Shanghai. Fortunately, the majority of the construction projects were now completed and we spotted very few cranes. The city sparkled with its gleaming new structures.

When we arrived at the luxurious Portman Ritz Carlton, a fax dated five days earlier awaited me with news that my jewelry had been found in the Xian hotel. I was overjoyed by the honesty of the Xian hotel staff. However, no arrangements had been made to ship them to our hotel in Shanghai. Catherine, a young hotel manager from England, proved most helpful and made all the necessary arrangements. We crossed our fingers that the package would arrive before our departure in three days. Tom planned to return to Shanghai in a few weeks and offered to bring it back to the States if it arrived late. If Plan A didn't work, we had a solid Plan B.

After finding our rooms and unpacking, our group met at a theater in the hotel complex for a 7:30 p.m. acrobat show. This all-out extravaganza featured a large cast of incredibly talented but uncomfortably too-young performers. Filled with thrills and amazing feats, the show kept us spellbound. The gymnasts flipped, twisted into pretzels and balanced one upon another up to the ceiling. One girl had hula hoops tossed over her until she resembled a human slinky. When we filed out of the auditorium another crowd waited to take our seats. It couldn't have been an easy life for these young performers.

At 8:30 a.m. the next day we departed for the Bund, a historic area directly across the river from Pudong. Many significant turn-of-the-twentieth-century buildings still graced the Bund and most were originally built as European banks. We walked along the river to a four-story Friendship Store. I wandered through looking for a Chinese-style dress for my daughter Emily. She was 5'11" and Chinese women were tiny. It proved to be a futile exercise.

We then drove to a historic preservation area in the center of old Shanghai. Now converted to shops, the century-old homes once constituted an opulent neighborhood. Today it brimmed with Chinese shoppers and tourists. As Mei-yu so wisely said, "Every day is Christmas in China." The crowds indeed resembled frantic last-minute holiday shoppers at Macy's in New York City.

We quickly threaded through the masses and entered a gate to a peaceful garden house at the edge of the turmoil. What a contrast! We marveled at the serene landscaping with its koi ponds, gentle green plantings and massive sculptured rocks. After forty-five minutes we re-entered the crowded shopping area and were given another forty-five minutes to wander. I was grateful to be back on the bus for the ride to our hotel.

With no formal activities for the afternoon, I joined Judy and Jack for lunch in the Ritz Carlton's Garden Room. Another woman in our tour group stopped by our table and invited me to walk with her after lunch. We crossed the street to explore a large exhibition hall. Our guide this morning told us we would find Chinese arts and crafts near it, but all we discovered was a health fair so we continued toward the Bund.

On impulse we turned into an alleyway leading away from the blocks of gleaming buildings that lined Nanjing Road and soon found ourselves in the midst of life as it probably had been for at least a century. We passed rows of tiny houses decked with laundry hanging from windows to dry. At each corner a woman sat on a blanket with an array of fruits and vegetables for sale. A man sat repairing shoes outside a small building and another had a bicycle repair business set up on the sidewalk. It put Nanjing Road into perspective and we now realized that all its glitz and glamour were no more than a façade. Real life happened just beyond it.

I had booked a 5:00 p.m. manicure at the hotel and arrived just in time for it. After a short rest I joined a dozen from our group who went for dim sum and then a view of the city at night from the Pudong TV station's lofty observation deck in the Pearl Tower. We boarded a bus with Lu, our Shanghai tour guide, who took us to an overly crowded tourist restaurant. I had my doubts and they proved true. Only the bok choy was edible. We each paid US$35 for the dinner and we suspected that Lu pocketed a tidy little profit.

Once at the Pearl Tower we took an elevator to the observation level. My suspicions earlier that day that much of Shanghai was a façade were confirmed from our vantage point high above the city. Glossy high rises lined all the important avenues and nothing but darkness lurked in the background. In 1999, the beautiful buildings painted a picture of a modern thriving city that lacked depth.

The next morning's 6:00 a.m. wake-up call barely gave us time to catch an early train to Suzhou, the city of canals and three hundred garden houses about an hour from Shanghai. The day turned out to be a glorified shopping op, first at an embroidery shop and, after lunch, a silk factory. Another so-so lunch at a local hotel didn't make the day any brighter. My find for the day was a lovely watercolor of a sampan that I discovered in an art boutique in the garden house we toured. It now hangs proudly in our home, reminding me of my Yangtze River trip.

On our return to Shanghai we stopped at the Grand Canal for a quick look at this man-made body of water that linked the Yellow and Yangtze Rivers. I stayed on the bus and those who ventured out reported that the canal needed a major clean-up. We made one more stop at a local hotel for its Happy House, a.k.a. WC, and then made the hour-long trip to our hotel.

Tonight I joined Joan, Ruth Ann and their husbands, Dave and Bill, for Continental fare at M, an upscale restaurant near the Bund. Dave, well versed in gourmet food, had read a rave review in an airline magazine. We were not disappointed. I ordered the house special, roast suckling pig. For dessert I ordered sticky toffee pudding with caramel sauce. I tried to remember where I had first sampled this delicious concoction and it came to me that it had been in Australia. I later learned that M had a sister restaurant in Sydney.

On our last day of touring we met at 9:00 a.m. for a short ride to the Shanghai Museum. This incredible new institution housed four stories of treasures. With two hours on our own I decided to head to the top and work my way down, passing displays of coins, period furniture, bronzes, jade, clothing, painted scrolls, china, porcelain, and more. One could spend days here. As Janet put it so well, "We should have come here first. It puts so much of China's history and culture into perspective." At least we would leave China with a wealth of knowledge and understanding after today's visit to this treasure.

We regrouped at noon and about ten of us joined Mei-yu and a Chinese friend to lunch and shop on Nanjing Road East. Mei-yu had mentioned a shop that discounted quality crafts up to ninety percent and I bought a pair of Fu dogs. Only when they were boxed and ready to go did I realize how much these fellows weighed. Leaving the box until the end of the afternoon's activities, we walked another block and took an elevator to the seventh floor for lunch in a private dining room. Mei-yu and her friend made all the selections and the food far surpassed anything to date for a mere US$7.50 per person. What a grand finale!

After lunch our group headed in different directions. Three of us stayed with Mei-yu and her friend to buy green tea and then do a walk-through of an enormous department store. Mei-yu's earlier observation that every day is Christmas in China certainly held true here. So many Chinese packed the aisles that we could barely make our way through them. Once on the street I headed to the discount store to collect my Fu dogs before returning to the Ritz Carlton.

We all regrouped at 6:00 p.m. for a farewell cocktail party. The mood, although festive, was equally bittersweet. We had all become good friends during the course of our China odyssey. Cameras flashed and memories were shared. Jane surprised us with a clever awards presentation, capturing the essence of each of us with humorous accuracy and providing a delightful conclusion to another gratifying expedition.

IRELAND

Doolin, Ashford Castle/Cong, Connemara, Kilkenny,
Ballycotton, Cobh, Cloyne, Ballymaloe, Sheen Falls, Beara Peninsula,
Dingle, and Dromoland Castle

October 2–17, 2002

OUR FIRST VISIT to Ireland in 1983 brought us to the eastern coast. We
were struck at the time by a sense of prevailing poverty outside of Dublin.
As we ventured into the countryside on day trips, we often passed long lines
of gypsy caravans along the roadside. Buildings needed paint and we did
not see much commercial activity. Almost nineteen years later, the country's
economy was on an upswing. American companies, primarily tech, set up
separate legal entities in Ireland and employment boomed. Although our
current trip took us to the western coast, this Irish lass looked forward to
seeing the country transformed from impoverished to plentiful.

Day one of our Irish adventure led us from LA to Doolin, a tiny village
on Ireland's west coast best known as the birthplace of traditional Irish music.
After an easy nine-hour flight from LA we arrived at Dublin International at
11:40 a.m. Our Aer Lingus club-class service was superb and we nestled into
quilted comforters for a few hours' sleep during the flight. Upon landing, we
stayed on board and soon backtracked westward to Shannon Airport. After
clearing customs, we rented a car and began our fifteen-day tour.

Our drive to Doolin took us along the N18 toward Ennis. Reminding
Wayne to stay left and look right on this bright afternoon, we exited the tiny
Shannon Airport. Just outside of Ennis we turned onto the N85, a roadway
so narrow that it seemed unlikely that two vehicles could pass each other. To
complicate matters, stone walls lined the highway to its very edge. We passed
a sign posting an ominous message that forty-six souls had lost their lives on

this stretch of road over the past four years. In spite of the warning, locals sped past us.

We stopped in the small village of Ennistymon at 3:00 p.m. for a quick snack. As we walked along the main street, we found a restaurant and ordered grilled-ham-and-cheese sandwiches. To our dismay we were served soggy prepackaged sandwiches heated in a microwave. Ah, well…better things to come, we were sure.

A ten-minute drive took us to the Cliffs of Moher, spectacular high bluffs perched above the coast. We decided to stop for a closer look. A short climb to the viewing area offered panoramic vistas of the cliffs and crashing waves far below. We walked a bit farther to O'Brien's Tower built in 1853 and climbed to the top for more spectacular views. From there it was a short drive to Doolin and our B&B, the Ballyvara House.

Two hometown friends had recommended Ballyvara and we had no trouble locating it. Itch, the innkeepers' terrier, greeted us as we walked to the door. Once inside, innkeeper Becky and her daughter Hailey showed us to our immaculate room. After hanging up some of our clothes we drove back into Doolin to check out the village's three pubs known for traditional Irish music.

We chose McDermott's, which seemed to have the most authentic atmosphere, for our first evening's pub dinner. When three musicians appeared with violin, mandolin and accordion in hand we knew we had made the right choice. The pieces they played sounded much like the music we heard performed by the Chieftains in July at the Hollywood Bowl. It was truly Irish music at its best, albeit played with fewer instruments. A young man stood near the musicians and did an occasional impromptu Irish jig while wearing hiking boots, no less. It was a magical first evening.

Before returning to our B&B we popped into McGann's for half an hour, sharing a table with a man from Boston, an Englishman and his French wife. Even though the pub was packed with guests from wall to wall, we all agreed that the music at McDermott's won the honors that evening.

We slept fairly well with the help of our sound machine covering the outrageous snores of the guest in the room next to ours. Even the soothing sound of the ocean playing at full volume barely muffled the auditory assault from the Italian just beyond our walls. Thankfully, he checked out the next morning.

After enjoying a full Irish breakfast of oatmeal, Irish brown bread, eggs, bacon, sausage, and grilled tomatoes we embarked on what should have been a mile-and-a-quarter hike to the Doonagore Castle, one of Doolin's historic landmarks. Wayne asked Becky for directions while I loaded my cameras and we set out on our trek on a brisk windy morning. Cars, trucks and buses whizzed past us as we walked and walked along the busy narrow highway, wondering if the castle would even appear. When it finally did and we turned down the roadway toward the ocean leading to it, we noticed a paved pathway running perpendicular to the highway. Our instincts told us to follow it on our return trip and it took us directly to the B&B. We had taken a much longer and more dangerous route on our walk to the castle. Ah, well…good exercise.

Returning to the B&B we hopped into our car and drove back to the Cliffs of Moher hoping for an opportunity to photograph them when the sun was at a better angle. It simply wasn't meant to be; the clouds returned just as we arrived. Nonetheless, we enjoyed revisiting this magnificent natural wonder. At our next stop, Gus O'Connell's Pub in Doolin, Wayne chose Irish stew for lunch and I ordered seafood chowder. Delicious! We then popped into a local shop owned by a transplanted New Englander and bought a couple of CDs featuring traditional Irish music to listen to as we traveled.

Driving north on N477 along the coast, our plan was to explore the famed County Clare Burren, a vast landscape of barren cracked glacier-era limestone with cliffs and caves, rock formations and archaeological sites. En route I spotted a small weathered cemetery filled with Celtic crosses that tilted down a hillside leading toward Doolin in the distance. Deciding it would make interesting photos, I asked Wayne to turn onto the road leading to it. While taking the photos I noticed a sign for a craft shop further down the road and we continued on. The shop turned out to be a good find and Wayne bought a leather belt with a Celtic symbol on the buckle. We chatted with the delightful Irish owner before continuing on our way.

Heading north, we soon arrived at the Burren. Cars had pulled off the roadway and we decided to do the same. We walked a short distance across the rocky slabs of limestone encrusted with tiny mosses and wildflowers that grew from seemingly barren crevices. From our vantage point at the edge of the ocean we could see for miles south to the Cliffs of Moher. Wayne had read that the Burren stretched from the ocean in County Clare inland covering an area of forty thousand hectares, approximately 150 square miles. As we stepped carefully over the slabs of limestone toward our car, we met a charming Irish woman who greeted us and introduced us to her terrier. "Isn't this the most beautiful place in the entire world?" she asked and of course we agreed.

We drove a bit further to the village of Fanore in hopes of finding a tea room. No such luck. As we discovered on our visit to Ireland nineteen years earlier, pubs prevail but food, coffee and tea are at a premium. I remembered a place in Doolin so we headed south to the Lodestone, a small café that served espresso and sweets. While talking with the waitress in this charming cottage-turned-restaurant we discovered that the dinner menu looked fabulous and smoking was prohibited. We decided to return that evening and give it a whirl.

The same waitress greeted us at 8:00 p.m. and seated us at one of three group tables. At her recommendation we ordered rack of lamb and honey-glazed duck after sharing a starter course of assorted cheeses. Each selection earned raves. As we dined, we chatted with Susan, a Canadian living in London. We had noticed her earlier that day in the small gift shop near the cemetery. After finishing our coffee and agreeing that we had chosen the best restaurant, the three of us decided to make the Friday night pub rounds on our mutual last night in Doolin.

Since O'Connell's was just up the street, that seemed the logical first stop. It was packed and it was hopping. A group of seven musicians appeared with their instruments: a banjo, sticks, guitar, mandolin, violin, and accordion, or squeeze box as it is sometimes called. They also had a traditional goatskin bodhrán, pronounced *bow-rawn*, a frame drum that gives the distinctive heartbeat to much of the Irish music. The performers played traditional Irish tunes while sipping Guinness and whiskey in the smoke-and-noise-filled pub.

We then drove to the north end of the village to McGann's where a smaller ensemble played for a smaller crowd. Our last stop, McDermott's, featured a disappointing rock and roll band—nothing like the authentic Irish music on the previous night. We said goodbye to Susan and drove back to O'Connell's for a last hurrah before returning to our B&B at midnight. Doolin and its Irish music would long remain among our fondest memories.

Saying farewell to Doolin the next morning we headed north toward Ashford Castle in County Mayo. Blustery grey clouds foretold the possibility of scattered showers. With each passing mile, however, the clouds dissipated and we soon were treated to a bright warm day.

Wayne headed our car onto the N67 along the inland route through the Burren toward the towns of Lisdoonvarna and Ballyvaughan. In spite of the gift of good weather the roadway became the drive from hell. The narrowest-yet path of a highway zigzagged from the villages into a mountainous area flanked by either tight stone walls or hedgerows. It seemed virtually impossible to pass the oncoming stream of cars, let alone the all-too-frequent truck or bus. Wayne did a masterful job but it nevertheless took all the joy out of what would have been an incredibly scenic drive.

After an hour of tension, we arrived in the picturesque seaside village of Kinvara. Just outside the town we noted another ominous sign stating that

108 people had lost their lives along this road over the past four years. Since I had almost had cardiac arrest as a passenger along this stretch, I might easily have become number 109. The tide was out and an impressive castle stood marooned in a tide pool at the entrance to the harbor.

We entered a roundabout and suddenly found ourselves on a divided four-lane highway. As Wayne noted, we had gone from the ridiculous to the sublime in a matter of seconds. This luxury did not last for long. Within ten miles we skirted the city of Galway at another roundabout onto N84 in the direction of Castlebar. Once again we encountered too-narrow roads with too many tourists driving too slowly and being passed by too many frustrated locals. We drove onward while dangerously encountering too many trucks and buses coming at us from the opposite direction. I just hoped my white knuckles would return to pink by the evening.

Just after turning onto the R334 we entered County Mayo and drove toward the village of Cong, home of Ashford Castle. Suddenly the imposing stone castle gate appeared before us at the end of junction R336. I couldn't wait to step out of our rental onto terra firma. The long driveway to the castle bordered a nine-hole golf course. While this might have been a treat for Wayne, it rained every day he had an opportunity to play.

As we rounded the last bend an enormous majestic Tudor-style castle appeared before us. Nestled at the mouth of a small river that flowed into a quiet lake, Ashford Castle rested regally amid formal gardens and many acres of woods. It ranked as a national treasure and we looked forward to our several-day stay at this unique venue.

Our room was not ready when we arrived so we decided to have a light lunch in the lounge. When we were finally led to our room we discovered that, in addition to being minute, it was located adjacent to a continually buzzing elevator. We returned to the desk and I very graciously asked the receptionist for another room. The castle was fully booked but she managed to find us a fabulous room with views of the lake and gardens on the fourth floor of the rear tower. It paid to ask with a smile.

Ashford Castle boasted a seven-hundred-year history. Originally con-structed in 1228 AD, it had been expanded over the centuries and now served as a five-star luxury hotel. The estate was purchased in 1852 by Sir Benjamin Guinness and he added two Victorian-style extensions. When he died in 1868 the estate passed into the hands of his son, an avid gardener who oversaw the development of massive woodlands and rebuilt the west wing of the castle. It was donated to the Irish government in 1915 and turned into a hotel in 1933.

We walked to the quaint village of Cong and passed the ruins of Cong Abbey. Just a short stroll from the castle, this hamlet was the site of the 1950 movie *The Quiet Man* starring John Wayne and Maureen O'Hara. Fifty years later the townspeople still told tales of their roles as extras in the film.

When we came down for dinner in the castle's dining room at 8:30 p.m. it was so crowded that we waited twenty minutes just to be seated. Once at our table, we had to flag down a waiter to place our order. The cavernous formal dining room was too brightly lit and although our meal was lovely, we were less than impressed with the ambience and the service.

Ah, the true meaning of a vacation! No alarm clocks. Today we awoke to a dense fog over the lake and decided to let the rental car rest. After a break from too much good eating, we opted for late coffee and a plate of local cheeses and then headed out to the wooded paths that bordered the castle's vast estate. We walked, and we walked. The paths led us through lush semi-tropical woods to the lake's edge.

The sun broke through the fog and by afternoon the day could not have been more beautiful. We thoroughly enjoyed our brisk stroll along the wooded paths and eventually made our way into the village. Following a footbridge over the river we reached the Cong Abbey founded in 1135 AD. Now in ruins, the abbey featured some of the best examples of medieval ecclesiastical architecture in all of Ireland. We explored what remained of it.

While walking through the village we discovered a small storefront restaurant called Micilin's that looked quite charming and stepped inside to inquire about a dinner reservation. No one seemed to be there but the aromas were tantalizing. We walked toward the kitchen and found the owner dressed in full chef's garb busily stirring his pots. He welcomed us and assured us that he would have a table for us at 8:00 p.m.

Ashford Castle, for all its grandeur, packed in busloads of aging, overweight and inappropriately dressed tourists. By mid-afternoon each day they choked the halls with suitcases and sat in the dining room in large, noisy groups. Although the food was good, the fixed-price menu included more courses than either Wayne or I wanted. The exquisite Waterford crystal chandeliers in the huge dining hall assaulted the tables with such bright light, it seemed we had a spotlight shining on us. When we asked that the one above us be turned down, we were told it wasn't possible. In contrast, Micilin's offered interesting menu selections in a relaxed atmosphere.

We were well rewarded for our decision. We shared an exceptional house pâté. I then ordered chicken in a wine cream sauce and Wayne had duck à l'orange. Both earned raves along with our sides of breads and vegetables. Margaret, our young waitress, charmed us and we decided to return the next night. Several people we met at Ashford Castle sat at a table near us. They had discovered Micilin's on a previous visit.

The next day it rained. It had to happen sooner or later. We were glad we chose yesterday to walk and today to travel. As I finished preparing for our drive through the mountains of Connemara, Wayne visited the hotel gift shop to buy a few extra rolls of film. While there he spotted an Ashford plaid wool sports coat that fit him perfectly. With my nod of approval, he made the purchase.

Robert, the hotel concierge, charted a route for us through the Connemara and we began our drive on this chilly overcast October morning. Skirting the lake, we began a half-hour drive into the mountains toward Maam, derived from a Gaelic word meaning mountain pass. Even though the road was narrow it seemed like a superhighway after yesterday's driving experience. Straight was not a word in the Irish vocabulary of road design and hairpin curves continued to be the order of the day.

Soon spectacular vistas appeared. We entered upland meadows as we headed north toward the village of Leenane. Sheep dotted the mountains on either side of us for quite a distance. With no shoulder along the road we couldn't stop for photos so these words would serve as our memories. Killary Harbour eventually came into view with fish farms covering its surface for several miles. Finally, a turnout appeared and we stopped in the drizzle for photos of some decrepit fishing boats moored along the edge of the harbor, the fog-covered mountains in the background.

Turning on our traditional Irish music CDs, we continued along the road through the valley to the south bordering the ocean. Wayne suddenly pulled over and shouted, "Look at that!" He had spotted a peat-cutting operation. Blocks of peat were stacked in symmetrical rounds. Trenches from the bog cutting ran in diagonal ridges from the road. We shot misty photos through the rain in hopes of capturing this interesting process.

Arriving at Kylemore Park at noon, we stopped at its namesake abbey to take a look at this impressive 1867 edifice. Like Ashford Castle, Kylemore Abbey was built by a wealthy man, a doctor who enjoyed hunting and fishing. Since 1920 it had functioned as a community for Benedictine nuns. Set into a wooded hillside along a lake, it was truly remarkable. Walking tours were available but we took a pass since it was now pouring rain.

Reaching the next village of Letterfrack we came upon the Avoca Handcraft Shop and decided to take a look. I picked up some early Christmas gifts, soaps and bath salts made locally. By now we were hungry and began to look for a restaurant or pub and discovered the Rose Cottage and Farmhouse Restaurant just outside the village. Good choice! John, the young chef, had studied in culinary school eleven years earlier and cooked in Galway and Clifton before returning to his home just a few months ago. How fortunate for us! His warming seafood chowder was superb. Wayne also ordered salmon and I tried my very first cod. His preparations were simply divine. We enjoyed chatting with John and offered him a stay in our Rincon Beach house in exchange for a dinner party or two while he was in residence.

A final stop at Joyce's Craft Shop in Recess resulted in one more sport coat for Wayne. I was astounded by the quality and reasonable prices of these jackets. We then completed the last part of our drive to Maam Cross, and finally back to Ashford Castle. Once again it was tour bus heaven and we had to thread our way through huge piles of suitcases and throngs of tourists clogging the parking area and passageways. This was not what we expected from a highly touted Relais & Chateaux hotel. We were glad to hear that friends of ours had a very different experience when they stayed at Ashford Castle years after we did, as they did not encounter busloads of tourists. Lucky them!

In a steady rain we retraced our footsteps to Micilin's for an 8:00 p.m. dinner. After a full day in a car even a soggy walk felt good. Margaret, the hostess, saved our favorite table for us. New friend Robert, the concierge at Ashford, told us that Micilin's chef Sean Devereux had served on the Queen Mary until it was decommissioned. Incidentally, having watched the movie *The Quiet Man* the night before, we now realized that Micilin was the name of the pony cart driver in the film. A tongue-in-cheek sketch of the actor pointing in the direction of the WC seemed to be the only visual reference to the restaurant's namesake.

On this chilly evening I selected seafood curry and Wayne chose the chicken dish I had ordered the previous evening. Once again, our dinners were outstanding. While chatting with Margaret after all the guests had left, Wayne asked if we could thank the chef. He came out of the kitchen and we were treated to a fascinating forty-five-minute dissertation of his time spent on the Queen Mary and cooking at private parties for the Queen Mum.

We decided to walk back to the castle in the rain rather than call for a courtesy cab. As we entered the lobby, I stopped to compliment a woman wearing a full-length plaid pleated skirt and matching shawl. While we chatted, Wayne turned to her husband and in amazement said, "Arch!" It turned out to be an acquaintance from his business time in Chicago almost twenty-five years earlier. Arch and his wife Anne were with a small Yale group, class of 1944, celebrating their reunion in England and Ireland. It was lovely to see them at Ashford.

Getting to sleep was a nightmare. The residents of room #500 above us returned just after midnight and must have been part of one of the many tour groups. Suitcase packing went on until well after 1:00 a.m. and resumed as the sun came up. Scratch this as an ideal room…

After awakening to thumps and bumps and then to our alarm clock, we had an early breakfast before checking out and embarking on a re-run of the white-knuckle-drive-from-hell back to Galway. As usual, a fair number of trucks charged full speed directly at us, usually a good bit in our lane. Wayne had talked with concierge Robert who suggested we take the longer legs of the triangular route to Kilkenny to avoid even more dangerous roads.

Following the N8, we drove east toward Dublin as far as Athlone. Beyond it at the small village of Moate we turned south. Just after noon in a blinding rainstorm we found ourselves on another narrow road with no shoulders, the N80. A sign announced that thirty-six people had died on this stretch in the past four years. Not good. Not good at all. After a few miles the road widened slightly and the rain subsided. Life maybe was good after all.

Reaching Port Laoise at 2:00 p.m. in pouring rain we spotted a pub for a late lunch. It turned out to be another ham-and-cheese-sandwich-on-white-bread joint. Fifteen more minutes along the N8 would have led us to Abbeyleix, a charming small village with several dining options. I noticed signs for Quinn's Tea & Coffee House and Preston House Café, among others. The quaint town filled with vine-covered cottages had been designated a Heritage Town and definitely rated a return visit.

En route to Kilkenny we passed a large factory just north of a town called Ballygalget. Although we had no idea what it produced, it was the first big business operation other than farming and tourism we had encountered in the past five days.

We arrived in Kilkenny at 4:00 p.m., missing our hotel, the Zuni, on our first pass through the town. Wayne actually stopped to ask for directions, a rarity for him, and we found it shortly thereafter. Recommended in Karen Brown's book, the hotel was a bit stark for our taste but quiet and well located. We unloaded our bags and proceeded into town in a drizzle for a quick look before dinner in the hotel's highly rated dining room.

After an hour's walk through the center of Kilkenny, the finest example of a medieval city in all of Ireland, we returned to the hotel for a rest after our long day's drive. At 8:00 p.m. we were led to our table in Zuni's ultra-modern dining room. As at Ashford Castle, one of our two servers came from Southeast Africa. The other hailed from Malaysia.

Zuni's cuisine brought us to this establishment and we were not disappointed. Both food and attentive service excelled. Wayne began with a goat cheese and onion tart and I had smoked mushroom soup. We asked our waitress to recommend the house specialty and she instantly suggested the bacon with colcannon cakes. In Ireland, bacon equaled lean smoked pork similar to a thick cut of Canadian bacon. Zuni's version of colcannon cakes consisted of seasoned mashed potatoes, cabbage and onion formed into patties, dipped in breadcrumbs and then quickly deep-fried. To die for! I had had a version of this typical pub dish on my first night in Doolin but it was nothing like this. We'd have to diet for weeks when we returned home.

After a wonderful full breakfast at Zuni we donned our rain gear—enough already with this rain!—and headed out for a look at Kilkenny Castle. As was the case throughout our visit, we encountered a friendly Irishman about our age walking his two Jack Russells along the river path and we chatted for a bit before leaving the castle grounds. We then crossed the street to the castle's vast stable complex that now housed a restaurant and a series of craft shops, and made a few more purchases before heading into the town center.

We popped into a pub attached to the Hibernia Hotel not far from Zuni. It was packed but we found a couple of stools near the door. Since the room was filled with smoke this was welcome. I ordered the wild mushroom and chestnut soup and Wayne followed suit. It tasted so divine that we decided to try the Hibernia's more formal dining room for dinner that night. We wanted charm in Ireland. We can find plenty of Zuni modern in LA.

Since the guide for the 3:00 p.m. walking tour we had signed up for was running late, we opted to skip it and create our own. We visited the imposing St. Canice's Cathedral, Anglican since the time of Henry VIII, and then Rothe House Museum and Garden, a typical home of the Tudor period. Continuing on our self-guided tour we stopped at the Black Abbey founded in 1225 AD. It became known as the Black Abbey in 1349 AD when the community within the priory was affected by an outbreak of bubonic plague, also known as Black Death.

Just after 8:00 p.m. we walked the short distance to the Hibernia Hotel's Jacobs Cottage for tonight's dinner, which did not live up to our expectations. Since the lamb shank on the menu wasn't available, our waitress suggested pork, mediocre at best. In retrospect, we should have stayed with Zuni, a proven success. However, eating lightly tonight after a week of fine dining may have been a blessing in disguise.

Assuming that we had a relatively short drive today, we took our time and departed Kilkenny at 11:00 a.m. As it would prove time after time along Ireland's roadways, the drive was not an easy one. Disturbing signs continued to post the number of lives lost along stretches of the narrow highways.

We turned onto the N25 at Waterford, a large port city, spelled Port Láirge in Gaelic. Many in western Ireland still speak their native language and signs are posted in both Gaelic and English. When Wayne looked for a news station the previous night, the only one he found was in Gaelic. Although he could not understand the woman reporting the weather, he could tell from her map that the rain would stop.

Hometown friends had suggested a stop at the Waterford Crystal Factory and we arrived there just before noon. The next hour-long tour was about to begin so we queued up for a bus ride to the factory. Our guide told us that William and George Penrose founded Waterford Crystal in 1783. Today the company employed sixteen hundred workers on its forty-acre site. We began our tour viewing a film from the millennium and then saw a small replica of the crystal ball that descended in Times Square on New Year's Eve 2000. New York City's version, the largest project ever undertaken by the Waterford Company, measured six feet in diameter, weighed two tons and took six months to complete.

Next, we watched demonstrations of glass blowing and shaping, cutting, etching, and polishing. Just before leaving the factory we met a master cutter who demonstrated his craft and answered questions. He told us he began to study these techniques at the age of sixteen and became a master cutter at age twenty-four. Not an overnight success story!

We had a quick lunch in the Waterford cafeteria before forging ahead toward Cork and Ballymaloe House, our next destination. Around mid-afternoon we entered County Cork and soon came to the seaside village of Youghal on the Atlantic coast along the southern tip of Ireland. For the first time in three days the sun attempted to peek through the grey clouds and we couldn't resist stopping for a look around. Brightly painted fishing boats rested on the muddy bottom of the harbor at low tide.

Continuing on to Midleton we looked for signs for Cloyne and then Ballymaloe. After a missed turn we doubled back and soon found our way to the charming farmhouse-turned-inn. Famed for its cooking school as well as its inn, Ballymaloe rests on four hundred acres about twenty miles east of Cork. As we drove onto the grounds we had to stop while a few sheep lazily made their way across the road. Ah, the pastoral life! No tour buses here!

We registered and were led to the West Room on the lower level overlooking the back garden and a pond in the distance. Above us was a television room which we doubted would get much use from us. Our bellman told us the inn was only half full so we anticipated a quiet three-night stay.

Dinner at 8:30 p.m. was served in one of five small dining rooms. Our five-course meal began with a chilled artichoke soup followed by plaice and venison for Wayne and oysters and guinea hen for me. Afterward, an incredible cheese trolley rolled up to our table, trailed by yet another filled with desserts and coffee to complete the evening. I was glad I didn't find a scale in our room!

We enjoyed meeting several of the young servers. One from Budapest who planned to leave for Bavaria the next morning invited us to her farewell party at the Black Bird Pub in Ballycotton. Although we were tempted, it was now 11:00 p.m. and we decided that late nights were meant for the younger set. Before we left, another woman who hailed from Cloyne shared her insights on the dynamic changes in Ireland during the past twenty years.

Irishly speaking, we awoke to another rainy day. A fabulous full traditional Irish breakfast in Ballymaloe's dining room did help to brighten our spirits. I even ordered fresh cod as an accompaniment and Wayne marveled at the quality of the porridge. After talking with hotel personnel and charting the day's trip, we departed for the village of Ballycotton and a walk through the Irish Heritage Center in Cobh.

We drove through the small village of Shanagarry to the sea coast. Although it was too dreary to go for a walk, we did spot an island with a lighthouse perched on it. We retraced our route to the Stephen Pearce Pottery Gallery in Shanagarry, a modern building showcasing well-executed pieces in earth tones. Wayne wondered if Stephen had a connection to the well-known glass artist Simon Pearce and we soon learned the two were brothers.

Our next stop was Ballycotton, spelled Baile Choitín in Gaelic, whose harbor rose to a cliff overlooking the Atlantic. We mailed a few postcards and took advantage of a brief break in the rain to take photos before exiting the village along yet another too-narrow road bordering the cliff.

We drove through Cloyne and headed southwest to Cobh, pronounced *Cove*, home of the Irish Heritage Center. On the outskirts of town, we noticed a ferry about to depart for Cork just across the narrow harbor and stopped to watch it in the light drizzle. Wayne pointed out a restaurant on the Cork side of the harbor where he had dined with business friends on a previous trip.

Driving into Cobh I was surprised by the gingerbread-house-esque trim on many of the homes. The lacy detailing reminded us of Alpine architecture. As we entered the town we were struck by the bright colors of the hotels, shops and pubs. The buildings reminded me of a box of crayons—bright reds, greens, purples, blues, and golds all lined up side by side. Just charming! In spite of the rain the town was filled with people and parking was at a premium. Glancing down a side road I spotted a single open space and we soon made our way to the Heritage Center.

Once inside we learned of the Irish emigration to America, Canada, South America, and Australia that occurred from the early 1800s to the early 1900s. One room recreated the sound and the fury of an actual sailing ship leaving what was then called Queenstown, now Cobh. In the 1840s the name was changed to Queenstown when Queen Victoria visited and then reverted to its original name of Cobh in the 1920s. Another section of the museum was dedicated to the *Titanic* and the *Lusitania*, both making their last port of call in Queenstown/Cobh.

Not far from town we passed a sign to the Fota House, Ireland's finest example of Regency-period architecture with superb neoclassical interiors. Deciding to stop, we entered the grounds and noted directions to either an exotic animal park or to the manor house and gardens. Choosing option number two we parked our car and spotted the impressive home in the distance. Already soggy, we grabbed our umbrellas and set off along a wooded path for a forty-five-minute self-guided tour of the newly restored first floor of the estate. We then walked through the rear garden and orangerie, or greenhouse, before returning to the car park just seconds before a downpour that lasted the entire thirty-five-minute drive back to Ballymaloe.

After drying out, we returned to the dining room for another sinfully delicious repast.

Strange banging noises early the next morning woke us up. We couldn't figure out what caused them but when I looked out our window, I was overjoyed to see our first sunny morning in five days. Our first stop was the dining room. Wayne ordered a full Irish breakfast and I decided to try an egg and fresh cod. Nearly an hour later we were still waiting and noted that many of the diners around us were well into their full Irish breakfasts. The kitchen on a Saturday, it seemed, did not run as efficiently, particularly when a wayward guest ordered cod. Lesson learned. Tomorrow I'd go for the full Irish breakfast.

We finally departed at 11:00 a.m. for Ballycotton, enjoying the sunny drive. Our receptionist had suggested a walk that veered onto what she called a goat trail down to the ocean. We retraced yesterday's route and left our rental high above the Atlantic in a small public car park. The island with the lighthouse we had seen the day before now glowed in bright sunlight and I snapped far too many photos.

A nearby path led us along a steep cliff lined with wild blackberries. Eventually we came to a very narrow dirt path heading almost straight down to the ocean. I forged ahead, glad that we had packed good hiking boots. Two-thirds of the way down we reached cement steps leading almost vertically to a rocky outcrop. The steps were old and only a few sections of the corroded railing remained. Wayne gingerly passed me and made it to the bottom. I reached it eventually by looking only as far as my next step would take me to avoid vertigo. Once at the bottom the vistas were awesome. We took more photos before heading back up the cliff. Getting up seemed much easier than the descent and we hiked along the upper trail for almost a mile before retracing our steps to the car.

Wayne wanted to revisit Ballycotton's harbor in the sunshine so we stopped briefly and walked along the dock before driving to Shanagarry's beach. We walked out on the sandy shore at low tide before driving to Cloyne for a highly anticipated lunch followed by a climb up the town's medieval tower. No luck on either count. The hot new restaurant we had heard about only served lunch on Wednesdays and Fridays. We missed it by a day. As for the tower, it was locked. We knew that Ballymaloe's gift shop had a café so we drove to our inn to give it a try. Good choice; it was terrific. Just as we finished the rain returned.

After our very late lunch we headed for the small village of East Ferry. The turnoff wasn't sign-posted and the road became no wider than a driveway. We finally said, "Enough!" Wayne had hoped to see a marina at the end of the road but at 4:30 p.m. in inclement weather, it just didn't compute. We drove on to Whitebait and found a car park high above the harbor on the opposite side of Cobh. Just then the skies turned black and the rain fell in earnest. It was a shame to say good-bye to a truly beautiful site.

Our final stop was Garryvoe, another booming tidal beach town near Ballymaloe. Returning to the inn, we relaxed in the sitting room and planned the next day's drive to Sheen Falls. On our way we noticed a family with a baby and a toddler camped in the television room located directly above ours. That accounted for the early morning thumping we had heard. Since children are not allowed in the inn's dining rooms, this family had commandeered the television room for breakfast, lunch and dinner. We had a chat with the receptionist and she assured us that she would ask the family to start a bit later the next morning.

So much for asking…. We awoke to more thumping and more rain. Some things never change. The people in the room next to us also complained to the management about the early morning noise above us so we were not alone in our dissatisfaction. Wayne went for coffee and bumped into the distraught father of the youngsters who sighed and said that his two-year-old had arisen at 5:00 a.m. It came as no surprise to us. Ballymaloe wasn't an ideal retreat for families with babies and toddlers and I felt sorry for the couple trapped inside by the rain.

Breakfast that day came instantly and we sat near an interesting couple from Ohio. They were traveling much the same route as ours and had stayed at Ashford Castle. Their favorite resort was Ballylickey Manor House near Bantry. They recommended we avoid Kinsale on our way to Kenmare because its annual food festival was in progress, causing traffic congestion for miles. We were disappointed but decided to put this highly touted seaside village on a future trip agenda. The couple also advised us against the Ring of Kerry, telling us they had driven it and found themselves sandwiched between tour buses all day. They recommended the nearby Ring of Beara as an alternative.

We headed west on the N25 in steady rain toward Cork before turning onto the N71 toward Kinsale and passed rolling hillsides with farmhouses nestled atop pastures that were pretty even in pouring rain. As we drove through the town of Bandon we commented on the brightly colored buildings in this city, just as we had seen in Cobh. No two structures nestled alongside each other were the same; a purple touched a gold and a rose rested against a turquoise. We finally concluded that the vivid rainbow colors brightened the otherwise drab days of rainy Irish existence.

We continued on through Clonakilty's impressively landscaped gated entrance to the city and marveled at its new industry and corresponding new homes. The Irish middle class prospered in 2002. Soon we were back on narrow death-trap roads and yet another sign appeared announcing gloom and doom statistics.

I had read about Drombeg Stone Circle, a near-perfect prehistoric site along this route between Rosscarbery and Glandore and wanted to see it. It was active between 1100 and 800 BC according to radiocarbon dating, and was rediscovered in 1957. One of the best in all of Ireland, it consisted of a seventeen-stone prayer circle, a kitchen with a three-by-five-foot stone cauldron that could be heated to the boiling point in eighteen minutes simply by adding rocks from a fire pit, and two round living quarters. Although it took our asking locals how to find it, we were glad that we stopped. Just as we arrived the rains descended so we toured under umbrellas. That's Ireland!

At 3:00 p.m. we drove through the small harbor town of Bantry before backtracking to Bantry House built in 1796. After a quick late lunch in its cafeteria we toured the manor house before continuing on in a raging downpour toward Sheen Falls. Outside of Bantry we passed Ballylickey Manor House, which our breakfast companions had raved about and we agreed that the setting recommended it.

The road began to climb upward and the rain cleared once more for a stunning view of Bantry Bay to the south. As we proceeded, we entered a spectacular but dangerously narrow roadway leading into a rocky pass through a mountain. To complicate matters, sheep chose to graze right along the road. Locals didn't miss a beat and drove like maniacs, whizzing by us in the opposite direction and only missing our car by inches.

Pausing at a narrow two-car turnout at the top of the mountain for a photo just as the rain stopped, another car pulled in right behind us. A couple from England hopped out and we chatted while snapping photos.

As we started our drive down the mountain a spectacular rainbow suddenly appeared in the valley below us.

It took us another twenty minutes to reach Kenmare and Sheen Falls, our next destination. Sheen Falls Lodge, our stay for two nights, is located at the base of a small waterfall. We found it with no difficulty at 5:00 p.m. and checked into our room with a magnificent view of the falls. After unpacking we took a brief walk around the grounds and falls before getting ready for dinner.

This evening's meal proved to be a masterpiece. We did not expect gourmet dining and this was a very pleasant surprise. Wayne's pork and my venison were superb. The only drawback with all this good eating was that the abundance of rain had kept us from our usual walking. We would have many calories to burn when we returned to the States.

Deciding to go light on breakfast we opted for the buffet the next morning. Luck was with us and we were greeted by Irish sunshine. We took a brief walk through the inn's wooded estate following the Queen's Walk for twenty-five minutes along the trails through a semi-tropical forest. Tiny ponds bordering part of the walkway were absolutely beautiful.

After too many miles on too many narrow roads, I suggested the night before that we hire a driver for our day's tour of the Ring of Beara. Wayne agreed in an instant. Returning to our room from our walk, we gathered cameras and prepared to meet our driver, Denis, who arrived on the dot and couldn't have been more charming. What a relief for both of us to have an alternate driver! Wayne sat in the passenger seat and enjoyed the scenery for the entire day while I sat in the back of the van and relaxed, feeling reassured that a local was at the wheel.

After about twenty minutes Denis (one n; he made sure we knew this) turned onto what I now called a one-lane road meant for two cars and our tour of the Ring of Beara began in earnest. Wayne and I never would have known of this route and it would have been a shame to miss it. We could see across the bay to the mountains of the Ring of Kerry and suspected that from our vantage point we had the best view. On this sunny day it was a sight to behold. We were glad we had chosen to explore this peninsula.

Wayne noticed houses scattered on the hillsides and asked Denis about the residents. He replied that only sheep farmers and fishermen lived in this scarcely populated area. As we had noticed the previous day, sheep far outnumbered the residents.

Denis stopped a couple of times but he obviously did not understand my passion for photography. Time after time he would speed past an absolutely breathtaking vista and then stop at turnouts that were far less scenic.

Sometimes he chose a spot that had absolutely no redeeming value. We just couldn't figure out his logic. Ah, well. Another day of mental memories...

When we came to the village of Eyeries, I had a change of heart. It was spectacular! As we drove to a vantage point above this colorful small town, I couldn't wait to grab my cameras. Denis continued downward into the town and stopped. However, the best shot was about a block's distance behind us. The lighting was perfect and I asked if I could walk back to shoot a few photos. "Absolutely!" he said. "However, I am driving up the road and you can take your photos from there." Trusting him I agreed and got in the car. Big mistake. My camera's telephoto didn't cover a distance of a mile and a half and that is precisely how much farther he drove. I'd have pictures of Eyeries that were the size of postage stamps. Very sad indeed.

We stopped in Allihies, once a copper-mining town, for a lunch of fish and chips at O'Neill's Pub before continuing on our way. Turning along the eastern end of the peninsula we had a view of Bantry before cutting across on the Healy Pass. This tiny path of a roadway snaked its way up the rocky mountainside to a souvenir shop at the very top which we thought was rather odd since so few vehicles traveled this route. Denis told us that many hikers followed this pass so the shop probably offered snacks and water as well as mementos.

The road then cut sharply downward and linked back to one we had started out on earlier in the day. We returned to Sheen Falls just before 4:30 p.m. and both agreed that, in spite of very few photos, our relaxing day's tour of the spectacular Ring of Beara would long be a treasured memory.

Taking advantage of a still-sunny afternoon we decided to walk through the village of Kenmare, winner of a Tidy Town award. With only two main streets forming a "T" it took no time at all to stroll up and down each side of the roadways. Then Wayne bought two local cheeses, a delicious semi-soft farmhouse from Bantry and a hard rennet from Schull. Very nice!

Dinner tonight at the Lime Tree was an excellent suggestion from our driver Denis. Located in a lovely old two-story house, it sat a block off the main thoroughfare. We were given a table for two near the fireplace in a quiet corner. I ordered fresh steamed mussels and Wayne had a seafood tart for starters. I chose lamb for my main course and Wayne went for the duck. All were delicious.

Our daily routine always began with opening our curtains for a rain check. Today's forecast called for more rain and, although none fell while we had coffee and toast in our room, we knew it would soon follow. We packed, checked out and stopped in Kenmare at Nostalgia, an Irish linen shop, to purchase a few more gifts before starting our journey to Dingle.

Denis had plotted a safe and rather lengthy route for us that our bellman disagreed with. We decided to combine the two and headed onto the R569 just as the rain began to fall. The first leg of the trip plotted by Denis, albeit less scenic, moved us along at a steady clip and avoided the almost-certain tour buses on the narrow roads of the first leg of the Ring of Kerry. We missed the Killarney National Park but suspected we had seen much the same geological scenery the day before.

Our bellman recommended the turnoff to Milltown, a country road shortcut. We reached this tiny village just before noon and turned onto the R561 toward the coast and the Dingle Peninsula at Castlemaine, heading on toward Inch. Once there we stopped at a turnout and marveled at the best stretch of sandy beach we had seen in Ireland. Driving on, the road rose sharply and narrowed so much that I felt I was literally hanging over a 500-foot ledge above the ocean. As a passenger in an English car, it was indeed frightening. To add to the mix, the roads were in sad condition and full of potholes. Thankfully, the steep narrow roads only lasted a few miles.

Arriving in Dingle just before 1:00 p.m. we missed our B&B, Emlagh House, on the first pass through town. When we finally arrived, a sign posted on the front door informed us that the innkeeper would return at 2:00 p.m. We decided to look for Doyle's Fish House, a restaurant we had read about, for lunch. It was closed until dinnertime but next to it was the Half Door posting an impressive menu. We decided to give it a try. Just as we were seated, I watched a fisherman deliver a large sack of mussels and ordered some. Talk about fresh! Wayne opted for oysters which were also wonderful. He topped them off with local salmon and I ordered crab au gratin.

We returned to our B&B and met the delightful owner, Marion, who recommended that we drive the thirty-mile ring around the Dingle Peninsula. First, we selected a room on the top floor of the inn, the Honeysuckle, with a harbor view toward the Ring of Kerry. Emlagh House was a treasure, only two years old and built in the style of an elegant English country house. Every detail was perfect and we would choose it again for another stay in Dingle.

We began our tour along the Slea Head Drive at 4:00 p.m. in clearing weather. Not, however, on better roads.... We stopped at the Celtic and Prehistoric Museum, operated by a New Englander who had lived eight years on a houseboat in Amsterdam. One of the highlights was a great woolly mammoth skull with tusks intact named Millie in honor of its discovery in 1999 at the almost-millenium. It turned out, however, that she was a he. We also stopped at the Dúnbeg Iron Age Fort dating from 500 BC–500 AD and then drove along beautiful scenic areas including locations for the films *Far and Away* and *Ryan's Daughter*. Once more the roadways were precarious.

I had jumped off bridges on bungee cords and parasailed off mountainsides but these roads made me crazy.

We chose Doyle's for dinner. Famed for its seafood, we couldn't skip it during our stay in Dingle. Arriving just after 8:00 p.m. we were ushered to a banquette next to a noisy table of six and asked to be seated a bit further away. Our dinner was good; not great. Lunch at the Half Door a few feet away far surpassed our meal at this world-renowned restaurant, but we enjoyed chatting with Fiona and John, our waitress and waiter.

Walking toward the car after dinner we heard pure Irish music coming from a pub. We stood at the entrance and listened to captivating music played on a flute, guitar, violin, and accordion. While in Ireland we learned two tricks in dealing with Irish pubs: find a place to stand just outside or sit near the door to avoid the smoke. Once inside, order a short Guinness and let it rest on the table. As long as your glass was full, you were a legitimate patron.

Ah, the luck of the Irish! Perhaps it paid to be fifty percent Irish on the last full day in the country. When we opened the curtains this morning the sun smiled right in on us. Marion greeted us in the inn's charming breakfast room and served us freshly squeezed orange juice and a fabulous full Irish breakfast. Before we departed, her husband Michael came to meet us. In addition to serving as innkeeper he worked as a farmer and local land developer. Charming couple!

We asked Marion to suggest a good gift shop in the village along with an interesting new route to exit the Dingle Peninsula. She mentioned Simple Pleasures, a lovely shop with a bright pink storefront and encouraged us to take the narrow but scenic Connor Pass across the peninsula. Deciding that we could handle one last too-narrow and too-steep road on our last day of driving, we embarked on another long and winding road.

On a sunny day, white knuckles and all, the sheer beauty overwhelmed us as we headed up a four-mile grade. We passed two young cyclists and marveled at their endurance. A parking area at the top held eight or ten cars and vans, all filled with tourists. The view downward in one direction offered a miniature view of Dingle. To the left we spotted a couple of upland lakes. On the opposite side lay the spectacular coast with sandy bays. This viewing point, the highest in all of Ireland, could only be reached by car or bicycle and we now knew why Marion encouraged us to take this spectacular route.

We continued down the narrow roadway with me cringing at each turn as we inevitably encountered another vehicle squeezing past us. Soon we came to the R560 along the north coast of the Dingle Peninsula. On our right were lush towering green hills dotted with plots of farmland. On the opposite side more farmland stretched almost to the sea. The coastal road bordered sandy beaches interrupted occasionally by a small village. Our drive was, as usual, slow going. With homes built right along the roads, Ireland may never be able to widen its highways. We often had to slow to twenty miles an hour or less as we followed trucks and tractors. Such was daily life in Ireland.

Arriving at Tralee at 1:00 p.m. we somehow missed the turn onto the N21 and drove through the town. The twenty-minute detour through this large town confirmed what we had heard of Ireland's surging economy. Tralee sparkled in the glow of recent growth and even had a large sports stadium.

Nevertheless, we both agreed that far too much of our vacation in Ireland had been spent making slow progress in our rental car. We had expected our point-to-point time to pass by quickly and would plan for much slower commutes if and when we returned. We looked forward to more strolls through charming villages and far less time inside our car. Hiring a full-time driver began to have its appeal.

We continued on through Adare and noted that, like the village of Kenmare, it won a Tidy Town award. Its castle, in ruins, appeared to be under reconstruction. The small village looked absolutely charming. Good friends considered Adare Manor one of their favorites.

Arriving in Limerick at 2:45 p.m. we took the N18 toward Galway and then to Dromoland Castle in County Clare, passing the old wharf area bordering the River Shannon. We noted a number of industrial complexes and even more under construction. Until the Irish roadways improved, however, all industrial development seemed to be located in proximity to Ireland's major airports and seaports.

Wayne noted that the car's odometer had reached the 1,000-mile mark. Hours of driving almost every day was not a vacation. If we returned to Ireland, we'd limit our scope. We'd concentrate on southwest Ireland. Another visit to Dooling and a visit to Kinsale when it wasn't inundated with food-festival tourists ranked high on our to-do list. We'd like to revisit Ballymaloe and stay in a room that wasn't beneath the television room. We might consider enrolling in its famed cooking school. We'd also like to try Adare Manor. Another trip was definitely in order.

Perhaps we'd revisit Dromoland Castle although the surrounding area didn't have much to offer. We chose it for our final night not only for its charm but also because of its proximity to the Shannon Airport. We checked into our room in the old part of the castle that dated from the 16th century and only saw one tour bus, a far cry from Ashford Castle. Even though there were a hundred rooms, Dromoland seemed intimate.

We walked for some time through the gardens and surrounding grounds. The formal gardens, a short stroll from the castle, displayed a wide variety of meticulously tended plants and flowers. We then meandered along an area bordering a wood and Wayne spotted a pheasant just off the path. I quietly focused my camera for an opportunity to capture this bird in the wild. Surprisingly, it stood still. When it did wander away, we followed its direction and soon came to a fenced area filled with pheasants. No wonder our photo model was so accommodating. With clipped wings, he was just out for a short amble.

We returned to the castle in time for afternoon tea. How civilized! Then we organized our suitcases one last time. Our 9:00 p.m. dinner exceeded our expectations and we both ordered perfectly prepared lamb in one of Dromoland's small, intimate dining rooms. A woman playing an Irish harp added a lovely touch.

Coffee and scones arrived at our door at 6:45 a.m. the next day and we soon said farewell to Dromoland Castle. Not wishing for us to miss one last adventure on Irish roads, the weather gods socked us in with thick fog and Wayne could barely see a few feet in front of him. When we finally arrived at Shannon Airport, we gave a sigh of relief and thankfully turned in our rental car.

After clearing immigration, we boarded a plane to Dublin before catching our connecting flight to LA. As we flew across Ireland, we had a last look at the patchwork of small farms that dotted so much of the emerald countryside. Clouds soon obscured our view and we settled in for our flight to America.

In spite of the abundant rain and treacherous roads, we treasured our time in Ireland. We smile when we recall the friends we met who charmed us with their Irish humor and hospitality. Warm memories carry us from the Cliffs of Moher and the Burren to Cong and the Connemara; from medieval Kilkenny to Ballymaloe; from Sheen Falls to the Ring of Beara and the Dingle Peninsula. We often listen to the music we brought home from Doolin and will never forget seeing our first Irish rainbow.

GERMANY AND RUSSIA
Berlin, Munich, Moscow, Uglich, Yaroslavl, Goritsy, Kizhi,
and St. Petersburg

July 30–August 16, 2003

NO MATTER HOW you slice it, the travel time from LA to anywhere in Europe takes many hours. Thankfully, Wayne booked us in first class on a flight departing at 6:00 p.m. so we could at least try to get a good night's sleep during the twelve-and-a-half-hour transit to Frankfurt, Germany, and subsequent transfer to Berlin.

As our taxi traveled through East Berlin, we marveled at the massive reconstruction taking place. I had expected to see the city still ravaged by years of neglect but this was not the case. Reconstruction would be a recurring theme during our visit to the eastern sector, now open since the fall of the Berlin Wall in 1989. We arrived at our hotel, the Adlon, located just inside the famed Brandenburg Gate. The bellman led us to a suite with a full view of the impressive landmark. Andrew Harper rated the Adlon as one of the best hotels in the world and we agreed.

With jet lag after a long day of travel we opted for a light dinner in the Adlon's sidewalk café. A charming German couple from Munich sat at the table next to us and we chatted about things to see and do when we arrived in their city later in the week. After dinner, the four of us walked through the Brandenburg Gate and around the Reichstag, Germany's newly restored and reinstated capitol building. It sparkled at night and we thanked our new friends Nicole and Rudy for their guided tour before retiring for the night.

A buffet of meats and cheeses, fruits and breads followed by an optional full order of eggs and sausage greeted us the next morning. We passed on the eggs, finding the buffet more than ample.

Europe suffered from the worst heat wave in a hundred years during the summer of 2003 and we were relieved that we had an air-conditioned suite. Berlin's temperatures ranged between a muggy ninety-five and a hundred degrees during the entirety of our visit.

We booked an air-conditioned BMW limo for a tour of the east and west sections of Berlin and met our driver, Volker, at 10:00 a.m. As we drove along the impressive Unter den Linden in the eastern section we soon passed the massive, sterile-looking Russian Embassy built just after World War II. It stood in stark contrast to the newly cleaned classic architectural gems along this main thoroughfare. As we looked back at the Brandenburg Gate, Volker told us that, inspired by the Acropolis in Athens, Prussian Sovereign Friedrich Wilhelm II commissioned this masterpiece to enhance the approach to the Unter den Linden. It was constructed between 1788 and 1791.

Our first stop, Policemen's Square, featured a number of noteworthy buildings. A highlight was a neo-gothic 19th-century church designed by Karl Friedrich Schinkel. Although eighty percent of the Baroque buildings were damaged or destroyed during World War II, restoration was in progress almost everywhere we looked. Glancing around us, Wayne and I concluded that the massive number of industrial cranes we had seen in Shanghai during the 1990s now resided in East Berlin.

Continuing on toward Museum Island, housing world-class art and relics in a number of buildings, we passed the ultramodern Jewish Museum, opened in 2001. Because of the current turmoil between Iraq and Israel, vigilant guards stood all along the museum's periphery. We talked with Volker, an educated man in his late thirties, about Germany's concern over America's invasion of Iraq. Most Germans, he told us, did not believe the invasion was wise nor did they believe Saddam Hussein's regime would end even though he was overthrown. As Volker pointed out flags symbolizing peace that hung from many of the buildings along our route, I reflected on the fact that time would tell whether or not the incursion was the right choice for world peace.

Our drive continued through an area called Kollwitzplatz, a conglomeration of shops, restaurants, apartments, and parks along the Karl-Marx-Allee. Restoration resonated in every block. We stopped at the remnants of the Berlin Wall, constructed in 1961 and finally toppled in 1989. It marked a dark chapter in the city's history as it separated East and West Berlin. Sections of the wall still stood, filled with graffiti. We walked along it and took a number of photos before continuing our tour.

Driving along the River Spree we crossed into West Berlin. It didn't seem like the same city. While East Berlin's classical architecture dazzled us with its beauty, West Berlin looked like any large turn-of-the-20th-century city.

The architecture seemed plain and the streets were crowded. Volker pointed out the Kaufhaus des Westens, or Ka De We, Berlin's largest department store. One building we passed, the Kaiser Wilhelm Memorial Church with its impressive tower, stood as a striking landmark in the western sector.

Heading back into East Berlin we passed the massive Column of Victory, moved from the Reichstag in the 1930s to its present location in the middle of a circular roadway near the Tiergarten. Returning to the Adlon, we said farewell to Volker and reorganized for our 4:00 p.m. tea at the glass-domed top of the Reichstag, just a short walk from the hotel. We had been advised to have reservations to avoid up to an hour's wait in line for an elevator ride to the top. Booking well in advance, we rejoiced at taking this advice to bypass the lengthy line in the staggering heat. The tea proved mediocre but the circular interior walkway leading to the top of the dome was fascinating, giving us clear views of the city in all directions.

Returning to our air-conditioned suite, we booked a 9:00 p.m. dinner at Lutter & Wegner at Charlottenstrasse 56, one of the oldest restaurants in all of Berlin. Even this late at night the temperatures soared and we opted for a table along the sidewalk. After an enjoyable two-and-a-half-hour dinner we returned to the hotel. Just before midnight I heard what sounded like thunder and when we opened the curtains we were treated to a fireworks display in a stadium not far from us. We literally ended our first day in Berlin with a bang!

The travel wearies caught up with us and we had a late start. After another marathon breakfast at the Adlon we took a cab to the Egyptian Museum in West Berlin. Its incomparable collection of treasured artifacts would soon move to a new home on Museum Island in the eastern sector. With no ventilation or air conditioning, the interior felt like an oven. Nevertheless, the heat was a small price to pay for time with the antiquities housed here. The highlight, a near-perfect bust of Egypt's Queen Nefertiti, simply took our breath away with its stark beauty. We wandered through room after room filled with Egyptian artifacts. Another favorite was the bust of the Berlin Green Man, a two-thousand-year-old sculpture so perfect that the image seemed to come alive. In the heat and crowds, we missed the mask of Nefertiti's mother. Next time...

After a good bit of time spent locating a taxi, we went to the center of West Berlin to check out the famed Ka De We department store. Initially we were disappointed, wondering why we had bothered. Merchandise, much of it from America, covered the massive floors. We had heard the store had a food hall rivaling Harrod's and we soon discovered an amazing array of exotic foods and beverages. It made our visit worthwhile.

We taxied back to the Adlon and had a late light lunch at the hotel's sidewalk café. Later that afternoon we walked a few blocks to the River Spree and boarded a boat for a one-hour city tour. The cruise took us past the famed TV tower, the Berlin Cathedral, Museum Island, the old train station now serving as a cultural center, the Reichstag, the new glass-encased train station, the Tiergarten, and more large cranes than we could count. At the halfway point the boat turned in the river and headed back to its mooring just off the Unter den Linden. We walked back to the hotel, stopping for a pretzel on the way.

Tonight we dined at Sale e Tabacchi, an Italian restaurant near Checkpoint Charlie, still standing in the middle of the street near the wall. Our first table in a crowded courtyard was right next to a woman who chain-smoked. A move to a second table seemed better until a couple sat next to us and smoked throughout the evening. We Californians were indeed fortunate to have non-smoking regulations in place. My meal, although very good, was spoiled by the constant infusion of smoke. Since the courtyard had walls surrounding it, ventilation was inadequate.

The Adlon served breakfast in a first-floor (second in America) dining room and we were thrilled to be seated by a window overlooking the Brandenburg Gate. At the table next to us we heard English spoken for the first time since we arrived. Germany's displeasure with America's recent invasion of Iraq apparently discouraged many American tourists from visiting the country. The couple, who hailed from Philadelphia, commented on this and during our stay in Berlin we encountered only two other twosomes from America.

After breakfast we took a taxi to the Pergamon Museum on Museum Island. Although many East Berlin museums remained under reconstruction at this time, the Pergamon proved accessible. However, from the moment we arrived at 11:00 a.m. for our scheduled admittance, the overwhelming heat staggered us. While the temperature outside climbed to a hundred degrees, the still air inside the unventilated museum felt twenty degrees hotter. We wandered through the two main exhibits featuring the remains of Pergamon housed in rooms undergoing extensive renovation.

As we turned into another section, we were dazzled by a rendering of the massive Ishtar Gate, the eighth to the inner city of Babylon, constructed around 575 BC. It took a personal visit to grasp the scope and splendor of walking through the blue tile arches that welcomed guests. Tiled walls on either side of the passageway featured a combination of real and mythical creatures that protruded in shades of vibrant gold, giving the animals an almost three-dimensional appearance. Most impressive were the striding lions. The brick-like tiles, including a number from the original gate, shone as if they'd just been formed. Although many were shattered over the centuries by wars and earthquakes, we were overwhelmed by the beauty and majesty of the reconstruction.

Continuing on through the main floor we marveled at the vast collection of ancient artifacts on display. Walking up a massive staircase to the next level brought us to some of the finest Persian carpets we had ever seen. Unfortunately, the heat on this floor literally forced us to take a too-quick look before exiting and gulping bottles of water. Proper ventilation and air conditioning would have saved the day.

As we walked toward the Unter den Linden we passed a building on our right that bore the scars of a barrage of bullets from World War II. We then came to an area near the River Spree with spectacular new buildings obscured under scaffolding. Near the State Opera House, still closed for renovation, we noted a horseshoe-shaped building under reconstruction. We later learned it was part of Humboldt University. The magnificence of both buildings shone through the repairs and would be treasures when completed.

We walked another mile to our hotel and each soaked in a cool bath before heading back along the Unter den Linden to Charlottenstrasse in search of the Four Seasons Hotel located near Policemen's Square. On our way we entered a narrow roadway that took us along the far end of the Humboldt University building. We passed a Catholic Church, one of only four in Berlin, built after World War II. Continuing on to Policemen's Square we entered the historic Huguenot Church. Only the vestibule was open, offering a 254-step climb to the top of the church tower. We took a pass on this extremely hot day.

Reaching the very modern Four Seasons Hotel we were struck by how empty it seemed. Not another soul appeared as we toured the main level. Beautiful pastries sat uneaten in a glass-covered cart in the area where afternoon tea was served. We opted to return to the Adlon's lobby for strawberry cake and coffee.

After a third cold bath for the day we sat once more on the Adlon's patio with a spectacular view of the Brandenburg Gate and ordered dinner. As one could have a relatively good and smoke-free dining experience on this well-located patio, it provided the perfect farewell to Berlin.

On another sunny, overly warm morning we took a taxi to the airport for a late morning flight to Munich. This would be a day of delays. Our flight departed almost an hour late and when we arrived at the Mandarin Oriental, a small hotel with seventy-three rooms in the heart of Munich, our room was not available. While waiting we had coffee in the lobby and, unlike in Berlin, we noticed many Americans. We really were easy to spot! After an hour's wait, we were led to our glamorous but cigar-scented accommodation. We opened all the windows and eventually the smell disappeared. A bottle of chilled champagne arrived from the management with a note of apology for the delay.

After settling in, we finally made it to the streets. Walking along the Maximilianstrasse we encountered a blast of heat even stronger than we had felt in Berlin. We popped into a few of the elegant shops along Munich's equivalent of LA's Rodeo Drive. Delighted to see that German fashion designer Jil Sander reappeared along the avenue—she had retired a few years earlier—I couldn't resist taking a peek. Germany was, after all, her home base. I purchased a white blouse sporting a collar with flair which needed a bit of altering. The accommodating clerk promised to have it completed and delivered to our hotel at no charge the following day.

In the midst of a meltdown we nevertheless ambled toward the central square just in time to watch the animation on Munich's charming glockenspiel. Rows of figures danced and rang bells as they rotated to the historic clock's music. We always enjoyed watching this when we were in Munich and we congratulated ourselves on our perfect timing.

My feet were badly swollen from the excessive heat and walking on cobblestones so I bought Birkenstock sandals in a small shop just off the main square. Ah, relief! I thought of our trip through Europe with our two daughters many years ago when they wore Birkenstocks almost every day. Now I knew why.

I remembered a garden café tucked behind the building housing the massive glockenspiel. It took a bit of sleuthing to find the arched entrance but we soon had a shady table and a cold drink. The walls of the buildings surrounding the garden were covered with amusing gargoyles. Walking toward our hotel we stopped for a moment at the famous Hofbrauhaus and Wayne ordered a cold beer while I munched on a giant pretzel. A small dog at the table next to us eyed my pretzel and, after pantomiming for the owner's permission to give the dog a small piece and getting a nod, I had a new buddy.

Wayne had made dinner arrangements with a business acquaintance in Munich. Gihan was originally from Sri Lanka and his wife Anita hailed from India. Both were now U.S. citizens and had lived in Munich for six years. They met us at the Meridian and drove us to a charming restaurant in a residential area. We sat in the garden for several hours enjoying wonderful food and stimulating conversation and thoroughly enjoyed our evening with this delightful young cosmopolitan couple.

Ah, a day in the Alps! Wayne rented a BMW and we drove toward the Bavarian mountains in our air-conditioned car. After nearly a week touring large and very hot cities it was a welcome change of pace. Our first challenge was to navigate our way out of Munich—no easy task. The car was equipped with a GPS system that spoke to us with the voice of a very proper English-woman. More than once the voice suggested that we, "Make a U-turn if possible." In the midst of bustling inner-city streets, it wasn't an easy task. Her instructions had us howling with laughter.

Once on the A95 we drove along a route bordered by forests and rolling countryside in the direction of Garmisch-Partenkirchen. The Alps rose in the distance and we reached them in no time as we sped along the roadway. We arrived at the Linderhof, King Ludwig's famed hunting palace in the Alps, at 12:15 p.m. We had hoped for cooler temperatures but even at this altitude it was hotter than blazes. We slathered on sunscreen and headed up the path to Ludwig's smallest but most exquisite gem.

Wayne had visited the Linderhof many years before, and we arrived just as the doors were closing when we traveled here with our daughters twelve years earlier. Although we enjoyed the grounds, I vowed to return for a peek at the interior. We purchased tickets for a 1:00 p.m. tour and headed to the opulent front gardens. To our surprise the façade of the palace was under massive repairs and draped in three stories of fabric painted with an exact replica of the building. We were charmed by this life-sized work of art.

After our tour of the stunning interior we hiked up another steep path to Ludwig's grotto complete with a man-made lake. An incurable lover of opera, he had the grotto constructed as a stage for Wagner operas. Although a German gave the presentation in his native tongue, we could understand enough to admire the effort that Ludwig had made. On this beastly hot day, we appreciated the coolness in this cave-like grotto.

We had passed through the small village of Ettal on our way to the Linderhof and noticed a massive church-like structure on one side of it. Since it was already 3:00 p.m. when we returned, we opted for a quick lunch before exploring. We feasted on country-style bratwurst with bacon and onion, and mashed potatoes with cooked cabbage. Our lunch cost almost nothing and after a long day of driving and touring, it tasted divine.

We crossed the street and toured the Ettal Basilica, an elaborate Baroque church at the far end of a huge courtyard bordered on all sides by buildings housing a Benedictine monastery. No longer functioning as such, it now hosted Sunday services conducted by visiting clergy.

We said our goodbyes to the Bavarian Alps and headed back to Munich. All went well until we reached the outskirts of the city. At that point Wayne decided he had had enough of the talking Englishwoman in the black box mounted to the car's dashboard and decided to navigate for himself. We drove for miles in what seemed like circles, never coming to a familiar road. After an hour of this I insisted that Wayne stop and ask for directions. Voila! In a matter of minutes we reached our hotel.

Tonight's dinner was arranged at Schuhbecks, just around the corner from our hotel and adjacent to the Hofbrauhaus. Our German tablemates in Berlin had recommended it highly. They told us that the chef was a TV celebrity in Germany on par with Julia Child. It sounded like a winner to us.

When we arrived, however, we were shown to a table in the back corner and the temperature even at this late hour hovered around a hundred degrees. With no breeze it was oppressive. We politely excused ourselves to our English-speaking maître d' and as we headed toward the door, he mentioned that he was from Modesto, California. He suggested that we wait near the front and assured us he would see what he could do for us. It took another forty-five minutes but we were eventually seated at a table next to an open window. Although still warm, we enjoyed eating our way through four delicious courses.

The next morning we decided not to fight the oppressive heat and opted for a relatively quiet day. We wandered along the Maximilianstrasse and looked into a few more of the shops before stopping for lunch at the Opern-Espresso just across from the entrance to the Munich Opera House. We enjoyed a leisurely late lunch before returning to the hotel to sort and pack for tomorrow's journey into Russia. We culled all of our "what if it's cold" clothes and arranged to have them shipped home.

My final splurge was a manicure and pedicure at a salon across the street from the hotel. The manicurist hailed from Cali, Columbia and we managed to converse with my singular year of conversational Spanish studied so many years ago.

We flew to Moscow in the morning and, after our week of three-digit temperatures in Germany, sighed with great relief upon feeling balmy weather in the high seventies. This summer's unusually high temperatures in Europe resulted in numerous heat-related deaths, including an estimated fifteen thousand in France and many more in Spain, Germany and England.

While flying from Munich to Moscow I sat next to a young woman and her daughter who were returning from Austria. She spoke English very well and actually taught it in Moscow. We chatted about the changes to the city in recent years. Her husband, a dentist, obviously profited from them, making it possible for his wife and daughter to travel. She said life was so much better than it used to be. I assumed she meant before the end of the Soviet regime.

After landing, Wayne maneuvered around, playing a game of Russian roulette at the customs line, and lost. He selected one that virtually did not budge and we sighed as we watched all the other passengers breeze through the process. We finally joined our Harvard group, all gathered around a sea of suitcases. After identifying our luggage, we headed outside to board our buses. Then we waited some more for two of our group who lingered behind to visit the airport shops.

Marshall Goldman, Associate Director of the Harvard Russian Research Center who would accompany us on the trip, rode on our bus. He was an expert on the Russian economy and fluent in the language. As we took the hour-long route into Moscow at rush hour, he rattled off numerous bits of information. He said the city's Mayor Yury Luzhkov was very popular but ruled much like Mayor Daley Sr. of Chicago. Legal? Who knew! There was corruption in his past but he got things done. Moscow was a beautiful city in 2003 but it wasn't always that way. As an aside, Luzhkov ran for president of Russia in 2000 and lost.

Marshall also informed us that Red Square remained closed to the public and so, after years of dreaming about wandering through this world-famous square, it would not happen. Threats from Chechnya continued to hamper security efforts and Moscow was not interested in offering Red Square as a potential target. It was very disappointing news for this tourist. More disturbing news: a serial killer was preying on women along the river. Welcome to Moscow!

Our in-city guide Elena pointed out places of interest as we drove to the Metropol, a historic 1907 Art Nouveau-style hotel located just outside of Red Square. At times we came to a dead stop and Elena seemed surprised. After twenty-five very slow minutes we passed an accident. Just as in California, drivers slowed to gawk at the aftermath of the collision. We then passed two ultra-modern shopping centers before crossing the Moscow River. Noting the huge traffic jam heading out of Moscow, we were relieved to be traveling in the opposite direction.

As we approached our hotel, we passed the Bolshoi Ballet Theatre located a short distance from the Metropol. Just a few blocks further up the street stood the formidable KGB building. I was struck by the contrast between the beauty of the Bolshoi that celebrated the art of dance and the starkness of the massive KGB building known for barbaric torture.

Following check-in, we hurried to a meeting room in the lower level for introductions followed by a talk by Charlie Riley, a University of Michigan graduate who ranked number two in the American Embassy. I couldn't resist a "Go Blue!" after his talk and that brought a smile to his face. Charlie's message was somewhat guarded and I suspected he was hesitant to say much, if anything, to this jetlagged group of tourists. His tone was positive and I must admit I felt honored to have this handsome, articulate man representing America in Moscow.

After the lecture we walked along a section of the outer periphery of Red Square and, to our delight, discovered that the guarded barricades blocking the entrances were waist high at best. With no people in the square we were able to see it in its entirety and we were simply in awe of its significance both historically and architecturally. Lit at night, it was dazzling.

Many young Russians wandered along the area surrounding Red Square, now permanently blocked from traffic. We noted how Western the people looked. Our expectation of lingering malaise and poverty did not materialize here. As we walked for a few blocks in each direction we felt perfectly safe. If life wasn't good here, it certainly appeared to be getting better.

Returning to the Metropol at 10:00 p.m. we decided to have dinner in its formal dining room. Enormous and elegant, it was crowned by a magnificent arched ceiling made of stained glass. Built between 1899 and 1907, its grandeur still shone. We had a light dinner of perfectly prepared blinis accompanied by red caviar, smoked salmon and crème fraîche.

Our day began with an early buffet breakfast followed by an 8:00 a.m. lecture from Marshall on Russian geography. He began by saying that many Russians had never forgiven Mikhail Gorbachev or Boris Yeltsin for allowing so much of the former Soviet Union to become independent. However, even though Russia had lost almost half its landmass, it was still the largest country in the world.

Marshall suggested that the only way for the Russian economy to grow was for the leaders of the country to motivate the peasants to "get off the stow" and work for a better life. Because the country was so vast and varied, this proved to be a difficult process. For centuries, Russia had been a country of a few wealthy controlling the vast majority of impoverished citizens. With no history of a middle class the peasants in the outlying areas simply could not visualize moving up within their society. Therefore, the wealthy few landowners, including royalty, ruled the vast peasant majority for centuries.

Russia began in Kiev in the Ukraine a thousand years ago. Odessa, in the southernmost part of the country, was actually on the same latitude as Montreal. The gulf stream protected it and enabled a longer growing season for crops. A vast part of Russia remained virtually unusable.

In outlying areas, farmers across Russia formed small villages to protect themselves from the cold. In their homes the stove became the centerpiece. Whereas Americans lived in cities and functioned from day to day on their own, Russians formed strong communal bonds that had lasted for generations.

What kept Russia from becoming a superpower? Unlike all the other strong nations that developed, Russia had very limited access to oceans. For centuries the Mongols posed the biggest threat to Russia, thus eliminating access to any warm water ports. Also, since most of the rivers flowed north rather than east to west, only travel by horse or foot enabled access to distant reaches. Even railroads were slow to reach Russia; leaders feared that invaders would utilize them. To solve this dilemma the Russians constructed a rail system using a slightly different gauge from the norm.

For a time, Kiev, the first of Russia's cities, held the title of *The Third Rome*. However, it missed out on both the Renaissance and Reformation eras. There simply was no challenge to its church. Because of its remote location coupled with limited ship access, very few cities engaged in trade with Kiev. The largest cause of its fall from prominence resulted from the lack of bourgeoisie. A middle class simply did not exist. Until World War I most Russians remained largely agrarian, uneducated and self-sufficient within district villages. It was a government from the top down, based on absolute control.

Following the lecture, we boarded buses for a tour of Moscow. Marshall joined our guide Elena and both imparted information as we rode through the city. Once more we passed the Bolshoi and then the imposing KGB building. Marshall told us that in 1991 the statue of KGB founder Felix Dzerzhinsky was torn down. Now housing government officials, the building continued to instill a sense of foreboding and one could only wonder what horrific encounters occurred within its massive walls during the height of the Soviet Union. Most of those who could have told the stories did not live to do so.

Skirting the outer edge of Red Square, the golden domes of the Kremlin shone in the distance. Moscow, founded in 1147 AD, today showcased far more churches than I had expected. Along St. Barbara Street we were surprised to see several Asian-style churches. As we drove on, the onion-shaped domes of St. Basil's Cathedral came into view.

Continuing on, we passed the Pushkin State Museum of Fine Arts built in 1912 and the Cathedral of Christ the Savior, the largest in Moscow. In 1931, Joseph Stalin blew up the original 19th-century church that stood on the site to build a massive towering head of Vladimir Lenin. When it was determined that his concept for the head was structurally impossible, a swimming pool took its place. The cathedral, reconstructed between 1995 and 1998 now stands as a tribute to the original church.

As we drove, we noted some lovely classical architecture. Many of the buildings were under restoration and we were pleased by the effort of the Russians to save them. A statue of Tolstoy loomed in a park near The Field of

Maidens. After Elena pointed out a medical school and a military academy, she added that the State used to provide complete medical coverage but that citizens could now opt for costly private treatment.

Shortly afterward, we arrived at the red-walled entrance to New Maiden Cemetery, the burial place of many famous Russians. Its elaborate grave ornamentation fascinated us. Some were intricate works of art while others were simply whimsical. Among the famous in the cemetery were Nikita Khrushchev, Raisa Gorbachev, the composer Dmitri Shostakovich and numerous other composers, writers and poets. I don't often recommend cemeteries but this one rated a visit.

When we left the bus, the ominous dark clouds in the sky prompted us to bring our umbrellas. At the halfway point of our cemetery tour, a heavy rain began to fall and we were thankful to have them for this soaker.

Our next stop was the New Maiden Convent in the southwest sector of Moscow. Boris Godunov became tsar in 1598 AD and his sister resided here. Although the Communists shut down the historic convent during their reign, it reopened on a small scale in 1991. We wandered through the gardens and admired the surrounding buildings before entering a small vaulted room attached to one side of the cathedral. Soon five young men entered and sang an a cappella Easter song followed by a hymn to Mary Magdalene.

Winding our way back toward Red Square, Elena and Marshall shared some Moscow insights with their captive audience. In the last fifteen years the number of cars in Moscow had increased from seven hundred thousand to 19 million. Although Russians preferred German and Japanese cars, the price tags and taxes prohibited the owning of foreign vehicles. There were fifteen million people living in the greater Moscow area. Most of the churches were Russian Orthodox. The Tatar-Mongol yoke lasted for two and a half centuries, during which time most of the craftsmanship skills of the earlier Russians were lost. The Russian State Library in Moscow was the second largest in the world, topped only by the Library of Congress in Washington, DC. The architects who designed St. Basil's Cathedral in the mid-16th century were later blinded by Ivan the Terrible so they could never duplicate their design. The Academy of Sciences, or Stalin's birthday cake building, was a prominent skyscraper in central Moscow, looming in the background of Red Square along the Moscow River. It was one of seven similar structures built by Stalin during his reign of power.

Our final stop for the morning was St. Basil's Cathedral. As we toured this enchanting structure known for its magnificent, colorful onion-shaped domes, I was struck by the small size of its interior rooms. Having seen photos of this cathedral that dominated Red Square, I expected grand spaces.

Instead, the monastic rooms offered solitude as well as safety from invaders. The frescoed walls remained well preserved, largely due to the lack of sunlight. We did notice that restoration was in progress on some of the frescoes.

The entrance to the cathedral enabled us to stand behind the low barricades along Red Square. It was a perfect spot for photos and we took ample advantage of the opportunity. Standing just outside of the square we photographed St. Basil's with its unforgettable domes.

After the short ride to the Metropol, Wayne and I hired our guide Elena for an afternoon tour of the Moscow subways. Since there was no group lunch or afternoon program planned today, the subway tour topped our list of to-do's. We invited Andy and Rhody, two others from our group, to join us and the four of us treated Elena to lunch at a nearby restaurant that she selected. Elena managed to get us into the upper level away from the tourist trade and we enjoyed more blinis and caviar. She told us that she missed the earlier days when she could enjoy caviar with her grandmother almost every day. Now it was a rarity.

We walked two blocks to the subway entrance near GUM Department Store. From the moment we entered the station we were dazzled. After descending for what seemed like forever on an escalator, we reached a strikingly beautiful area with exquisite sculpted ceilings, bronze-and marble-bordered walls and colorful murals. Elena took us to five other stations, leading us through the maze of tracks and transfers. Each station reflected a Communist theme praising workers, honoring the military, exalting children, and more. Both couples gave Elena US$20 and we later learned that this equaled about half a week's pay for her. She was a delight and we never could have toured the Moscow subway without her guidance.

After returning to the hotel and saying goodbye to Elena, Andy and Rhody, Wayne and I decided to walk a couple of blocks to get a better view of the KGB building and take photos. From years of reading novels and hearing news based on this daunting site, we simply couldn't resist a closer look. Gloomy Moscow weather added to the intrigue and it remained overcast as we walked past shops and small restaurants. At close range we found it difficult to take in the enormity of the structure. It was impossible to capture on my camera but Wayne made it happen with his wide-angle lens.

We walked back toward the hotel and then continued on to the arched entrance of Red Square and took more photos. Having toured St. Basil's earlier in the day, we could now capture it on film from another perspective. Farther along the pedestrian walkway just outside of the square we noticed a barricaded area which we soon discovered was Russia's Tomb of the Unknown Soldier. Two uniformed soldiers stood inside the enclosure. As we watched, two brides in beautiful white gowns appeared at the barricade with their husbands and one of the soldiers lifted a gate to let them enter. Each bride placed a bouquet on the tomb and photographers captured the moment on film. We couldn't resist a photo or two as well before returning to the Metropol to prepare for our 5:30 p.m. reception and 6:30 p.m. dinner at the Godunov Restaurant just a short walk away.

The next day began with breakfast in the hotel followed by talks from two young American journalists. The first, a woman who had studied with Marshall Goldman, wrote for the *Moscow Times*. She told us she had permission to write anything but that did not guarantee her words would be published. In Russia, she said, there are often many different versions of the truth. Reporters in Russia are paid to report a story favorably.

The second young woman, who wrote for the *New York Times* Moscow Bureau, also commented on how the Moscow news was filled with stories written by public relations people. She told of flying to a village in Siberia to gather information for a story on the ecological impact of oil drilling in the area. As she stepped from her plane a team of reporters from the local TV station, conveniently owned by the oil company, met her and questioned her motives for the visit. No one from the oil company would talk with her. It virtually owned and controlled all the news.

Our guide for the day, Natasha, met us for a tour of the Tretyakov Gallery. Constructed between 1902 and 1904, this Russian fairy-tale-style building housed a collection of national art donated in 1892 by wealthy merchant Pavel Tretyakov who hoped his two-thousand-piece gift would someday grow into a museum. It did and now a vast array of Russian art from the past two centuries was on display. This impressive collection ranged from classical to modern art and we were particularly touched by the brilliant colors of the impressionistic works by Russian artists who studied in Paris in the late 1800s.

Following the gallery tour we stopped at the Pushkin Restaurant for lunch. We then toured the Pushkin Museum. Although we enjoyed the visit, we missed seeing many of the works from the museum's famed impressionist collection because they were on loan to the Los Angeles County Museum of Art. We had not had an opportunity to visit the collection in LA and it left shortly after our return.

After checking out of the Metropol the next morning, we boarded buses at 9:00 a.m. for a tour of Moscow's Kremlin. Natasha explained that the word kremlin means *fortress* and many Russian villages had one. Moscow was founded in 1147 AD by Russian Prince Yuri Dolgorukiy. While St. Petersburg was Russia's window on Europe, Moscow was often referred to as its heart.

Our first stop in the vast compound was the Armory Chamber Museum featuring a wide variety of coronation items, vestments and costumes worn by royalty, Catherine the Great's wedding gown, royal carriages, fine china and crystal, crowns, armaments, and a collection of Fabergé eggs. From there we toured a group of small cathedrals and admired their domes glistening in the noonday sun.

We had a free afternoon and decided to do a repeat of our caviar and blini lunch at the Metropol's elegant domed restaurant. This time we splurged and ordered the finest black caviar. As we dined the sun illuminated the stained-glass ceiling, making the vibrant colors sparkle.

After lunch we walked to GUM, Moscow's famed department store. The collection of storefront shops housed within the massive building fascinated us. Many of the shops found in the U.S. were now offered here. Wayne bought an inexpensive watch and I purchased a travel alarm clock. We then took the subway to the area where we would begin a cruise, carefully counting the nine stops it took to reach it.

We had hoped to book a suite for our river cruise from Moscow to St. Petersburg but by the time the trip brochure reached us on the West Coast they were taken. When we boarded and looked into our assigned room with its incredibly tiny space, Wayne rightly said, "This is never going to work." With a bathroom barely big enough for one and just enough room to maneuver between the two twin beds, the room was not large enough to properly accommodate even one guest.

Remembering that a couple on my river cruise in China managed to book a suite at the last minute, I suggested Wayne try his luck at the front desk. He returned to report that all the suites remained reserved but he made an executive decision and took an available room three doors down the hall. Even though the Russian-owned ship's crew made no accommodations to lower the rate on the second room, he took it knowing we would be on board for a number of days and having the extra space would make us more comfortable. The women in the two rooms that separated us wondered what was going on until we explained that we were actually married to each other. It was a brilliant move on Wayne's part and the couples in tight quarters were ready to jump ship by the end of the cruise.

Marshall held the first of our pre-dinner onboard lectures in the ship's conference room. He told us that from the mid-13th century to the late 15th century, Russia was controlled by the Mongols and Tatars, and local rule prevailed. Ivan the Great freed Russia and governed from 1480 AD to 1505 AD. Peter the Great, who reigned as Tsar from 1682 AD to 1725 AD, unified Russia. He wished to develop a warm-water port and spent time studying shipbuilding in Holland and England. Under his rule, St. Petersburg rose from the swamps to become the Jewel of Russia. This took an enormous toll on the population, however. Many died during the construction phase and all Russians were taxed to pay for the elaborate city. In a largely agricultural society based upon serfdom, the peasants were particularly squeezed.

Catherine the Great came to Russia from Germany as a teen. She came to power following a coup d'état that she organized to overthrow her husband, Peter III. She ruled from 1762 to 1796 AD and under her leadership, culture thrived. She promoted western intellect, art and architecture. Napoleon invaded Russia in 1812 and was defeated. Poland and Finland came under Russian control in the 19th century. Russia always seemed to be adding and then subtracting territories in spite of its relative isolation.

Under Gorbachev and Yeltsin, Russia relinquished control of Central Asia, the Caucasus and Belarus. This did not please the majority of Russians; they were used to and actually liked absolute power.

The Russian peasant embodied everything Russian until the early 20th century. Those who lived in the cities viewed peasants as idle, ignorant, backward, and dirty. The peasants, for many generations, lived in isolated enclaves and depended on communal support. Under the control of land owners, they had an affinity for top-down control.

After the lecture we spent some time on the observation deck and watched the activity—or lack of it—along the Volga River. Moscow soon disappeared and miles of birch forests lined both banks. Occasionally a group of boaters or bathers would appear along the river and they almost always returned our waves of hello.

We returned to the lecture hall for a talk by two of the ship's employees, Katerina and Rita, who introduced us to lacquer miniature boxes, a thousand-year-old tradition. They explained that the best ones came from four villages near Moscow—Palekh, Kholui, Mstera, and Fedoskino.

The boxes were crafted from papier-mâché and then lacquered and hand painted. Each took three months to create. First, cardboard was placed in a press to form and dry. Then it was cured in linseed oil and heated at 150 degrees for two months. Craftsmen created the various shapes and attached metal hinges. Every box was then sanded, planed and shaped so that its lid fit perfectly. Then the bottom was attached. Priming took place in four stages with a sanding after each application. Local clay, linseed oil and ashes comprised the primer. The interior of the box was then painted with three or four coats of red and the exterior, black. Next, lacquer was applied and the box was polished with pumice powder and buffed with rabbit fur.

White paint was applied with squirrel-fur brushes. Then the original designs, ranging from Russian folk tales to architecture, were applied with a fine rabbit-fur brush. The techniques were similar to icon painting. Colors were produced from egg emulsion tempera blended on a stone slab. Gold was added last. The boxes were treated with a final polishing before they were signed and ready for sale.

Papier-mâché was used to produce a smooth shape that wouldn't warp or create bubbles when painted. The lid made a soft sound when closed. In fact, one could check for authenticity based on the sound of the lid. Many sold in Russia were actually made of plastic and had decals. Others had bubbles in the paint and the lids made a clunky sound. One should always look for the seal on the bottom of a box to determine its authenticity.

We thoroughly enjoyed the talk and, although I had already purchased four of the boxes in the ship's store, I selected a fifth from a grouping on a display table. This one was a Kholui with the kremlin from a small village near Moscow.

We joined our group for lunch and then returned to the upper deck just as we approached a large lock at least thirty feet in height. In front of us was a scrap-metal barge also waiting its turn. On it, we were amused by a woman with a cat on a leash. After about twenty minutes the water level in the lock rose and soon the two boats moved forward.

At 4:30 p.m. we arrived at Uglich, our first port since departing from Moscow. Irina, our lovely young guide, walked us to the center of the town, rich in history. We first visited the Church of Dmitry on Blood, dedicated to a son of Ivan the Terrible. Its deep red color crowned with five blue onion-shaped domes represented a significant part of Uglich's dark history. The church had an outstanding collection of icons and, after paying a dollar's fee, we were allowed to take photographs. I felt somewhat guilty using a flash camera on these priceless 15th-and 16th-century treasures. Nevertheless, I couldn't resist capturing a few of the images on film.

Following Ivan the Terrible's death in 1584 AD, his son Fyodor was named tsar. As he was disabled and incapable of performing his duties, Boris Godunov served as regent and ruled for Fyodor. Fearful of losing his powerful position to Fyodor's younger brother Dmitry, Godunov exiled the boy to Uglich. In 1591 AD, Godunov had Dmitry murdered and then claimed that the boy had fallen on a knife during an epileptic seizure, which Dmitry was known to have. In 1598 AD, Fyodor died in his sleep without an heir, freeing Godunov to serve as tsar for seven years, by which time the plot to kill Dmitry had unraveled. Uglich became a pilgrimage site and Dmitry is still honored as a saint. A mural in the chapel depicted the execution of Godunov and the expulsion of his followers in Uglich to Siberia.

Next on the tour was a small 14th-century castle that was now a museum. Then Irena led us through the village past rows of booths filled with trinkets and on to the vodka museum. This proved to be a disappointment, though, so we returned to the blocks of stalls selling replicas of lacquer boxes, charming painted Christmas ornaments and other inexpensive souvenirs. Uglich was noted for its enameled watches and our honest guide Irena told us that although they did not last for long, they were lovely to wear. I resisted the watches and bought some painted wooden ornaments.

We returned to the ship at 7:30 p.m. for dinner and the start of an overnight sail. The food on the ship, although ample, lacked much taste or originality. After dinner we went into the lounge where a young man named Alexander played a medley of Russian folk songs.

We awoke in our next port, Yaroslavl, a large city with a population of six hundred thirteen thousand. Following breakfast, we began our tour. Once beautiful, the city now appeared tired and worn. According to today's guide, its four main industries were tires, cigarettes, vodka, and beer. We stopped at the 12th-century Transfiguration Monastery and toured the central chapel. Rain began to fall as we walked from building to building in the complex. Hand bells on a frame in one of the courtyards rang in spite of the steady downpour.

A service was in progress in the main chapel, the Church of Elijah the Prophet built in 1650 AD, so we were not permitted to enter. However, someone approached our guide and escorted us into a side chapel. We sat in chairs and soon a four-man a cappella choir entered and began to sing. The group performed one folk song and one traditional religious piece. With its vaulted ceilings and painted murals, the small chapel echoed with the haunting songs. When CDs were offered for sale after the performance, many of us purchased them.

Our bus drove into the central area of Yaroslavl and deposited us for a forty-five-minute shopping/sightseeing opportunity. Since the rain continued to fall, we opted for a nearby shop with more lacquered boxes. After our shipboard lecture, I was a bit dubious as to their authenticity but our local guide assured us they were of good quality. We looked but didn't buy.

Wayne decided to wander through the town a bit while I opted for a dry seat on the bus. When he returned, Wayne reported that he had ventured into a local food market and was amazed to note that most of the products were locked away from customers. Once a customer paid for an item, the clerk unlocked a cabinet and exchanged the item for the sales receipt. In retrospect, I wished that I had gone with him because we never did find another food market.

On our final stop we were ushered into an old building filled with seats facing a stage. A group of performers in Russian costumes danced, played traditional Russian instruments and sang folk songs for forty-five minutes. Even though the show was geared for tourists, we enjoyed it.

At 2:30 p.m. we joined many of our group on board the ship for a Russian language lesson with the ship's Marina. She explained the Russian alphabet and taught us a few basic words and phrases. We finished with two Russian songs and Wayne was selected to lead us in one sung in rounds. We'd never master Russian but it was great fun to give it a try.

After a delightful dinner with a couple in our group, Wayne and I opted for some exercise and decided we would walk eight times around the ship's upper deck, a distance of roughly a mile. The ship entered a large lake and a strong wind made it almost impossible to walk. After four rounds we gave up. The 1935 film, *Anna Karenina*, staring Basil Rathbone and Greta Garbo, was showing in the ship's lecture hall so we watched it until 11:00 p.m.

The next afternoon we visited Svirstroy, a small impoverished village filled with warm-hearted peasants. A group of women greeted our ship as we docked, offering simple bouquets of flowers for sale. We walked with Marshall and his wife and when one of the villagers offered us tea in her home, he encouraged us to take her up on it. Wayne and I entered her meager home and, with only sign language to communicate without the company of Russian-speaking Marshall, we had a delightful time. She served us tea and homemade cake and then gave us a tour of her simple home. It was lovely to spend even a short amount of time in a Russian household and we thanked her for her hospitality. Of course, we also left a few rubles.

The next day our river cruise continued on to Kizhi, an island in the center of Lake Onega and home to The Church of the Transfiguration, one of Russia's most spectacular wooden domed churches built without a single nail. Topping the multi-story frame structure were a series of twenty-two onion domes that spired toward the heavens. Words could not do it justice; it had to be seen to be fully appreciated.

At last we arrived in St. Petersburg, Russia's port city on the Baltic Sea. Our ship docked alongside many others at night and we reveled in the sight of this magnificent city. With its world-class museums, magnificent architecture and series of canals, it was often referred to as the Venice of the North. Although it had fallen into disrepair in modern times, the Russian government gave St. Petersburg an impressive face lift in anticipation of its three hundredth anniversary in February of this year and we were fortunate to see it at its very best.

The next morning, we ventured out early for what was supposed to be a

VIP tour of the State Hermitage Museum to view its treasured art collection. Founded in 1764 AD by Catherine the Great, today's collection exceeded three million works of art. We stood in an area about the size of four football fields filled with tourists waiting for the doors to open. The promise of entering an hour ahead of the throngs never happened. Our guide hustled us through some of the prime areas and we had very little time to explore this important collection of arts and antiquities. We would just have to return at a later date.

After lunch at a local restaurant, we went to the Church of the Savior on the Spilled Blood. Alexander III began construction of this Orthodox church in 1883 and dedicated it to his father, Alexander II, who had been assassinated two years earlier. Now a museum, the walls of this Orthodox church were covered with priceless icons. Topped with a series of onion-domed towers, its colorful interior icons, all set in mosaics, continue to draw visitors from around the world.

From there we went to the Winter Palace, located across from a park in central St. Petersburg. With more than fifteen hundred rooms, it served as the residence of Russian emperors from 1732-1917. Now forming part of the Hermitage Museum complex, the Winter Palace sat adjacent to the site of Peter the Great's original palace. In its current form, it took just over one hundred years to construct and was completed in 1837. Many architects contributed to the massive structure, most notably Italian Bartolomeo Rastrelli's Baroque style. Following a fire in 1837, its 705-foot-long exterior remained unchanged but the interior adapted a Rococo style reflecting the times. We were awed by the opulence of the palace.

As we exited from the rear of the palace, I noticed several artists selling their paintings. One small work caught my eye and it turned out to be an illustration created for a children's book. The watercolor depicted a cheery bearded man with a dancing bear surrounded by gleeful children. The artist spoke English very well and told me it had been painted by his wife. I bought it and it still hangs in our home.

Nothing could overwhelm this world traveler quite like Peter the Great's Summer Palace built on the outskirts of St. Petersburg between 1710 and 1714 AD. Walkways along its gracious block-long reflecting pool lined with a series of fountains led to the main entrance of the palace. Once inside, room after splendid room simply dazzled us. A highlight was the Amber Room, once dubbed the Eighth Wonder of the World until the Nazis looted it during World War II. The room's amber panels, packed away in crates, disappeared and were never found, but replicas were completed in 2003, just in time for our visit. We spent a good part of the day touring, exploring the gardens and park-like setting, taking photos, and simply delighting in the splendors of the palace and its vast grounds.

Over dinner on the ship we all spoke of the magnificence of St. Petersburg. Wayne and I decided to venture back onto the streets for one last look at the city and we bumped into Marshall and his wife. When we mentioned that we had toured the subways of Moscow, he offered to accompany us on a ride through St. Petersburg's subway system. We gladly accepted and he led the way. Built in 1955, it competed in beauty with the interior of the Hermitage with its crystal chandeliers and gracious ornate columns. The ride through the subways in St. Petersburg proved the perfect conclusion to our time in this spectacular city. Coupled with our experiences in Moscow and the sights on the river cruise, our tour of Russia would long remain a favorite memory.

DORDOGNE

Bordeaux Sarlat, Rocamadour, Les Eyzies-de-Tayac-Sireuil,
Cap Blanc, Rouffignac-Saint-Cernin-de-Reilhac,
Saint-Amand-de-Coly, Beynac-et-Cazenac, and Domme

October 16–24, 2003

ARCHAEOLOGY had always intrigued me so when we received a brochure
from the University of Michigan outlining an eight-day trip to the Dordogne
region of France with visits to several prehistoric caves, I couldn't resist. With
my trusty husband Wayne in agreement, we signed up for what proved to be
one of our favorite adventures.

We flew to Paris and caught a connecting flight to Bordeaux. Once in
Bordeaux we met our U of M group and boarded a bus for the final two-and-
a-half-hour leg of our journey. After a long day of travel, we arrived at the
Hôtel Madeleine in the charming French village of Sarlat-la-Canéda.

Once unpacked, Wayne and I walked along winding cobblestone roads
bordered by centuries-old stone buildings. Perhaps because Sarlat is so far
removed from any airport and is difficult to reach, the streets were virtually
empty. We could not believe the beauty of this authentically restored medieval town.

Dinner at 7:30 p.m. in the hotel's dining room with our twenty-seven
fellow travelers gave us an opportunity to get acquainted. Most in our group
opted for a good night's sleep but Wayne and I couldn't resist a nighttime
stroll. Lit with gas lights, the village sparkled.

After breakfast the next morning our speaker, Véronique Plesch, a Colby College professor specializing in medieval French literature, talked about French food. She began by pointing out that fat was the unifying factor in French cooking. Here in the Dordogne, duck and goose fat were mainstays. She noted that foie gras was sold on every street and the best way to enjoy it was *entier*, meaning whole, duck or goose liver. The ancient Egyptians and Romans were the first to indulge in this rich delicacy. Bloc foie gras was made from trimmings and usually canned in paste form. We tasted bloc later in the day and decided that it was both delicious and affordable.

Véronique talked about the variety of courses that composed a typical French dinner and then sang the praises of Auguste Escoffier (1846-1945) who set the bar for French cuisine. He promoted excellent food in hotels and restaurants and his influence was still felt today.

French citizens shopped almost daily and created meals around the fresh ingredients they found in markets. American cooks, on the other hand, often read a recipe and then shopped for its ingredients. She concluded by saying that French cooking was a tribute to an ever-changing France. Judging from our many journeys throughout France, we had to agree. French chefs had set an unbeatable bar for excellence.

After the lecture we began a walking tour of Sarlat with our guide for the week, Angelika. She told us the village of Sarlat, declared a national monument in 1962, received funds from the French government to restore the twenty-two-acre classical medieval central village. We later learned from our hotel proprietor that the restoration took ten years to complete. All the work was done by hand in an effort to replicate the original building techniques. Today the stunning stone buildings and gas street lights in the central area were a gleaming tribute to the past.

In earlier times the village was called the Black City. Grime covered the walls of the buildings and garbage and sewage covered the streets, sometimes to a depth of two or more feet. The streets were cleaned only when a notable dignitary visited the city. Needless to say, disease prevailed. By the 19th century, sanitation became a concern but the city continued to decay. With no fewer than seventy-seven historical monuments in Sarlat, the restoration project saved a gem that today dazzled an annual one million visitors.

Houses and other important 15th-and 16th-century buildings now looked much the same as they did when they were first constructed. Walking through the narrow, cobbled streets was an architectural and artistic treat. Some of the earlier structures, built with half timbers, had disappeared over the centuries but after the Hundred Years' War, limestone blocks became the material of choice in construction. Stone-tiled roofs can last for several centuries if properly maintained. Today, twenty-five hundred people lived in the historic center.

When the tour ended, Wayne and I visited Sarlat's incredible Saturday market. Vendors lined most of the streets in the village selling a variety of foods. We bought fresh goat cheese, a small loaf of bread, goose and duck bloc foie gras, olives, and salted almonds to supplement our already ample hotel fare. Following lunch at the hotel, Wayne and I decided to revisit the street market. On this glorious sunny day, we couldn't have chosen a better way to become familiar with this charming village.

We all regrouped at 4:00 p.m. for a lecture given by the hotel owner/chef on the history of Sarlat. He spoke in French and one of our guides translated. As animated as he was, the actual information he imparted in the hour-long presentation proved minimal. Angelika covered in five minutes this morning most of what took an hour to hear in French and then be translated. After a food fest in our room we joined our group at 7:00 p.m. for a reception and then dinner in the hotel. We met several interesting couples and thoroughly enjoyed the lively conversation.

After an early wake-up call followed by breakfast, our group boarded a bus at 8:00 a.m. for an hour's ride to Rocamadour. Today's gloom promised rain so we took our umbrellas just in case the skies were to open. The ride to Rocamadour followed the Dordogne River Valley into the district of Lot. As we passed numerous walnut groves Angelika gave us more history pointers. Prehistoric man lived in these valleys three hundred thousand years ago as evidenced by findings in caves. In more recent times the area was conquered by tribes from the east and then by the Celts and Romans. Under the Romans the area was known as Gaul. The Romans blended their traditions with some of the Celtic traditions and that influence remained to this day. Villages with names ending in *ac*, some of which we would visit, signified early possession by the Romans.

During the 3rd century AD, barbarians invaded and conquered the area. By the 5th and early 6th centuries AD the area fell to the Visigoths. Under Clovis, the Franks from Cologne pushed the Visigoths into Spain. Under Charlemagne, overlords took control of large areas which they defended against their rivals with fortifications. At this point in France's history the vassal-serf system developed. Many of the small villages in the area were remnants of this earlier settlement.

We passed several impressive chateaus perched atop steep limestone cliffs. Noticing a large gaggle of geese along the roadside, Angelika told us we would stop for photos on our return trip. Not many goats or sheep were visible today but we were told that Rocamadour produced a wonderful goat cheese. Farms dotted the countryside with harvested corn used to fatten the ducks and geese. Noting all the rocks dotting the countryside it had to be a monumental challenge to clear and then plant the acreage. Angelika told us the locals like to say that nothing grew in this area as well as rocks.

Arriving at the top of Rocamadour, a small cliffside village in South Central France, we heard a bit of history before leaving the bus. Rocamadour developed because of a series of miracles that supposedly took place here and it was known for its complex of religious buildings. A highlight was the Chapelle Notre-Dame and its famous artifact, the Black Madonna, a small statue of the Virgin and Child. Carved from walnut and most likely painted, no one knew the story of its origin.

As the morning's tour ended, we gathered for lunch at a local restaurant and sat with Margot and Peter, the couple representing the University of Michigan. As promised, we stopped near the gaggle of geese on our way back to the hotel for photos. Angelika had brought a bag of stale bread which we tossed to the birds. They squawked and flapped their wings, much to the delight of those taking photos. As predicted, it began to rain and we continued on to Sarlat in a light drizzle.

At 6:30 p.m. our group assembled in the hotel for a welcome from the U of M couple traveling with us and then sampled some regional cheeses and wines. Following this we gathered in the dining room for dinner and enjoyed listening to a fellow traveler who served as department head of the School of Anthropology at Michigan.

The next morning, Véronique joined us once more for a lecture on regional cave history. She presented a series of slides and gave a general overview of the time frames and types of cave art in the area. She mentioned the small figurine of a female goddess, Venus of Willendorf, dating from 25,000 BC. These early goddess statues seemed to exaggerate the breast and womb areas of the subjects. Animal figures, on the other hand, were carved realistically.

Figures in Dordogne were etched or painted on cave walls and no humans were represented. Lascaux, dating from 15,000 to 10,000 BC, was discovered in the 1940s and became one of the most popular sites in the region. Due to overuse and decay of the art, the site was now closed to the public, but an exact replica incorporating the images was now open for tours. In the original cave, early artists utilized the shapes of the cave walls in the animals they painted; the hump of an animal would be painted on a bulge in the cave wall. Other cave paintings were stenciled using human hands to outline each animal in a uniform pattern. At the Cap Blanc rock shelter, actual carved figures covered in clay had survived.

Véronique presented three theories to explain the cave paintings:

1. **Interior decoration** Most disagreed with this theory because the art did not coincide with the area in which the cave dwellers lived.

2. **Hunting magic** Capturing animals on the walls of caves symbolized luck in capturing the animals in reality. The problem with this theory was that only ten percent of the arrows depicted on cave walls were actually aimed at the animals. Additionally, many of the larger animals were not consumed for food.

3. **Pictures as messages** Some experts believed that the drawings represented symbolic art. It helped to explain series of dots and rectangles that appeared on cave walls in France and Spain. Even though these had yet to be interpreted, they seemed to indicate some sort of ritual function or rite of passage.

After the lecture we were divided into groups and the first one boarded a bus for Les Eyzies-de-Tayac-Sireuil, one of the caves we would visit. Since our section wasn't scheduled to leave until 1:00 p.m., we had coffee in the hotel dining room. Dick, the head of the U of M Anthropology Department, was with us and led a fascinating discussion about his theories behind cave art.

From 25,000 to 14,000 BC, people habitually returned to the same place as their ancestors and left their mark. Thus, much of the cave art is layered with one figure over another. The layering took place not at one time but over generations, sometimes over thousands of years, as evidenced by the types of animals depicted. After the peak glacial period around 18,000 BC many animals drawn in earlier paintings moved to the north and new animals took their place in the region. The reason for this was that the Dordogne was largely open meadows before the Ice Age. As the ice moved through, it deposited the seeds of trees and much of the plains became forests. Animals such as reindeer needed to graze and moved northward in search of grassy pastures. Climate came first and the environment followed.

As Véronique had also mentioned, Dick pointed out how the natural form of the caves were utilized in the formation of, for example, humps on bison. The artists used ochre-based materials from the iron-rich soil to create shades of red, violet, brown, and black. White color came from aluminum-based soil. Charcoal drawings were produced by using the burned ends of sticks. Using minute samples of the charcoal sketches about the size of a sesame seed, scientists could determine the age of the art within two thousand years.

Paintings were made utilizing wads of grass, shammy-like pieces of animal hide or perhaps chewing on the stem of a plant to create a brush. Bone tubes were used to blow paint onto the walls. The much later appearance of handprints seemed to indicate the recognition of self-worth. Other art forms such as clay figures and weaving had also been found in some of the caves.

Dick said the cave art could simply have been decorative but he didn't think that theory was correct. Some could have been hunting magic but not all the bones of the animals depicted had been found in the caves. They could simply have been a symbolic representation of the animals that existed at that time. Dick's theory was that prehistoric man celebrated with art the world in which he lived and he also recognized the existence of an underworld. He felt that cave art represented birth and reproduction as evidenced by some of the animal figures that were curled up as if in infancy. Some of the horse figures looked pregnant. Thus, the paintings signified the giving of, and ongoing, life.

Our group also discussed the theories of the evolution of modern man. The Eve Theory, universally accepted, illustrated that modern man, Homo Erectus, moved out of Africa eighty-six thousand years ago, eventually following routes through Israel into the Far East and through the Mediterranean into Europe. Until recently, the widely held belief was that when our ancestors, the Cro-Magnons, encountered the Neanderthals, they killed them. Milford Wolpoff, a paleoanthropology professor at the U of M, believed in the Replacement Theory, meaning that the Neanderthals mated themselves to death by crossbreeding with Cro-Magnons.

Dick accepted this theory and illustrated his point with the Australian Aborigines who probably arrived by boat from Southeast Asia some forty thousand years ago. They were not replaced by the people migrating out of Africa; they simply evolved. Thirty thousand years ago Australia was a land of beasts with birds twice the size of today's ostrich and giant kangaroos. The Aborigines burned the forests and pushed these animals into extinction.

Wayne asked for an explanation of the development of various races. Dick described that as man moved northward, his supply of vitamins and calcium diminished. With less sun there was a shorter growing season, resulting in a less abundant supply of foods that provide vitamins and calcium. Over time, this affected skin pigmentation.

We met our group for lunch before boarding a bus for our ride to Font-de-Gaume, a historic cave discovered in 1901 just outside Les Eyzies-de-Tayac-Sireuil. Even though the skies turned grey and rain began to fall as we ascended three hundred yards to the cave entrance, nothing could dampen this experience. Now one of the only prehistoric caves open for public visits, we were part of the 120 permitted through it each day. We needed to divide into groups of twelve, the maximum allowed to tour at any given time.

We followed a narrow passage and after about fifty yards came to the first of four stops. Our French guide turned on an electric light and suddenly two reindeer appeared on the wall of the cave. As we had learned from our earlier lectures, the artists of 14,000 BC utilized the natural cave formations to create their art. Photos did not do it justice; one needed to see the drawings in three-dimension. One of the reindeer was depicted with an extended tongue licking another whose head was lowered. Quite amazing! In another area we saw a pair of horses and one of them, as Dick had mentioned this morning, appeared to be pregnant. We then saw two paintings of bison.

At one point, our guide used a pen light to show us the difference between using electrical lighting and what it must have looked like in the caves by torchlight. She shut off the bright electrical lighting and shone her flashlight on the subjects. We were now able to distinguish coloration and form in a much clearer manner. Our guide said that since the ventilation in the cave was poor, the artists carrying torches could only work for short periods of time before the cave filled with smoke.

After completing the tour, we headed into the village of Les Eyzies-de-Tayac-Sireuil for a tour of the National Museum of Prehistory. Angelika led our group for an hour-and-a-half study of tools dating from 150,000 BC. We then visited two other rooms filled with artwork and depictions of prehistoric burial sites. The museum, an earlier chateau built into the limestone cliffs of the village, sat majestically above the village and was surrounded by a moat. We returned to the hotel at 6:00 p.m. and reminisced about our fascinating day before joining the group for dinner.

The next morning we boarded a bus for a tour of Cap Blanc, a privately owned site with exceptionally well-preserved prehistoric wall art. This 14,000-year-old site, unlike the caves we had visited, was so named for a cap-like lid that provided shelter for those who lived here. The collapse of about twenty meters of the lid sealed the site for thousands of years and protected its drawings from deteriorating. When the site was discovered in 1909, the ochre-based colors were visible. Early archeologists did not know how to preserve these works so no color remained today.

After lunch at the hotel we regrouped for a bus ride to Lascaux II, an exact replica of the phenomenal site discovered in the early 1940s by four local boys. The French allowed access to numerous tourists and within fifteen years the ecosystem was altered to the point that the cave paintings were attacked by mold and mildew. Today only groups of five were allowed to view the original cave drawings three days each week. The rest of us were fortunate to view the 17,000-year-old art in an amazingly realistic duplicated cave called Lascaux II. Led through it by a guide from the Netherlands, we learned that man painted what he didn't hunt. The same animals keep reappearing in each ancient site so it was assumed that they represented some type of ritual. Lines and boxes etched or painted on the cave walls seemed to reinforce this theory but no one knew what these markings represented.

From Lascaux II we bused to the village of Rouffignac-Saint-Cernin-de-Reilhac for a one-hour tram ride into the 850-meter-deep Rouffignac Cave. This site was also privately owned. Our group somehow had been relegated to last and we waited until 4:30 p.m. to enter. Having been forewarned that the cave was cold and damp we bundled up accordingly. Anyone with the least bit of claustrophobia declined this adventure but the rest of us climbed aboard an open-air tram for an unforgettable ride back in time.

The Rouffignac cave art dated back eleven thousand years and contained more than 250 engravings and cave paintings. Evidence of cave bear scratching covered the surfaces high above us and there was no doubt these enormous prehistoric creatures, extinct for more than eighteen thousand years, once used these caves for hibernation. Our guide's French accent was difficult to understand but he nevertheless pointed out figures of bulls, woolly mammoths, horses, bison, and reindeer. He noted that more than ninety percent of prehistoric cave art included these five figures. Plants, sun and moon were never drawn. Seldom were people depicted, though occasionally a handprint appeared. Today's tour lasted much longer than we anticipated and we didn't get back to our hotel until 6:45 p.m.

While en route to Rocamadour, we passed the imposing Château de la Treyne on a cliff rising above the Dordogne River, now functioning as a small hotel with dining. Too spectacular to pass up, we opted out of tonight's dinner at our hotel and made arrangements to return with the Daniels, a delightful couple we met on the tour. We also invited Antoinette, one of our local guides, promising her a very special dinner in exchange for the forty-five-minute drive each way.

Wayne and I scurried to get ready, met our friends and Antoinette at 7:00 p.m. and arrived at the chateau just after dark. Words could not adequately describe the magnificence of this 14th-century structure. We were ushered into a paneled sitting room with a blazing fire and offered aperitifs and appetizers. After selecting our dinners from the menu we entered the elegant dining room. Our meals neared perfection with samplings of house foie gras, risotto and seared scallops. These were followed by duck, lamb, desserts, and coffee. Antoinette graciously declined alcohol and returned us to our hotel in Sarlat at 11:30 p.m. We all agreed that we had sampled a bit of Dordogne heaven.

The next morning was free so Wayne and I opted to visit the Wednesday open market in the center of the village. Unlike the Saturday market, it was quite small. We wandered through the streets admiring the vendors' meats, cheeses and fresh produce. At one stand we purchased a boxed walnut cake to bring back to the States. We then sampled and bought incredibly delicious Dutch Gouda from an Englishman with a booth in this French marketplace.

After lunch at the hotel we met for a bus ride to Saint-Amand-de-Coly, a small medieval village with an impressive restored cathedral as its focal point. We had time to wander through the streets and it was like visiting a ghost town. As we were leaving, we noticed a teen tossing a basketball near his home. Otherwise, we never saw a soul. Very strange...

We had enjoyed our dinner the previous night with the Daniels and opted for another off-campus dinner with them. Wayne had read about Le Centenaire in Les Eyzies, a small Relais et Châteaux hotel with a two-star restaurant, and we all decided to give it a try. Our taxi driver delivered us in pouring rain and we entered a rather ordinary building. We opted for the five-course prix fixe menu. The food was very good but the room lacked atmosphere. We all agreed that our evening at Château de la Treyne had spoiled us completely.

The next day's tour began just before 9:00 a.m. and we boarded our bus for the drive to Château Beynac in the village of Beynac-et-Cazenac. Perched high on a cliff at breathtaking heights, the castle stood as a stone sentinel for nine centuries. In 1961 a Frenchman purchased the decaying castle for one franc with a promise to restore it. After forty years the restoration had progressed but would not be completed for another forty years. The owner was now in his 90s and it was uncertain who would continue the work.

Our French guide took us from the ground level constructed in the 12th century up a series of levels ranging from defenses to living quarters. Those hardy enough to climb sixty steep steps to the castle's tower were greeted with an impressive view of the Dordogne valley.

Next on the agenda was a forty-minute boat ride along the Dordogne River. The day had turned bitter cold and some in our group opted not to go. We brave souls rode to a site not far from Beynac with another imposing castle owned and restored by a wealthy Texan. It was not open for tours. After returning to the dock we all walked to a nearby restaurant for lunch.

We then bused to the picturesque village of Domme, a planned medieval village perched high on the cliffs above the Dordogne River. A train, à la Disneyland, took us to the top of the cliff and into the village for a forty-minute, self-guided walking tour. Unfortunately, the skies opened and we toured in a steady cold rain.

When we returned to the hotel, we ventured out to buy cheese and bread for a bring-an-hors d'oeuvre farewell party in the lounge before dinner. Once at the gathering we sampled a variety of local foods before our final repast. We took home memories of new friendships, stunning small French villages and incredible prehistoric cave art. The beauty of the Dordogne and its archaeological treasures would remain with us forever.

SPAIN AND PORTUGAL
Santiago de Compostela, Guimarães, Amares, and Porto

September 20–October 4, 2009

AS A FRESHMAN at the University of Michigan, I decided to forego one more year of Latin to complete my college language requirement and took a year of conversational Spanish. The course included many hours in a lab repeating useful words and phrases. Our teaching fellow, a lively redhead just back in the States from a year in Spain, kept us on our toes in her classroom. I came away with a limited but useful vocabulary and the ability to converse in present-tense Spanish. Until I moved to Southern California many years later, I rarely had an opportunity to use my newly acquired, albeit limited, language skill.

When the Santa Barbara Museum of Art offered a trip to Spain, Wayne and I jumped at the opportunity. After all my years of overseas travel, this would be only my second trip to a Spanish-speaking country. We cashed in miles we had accumulated for first-class seats and the airline complied with an indirect route. Four baggage scans and many hours later we arrived at Heathrow and boarded a plane for our final destination, Barcelona. Our plan was to meet the tour group after adding a few extra days to visit this city and then Madrid.

We arrived at Hotel Claris and checked into a small ultra-modern two-story suite. A staircase led to a sitting room which we never did use. Once settled, we ventured out mid-afternoon in warm sunlight for a quarter-mile walk to Antoni Gaudí's magnificent unfinished cathedral, the Sagrada Familia. As we strolled along a wide boulevard lined with small shops and exclusive apartments, we suddenly felt something wet on our backs. Wayne turned around and I noticed a blob of yellow paint on him. He found the same marks on my new white shirt. We looked up and realized we were walking directly beneath a painter working several stories above us.

A man in a sport coat appeared at our sides, shaking his head in disgust. He took out a pack of tissues and motioned us into the foyer of the nearest apartment building. Fighting jet lag and not thinking clearly, we followed him and he began to wipe Wayne's back. He put his hand on Wayne's hip pocket and Wayne immediately brushed it away. As a savvy traveler, I carried no purse and wore no flashy jewelry. Wayne's cash was in a money belt safely tucked inside his slacks. We opened the door and returned to the street in a big hurry.

As we assessed the situation, we realized that our helper must have had a hole in his jacket pocket just large enough for him to shoot a water pistol filled with paint at two unsuspecting tourists and then feign sympathy. We put ourselves in harm's way when we naively followed this would-be robber into the building's foyer but fortunately he came away empty handed.

We continued on and soon the towers of Sagrada Familia rose majestically in the foreground. Once in full view it simply captivated us. Gaudí's passion and creativity came to life in this yet-to-be-completed cathedral. The mere size of the structure boggled one's imagination. At every turn, more elaborate embellishments appeared. This work-of-art-in-progress simply had to be seen to be fully appreciated. We entered and walked around the periphery of the interior, watching men at work and realizing that it would take several visits to absorb the magnitude of this masterpiece.

When we returned to the Claris and told the hotel manager of our paint plight, he was aghast. Apparently con artists often lured unsuspecting tourists into buildings and robbed them. Even though our would-be thief came away unrewarded, the hotel manager told us we were lucky. We'd chalk this Barcelona episode up to a good lesson learned. All's well that ends well. Thankfully, the hotel's laundry removed the paint from our clothing.

We changed out of our splattered clothes and headed back into the streets. In spite of our earlier misadventure we fell in love with bustling Barcelona. A block from our hotel stood the Hotel Majestic and shops lined either side of the street. Not far away we happened upon Casa Batlló, considered one of Gaudí's works of genius. In 1904 he redesigned the façade of a home built in 1877, creating a corrugated surface using stone, glass and ceramics.

For dinner that evening we walked a few blocks just after 8:00 p.m. to Cerveceria Catalana, a well-known tapas bar. Even at this early-for-Barcelona dining hour, people crowded around the counters three and four deep. It helped to be tall and, having done some homework on what to order, I called out for an assortment of tapas. We wedged into a corner and dined on our picturesque and delicious choices. Wayne felt a bit claustrophobic in the sea of diners so we passed on a second round and headed back to the Claris feeling content.

We slept soundly and had coffee in our room before walking to the Plaça d'Espanya to purchase two 2-day Red and Blue Line bus passes for 54 euros, about US$81. Several friends mentioned that riding the buses offered the best way to see the city, and we soon discovered they were absolutely right. Created for the 1992 Summer Olympics, the bus lines traveled to all the major tourist spots and riders could hop on and off at their leisure. We boarded the Blue Line and plugged the headsets that came with our tickets into the English-speaking channel. A clear voice gave us highlights of each area we passed and we followed along with a booklet that was also provided.

Approaching a grand promenade surrounded by stunning buildings built for the 1929 World's Fair, we decided to hop off the bus. Wandering along the walkway we made our way up a series of stairs leading to the Museu Nacional d'Art de Catalunya, an impressive structure at the top. Divided into two sections, the first featured works by Ramon Casas and other regional painters. The second showcased contemporary paintings that included a number by Picasso. We thoroughly enjoyed the art and architecture of this small but mighty museum. Since it was 2:30 p.m. we opted for a light lunch in the museum's elegant dining room which featured three-story windows overlooking Barcelona.

We returned to a Blue Line bus, catching this one at the top of the hill. Our recorded voice pointed out that many of the 1929 World's Fair structures were also used for the 1992 Summer Olympics. We passed the Olympic Pool and broadcast towers before heading down the hill overlooking Barcelona's harbor. When we reached the Miró Museum, a modern structure housing a multitude of the artist's treasures, we stepped off the bus once more. Wayne and I enjoyed seeing Miró's art displayed chronologically in a series of galleries and we both agreed that his earlier works far surpassed his later efforts. In our opinion, he became less creative and more commercial over time. We visited the outdoor garden filled with the artist's delightful sculptures before queuing up for the next Blue Line bus.

Our tour continued to the harbor where the QE2 sat at anchor. After passing the statue of Columbus in the circle at the beginning of Las Ramblas, we hopped off to walk the length of this famous boulevard. The wide walkway overflowed with townspeople and tourists, young and old. Small stalls selling souvenirs lined the center of Las Ramblas, stretching for blocks.

Street performers and mimes vied for coins from passersby. The atmosphere along the automobile-free boulevard was a blend of flea market and carnival.

Arriving at another Gaudí home, Casa Milà, we decided to take a self-guided tour. Built between 1906 and 1912, it was the artist's last work of civic architecture, known as La Pedrera because of its resemblance to a stone quarry. Every detail fascinated us as we wound our way upward to the top floor featuring exhibits and examples of furniture created by the architect. Like other works by Gaudí, we found its spire-filled rooftop captivating. We purchased a CD in the gift shop only to later discover it wouldn't work in our American video player.

We walked a block beyond our hotel to a pastry shop we had noticed earlier. With the exchange rate for the euro at US$1.40, room service came with a hefty price tag. We decided to buy a couple of pastries for tomorrow's breakfast to accompany our room service coffee.

Tonight's dinner reservation made well in advance was at Restaurante Lasarte, rated with two Michelin stars (three today) and ranked number two on the Zagat list of best Barcelona restaurants. Located a few blocks away in the Hotel Condes, the small, ultra-modern dining room seated about twenty guests. Service was stellar, the presentation a work of art and the food superb. Chef Martin Berasategui's genius shone throughout our selections. We began with a watermelon soup topped with finely diced carrots and tomatoes. This was followed by warm scallops topped with truffle mayonnaise. Other highlights were Wayne's caramelized mille-feuille of green apple, foie gras and smoked eel and my crunchy oysters with grapefruit, walnuts and sage cream. Every plate was a work of art and equally delicious. Before we left, our waiter presented us with a signed copy of the menu. Tonight's was indeed a memorable dining experience.

We awoke to another warm, sunny fall day and after enjoying our pastries, walked in the direction of the Barcelona Cathedral in the medieval section of the city. Map Man Wayne led the way but somehow missed his mark. We wound through narrow streets lined with shops and finally emerged in a square featuring a not-very-grand church. By the time we reached it the temperature loomed in the upper eighties, accompanied by a high humidity level. After a quick look inside, we walked to a boarding area for the Red Line bus.

Today's route took us past Sagrada Familia, Gaudí's dream for forty years of his life. Since his death in 1926, anonymous donations had funded the continued construction of the cathedral. There was currently a push to complete the project and I overheard someone say it was expected to be finished in the next twenty years. Time would tell, I guessed...

We sat on the top deck of the bus for the next forty-five minutes as we rode past Gràcia, Parc Güell, Tibidabo, Sarria, and Barcelona's Futbol (soccer) Club. We jumped off at the Francesc Macia Diagonal and, after a frappuccino and sinfully good cookies at Starbucks, we caught the Blue Line, retracing some of yesterday's sights and discovering new ones. We recommend the buses highly but advise future travelers to be prepared for the stops. We missed Parc Güell because we didn't move quickly enough from the upper deck. Next time…

We exited near Gaudí's ornate Casa Batlló with its fanciful pink and blue roof tiles dripping down like the topping on an ice cream cone. Its exquisite interior was quite different from Casa Milà. Varying patterns of blue and cream tiles lined the interior corridor leading to the rooftop. We were awed by the elaborate details, some sculptural, that adorned this lofty area with splendid views of the city. I took a number of photos of the minute details. My love for all things Gaudí increased with each new example of his genius. Some called it bizarre; I called it brilliant.

Before returning to the Claris we stopped at a sidewalk café along the Passeig de Gràcia for a double espresso. We hadn't made dinner reservations and decided we would find another tapas bar near our hotel. I promised Wayne we could spend a little more for a table of our own.

While resting our feet, I made several observations based on our two and a half days in Barcelona. We were entranced by this elegant city's blend of classical and modern architecture. Other than our attack by the Spray Paint Bandit, whom we cleverly outfoxed with our well-concealed valuables, we found the people courteous and most appreciative of our attempts to converse in Spanish. The city was immaculate. Late September weather, albeit a bit warm and humid, was quite delightful. Exploring Gaudí's works first-hand merited a visit to Barcelona. We do regret missing Parc Güell. We'd like to live long enough to see Sagrada Familia reach completion. This may very well be a mission we bequeath to our daughters.

We chose Tapa Tapa and did indeed secure a table for this evening's tapas. Our waiter brought plastic place mats with photos of the wide variety of tapas available to sample. We selected a xarcuteria assortit, calamari, camembert cruixent, croquetes, tempura de verdures, and langostinos. It was a bit like eating in a cafeteria but the food was just fine.

After dinner we decided to walk a mile to Sagrada Familia for a look at this magnificent building's exterior lit at night. Once we arrived, we both felt that as lovely as it was under spotlights, the cathedral showed all its glory in pure daylight. Nevertheless, the walk felt good and we returned to our hotel to pack our bags for our flight to Madrid.

Leaving the hotel the next morning, the doorman offered us a private driver for the same price as a taxi and we accepted. Our driver asked if we spoke Spanish and we replied, "Un pocito." We surprised ourselves by carrying on a somewhat cohesive conversation on our way to the airport. Languages are like riding a bike; Wayne's high school Spanish and my year of conversational Spanish came back when we needed it.

The international airport in Barcelona, a modern facility, made check-in a breeze and we had ample time to explore the duty-free shops. I bought a bright green canvas tote bag emblazoned all over with *Barcelona* to replace the disintegrating paper bag I was using to carry the trinkets I had accumulated. I've employed the Moscow Rule of Shopping on many overseas ventures and this was no exception. Loosely translated, this means that *if you see it, buy it because it may not be there when you come back for it.*

Our personable Madrid taxi driver, dressed like a businessman, indicated points of interest as we drove to the Hotel Orfila, at one time a small palace, built in 1886. After checking in we asked the concierge to book a dinner reservation at a restaurant my good friend Pat, who once lived in Madrid, had recommended. Unfortunately, we were unable to make arrangements for either of the nights we would be in the city.

After unpacking in our spaciously elegant room we hailed a taxi for a ride to the Plaza Mayor in the heart of Madrid. The massive square, surrounded by shops, bars and restaurants, seemed rather peaceful in the late afternoon. Like all of Spain, activity picked up as the evening progressed. Many of the businesses were closed at 4:30 p.m. and wouldn't reopen until 7:00 p.m. As in most of Spain, dinner in Madrid typically began at 10:00 p.m. or even later.

With time to spare we took a taxi to the Thyssen-Bornemisza Museum showcasing its wealth of art collected by this influential family over a period of two generations. We were dazzled by the breadth and scope of the collection, featuring early works by Jan Steen and Franz Halls and many works by Jacob van Ruisdael depicting the flat gray scenery of 17th-century Netherlands. One room displayed collections of Dutch still life and porcelain.

Noted works by 19th-century English and American painters adorned the walls of another gallery in the museum. Portraits by Gainsborough and landscapes by John Copley, *Portrait of George Washington's Cook* by Gilbert Stuart, *Portrait of Millicent, Duchess of Sutherland* by John Singer Sargent and *The Falls of Saint Anthony* by western artist George Catlin were but a few of my favorites. Others included works by William Merritt Chase and Winslow Homer.

World-renowned European artists were prominent as well. Picasso's *The Frugal Meal* was a painting we'd viewed in an exhibit in the States. A wealth of art by greats such as Corot, Morisot, Manet, Pissarro, van Gogh, Renoir, Monet, Matisse, Bonnard, Gauguin, Degas, Toulouse-Lautrec, and Cézanne hung proudly in these corridors. We continued to view art throughout the galleries until the 7:00 p.m. closing and agreed that the collection was rich in every sense of the word. It ranked high on our list of museum favorites.

We decided to walk what was roughly a mile back to the Hotel Orfila. Along the way we stopped at a rather ordinary American coffee vendor for rather ordinary cups of coffee. Returning to our beautifully appointed room we relaxed a bit before ordering room service plates of local cured ham and cheeses at 9:30 p.m., an early dinner by Madrid standards.

Our first impressions of Madrid failed to match those of Barcelona. While Madrid boasts a varied array of architectural masterpieces, it lacks the whimsy of Barcelona. Madrid seemed stately and cosmopolitan while Barcelona exuded a playful flair and the abundant influence of Gaudí. In all fairness, Madrid's famed boulevards were in various stages of repair and sported bright yellow tape to keep passers-by out of open trenches. With a staggering twenty percent unemployment rate, the government now paid able-bodied workers to carry out these civic projects.

We slept well and after a light breakfast took a taxi to Madrid's Prado Museum, again passing block after block with sections of roadway under reconstruction. Our driver told us that the government was sponsoring a one-year project to repair roads and walkways in the city. We'd have to return someday to see the finished results and enjoy Madrid without repairs underway at almost every intersection.

Ah, the Prado! It truly is one of the world's great museums, paying particular tribute to centuries of Spain's most revered artists. Founded in 1819, it housed *Las Meninas* by Diego Velázques, *The Clothed Maja* by Francisco de Goya, *The Garden of Earthly Delights* by Hieronymus Bosch, *Still Life with Game, Vegetables and Fruit* by Juan Sánchez Cotán and *The Cardinal* by Raphael. The massive Prado, filled with art treasures, simply must be experienced at least once in one's lifetime.

At 2:15 p.m. we walked to the Ritz, not far from the museum. As we approached, we noticed a large crowd near the main entrance holding protest signs. We darted through and enjoyed a leisurely light lunch of Iberian ham and toast with a spicy tomato spread followed by coffee. When we exited, we were serenaded by the band of protesters blasting out ear-splitting high-pitched sounds on plastic horns. Their deafening blares failed to win our sympathy.

Our next quest was to find the Reina Sofia Museum. After mistaking a train station for the museum, we were given directions by a helpful local couple. The building, originally a hospital completed in 1805, was reconfigured to accommodate the museum in 1988. Primarily dedicated to Spanish art, it houses Picasso's massive 1937 *Guernica* and works by Juan Miró, Juan Gris, Pablo Serrano, Lucio Gordillo, and many more.

Retracing our steps in the direction of the Ritz, we decided to walk through Madrid's Public Gardens. We paid the 2-euro entrance fee and took leisurely strolls along a series of pathways that bordered meticulously manicured gardens.

Hailing a taxi near the Ritz, we began the return to our hotel. As soon as we closed the taxi doors, we realized we had picked the driver from hell. Filled with road rage he ranted and raved, honking incessantly at anyone and everyone. He spoke no English but we got his message. We finally had enough and hopped out a few blocks from our hotel. Much to our delight, our walk took us through charming neoclassical neighborhoods. While our hotel may not have been located in the heart of Madrid, it was in a lovely residential area.

The concierge made reservations for us at El Cenador del Prodo, a fading star near the Plaza Mayor. Its décor could best be described as tired; it had certainly seen its better days. The service, however, was good and the food was just fine. We learned all too late that, as we did for Barcelona's Restaurante Lasarte, we should have made our Madrid dinner reservations well in advance.

The next morning, we met our driver Julian and buckled up in the back seat of his roomy Mercedes for a day trip to Toledo. As we traveled, he filled us with the city's history.

Our route took us through La Mancha dotted with flat farmland and an occasional factory. We arrived at noon with the intention of visiting the city's historic hospital-turned-museum, Hospital de Tavera. Much to his dismay, Julian found it impossible to approach the museum. Roads were barricaded and police stood guard. We wondered if something as drastic as a bomb threat had occurred but we later learned it was nothing more than a special police celebration.

We opted for Plan B and our driver took us to an overlook high above Toledo. What breathtaking views from this vantage point! The medieval city below us with its towering central cathedral shone like a jewel as we drove down the hill to its entrance. Surrounded on three sides by the Tagus River, it was necessary to access the walled city via centuries-old pedestrian bridges. We crossed one dating from 1490 AD that was still in use to this day. The massive Visigoth wooden gate clad in iron opened to a bridge crossing the river, leading us to the cobbled streets of Toledo.

Once inside the city, Julian explained that Toledo, now a UNESCO

World Heritage Centre, remained divided into three sections—Moorish, Jewish and Christian. Under the rule of Alfonso VI in 1085 AD, Toledo became the most important political and social center of Castile. It remained a fusion of Christian, Arab and Jewish cultures until the reign of Philip II began in 1556 AD when he proclaimed, "Out with the heretics!"

The Moors were exquisite craftsmen and their exodus proved to be a great artistic loss for Spain. From 1609 to 1611 AD, eight thousand Muslims left the country. From 1618 to 1648 AD, Philip IV conducted a thirty-year war and either banished or executed many Jews, who were the intellectuals of Spain. The loss of both the Moors and the Jews had a devastating effect on Spain's artistic and intellectual development over the next few centuries.

We visited a metalworks shop in the old Jewish section that featured handmade knives and jewelry uniquely fused with gold wire. Wayne bought a hunting knife for a good friend who has a cabin in Montana and it remains a gift that he treasures.

Julian then took us to a church with paintings by El Greco before we lunched at La Juderia, a restaurant situated in an old home. Our driver, who was Jewish, knew the owner and we were well fed. The proprietor actually moved a couple in the crowded courtyard who were seated at a prime table and gave it to us. The cooking exemplified home-style cuisine and we enjoyed the experience.

After lunch we walked a few blocks to the imposing Toledo Cathedral, one of three High Gothic cathedrals in Spain. Begun in 1226 AD under the rule of Ferdinand III, construction of the towering altar in the main chapel began in 1496 AD and took six years to complete. Vaults were added in the 15th century by the aristocratic de Luna family and a chapel was added in the 17th century in honor of Ildefonsus, Toledo's patron saint. El Greco arrived in Spain in 1576 AD and eventually settled in Toledo, where he was commissioned to paint altarpieces and other works of art.

We walked back to Julian's car and as we exited the city were surprised to find the museum still closed to the public. On our return trip to Madrid we drove past a Gaudí home located not far from our hotel. Unlike any we had seen in Barcelona, the exterior had three-dimensional long-stemmed flowers and ornate ironwork all in the same pale grey tones.

With a long day's touring behind us we opted for a quiet night. We walked in the hotel's residential neighborhood, stopped for an espresso at Bar Gaudí and then meandered along a section of Paseo de la Castellana that wasn't in the midst of reconstruction. With a half moon shining above us and buildings lit at night, the evening provided a magical farewell to Madrid.

The next morning, we rearranged our suitcases for eight days in paradors and pousadas, or inns, throughout northwestern Spain and Portugal with our group from the Santa Barbara Museum of Art. We hired a driver, a woman with little English, who wasted no time getting us to Avila, forty-two miles from Madrid. Ignoring the posted 100 kilometer speed limit, she raced along the highway at 140 kilometers, about ninety miles per hour, and only slowed when the car's radar detector alerted her to impending police.

We passed factories and farms and noted that the countryside, dotted with olive orchards and rolling hills, resembled central California. As we approached Avila, we observed an ominous bank of grey clouds, the first we had encountered in a week. Just past El Escorial we drove into foothills bordering a mountain range and soon entered a long tunnel stretching for two or three miles. We passed the exit to Segovia, part of our tour later in the week.

As we exited the highway toward Avila a light rain began to fall. Patches of blue sky peeked through the clouds and we surmised that the sprinkles wouldn't hamper us. Avila was much larger and more modern than we had anticipated. We drove several miles before reaching the medieval center and then wound our way up a narrow road to the 12th-century walled city and our inn, the Parador Raimundo de Borgona. After paying our driver and collecting our bags we headed to the check-in desk and met two fellow travelers who hailed from Houston.

We were ushered to a room at the end of an addition to the parador. Opening the curtains, we chuckled that the view overlooked garbage containers along the street. At least it was quiet. We unpacked for our three-night stay and then sat in the courtyard sipping espressos before venturing out to stroll along the walkway atop the massive stone walls encircling the medieval city. The hillside fortress of Avila, the highest capital city in all of Spain, was surrounded by walls standing thirty-six feet high, one and a half feet thick and extending seventy-five hundred feet, the distance of one and a half miles. Completed between the 11th and 14th centuries, we marveled at these stone and mortar walls that withstood the test of time.

That evening we met our fellow travelers at a cocktail party hosted by our tour guide, Paula. We then enjoyed dinner as we sat at long tables in the dining room. As is typical of museum tours, our group of twenty-six hailed from all parts of the U.S., including Pasadena, San Francisco, San Diego, Houston, and several East Coast cities. Everyone looked forward to the adventures ahead of us.

Our day began with a breakfast buffet at the parador before meeting our group in the lobby for a walking tour. In Spain, tours must use a local guide from each city and today Blanca escorted us along the interior of the walls as she enlightened us with local history. Avila's cathedral, the oldest in Spain, had its beginning in the 12th century. First built in the Romanesque style, 14th-century additions adopted Gothic architecture. In the cloister, visitors could look at a two thousand-year time line depicting worship in this location. Warm sandstone unique to this area flecked with burgundy created by iron content was used in the construction. Unlike so many other ancient cathedrals with dull grey interiors that we had seen over the years, this one virtually glowed.

A girl's got to do what a girl's got to do and when the tour ended I asked Blanca if she could recommend a nail salon. She graciously led us to one and I spent the time practicing my limited Spanish as the manicurist worked on my well-worn nails. It always amazes me how my ability to communicate comes back when I travel in Spanish-speaking countries.

With a free afternoon, Wayne and I roamed the streets of Avila. Wayne, a shoe and luggage fan, spotted a pair of walking shoes in a shop window and purchased them for just under US$100. We then stopped at El Buen Yantar on the central square for a late lunch of Spanish meats, including chorizo, pork loin, ham, and salami.

That evening we gathered at the parador for a lecture on the history of Castile. Our lively lecturer told us of Isabella and Ferdinand, whose marriage in 1469 AD at the ages of eighteen and seventeen, respectively, united the kingdoms of Castile and Aragon. It was a political alliance and not a love match. Their aim was to strengthen the power of the royalty by weakening the power of the noblemen. They also wanted to control the church and to accomplish this they made the archbishop the third most powerful person after themselves.

In 1492 AD, during the Spanish Inquisition, Spain conquered Granada and decreed that all Jews either be baptized or exiled. Those Jews who remained and refused to convert were publicly burned to death. Coincidentally, El Greco painted during this period. In the year 1492 AD the Moors were also defeated and expelled. Those who did convert were called Moriscos. As we learned from our guide in Toledo, many of the Moors and Jews simply left Spain and their absence created an intellectual and artistic void. Of course, 1492 AD also marked Christopher Columbus' discovery of America. On August 2 of that year, Isabella approved the sailing of the Niña, Pinta and Santa María and the three ships landed that October on Hispaniola in the Bahamas. In 1497 AD Amerigo Vespucci, also sponsored by Spain, was credited for landing on the mainland of the Americas near Rio de Janeiro and later naming his discovery after himself.

In the Middle Ages, royalty often intermarried and their gene pools became gene puddles. Isabella died in 1504 AD and was buried in Granada. Ferdinand died in 1516 AD. Joan the Mad, their third child who survived a sister and brother, married Philip the Handsome, who died at the age of twenty-nine. She kept his body for decades, hoping he would revive. Philip was buried forty-eight years after his death when Joan finally died. Alfred Hitchcock could have had a heyday with this tale.

Charles I, son of Joan and Philip, felt he was the guardian of Christian Europe. His son, Philip II, named Madrid the capital of Spain. He ordered the construction of El Escorial in 1557 AD. Built in twenty-one years, the city now houses one of Spain's finest art collections and libraries. In 1588 AD the Spanish Armada attacked England and was defeated. This marked the beginning of the end of Spain as a superpower.

Our group met early the next morning and boarded a bus just outside the city walls for a one-hour ride to Segovia. Paula mentioned that Spanish children were now eating fast foods and sugary donuts and, as in the States, obesity was becoming a problem. Just a few short years ago children and adults ate only meat, fish, vegetables, fruit, and good olive oil. Signs of the times…

We drove past rolling hills and small farms. Mountains loomed in the background. A scattering of tiny cork oaks blended with olive trees all along the way. The emerald hues of the trees against the golden fields reminded us once more of summer in California. Dark clouds warned of impending rain. We continued into high chaparral where vast fields of gigantic white energy-producing windmills dotted the hilltops.

We marveled at the excellent roadways. The bus drove through the village of La Zarzuela and we noted signs stating that we would reach Segovia in twenty-five kilometers, about sixteen miles. We spotted horses and cattle in fields. Every farm had its own small grape arbor, most likely to produce wine for family and friends. In the midst of a particularly dry landscape a vibrant field of sunflowers suddenly appeared.

As we neared Segovia, Paula mentioned that cultural Spain remained a puzzle. Although unification was forced by Isabella and Ferdinand, it did not sit well with all of Spain's citizens. Even now, there was no love between Barcelona and Madrid. Each viewed itself as culturally superior to the other.

Nearing our destination, we noticed large apartment complexes, often unfinished or empty. The current poor state of the economy in Spain dictated their lack of occupancy. Segovia's population in 2009 stood at fifty-two thousand as compared with Avila's sixty-four thousand. Although Segovia's outer periphery seemed new and modern, we knew from our experience entering Avila that the historic center would tell a much different story.

Today's local guide, Maria, walked our group to the Segovia Cathedral, built in the 16th century. The cathedral's construction began in 1535 AD and took 150 years to complete. Built in the Gothic style, its interior rose a towering fifty-four meters from floor to ceiling, one of the highest in Spain. Above the choir seats, we noted Moorish-style carvings. Quite impressive!

While walking, we passed men on scaffolding and stopped to watch as they traced intricate Moorish patterns onto a border at the top of a building and then etched the patterns in bas-relief. The designs would later be painted in typical Moorish colors of blue, green, gold, and rust. I had wondered how the trim on the homes and buildings in Segovia were created and now I had an answer; each was meticulously crafted by local artisans.

At 1:30 p.m. we stopped for lunch at a small restaurant, Mesón de Cándido, on the main square. Our top floor window table provided us with a spectacular view of the Aqueduct of Segovia, one of the best-preserved elevated Roman aqueducts and the symbol of the city. Now a UNESCO World Heritage Site, it is generally believed that its construction was ordered by Emperor Domitian and completed in 98 AD. We were delighted to have a birds-eye view during our traditional lunch featuring suckling pig and a custard cake. We thoroughly enjoyed our tour of Segovia, a city that holds a special place in my heart.

When we returned to Avila, Wayne and I walked for an hour and had coffee in the main square. We then packed a hefty box filled with books, trinkets and the knife we bought in Toledo, assuming it might raise red flags if we tried to carry it across borders. Hopefully, it would arrive safely when we shipped it stateside.

The next morning we were up at 6:30 a.m. for a quick breakfast before walking through the walled city of Avila for the final time and boarding a bus for a long day's ride to Santiago de Compostela. As we began our journey, Paula told us about the languages in Spain. In Madrid, Castilian was spoken, as legend had it, in deference to a lisping 16th-century monarch. The only documented monarch with a lisp was Pedro of Castile, 1334 AD–1369 AD, but he died two hundred years before the Castilian dialect developed. In Barcelona the dialect was Catalan. The Basque had a language of their own but many now spoke Castilian, or what was considered "pure" Spanish. In Santiago de Compostela the dialect was Galician.

Paula mentioned that the northern part of the country was the wealthiest. When the dictator Franco died in 1975, democracy began in Spain. All four languages were again permitted and families could determine which language their children learned in school. Children began their studies at age six in either a public or private school. In Spain, education was compulsory through the twelfth grade while in Portugal, only nine years were required. There were scholarships for college but they did not cover living expenses so parents needed to assist financially. Children in Spain lived with their parents until their first job, university, apartment, or marriage. However, marriages were decreasing as more and more young people chose to live together. There were, at the time, fairly low birth rates in both Spain and Portugal.

The bull is an important symbol in Spain. We had noticed ancient rustic life-sized sandstone bulls scattered throughout Avila. On today's drive we spotted several huge flat billboards depicting a bull. Although no advertising was permitted along the highways, the enormous bull representing a cherry wine company had taken a wordless but lasting stand.

Eventually we reached Salamanca, a cosmopolitan city of one hundred fifty thousand. Salamanca University was the oldest and most prestigious in all of Spain, founded in 1218 AD by King Alfonso IX. We stopped for a visit and today's city guide, Carmen, told us that the college first belonged to the Catholic Church. By 1492 AD it boasted eight thousand students. Today there were fifty-five thousand. Salamanca was called the Golden City because of its buildings constructed from local gold-hued sandstone.

The city's cathedral, built in the 12th century with a Romanesque dome over the altar, eventually became too small. The new cathedral, begun in the 16th century, expanded around the existing structure over a period of 220 years. Rows of stacked artwork hung on the walls, reminding us of the many icons on the walls of churches in Russia. Ten years before our visit, a 13th-century fresco in almost mint condition was discovered under many layers of paint. Much of the newer cathedral was created in a Moorish/Romanesque style.

In a recent cleaning procedure, five hundred pounds of dust formed from burning candles and incense over the centuries was removed from the ceiling. Before leaving, Carmen pointed out that in Spain, the choir was almost always situated in the center of the interior. Nobility sat in front of the choir and the commoners were relegated to the back.

Carmen paused near a facade covered in pictorial symbols, each telling a story. She pointed out one in particular featuring a frog on top of a skull. Since the frog represented lust and the skull death, the story told in this symbol is a simple warning to medieval students: you do it, you die. Much to our surprise, we noticed an astronaut represented in one of the symbols. Carmen told us that during a 1992 restoration, the artisans added this contemporary symbol to the façade.

We had toted umbrellas and the rain finally began as we ended our tour and boarded the bus just before noon. It seemed the rain in Spain did indeed fall mainly on the plain. We were all glad to be on the bus and relatively dry as we headed for Zamora and a lunch stop. This city wouldn't make it to my A, B or even C list for a second visit but we did enjoy a delicious lunch in one of its restaurants.

As we drove on, we recalled that Spain had experienced a severe drought and, crossing a river, noticed how low the water level actually was. It painted a dramatic picture of the severity of the drought.

We continued driving northwest across barren land for another hour and a half before approaching foothills covered with cork oaks. An ear-popping climb leading into Galicia provided views of vast fields of enormous energy-producing windmills on the upper peaks. Spain boasted a goodly number of energy farms like this one. As we continued to wind our way along steep cliffs, the sky turned from grey to black and a downpour ensued. By the time we entered Galicia it subsided considerably and, after many clear days in Spain, we were glad to spend the only rainy one we encountered on the bus.

As required by law in Spain, at 4:30 p.m. we made a forty-five-minute rest stop for our bus driver in a village with nothing more than a gas station, several bars and a few houses. We sat on the veranda of one of the bars sipping coffee and a woman in our group announced that she wanted to visit the rapids just down the road. I thought it odd given the severe drought in Spain and asked, "Are there really rapids nearby?" "Yes!" she replied. We joined her for a 200-yard walk along the roadway and reached a garden surrounded by a chain link fence. "There they are!" she exclaimed. We soon realized that she had said rabbits, not rapids, and we watched the furry fellows hop around the field.

We reached Santiago de Compostela early that evening. Arriving at Parador Hostas dos Reis Católicos, we were all struck by its grandeur. Having served as a hospital for many centuries, its conversion into a parador worked to perfection. After collecting our luggage, we joined our group for dinner. Paula announced that sunshine was predicted for the next day and we all thanked the weather gods for smiling on us.

Today's local guide met us in the lobby after breakfast and filled us with factoids as we walked through the historic center. Santiago's population, combining the historical center and the newer village, was ninety thousand. Most of the buildings in the historic center were built in the 15th, 16th and 17th centuries, the latter in the Baroque style. Some of the older buildings now sported Baroque façades yet the interiors retained their Romanesque 12th-century style. The cathedral exemplified this. It was dedicated to Santiago, better known to us as Saint James. One of Christ's apostles, James came in peace to preach in Galicia yet became known as the saint of war during the Middle Ages. The cross and dagger, originally the symbol of the war against Muslims, was now associated with Saint James.

The cathedral sat atop the original one that took over a century to build and was eventually destroyed by the Moors. It is believed that the remains of Saint James were buried here and, for centuries, pilgrims from all over Europe have traveled to Santiago to pay homage. Many would walk for weeks or months and we spotted a number of them during our stay. July 5th marked the discovery of the city's ancient cemetery and was now an official holiday in Santiago.

Once inside the cathedral our guide pointed out a small statue of Saint James atop a low column. For centuries, students knocked their heads against the statue three times, hoping that the architect Maestro Mateo's intellect would rub off on them. During the 1950s, the tombs below the cathedral were examined and revealed burials from the 1st, 5th and 9th centuries AD. In this cathedral, unlike most in Spain, the choir was not situated in the center. We walked past an exquisite Baroque organ with approximately three thousand pipes and a Baroque/Rococo altar.

The *botafumeiro*, a massive incense burner, hung prominently from a pulley system designed to support it. Measuring more than three feet in diameter and weighing 119 pounds, its intent was practical as well as symbolic. Since the pilgrims traveled for weeks without bathing, one could only imagine the stench of hundreds gathered in the pews upon their arrival. The incense burner, built in the 16th century, took eight men to raise and then swing at seventy kilometers per hour, or forty-three-and-a-half miles per hour, in an attempt to masquerade the foul smell.

Termite damage discovered in 1998 in one chapel required extensive restoration. As workers removed centuries of whitewash from the walls, they discovered the original frescoes dating to 1596 AD, the time of the plague in Spain. Our guide pointed out that the cathedral was like a child, growing and then growing some more.

The clam shell is the symbol of Santiago. From the 9th through 11th centuries, pilgrims visiting Santiago would continue on to the coast to see the sun set over what they had assumed was the end of the earth. While there, they collected shells. Santiago began to sell shells to pilgrims and later, shells made from either silver or jet, long thought to be magic, became typical souvenirs. Today's jet shells no longer came from petrified trees but from charcoal.

We noticed round, flat almond cakes in the windows of many of the shops. Our guide explained that these Tartas de Santiago, made from sugar, eggs and ground almonds but containing no flour, were unique to Santiago and very popular.

Our last stop took us to the Tuesday outdoor farmers' market at the edge of the historic center. The vendors, many quite old, gathered around the exterior of a daily market hall selling meat, fish, cheese, pastries, and produce. The majority of the merchants were women and I took a photo of one counting out one hundred small peppers and placing them into plastic bags. At our breakfast buffet I tried a small roasted pepper and liked it very much. Woven baskets filled with fruits, vegetables and chestnuts lined the outer walls of the building and I took another photo of an old woman removing large white beans from their pods. Unlike other areas of Spain, the women in Santiago tended to be portly and today's vendors were no exception.

Wayne and I entered one of the long corridors inside the hall and purchased a small round of queso fresco and some fresh crunchy bread for our lunch. On our way back to the parador I spotted some Tartas de Santiago in a shop window and we added one to the picnic-in-our-room bundle. We'd each have a slice and give the rest to one of our fellow travelers who couldn't eat anything made with wheat flour.

Now ranked as a five-star hotel, Parador Hostas dos Reis Católicos was built as a royal hospital in 1499 AD. Like many of Santiago's centuries-old buildings, it had a Renaissance-style façade with Baroque balconies that were added later. Its many common areas, gardens and central courtyards were charming. We also liked the rustic dining room with numerous bench-lined alcoves. After we left the parador in Santiago we learned from Paula that the dining room had originally served as the hospital's morgue.

We spent the rest of the afternoon wandering through the historic center and even ventured a few blocks into the newer city. Preferring the older section, we returned and explored along narrow streets and alleys filled with shops, cafés and restaurants. I bought an inexpensive silver-plated shell pendant as a souvenir. We returned to the parador's outdoor café at 6:00 p.m. and Paula joined us for wine and conversation.

Deciding to forego dinner outside the parador on a free evening, we opted to polish off the rest of the cheese and bread in our room. Then we listened to the cathedral bells toll each hour as we packed, read novels and finally drifted to sleep.

After a lovely breakfast in the dining room/morgue we checked out and then boarded a bus for another day of travel, this time into Portugal, stopping mid-morning for a tour of Bom Jesus do Monte in Braga, Portugal. Our next stop in Braga was for lunch at the Hotel do Elevador high atop a hill. We rode up in a funicular and peeked in yet another chapel before entering the dining room for a delightful lunch with spectacular views of Braga below us.

To get back to the bus we opted to walk down a long series of stairways that cascaded down the hillside. Statuary adorned each set of stairs and I must have taken twenty photos in search of the perfect artistic shot.

We drove further south until we reached Guimarães by mid-afternoon. Along the way we passed cork oak groves, farms and small villages. Most homes had grape trellises that seemed to stretch skyward to heights of eight or ten feet. Someone later explained that they prevented animals from devouring the grapes. We also traveled through patches of fog, reminding us that we were relatively close to the Atlantic Ocean.

When we crossed the border, Spanish paradors became Portuguese pousadas. The two shared the same translation of *a place to sleep*; only the languages differed. Our hotel in Guimarães, Pousada de Santa Marinha, sat atop a hillside overlooking the town. From this vantage point we could see for miles. The pousada, a 12th-century Augustinian monastery before its conversion into a hotel, impressed us with its stately appearance and lovely grounds. Even the small cemetery to the left of the entrance had a certain charm, sporting bright, colorful flowers on each grave. Our group dined at the pousada that evening and we shared lots of laughs.

Our local guide the next morning, a fast-talking and even faster-walking young woman, met us in the village for a three-hour tour of historic Guimarães, pronounced *Gee* (hard G)-*mare-a-we*. We wound through a series of streets lined with distinctive shops and homes, many around plazas, to a restored monastery filled with tapestries and furnishings from the reign of Alfonso VI in the 17th century. We then walked uphill to a 10th-century castle that was not open for tours.

Wayne and I left the group just before noon and walked back to the historic district of Guimarães to buy a few souvenirs. Most of the clerks spoke English well and were very helpful. I bought some embroidered sachets and some glazed tiles typical of the town.

We had a light lunch on one of the squares and then, with another couple from our group, toured a small nearby museum, the Museu de Alberto Sampaio Guimarães. Set in a former monastery, it turned out to be a special surprise for all of us. The walls of the main gallery were painted fuchsia, a perfect background for many historically significant works of art as well as a number of 16th-century religious paintings that hung on them.

We then boarded a local bus for the winding ride to the top of the hill and our pousada.

Later that afternoon we all met in a lecture hall for an educational program focusing on the historical perspective of Portugal. We learned that Porto had one and a half million residents and two hundred sixty thousand lived within the city proper, second only to Lisbon, the capital. Lisbon residents liked to say that Lisbon was the capital and the rest of the country was just landscape. The residents of Porto disagreed.

Porto, a natural port, provided a great location for trade to northern Europe. The name Portugal means the land of ports. During the 15th century, ship building thrived here. When the English were at war with France in the 17th century and couldn't buy French wine, they began to import port wine. It is an English favorite to this day.

At the end of the 19th century the first movements against the monarchy began in Porto and in 1910, the many centuries of its rule ended. Although the form of leadership varied since then, including tyranny and dictatorship, Portugal now enjoyed a democratic government.

After the lecture we boarded a bus for an hour's ride and dinner at Pousada Santa Maria do Bouro, an elegantly restored 12th-century Cistercian Monastery in Amares. What a treat! Even at night the charm of this pousada captivated us. We walked through the lobby and common areas to our private dining room and thoroughly enjoyed our meal and the attentive service.

The next day we explored the city of Porto, founded in 1123 AD and known for its stately bridges and port wine production. As we approached, we first stopped high atop a centrally located hill overlooking the city. At the summit was the impressive Porto Cathedral with a surrounding courtyard offering spectacular views of the city below. After centuries of construction, the cathedral was completed in 1737 AD. The original structure, Romanesque in style, was the city's oldest monument. Later additions reflected its Gothic and Baroque elements.

Our bus wound its way through the main shopping district of Porto and we noticed that most were closed on Sundays. Many of the early 20th-century buildings had façades covered with decorative blue and white ceramic tiles. Paula explained that the tiles were easy to clean and provided good insulation against wintertime humidity.

We stopped for a whirlwind tour of the Stock Exchange Palace, a striking Neoclassical building with Palladian influences completed in 1850. A national monument, the building is now a UNESCO World Heritage Site. A glass dome perched over the interior courtyard was added when the government appropriated the structure that originally served as a monastery. Winding up an elaborate two-story staircase, we were surrounded by gold-leafed rectangles filled with coats of arms and other significant symbols painted in bright colors. On the upper level we toured the Arab Room, decorated in the exotic Moorish-Revival style so fashionable at the time.

The bus then took us along the ocean with its palm-lined promenade. On this sunny Sunday afternoon the townspeople strolled along it in masses. We spotted an enormous ship on the horizon and many sailboats hovered closer to shore.

Passing a 16th-century fortress en route, we returned to the center of Porto. Driving along the river, we noticed brightly colored homes on the opposite side. We then passed under a bridge built in 1936 that spanned the river. For seven years it claimed the title as the largest bridge in the world. Records were made to be broken and this one didn't last long.

Our next stop was in the Ribeira district for lunch at Chez Lapin. Although it had an abundance of local charm, we were packed as tight as sardines in a dining room with waiters rushing up and down the narrow passageways separating the tables. The food, served family style to each long table, was actually tasty and we noticed a framed proclamation stating that this restaurant made the Fodor's Choice list for 2007.

We learned that this weekend was a national holiday celebrating Portugal's independence from the monarchy and the streets and restaurants overflowed with locals. After lunch we crossed the river and drove along the quay to a port factory. It was such a beautiful afternoon that Wayne and I opted for a walk along the quay instead of the winery tour.

Holiday celebrations abounded and street entertainers amazed and amused us as we strolled along the river. A group of Brazilian musicians played a single string instrument resembling a walking stick. Another group performed Capoeira, a martial art disguised as dance. Slaves had learned they could defend themselves against cruel masters using these lethal maneuvers. By combining the moves with dance, they fooled their masters into believing they were part of a ritual performance.

We boarded the bus late in the afternoon for a return trip to Guimarães. After packing once more, we joined our group for a farewell dinner at the pousada. Sitting at a table with new friends, all agreed we were a fabulous group of travelers and that Paula, our guide throughout the trip, was just the best. Our adventures in Spain and Portugal would long be remembered with fondness.

EUROPE WITH A DANUBE RIVER CRUISE

Germany, Austria, Slovakia, Czech Republic, Bulgaria, Croatia,
and Montenegro

September 4–25, 2018

OVER THE YEARS, my husband and I have enjoyed a number of trips sponsored by the University of Michigan. We signed on for a Danube cruise and sandwiched it between a revisit to East Berlin with a stop in Dresden at the beginning and Dubrovnik and Montenegro at the end. On the appointed day we began with a bargain first-class, twelve-hour flight to Warsaw, Poland, and then transferred to Berlin.

The river trip from Passau to the coast of Bulgaria constituted a large part of our journey. Just before our departure we noticed an article in the *LA Times* mentioning that the worst drought in two hundred years halted boat travel on the Danube. We called our travel provider and no one at the agency had heard of closures. Undaunted, we decided to charge ahead and go with the flow, or lack of it as the case might be.

We reached Warsaw with an hour to make our connection to Berlin. To our surprise, we were herded into another long customs line even though our luggage remained with the airline. Joining a queue of passengers, we did our best to get through the tangle. With my knee replacement I am always subjected to a pat-down and a brusque woman insisted that I show her my scar—not easily accomplished wearing skinny jeans. To add insult to injury, I was pulled aside for what the security guard told me was a random check. After explaining that we were in jeopardy of missing our connecting flight, he did a quick inspection of my carry-on and let us proceed to our gate.

Our experience at the Berlin Airport only added insult to injury. We had a smooth flight to Berlin and looked for a baggage claim sign when we landed. Seeing none, we assumed that it must be on the floor below us. We exited, only to discover that our bags actually were on the floor above us and when we tried to re-enter, we were blocked by a guard.

After shuffling from one point to another we met a helpful agent who seemed all too familiar with our predicament. He took our claim ticket numbers and informed us that it would be a long wait. An hour later he let us know that our luggage was in the baggage claim building located outside the terminal. We trekked to the building only to discover a dozen people ahead of us in a line that barely moved. A howling two-year-old didn't help matters.

I sat next to a lovely woman from Berlin while Wayne stood in the line. She told me this mix-up happens often and she was waiting for a house guest who also left the arrival area without his luggage. She said a new airport was almost ready to open and baggage claims would be simplified. However, the government had held up its opening for years.

After half an hour and only one agent to process the claims, I gave in to Wayne's suggestion and took a taxi to the Adlon, our hotel for the next three nights. Not long after I arrived and checked in, my phone rang with news from Wayne that his name had magically been called and he was on his way. He had no idea how he moved to the front of the line. I'd like to think that our being patient with a series of agents made the difference.

After a long and exhausting two days in transit we called it a night when Wayne arrived at 10:00 p.m. and we slept until 5:30 a.m. Opening our curtains, we were greeted by spectacular views of the Brandenburg Gate and the Unter den Linden. We headed to the dining room and our charming waitress seated us at a breakfast table overlooking the Brandenburg Gate. I would never tire of this view! We enjoyed the selections of smoked salmon, cold meats, cheeses, dark bread, and added a pretzel for Wayne.

We took a four-and-a-half-mile walk past the Holocaust Memorial, the Berlin Wall Memorial, and the site where Checkpoint Charlie once stood. On a visit fifteen years ago, our driver took us past Checkpoint Charlie, still in its original location. Today it is part of the Allied Museum and is considered a major tourist attraction. Years ago, we also toured large sections of the Berlin Wall still in place and covered with colorful graffiti. Things changed over time and now sections of the wall were displayed in a memorial park within walking distance of the Unter den Linden. On our return to the hotel we passed Humboldt University, the Berlin Opera House and the foreboding Russian Embassy.

As we have revisited favorite cities through the years, we've been reminded that change is inevitable. We were struck by the number of tourists in East Berlin, and the newly cleaned buildings fifteen years ago along the boulevards now sported layers of dirt from the exhaust of nonstop traffic. On that previous visit, there were almost no buses and the gracious Unter den Linden wase virtually empty. Today tour buses lined the streets for blocks along the Tiergarten and we saw many parked on Museum Island. East Berlin had been discovered. Nevertheless, we would always have fond memories of this charming city.

We bought ham and cheese sandwiches along the way for a picnic in our room and decided to rest until mid-afternoon. Late in the afternoon we walked through the Tiergarten, adding another mile and a half to our daily tour.

That evening we taxied to Facil, a two-star restaurant in the Mandarin Hotel. I was feeling a bit weary but wanted to take advantage of the hefty guarantee we paid in advance. Simple courses were not an option but each delighted us. The lovely ambience of the glass-enclosed restaurant raised our final score for Facil to three stars. After two hours of dining we opted to walk back to the Adlon.

Rain greeted us as we looked out our window the next morning but had stopped by the time we finished breakfast. With tickets for an 11:30 a.m. admission to the Pergamon and day passes for the rest of East Berlin's Museum Island collections, we headed out to indulge in a day of antiquities. At the Neues, our first stop, we revisited the striking bust of Nefertiti, wife of Egyptian King Akhenaten, dating from the early 1300s BC. When we first visited, this masterpiece resided in a museum in West Berlin. Today she held court at this beautifully restored landmark. As it had before, her beauty captivated us and the only disappointment was that photography of her bust was not allowed, even though it was in the rest of the museum. Before we left, we purchased two postcards of Nefertiti in the gift shop.

Our day passes enabled us to avoid long lines at the other museums. We crossed the street to the Pergamon, bypassing a queue of tourists a block long. I thanked Wayne for purchasing tickets in advance. The highlight was passing through the stunning replica of the Ishtar Gate of Babylon, the eighth to the inner city constructed in 575 BC by King Nebuchadnezzar. The walls, finished in blue glazed bricks, had bas-reliefs of animals and mythical figures made from molded bricks in gold tones. This passageway alone merited a visit to the Pergamon.

The day's final museum tour was the Altes Museum filled with Greek artifacts. The Neoclassical-style building designed by Karl Friedrich Schinkel was completed in 1830 and restored in 2010–2011. Berlin's first museum, it stands as the centerpiece of Museum Island, all of which is a UNESCO-listed heritage site. We spent ample time admiring the vast collection of classical antiquities which included a number of large red clay urns embellished with scenes depicting life in ancient Greece.

Several months ago, I booked a dinner reservation for tonight at Reinstoff, another two-star restaurant. With age and jet lag catching up with us, Wayne called at 4:00 p.m. to opt out and the receptionist graciously allowed us to cancel without incurring a charge. We enjoyed a light dinner at Quarre, a brasserie-style restaurant in the Adlon. Our charming young waitress suggested the potato soup and it was outstanding. I never would have ordered it without her encouragement. My grilled salmon with steamed spinach was perfect and Wayne's wiener schnitzel and German potato salad filled the bill for him.

We checked out of the Adlon after breakfast and taxied to the central train station. With no attendant in sight Wayne read a sign posting our 11:19 a.m. departure on Track 3. We waited patiently and then noticed that Dresden, our next destination, had disappeared from the Track 3 board. When we finally found the information booth in this massive station, we learned that our train was switched to Track 12 and had already departed. The attendant exchanged our tickets for a 1:19 p.m. departure and this time we made sure we had the correct boarding information. Delays seemed to be playing a significant role and this was just one more.

Wayne, ever gallant, insisted on rolling his suitcase and mine on and off the station's escalators. On one of his last carries, two heavy bags capsized and knocked him down a couple of stairs. He jammed his foot and had a nasty gash on his right arm. Dr. Barb always carried a supply of antibiotic cream and bandages so I patched him up for the time being. With a nearly two-hour wait he was able to raise his sore foot on a suitcase to prevent swelling. We finally boarded and the train departed at precisely 1:19 p.m. We sat back and enjoyed the two-hour trip taking us through woods and past farms and an occasional village.

Our train arrived just after 3:00 p.m. and we checked into Hotel Taschenbergpalais on the edge of Dresden's Old Town. As our receptionist pointed out, the city's New Town is now older than its counterpart.

The architecturally significant buildings in Dresden, often referred to as the Venice of the Elbe, were obliterated near the end of World War II. Twelve hundred English and American bombers flew nighttime raids on February 13, 14, and 15, 1945, and nearly destroyed the city of Dresden in retaliation for Germany's bombing of England. When the war ended, almost all the historically significant buildings were painstakingly reconstructed using the charred stone blocks recovered after the bombings' firestorms. Visitors now had the sensation of walking through a centuries-old city. Although many countries offered to help with the reconstruction, the East Germans relied on the German Democratic Republic to finance the work and provide the manpower and artisans. The results were astonishing in spite of the blackened stones used in the reconstruction.

That evening we taxied to Carousel, a restaurant in the Hotel Bulow in the New Town just across the Elbe River. My research gave it a high rating and we were not disappointed. The etched glass ceiling above us enclosed what had once been an open-air courtyard. Guests sat at one of ten elegant tables and I was thankful we booked well in advance. Each artful dish not only looked beautiful but tasted even better. We began with a vegan foie gras that both would have guessed was the real deal had our waiter not told us otherwise. Wayne's entrée, a perfectly prepared venison fillet, got high marks as did my Norwegian lobster bisque. A variety of small chef's dishes were interspersed throughout the meal and we finished two and a half hours later with rich decaf coffee. In a word, perfection!

We began our only full day in Dresden with a tour of the Zwinger Palace, a complex that was one of the most important Baroque-period buildings in all of Germany. Originally constructed between 1710 and 1728 AD for Augustus II, it now served as a museum and housed a small but mighty collection of Renaissance art and a vast collection of Chinese and Meissen porcelain. The palace, heavily damaged by the bombings, displayed a façade of fire-blackened stonework. In recent years much of the blackened exterior had been restored to its original beauty and we noticed another wall scaffolded for repairs. It was fascinating to see the difference between the sections that had been restored and those that were in the queue for a cleaning. The palace complex with its magnificent gardens was well worth a visit.

With tickets in hand for a one-hour tour in English, we then visited the Semperoper. Opera in Dresden goes back to the mid-16th century and Dresden earned its place as one of the centers of opera in Europe. Gottfried Semper's first theater, build in 1841 AD, burned in 1869. The Semperoper was completed in 1878 and stood until it was destroyed by air raids in 1945. Meticulously reconstructed, it officially reopened in 1985. It now played host to opera, ballet and classical music.

Next on our agenda was a visit to the Green Vault of Polish King Augustus II, best known as Augustus the Strong. Now a part of the Dresden State Art Collections, the museum, founded in 1723 AD, featured a variety of works from Baroque to Classicism. Only the Vatican Museum could claim to be older than this one located in a section of the Dresden Castle. The exhibit contained more than two thousand artifacts representing ten percent of his original holdings. Augustus was a passionate collector of Chinese and Japanese porcelain and he displayed exquisite pieces in his Green Vault to impress visitors. Wanting to know the secret used to produce porcelain, he imprisoned alchemist Johann Böttger until he discovered the formula. He then established the first porcelain factory in Meissen and the rest is history.

After a very long day we opted to have dinner in our hotel, then took a short walk before repacking for the next day's train ride to Prague in the Czech Republic. We thoroughly enjoyed our time in Dresden, a city rebuilt with the strength and determination of its residents.

The next morning, we took a taxi to the central train station. Wayne, always intent on arriving early, allowed a forty-minute wait for our 11:10 a.m. departure. We chatted with a couple from Wisconsin whose itinerary was much the same as ours. Moving to the first-class boarding area we then talked with a young man from a village near Frankfurt who was meeting his girlfriend and then heading to a wooded area to camp. With unusually warm weather and extreme drought, they were guaranteed a perfect experience.

We boarded the train which once again left exactly on time. Randomly selecting places to sit, we soon realized that seats were assigned for this leg of the trip. Ironically, we landed in the correct first-class car just a row from our assigned seats. Since it wasn't full, Wayne stayed where he was and I moved back a row to my legitimate spot, offering both of us a forward view from a window. Wayne chatted with a couple across the aisle who hailed from Minneapolis and I enjoyed looking at the many small villages bordering the Elbe. The river remained extremely low and I took photos showing it down at least five feet from its normal level.

After an hour on the train we entered the Czech Republic and an hour later pulled into the Prague station. Then the craziness began. We looked for an elevator and, seeing none, began a long walk pulling our heavy bags toward a distant sign posting an escalator. When we arrived, we discovered that it went up and not down, the direction we needed. We continued to roll our bags along the walkway and when we arrived at what appeared to be the final staircase, we bumped our bags down it. Only then did we learn that we had just missed the escalator heading downward.

When we exited the terminal, we noticed two taxis just outside and a man gave Wayne a price for our drive to our hotel. Wayne misunderstood the quote and instead of US$4, the five-minute ride cost us US$40. Ah, well.... We arrived at the Art Deco Imperial Hotel and if a pricey taxi ride was the worst faux pas we made on this long journey, so be it.

Joannie, our tour director, greeted us enthusiastically when we entered the hotel. The first question we had for her was whether our boat would sail on the Danube. She assured us that it was all systems go. Our room wasn't quite ready so we had coffee in the bar and it wasn't long before the room keys were brought to us. We assumed that joining 140 fellow travelers from the University of Michigan, the University of Illinois, Cal Poly and a large Smithsonian group meant bare bones accommodations for our three days in Prague. Instead, we entered a lovely room that featured a large bathroom with a tub and shower and offered a nice view from our sitting area.

After unpacking we walked in the vicinity of the central square and stopped at the Palladium Mall, a building filled with shops and food stands. Since the heat wave showed no signs of breaking, we bought lightweight T-shirts and would ship a box filled with heavier fall clothing back to the States. A reading of a humid eighty degrees today almost guaranteed that the temperature would remain unseasonably warm for the duration of our trip.

That evening we joined our tour group in a very crowded room off the hotel lobby. We met a number of people from the University of Michigan as well as others on the tour. We skipped the appetizers knowing we had an 8:30 p.m. dinner at Next Door on a side street adjacent to the hotel. My research paid off on this winner. Wayne ordered a pheasant pâté followed by pork with chanterelles and I had an absolutely fresh salad with a light house dressing and then a delicious mushroom soufflé. We shared a traditional dessert, curd dumplings with plums and poppy seed ice cream, a perfect end to our first day in Prague.

We joined our U of M group for a guided two-and-a-half-mile walking tour through Prague's Old Town in the morning. The architecture of this centuries-old medieval city dazzled us. Prague dated from Roman times and boasted a collection of buildings in the Gothic, Renaissance, Baroque, Rococo, and Classical styles. We soon came to Prague's famed astrological clock, the Orloj, a centerpiece of the Old Town Square. The clock, dating to 1410 AD, was the oldest-functioning astronomical clock in the world. Unfortunately, it was almost entirely hidden by green mesh while undergoing restoration. Suffice it to say that the clock was the longest-functioning astronomical clock excluding a few times-outs for repairs and this was one of those time-outs.

Continuing on toward the Charles Bridge we made a quick visit to the Basilica of St. James. This Baroque church first opened in 1232 AD and continued to expand through the 14th century. The treasured *Madonna Pietatis* hung above the altar.

When we reached the Charles Bridge it was literally covered with tourists from one end to the other. This historic crossing was completed in 1402 AD and measured 1,693 feet. It spanned the Moldau River connecting the city's

Old Town with the Prague Castle and New Town. Almost every square inch of Prague seemed to be impacted by tourism and from today's walk through this architecturally exceptional city we could understand why. We slowly forged our way to the center of the bridge, which offered spectacular views in both directions.

Before today's tour began, our guide handed out to each of us a compact sound transmission device called a Vox which enabled us to listen to her remotely. Along with highlighting points of interest, she shared information about the city's history and its inhabitants. Prague was fortunate to have maintained its medieval glory because it escaped bombing during World War II. Hitler had had plans to destroy the Old Town and build a modern city but was defeated before this could happen. There were 1.2 million people in Prague and two hundred thousand dogs. In addition to their dogs, residents loved beer and consumed an average of 140 liters per person each year, the most of anywhere in the world. Our guide warned us of tourist shops selling Russian stacked wooden dolls, fake rubies and poor-quality crystal. She also advised us not to take pricey Russian taxis. We suspected we had done just that yesterday.

After two and a half hours, our guide offered to lead our group back to the hotel. We opted to keep touring on our own. Wayne and I wandered through the New Town in the direction of the Prague Castle perched high above the city. Built in the 9th century, it now served as the official office of the President of the Czech Republic. It was the largest ancient castle in the world and one of the most visited. We reached it after climbing 208 arduous steps up a hillside, arriving at noon just as a Changing of the Guard ceremony took place. Getting a good look proved difficult as we peered through throngs of tourists.

The lines to enter the castle were so long that we opted to walk back down the 208 steps to find a wood-carving shop I had spotted earlier in the New Town. After a quick stop in the shop to purchase ornaments we headed back to the Charles Bridge. En route, Wayne, our resident ice cream fan, bought a large cone baked on a street-side grill which was then rolled and filled with rich vanilla ice cream. He offered me a taste and it was delicious.

Tonight's dinner at Alcron in the hotel with the same name would remain a favorite memory. We opted for chef Jakub Cerny's six-course tasting menu. Highlights included pumpkin soufflé with chili, oxtail consommé with morel mushrooms and an apricot dessert with curry ice cream. Our waiter and his assistants were delightful and, other than a twenty-minute wait for a taxi after dinner, the evening was perfect.

The next morning, we took another walking tour that focused on Art

Nouveau and Cubist architecture. Our guide pointed out buildings along the way that exemplified these styles. We passed a number of them on yesterday's city tour and today we learned about these historic buildings. Many of the landmarks such as the Grand Hotel Europa represented Prague's social and political history.

When we reached the Municipal House, completed in 1912, we took a guided tour of the three gentlemen's quarters and the three ladies' quarters. Serving as meeting places, each area had its own unique characteristics. Murals decorated the walls and ceilings depicting Prague's history. Portraits of the city's famed writers and composers showcased Smetana, Dvorak and more. Décor in the ladies' quarters featured three variations of Art Nouveau on each of the walls and ceilings.

We then moved into the foyer located one floor above the main entrance and Wayne and I stood near a heavy door with cut-glass inserts. As we peered inside, we realized it was Smetana Hall, a small concert venue, with an orchestra assembled on the stage. Almost immediately the conductor began a rehearsal and we heard a beautiful soprano voice accompanying the music. We were mesmerized by the haunting performance.

After a stop at the first-floor café for coffee and a pastry, our guide led us along a linden-lined boulevard restricted to pedestrian traffic. Elegant shops bordered it on either side. Our guide continued to point out Art Nouveau and Cubist structures and at the end of the thoroughfare I stopped to take a photo of a sign crisscrossed with four or five street names. It seemed to point in every direction. When we turned our listening device on, we could only hear a faint murmur. Our guide moved quickly! With numerous directions to choose from, we randomly turned down one of the roads. It wasn't long before the audio transmission went silent and we made our own way back to the hotel.

Wayne kept mentioning the soprano we had heard earlier at the Municipal House and I suggested we ask the concierge if tickets were available for the concert. She checked and we were able to get good seats for the season premiere of the Prague Symphony Orchestra. The performance that evening included works by Strauss, Mahler and a Czech composer. We cancelled our dinner reservations at V Zatisi, a highly rated restaurant that I had booked well in advance, and opted instead in favor of take-out sandwiches from the Palladium Mall and an evening of classical music to celebrate our final night in Prague.

After lunch we met our antique-car driver for a one-hour tour of Prague. Telling her that we had traipsed all over Prague's Old Town and New Town, she drove us through other parts of the city. It wasn't as scenic as we had hoped but it was interesting to see Prague through the eyes of a woman who was born there. One of the highlights was the John Lennon Wall filled with graffiti. Our driver told us that locals developed systems to leave notes for each other on the walls which went undetected during the years of Soviet occupation.

After dinner we walked the few short blocks to the Municipal House. Heading up two flights of stairs to Smetana Hall we found our seats in row nineteen. With tickets for the third and fourth seats from the aisle, we knew we were in for a special musical evening. Before the performance began, we noticed a few people having photos taken in the aisle with their cell phones and we asked an usher to take one of us with the stage in the background. He graciously took several and one later appeared on our 2018 Christmas card. No mental memory-making tonight. We were captured on film—or on my iPhone, to be exact.

The intimate hall with excellent acoustics provided the perfect backdrop for tonight's performance. Finnish guest conductor Pietari Inkinen began with the *Festival Overture* by Czech composer Josef Foerster. Then the orchestra performed Richard Strauss' *Four Last Songs* sung by one of the leading Wagnerian sopranos, Lise Lindstrom. A native of Alameda, California, she sang the piece with power and passion. This was the voice that had captivated us on our morning's tour of the Municipal House. After the intermission the orchestra performed Gustav Mahler's majestic *Symphony 1*, also known as the *Titan*. The symphony is one of my all-time favorites and hearing it in Smetana Hall would remain a treasured Prague memory.

We boarded a bus early the next morning for our ride to Passau to board the *MS Amadeus Silver*, a Lüftner Cruises ship. It took almost forty-five minutes to exit Prague through heavy traffic. Eventually we traveled along a narrow roadway flanked by woods and farms but saw no animals in the fields for the first hour. Finally, small herds of sheep appeared here and there. After an hour and a half, we entered the first large town, Strakonice, in the South Bohemian Region of the Czech Republic and home to a 12th-century moated castle of the same name located along the Otava River.

We then climbed to a height of three thousand feet near the top of the Czech Bavarian Mountains. They created a natural border between the Czech Republic on one side and Germany and Austria on the other. We drove through the Bavarian Forest following narrow roads. Our bus driver skillfully avoided oncoming trucks, barely missing one as we came around a curve. We all applauded.

As we approached Passau, our guide mentioned that this German town on the border of Austria lies at the confluence of the Danube, Ilz and Inn

Rivers. The city sits on a peninsula with the Danube and the Inn on either side. We reached the *MS Amadeus Silver*, our home for the next six days, early in the afternoon and headed to our suite with keys in hand. Unlike other riverboat staterooms we'd had in the past, this one had plenty of space with an ample bathroom, good storage and closets, a seating area, and a sliding glass door leading to a balcony with a table and two chairs.

Wayne's baggage was already in our room and I suspected mine would arrive on one of the buses still on its way. We headed to the dining room and enjoyed a lunch buffet followed by an elaborate array of desserts. The pastry chef cut portions of cakes and told us about each selection. I tried several and topping the list was the most incredible opera cake I had ever tasted.

After lunch we met a local guide for a delightfully informative tour of Passau. We walked carefully along cobbled streets through this charming small town and passed through the artists' alley paved in colorful stones before stopping at the Glass Museum housing the world's greatest collection of European glass. With more than thirty thousand pieces, the exhibits offered a comprehensive view of glass art from Baroque to modern.

We then toured St. Stephen's Cathedral, a Baroque masterpiece completed in 1693 AD that featured the world's largest church organ. As we looked across the Danube, we saw a castle on the opposite banks dating from 1499 AD.

In 2018, the city's largest industry was the manufacturing of auto parts. The population was about fifty thousand including the twelve thousand students at the University of Passau, which offered courses in economics, theology, cultural studies, computer science, and a highly regarded law school.

We stepped into the New Bishop's Residence, built in the early 18th century. A brilliantly colored fresco rose high above us on the entrance ceiling. We exited and followed a series of steps down to the river before making our way back to our dock.

After resting for an hour, we joined fellow passengers at 6:00 p.m. for a formal greeting from the ship's director. He explained safety features and welcomed us aboard. Wine and soft drinks were passed as well as an array of appetizers. At dinner, we sat with Cindy and Rob from Ann Arbor, and made selections from the menu, all delicious. The chocolate soufflé dessert dazzled us. While we dined, we felt our boat leave its berth in Passau to begin an overnight journey to Melk, Austria. After dinner, we went to the top deck for a view, but the cool evening breeze convinced us to call it a night.

We arrived early in the morning after passing through a series of locks. Our tour group met at 10:00 a.m. for a five-minute bus ride to the impressive Melk Abbey, a Benedictine monastery built between 1702 and 1736 AD. If first impressions are worth noting, the size of this stunning Baroque complex simply overwhelmed us. We queued with a number of tour groups in the vast courtyard to wait for the signal to enter.

Our guide Karl, a knowledgeable and interesting young man, made our visit come alive. He later shared that he was an artist who had worked in Vienna creating sets for operas. Tiring of the long commute, he decided to become a guide at the abbey to be closer to his wife and young children. It was our group's good fortune to have him as our guide. He mentioned that three hundred people worked at the abbey and as many as two thousand tourists visited per day.

We began our tour in the Imperial Hallway stretching half a block in each direction. Karl explained that only members of the royal family were permitted to stay in the guest quarters. If traveling by carriage, the abbey was a one-day trip from Vienna. We walked up sixty-four steps on a curving marble stairway to an area with life-sized portraits of Empress Maria Theresa and her husband Leopold. The arranged marriage turned into one of love and they produced sixteen children, one of whom was Marie Antoinette. Karl teased that the flattering portrait of Maria Theresa might have been photo-shopped to make her look so trim.

A monastery had existed in Melk from very early times and a school and writing room were mentioned in a document dating to 1160 AD. In 1297 AD, the monastery caught fire and was almost totally destroyed. The church and monks' living quarters were reconstructed in the early 1300s. Fast forward to the 1700s, when the cathedral and abbey were created in their current Baroque form. The ideal of this style was an attempt to recreate the splendor of heaven on earth. Intricate carvings embellished with gold leaf, massive murals on walls and ceilings, and mirrors to enlarge spaces and reflect elegance graced the rooms of the imperial suites. There were five hundred rooms in the Melk Abbey, making it one of the largest in all of Europe.

Karl led us through a number of the chambers, including one with a 500-year-old series of large paintings depicting religious scenes that folded together to make them portable. Since most citizens could not read at that time, the folding paintings were used to teach lessons in Christianity. Another room had a centuries-old globe showing California as an island in the Pacific. We chuckled since many still considered it an island unto its own.

The Marble Hall dining room had numerous plaster columns painted in faux marble, adding a touch of Baroque symmetry without the weight of real marble columns. An ornate grate at least six feet square lay in the center of the floor, below which fires were built to provide heat in the winter. Karl noted that this elaborate dining room sometimes remained empty for as many as twenty years since only royalty were allowed to use it.

The last interior visit was the library, housing nine thousand books. We exited onto an open balcony that provided a panoramic view and Karl shared some additional points of interest with us. Emperor Joseph II created reusable wooden coffins. A body would be placed in a shroud and as the coffin was lowered, a release lever would drop its contents into the grave. The empty coffin was then raised and readied for its next occupant. The emperor also closed eight hundred abbeys but, because of its fame and academic stature, Melk escaped closure. Today there were one thousand middle and high school students who attended classes at the abbey. They paid full, but reasonably priced, tuition. No longer a Catholic school, it followed a traditional teaching program.

The exterior walls of the abbey were painted a mustard color, referred to as Schoenberg yellow. We walked down a series of steps to a Baroque church. After taking in its beauty, we walked through the abbey's manicured gardens before boarding our bus at noon for a return to our boat.

We sailed toward the village of Dürnstein, first mentioned in 1192 AD when King Richard I of England, known as Richard the Lionhearted, was held captive in the castle high above the town. Wayne and I opted for lunch in the dining room rather than the more casual buffet in the breakfast room and sat for an hour watching the scenery from the Wachau Valley pass by on our two-hour cruise down the Danube.

We took photos through the window of medieval castles nestled along the river and of one perched on a high, rocky hill. After lunch we went topside and took more photos of terraced vineyards that dotted the steep valley hillsides for many miles. Then we sat on our own balcony and enjoyed the view. Suddenly we were caught in a downpour that lasted about twenty minutes. By the time we docked only a few clouds remained and we had a dry walk through the small town. Although charming, it was filled with tourist shops all seeming to offer the same wares. We did purchase a few wooden Austrian ornaments.

After an informal reception for the U of M guests we had a lovely dinner in the ship's dining room with Cindy and Rob and new friends Julia and Larry, who hailed from Grand Rapids, Michigan. At dinner, Wayne discovered that one of his close college friends was Larry's law partner. Small world!

While outlining tomorrow's activities in Vienna, our tour director Jeannie told us that its streets are figuratively paved in gold with culture and music and described it as a timeless and memorable city. Her enthusiasm always added a spark of anticipation.

During the night, the ship sailed from Dürnstein and arrived in Vienna at 4:00 a.m. When we opened our curtains in the morning, I was unenthused to see we were docked next to another riverboat. Instead of a view of Vienna we had a view of neighboring passengers.

After a brief lecture on the city of Vienna we boarded buses for our tour. We passed the famed ferris wheel seen in the classic film, *The Third Man*. Our delightful guide pointed out significant buildings as we approached the Vienna Ring, or Ringstrasse. She mentioned that Austria's 600-year Habsburg rule ended in 1918 and it was the first country to join with Hitler. By 1945 nearly fifty percent of Vienna was destroyed but significant structures were spared.

Vienna's water source was thirty-four miles away in the Vienna Woods and the mountain spring water was safe to drink right from the tap. At the time of our visit, the population was 1.8 million. Under Emperor Franz Joseph I, Vienna's architect Otto Wagner designed classic Art Nouveau buildings in the late 1800s. The Ring Boulevard took thirty years to construct. Viennese call their city Wein pronounced with a "V".

We began our walking tour at the famed Spanish Riding School of Vienna. There we saw seventy-two stalls filled with the equally famed Lipizzaner Stallions. It would take eight years of training before a horse was ready to perform and years of work and training before a rider was accepted and paired with a horse.

In the 1580s, Archduke Karl von Habsburg began breeding his own horses for use in wartime. The sturdy stallions were trained to protect their riders from, and inflict injury on, opposing foot soldiers by performing acrobatic movements such as the capriole, in which the horse would leap in the air and kick straight back at a threat with its hind legs. The school, committed to preserving this pure form of classical horsemanship and its cultural importance, now provided demonstrations of their stunning performances at venues worldwide.

After walking along one of Vienna's most elegant shopping streets, we stopped at the Imperial Palace of the Hofburg. For more than six hundred years it served as the residence for Austrian sovereigns. The core of the medieval fortress had been preserved but each emperor expanded the palace. In the middle of the 16th century the exterior gained its Renaissance appearance. Room after elegant room featured portraits of royalty along with much of the palace's original furnishings. When we visited the Schönbrunn Palace thirty years ago on our first visit to Vienna, we admired the ornate ceramic heaters in each room and the heaters in the Imperial Palace were just as beautiful.

After a quick visit to the very crowded St. Stephen's Cathedral, Wayne and I walked in the direction of the Vienna Opera House. On our way I spotted a silver necklace in a shop window that spoke to me and my dear husband bought it as a Viennese memento.

We chose the Hotel Sacher for coffee and a light lunch, but its famed street café had a line that stretched a full block and was not an option. Walking around the corner we discovered the Blue Bar, an elegantly appointed room accessed via the main entrance to the hotel. Only two other tables were occupied and we enjoyed our leisurely lunch, a goose liver tart with hazelnut brioche and apricots followed by a glorious slice of Sacher torte covered with rich whipped cream.

After lunch we crossed the street to the Albertina Museum filled with incredible art. Established in 1776 AD, it ranked among the important museums in the world with one of the most comprehensive collections of modernism in Europe. We were dazzled by works of some of the world's most renowned artists including Picasso, Renoir, Giacometti, Modigliani, Chagall, Ernst, Miró, Monet, and more. To our delight it was relatively uncrowded. The Albertina would remain near the top of our list of favorites.

We returned to the boat late in the afternoon filled with wonderful memories of Vienna. Although as spectacular as we remembered it from our first visit thirty years ago, we were astonished by the number of tourists who seemed to fill every walkway and crowd into each significant attraction. At times it was almost impossible to walk along the Ring. Wayne and I remembered wandering leisurely down the street leading to St. Stephen's Cathedral. Back then we walked for blocks hardly encountering a soul and we toured an almost empty cathedral. On this visit it was nearly impossible to enter. We sounded like oldies but we missed those earlier times.

After breakfast the next morning we joined fellow passengers for a lecture on Slovakia presented by local expert Martin Sloboda. He talked about the history of his country since World War I. The concept for the formation of Czechoslovakia was actually developed by Czechs from Pittsburgh and Cleveland. Many had migrated to these cities to work in steel mills with plans to return to their home country and buy land. Most, however, stayed in the States. The 1918 Pittsburg Agreement crafted a plan to create a single country with the two ethnic areas, Czech and Slovakia, retaining their own separate identities. They spelled the umbrella country Czecho-Slovakia. The separation never happened and the country was consequently governed with no hyphen as one country.

After World War I, Czechoslovakia had the eighth largest economy in the world, primarily resulting from its production of munitions. In October 1938, Hitler met with the French and English and convinced them that because it had pockets of German speakers, Czechoslovakia should become part of Germany. The Allies agreed and Hitler made it happen within twenty-four hours. The Czechs were blindsided and felt abandoned by the Allies. In 1939, Hitler took Poland and then France half a year later.

At the end of the war there was a free election in Czechoslovakia and the Communist party won. Slovakia did not vote for it but the Czechs outnumbered the Slovaks two to one. The Soviet Union then took over the government in 1948 and held a firm hand over Czechoslovakia until 1968 when the Prague Spring challenged its powerful hold.

In November of 1989 the Soviet Wall came down and one week later the Velvet Revolution took place in Bratislava. It ended peacefully with the election between Václav Havel and Alexander Dubček. Havel won and decentralization of the country began. In 1992 the country was split by Havel and Dubček. Seventy percent of the citizens did not want the split but it happened quickly and smoothly. It was now referred to as the 1993 Velvet Divorce.

Slovakia's GDP dropped significantly after the breakup. Over the ensuing twenty-five years it had recovered and the country became a major producer of autos for a number of companies. For a small country of 5 million people, it was a huge exporter. Not long ago it qualified to join the European Union. As an aside, Martin mentioned that American astronaut Eugene Cernan and artist Andy Warhol were both Slovakians.

When the lecture concluded we joined our local guide Katerina for a walking tour of Bratislava. We passed along a traffic-free boulevard and soon came to St. Martin's Cathedral, the site of Maria Theresa's coronation. Eighteen coronations had taken place in this cathedral.

Katerina shared photos of her youth with us. She was fifty years old and had grown up among the World War II ruins that remained in place for years. Hers had been a black and white world. She had one photo of herself as a small child sitting on piles of rubble. Another photo showed her making her First Communion. It took place surreptitiously in her parents' apartment. Because the practice of Catholicism was forbidden, the priest arrived in civilian clothes and changed into his vestments inside the apartment before performing the ceremony. He then changed back into street clothes before leaving.

At the end of the tour we entered Konditorei Kormuth, a pastry shop with décor that simply dazzled us. We passed through a series of small rooms, each tastefully covered from floor to ceiling with unique paintings and elaborate frescoes in the Renaissance style. Originally a residence, the building was hundreds of years old. We had coffee served in china cups accompanied by sweet half-moon-shaped bagels in one of the small rooms.

After traveling all night, we arrived in Budapest early the next morning and had our first view of this magnificent city from our stateroom's balcony. Shrouded in the early morning shadows, most memorable were the Elizabeth Bridge and Parliament Building nestled along the edge of the Danube. Not long after we docked, another boat tied alongside of us. Fortunately, it wasn't as high as ours and we could still see quite a bit of Budapest from our balcony.

Our city bus tour departed at 8:30 a.m. on a sunny Monday morning. All went well until I reached into my purse for my iPhone and realized it was still plugged in for a recharge in our room. As the resident photographer, I borrowed Wayne's phone frequently for photos.

The tour began on the Pest side of the city and took us past the Opera House, now under restoration and closed for tours. We drove along Andrássy Boulevard, dating to 1872, showcasing block after block of elegant homes and equally stylish boutiques on the lower levels. We made a brief stop at Heroes' Square at the end of the thoroughfare. On either end stood the Museum of Fine Arts and the Hall of Arts, neither open on Monday. Statues of significant national figures dotted the plaza.

We doubled back toward the Danube and crossed to the Buda side via the Chain Bridge. The Royal Palace, also referred to as Buda Castle, and Matthias Church graced the top of a steep hill overlooking the Danube and Pest. After an hour on the bus in slow traffic, Wayne and I opted to leave our tour and walk down the steep hillside to the river. We stopped at the bottom for double espressos at Café l'Antico adjacent to the French Institute. From there we made our way along the river to the Chain Bridge and crossed the Danube on a pedestrian walkway.

Following the river, we walked up a street to Váci Utca, the most renowned shopping street in Budapest. At the end of the mile-long walkway, we arrived at the Great Market Hall, a massive building dating to 1897. Locals shopped the ground-floor markets here for meats, fruits and vegetables, spices, and pastries. I bought packets of sweet and spicy paprika to take home as gifts. We went to the second level filled with touristy items and discovered that many were made in Russia.

After making the wrong turn along the river in search of our boat, I asked two ship's stewards if they could point us in the right direction. We arrived just before lunch and I noted that my Fitbit had tallied a four-and-a-half-mile walk. We treated ourselves to a delicious piece of cake after lunch in honor of all the calories we had burned that morning.

Resting for a couple of hours, we then headed out in quest of the famed Gerbeaud Café on Vörösmarty Square. The café had been in business for more than 150 years and its cakes and pastries included many Hungarian classics. We ordered espressos and Gerbeaud chocolate cake for Wayne and an Esterházy torte for me. The only drawback was our long wait to order. The waiter in our section of the outdoor café purposefully ignored us, sensing, we suspected, we were Americans. We finally got the attention of a waitress in another section and she took our orders. Although we added another two and a half miles to our day's tally, the calories we consumed at Gerbeaud now surpassed those we burned in transit.

Tonight we joined Cindy, Rob, Julia, and Larry for dinner, all now good friends. After dinner the director invited everyone to come to the top deck to see the Budapest skyline at night. What a spectacular sight! The Parliament building, now fully lit, shone in varying shades of gold. As our ship cruised past it, we took many photos, hoping to capture a perfect remembrance. What a delightful way to say goodbye to this magnificent city!

Our overnight voyage on the Danube ended early in the morning in Kalocsa, one of the oldest towns in Hungary and well known for its paprika peppers. Each day at port, our ship provided tours to the surrounding areas. Today's tour of Pécs, pronounced *paytch*, included a visit to Roman ruins and a catacomb. The *Amadeus Silver* passengers who wanted to join the tour departed at 8:45 a.m. for the two-hour bus ride. I woke up with a sore throat and decided to rest on board. A dozen others opted out of the tour so I had company. While many of the passengers toured Pécs, the ship continued downriver for two hours and docked at Mohács.

As Wayne departed on the morning bus, he sent me a text suggesting I get a massage. I booked a one-hour session with Nina who hailed from Bali, followed by lunch and then a nap—a real luxury.

Wayne returned shortly after 4:00 p.m. and shared his experiences in Pécs. He told me the village dated to as early as the 4th century. The Ottoman Turks and the Hungarians fought for centuries over possession of Hungary. Pécs was now a college town with twenty thousand students and Sts. Peter and Paul's Cathedral, once a mosque, was a highlight of the tour. He also described the growing and drying of red peppers for paprika. The group enjoyed a lovely lunch in town before returning to the boat.

We continued along the Danube and shortly before we crossed into Belgrade, Serbia, everyone had to pick up passports and get them stamped by officials who boarded the *Amadeus Silver*. A Smithsonian speaker gave an hour's talk with slides showing how the Balkans changed hands over the centuries. Today's Balkanization, the most current formation of independent countries, was largely the result of religions—a not-always-harmonious blend of Serbs/Russian Orthodox, Croats/Roman Catholics and Muslims—and languages. The civil unrest of the late 1980s and 1990s left thousands dead and destroyed centuries-old landmarks and villages, but the current peace accord seemed to be working.

We slept well but kept our titles as the sniffle-and-sneeze team. Wayne brought a Z-Pak with him and felt much better. I went with the flow and just hoped to get over this soon. One couple boarded the ship sounding like death warmed over, coughing and sneezing around all of us, and a number of passengers caught their bug. I wasn't about to let it keep me from this morning's tour of Belgrade.

We joined our group for a bus ride through the government and embassy area on our way to the Belgrade Fortress in Kalemegdan Park. Belgrade was founded in the 3rd century BC by the Celts. Byzantine Emperor Justinian I rebuilt the fortress in 535 AD. Over the centuries it changed hands frequently, falling under the rule of Austria and the Ottoman Empire. The massive structure, built from white sandstone, underwent several periods of reconstruction and reached its present size in 1736 AD. It withstood the first Battle of Kosovo in 1389 AD, a war that had no winners since the leaders of both Belgrade and Serbia perished in the battle. As we learned from the earlier lecture, different religious beliefs and languages had always played a significant role in the Balkans.

In 2018, 2 million people lived in Belgrade and more than 7 million in Serbia. Its religious background was largely Russian Orthodox. Because of its central location, it had always served as a bridge between the East and the West. The Turks held control for five centuries and brought the Muslim religion to the area. Serbia served as the buffer between Muslims and Christians. In an accord signed in 1844 all agreed to live at peace within the country. Breaches began shortly thereafter and escalated in the latter part of the 1900s.

In 1978, NATO bombed Bosnia in an effort to stop its ethnic cleansing of Bosnian Muslims. The bombing was strategically focused and significant historical sites were spared. Our guide, an Orthodox Christian, felt that the NATO bombing was senseless. She acknowledged that although Milosevic and his government were the real targets, two thousand residents were killed. Our guide's daughter, who was only three at the time, couldn't understand why bombs were exploding all around her. When her mother explained that it was because of Milosevic's policies, her daughter suggested he move to the Arctic and rule the penguins. Many young residents couldn't understand why the land of Mickey Mouse and Donald Duck was bombing them. I suspected that the persecuted Muslim population had a totally different take on the situation. The atrocities were unspeakable.

Our next stop was the Church of Saint Sava, a Serbian Orthodox church.

Ranking as the largest Orthodox church in Serbia and one of the largest in the world, it had been under construction since 2000 and was sometimes compared to Gaudí's unfinished cathedral in Barcelona. When completed, it would accommodate twenty thousand worshippers. There were no pews, as Orthodox Christians stand throughout church services. Only the very old and infirmed were permitted to sit. As large as it was, it would never be called a cathedral. That title was reserved for Roman Catholic churches. Orthodox priests were required to marry. If a man wished to dedicate his life to the church he could become a monk and remain single.

Because construction continued on the main church, we toured a small chapel on the lower level. Funding for this chapel was a gift from Russia. It was small but truly grand. In Orthodox churches, statuary was not permitted, nor were stained glass windows unless they were narrow panels. Light came from a series of windows in the dome. Every inch of this chapel was covered with frescoes representing biblical stories in bright colors applied against a sky-blue background. It was simply exquisite.

Later that afternoon we heard a talk given by a young local historian. He focused on the last one hundred years of his country's history. After World War II, the communist revolutionary and statesman Josip Broz "Tito" ran unopposed and garnered one hundred and ten percent of the vote. Sounds a bit like old Chicago politics.... The rich hated Tito and his brand of communism. Their houses were often taken from them or divided so that other families could live with them. In 1948, Tito broke off all relations with Russia. He ruled for twenty-five years and was regularly referred to as the gentle dictator. He encouraged mixed marriages and by the time of our visit, there were at least seven thousand children from mixed marriages in Serbia.

We sat with our good friends Julia, Larry, Cindy, and Rob for dinner. Afterward the boat's staff paid tribute to our head tour director, Jeannie. Today marked her birthday and she was truly taken aback by the celebration. She was presented with a huge cake and we were all invited to share it with her.

After breakfast, we went to the upper deck and for the first time in more than two weeks we felt cold. Thankfully, we saved one cool-weather outfit just in case it did get chilly. We took photos as we cruised through the Danube Gorge, also known as the Iron Gates, one of the most scenic spots along the narrowing river, showcasing spectacular Serbian mountains to starboard and rocky Romanian cliffs to port.

We passed a cliff on the Romanian side with the massive face of a man carved into it. The figure, Decebalus, was the last king of Dacia. He took on the armies of Emperor Trajan and was regarded as an important Romanian folk hero. Completed in 2004, it took ten years to create and was the tallest rock relief in all of Europe.

Wayne and I returned to our suite and from our balcony watched the Romanian countryside pass by until we were once again invited to the top deck to watch our boat enter the famed Iron Gates. This joint project was funded by Romania and Serbia. There was no friendship between these two countries but both acknowledged that the locks were vital to prevent flooding and to allow safe passage through the rock-filled gorge. Before the locks and dam were opened in 1972, boats traveling this segment of the Danube had to rely on the skills of a pilot to navigate safe passage.

We entered the first chamber alongside another tour boat. The water level dropped at least forty feet in about twenty minutes. We all tried to guess how the gates would open to let us into the second chamber. Some thought they would swing open. I guessed the gate would slide open. We were all surprised when the gate lowered until it was safe to move forward into the second lock. The drop in the next lock happened more quickly and we soon were cruising down the Danube.

The crew pulled out all the stops for our final full day aboard the boat. As we sailed through the Iron Gates gorge and moved through the locks, they plied us with baklava and pastries. When we arrived for lunch in the dining room, we were presented with a whole suckling pig surrounded by fresh flowers accompanied by a variety of sausages and vegetables. Following this we were treated to an array of pastries all baked on board and heard that our final dinner would be a six-course affair. So much for retaining our girlish and boyish figures...

During lunch we docked at Drobeta-Turnu Severin, Romania. There were one hundred thousand residents in this town originally settled by Emperor Trajan. Destroyed by the Huns, it was rebuilt by Justinian from 527 to 565 AD and the Romanian language had a Latin base resulting from this early conquest. We toured the meager remains of the Roman occupancy in blistering heat. Our next-door suitemate Judy opted out of the tour and stayed on board to reorganize her suitcase. Brilliant choice! There was little to see in the oppressive heat and we were glad to return to our boat.

Tonight's dinner, a six-course extravaganza, marked the end of our time on board the *Amadeus Silver*. We sat with new best friends Cindy, Rob, Julia, and Larry and gave the ship's crew a rousing round of applause as they paraded through the dining room.

After sailing all night, we docked at Vidin, Bulgaria, and had our final shipboard breakfast before joining our newest guide, Theodora. We instantly liked her spunk and sense of humor. Heading into Vidin, we noted the sad state of most of the homes. Paint peeled from buildings and gutters hung from sagging rooftops. The structures spoke of many years of neglect.

We visited a small Orthodox Church partially built into the ground during the Ottoman rule. Somehow it escaped transformation into a mosque. Although it had a musty smell and its frescoes were badly faded, it spoke of survival. We continued on a short distance to the Vidin fortress, passing more houses crying out for some TLC. A few were literally falling apart. The Baba Vida, a medieval fortress, was Vidin's primary landmark and the only walled castle in the country that had been preserved. Three of its original nine towers remained intact as did the original battlements.

After our visit to the fortress we were bused for an hour to our lunch stop. Parts of the countryside resembled the golden hills of California. Stopping in Belogradchik, we entered a vast dining hall filled with tourists. Luckily, Theodora led us into a private room with views of the village's famed red rock cliffs. They reminded us of Sedona, Arizona. Lunch was a simple buffet of cold meats and cheeses with a traditional tomato and cucumber salad.

We continued our bus ride along a very narrow road bordered by farms. By the end of September many of the crops were harvested. Theodora told us that most of the farmland was owned by businessmen and the primary crops were wheat, corn, barley, and a variety of rapeseed used to produce canola oil. We learned that Bulgaria also grew vast amounts of roses and the petals were processed into the very pricey rose oil exported throughout the world. Fields of sunflowers were already harvested for their seeds.

Theodora filled us with information about her country as we continued our four-hour bus ride. Bulgaria's geographical position made it a strategic crossroad into Turkey, Asia and Africa. We noted a sign along the way for the town of Montana. Theodora assured us that the town's name had nothing to do with the state of the same name in America.

Trucks filled the narrow roadway and far outnumbered cars. We noted very few commercial buildings along the way until we neared Sofia and we passed several huge abandoned factory complexes. Theodora told us they had been communist chemical plants that produced fertilizer. When the communists left Bulgaria, they shut them down and thousands were out of work overnight. Over the last thirty years, 164 villages had disappeared from the Bulgarian map. No wonder we were witnessing evidence of extreme poverty.

Arriving during rush hour we slowly made our way to the Sofia Hotel Balkan built in 1956. It reminded us of the Metropol in Moscow. Our room, located at the end of a long hallway, was beautifully appointed and very quiet. On closer inspection we noticed signs of neglect and disrepair. The carpet was dirty and had split open along one of the seams. Updates apparently had not been a priority since the end of communist control.

We joined Julia, Larry, Cindy and Rob in the hotel's café for dinner. Our waiter Pete, short for his lengthy Bulgarian name, was obviously in training. We had to ask for water and then for napkins, both of which he delivered with a smile. We ordered our dinners and they came out one or two at a time. My chicken arrived twenty minutes after the first dish was served. We went with the flow and chatted a bit with young Pete. He seemed to appreciate our patience and when we went into the bar for dessert and coffee, he made sure that we were all given our own plates of pavlova even though each couple asked to split an order.

Theodora had given us a treasure trove of Bulgarian history the day before during our long bus ride. Armed with this information we met her in the lobby the next morning for a walking tour of central Sofia. It happened to be a national holiday and all the streets in the central city were closed to traffic. Just like Dorothy in The Wizard of Oz, we walked along streets that were paved in yellow bricks.

As we exited our hotel, we had an excellent view of the statue of St. Sofia. Theodora pointed out the former Bulgarian Communist Party headquarters. A red star used to sit atop its tower. After the Communists left in 1999, the Bulgarians removed it using a helicopter.

We then visited the Church of St. George, a Roman rotunda dating to the 4th century AD and considered the oldest building in Sofia. Although some modern repairs had taken place, the structure retained much of its original red brickwork. It had undergone several religious iterations but today it functioned as a Christian church and daily services were offered.

Continuing along the yellow brick road to Prince Alexander of Battenberg Square we noticed two uniformed guards standing at attention in front of a government building. We heard a chorus singing not far away and as we walked further, we realized we were in the midst of an Independence Day ceremony. It surprised us that the crowd was so sparse. After listening to speeches we couldn't understand and to the choir singing traditional Bulgarian anthems, we moved on to the Alexander Nevsky Cathedral built in the early 20th century. Constructed in Neo-Byzantine style, it is one of the largest in the world.

We returned to our hotel just before noon and walked to a small outdoor restaurant located just around the corner, choosing a table in the shade since the temperature had soared into the high 80s. Although grateful for virtually no rain on our trip, we had hoped for more typical fall weather. After a light lunch, we continued onward.

Our next stop was the National Archeological Museum. Housed in a former Ottoman mosque, the museum opened in 1905. Tastefully displayed were ancient pottery, gravestones, weapons, helmets, tools, and so much more. The museum's timeline began on ground level with prehistoric artifacts divided into Early, Middle and Late periods. The Main Hall focused on pieces from ancient Thrace, Greece and Rome. The second floor housed medieval treasures. With a focus on Bulgarian artifacts, this small but stellar museum would long remain one of my favorites.

Meeting and chatting with a man about our age from the Netherlands added another highlight to our museum visit. When I mentioned that we had seen the Vermeer show at the Mauritshuis in the Hague in 1996, he lit up and said that Vermeer was his passion. He has seen all of Vermeer's paintings except one belonging to Queen Elizabeth. He visited the three at the Frick and one each at the New York Metropolitan Museum and the National Museum in Washington, DC.

A farewell dinner at the hotel concluded the experiences we shared with so many new friends. Tonight's program of Bulgarian dances executed by a group of young performers wearing traditional costumes was a delight.

We awoke at the ungodly hour of 3:00 a.m. and headed to the Sofia Airport. Our game plan was a flight to Munich with a transfer to Dubrovnik, Croatia. Travel went smoothly and we arrived in Dubrovnik at 10:00 a.m., made our way through passport control and met our driver for a ride to our next hotel, the Pucić Palace. He drove us along the Dalmation Coast and dropped us at the mouth of a pedestrian-only passageway that wound through the Old Town. A hotel porter met us at the drop-off point and rolled our luggage through the narrow alleys. When we arrived, our room was not ready but the charming concierge gave us tips on where to walk and a place to stop for lunch.

As we walked along a narrow roadway paved in polished marble, we were immediately overwhelmed by throngs of tourists filling every square inch of the streets. Shops along the way sold souvenirs, jewelry, ice cream, and more. Cruise ship guides waving flags high above their heads led long lines through the streets, reminding us of Vienna. The charm of this stunningly beautiful town was literally smothered by too many visitors at one time. We later learned that Dubrovnik's residents had had enough of the cruise ship traffic and were considering reducing the numbers of visitors to thirty-five hundred a day from the seven-to ten-thousand now flooding the streets on a daily basis. In my humble opinion, thirty-five hundred would still be too many.

We found the suggested restaurant, Dubravka 1836, nestled at the foot of the fortress wall where it met the Adriatic Sea. At first, we were seated at a table with a fabulous view but in direct sunlight. Just before we ordered, the umbrella'd table next to us became available and we asked if we could take it. Our seafood lunch, enhanced by a spectacular shaded view of the impressive fortress wall and turquoise sea, could not have been any better.

We checked into our room and noticed it had a small balcony overlooking a courtyard. What a lovely spot for morning coffee! Our small hotel was the only one within the old walled city and we appreciated how well situated we were. Our travel agent deserved a round of applause.

Dubrovnik had a long history with evidence of a settlement as early as the 7th century AD. Through the years, it had been ruled by the Byzantines, Venetians, Hungarians, and French. The first mention of Dubrovnik was in 1181 AD. By the 16th century, it had a powerful merchant navy that traded all over the known world, but began its decline in the 17th century as the English and Dutch grew in naval strength.

Dubrovnik was besieged in October 1991 when Yugoslavia started to disintegrate and war broke out between Serbia and Croatia. Much of the Old City was destroyed but most had been restored. New red roof tiles mixed with weathered tiles dating back in time were the only hint that a war had taken place.

We enjoyed an early dinner at La Capella, an outdoor restaurant on a first-floor deck in the Pucić Palace. One of the starters we ordered, fresh sardines, arrived in a small metal oval-shaped dish with a flat top off to the side, resembling a can of sardines. That was where the comparison ended, however, and the fresh sardines were delicious. After dinner we walked through the streets of Old Dubrovnik and enjoyed mingling with locals sans the throngs of cruise shippers.

No need for an alarm clock today. We woke up at 6:30 a.m. to the sound of tables being set up for a farmers market in the courtyard just outside our window. We later visited this charming small bazaar and I bought a box of fresh blueberries, the first I'd encountered in three weeks. I'd have them for breakfast the next morning.

The day began with high humidity and warm temperatures with the possibility of a chance of rain. We met our Croatian driver Marco for a day's tour of Montenegro. Marco, a 26-year-old studying hotel management, took us along the coastal roadway past Konavle, home to the parents of a good friend. His parents emigrated to Gilroy, CA, the garlic capital of the world, and garlic was still the main crop of the Konavle Valley.

On our drive to the border we asked Marco to tell us about himself, his country and Montenegro. He told us Zagreb was Croatia's capital and eighty percent of the country's residents were Roman Catholic. As we had heard, he confirmed that Russian oligarchs were buying up most of the property along the Bay of Kotor in Montenegro. Marco also said tension remained between Serbia and Croatia and that Serbia had still not apologized for its 1991 attack.

We reached the border control and encountered an unusually long line of cars and buses making their way into Montenegro. It took forty-five minutes to clear the Croatian border and then another hour to get through Montenegro's border control. So much for a full day of sightseeing...

A friend in California had told us to look for the differences between Croatia and Montenegro and as we crossed the border the differences were instantly apparent. Homes and buildings on the Croatian side were solidly built with uniform-sized stone blocks and in good repair. Dark green shutters and red tiled roofs adorned most of the buildings in Dubrovnik. Homes in Montenegro appeared to be in various stages of disrepair and were not as well built. The contrast was startling and we sensed extreme poverty in Montenegro.

As we drove in on this overcast day we were nevertheless overwhelmed by the beauty of the sheer mountains on one side of us and the Bay of Kotor on the other. The setting was storybook gorgeous. Marco drove us to Perast to meet a friend of his who arranged motor boat rides to a small island just off the coast. We paid twenty euros for our boat ride to the island and were told we had a thirty-minute window to tour.

When we arrived, we looked into a small church that covered most of the island. Just as we exited it began to rain. The raincoat and umbrella I had carried through all eleven countries remained in our driver's car on the mainland. I fashioned a rain hat out of a plastic bag and we waited for our boat to appear. In retrospect, the trip to this island was a waste of time and money.

We drove to the village of Kotor which was filled with tourists. My vision of a charming waterside town was quickly shattered. A huge cruise ship anchored right along the road loomed above us. We evidenced more of the shoddy Russian construction that we had noticed all along the Bay of Kotor. The Russians had a huge presence here and many oligarchs moored their yachts in the harbor. They even built an airport nearby for easy access. The photos of Kotor in tourist brochures I had so admired were obviously taken from a distance. I had to admit that even my long-distance photos looked good. Up close, not so much.

Marco drove on to the village of Budva bordered by more uninteresting Russian apartment buildings and shopping complexes. The contrast between the Russian yachts in the town's harbor and the shoddy buildings along the shore was dramatic. Marco led us past open markets—tourist traps in reality—to a restaurant along the bay with indoor and outdoor dining areas. Although it rained heavily as we drove to Budva, it had stopped and we opted for outdoor dining along the harbor. The restaurant was short on ambience but long on good food. We spotted a number of mussel farms along the Bay of Kotor and I enjoyed a big steaming bowl of them. Wayne ordered baby octopus, another local specialty.

Just as we made our way to the car and started our drive to the ferry in Lepetane, the rain caught up with us. It took another thirty minutes to drive onto the ferry for a ten-minute ride across this narrow point in the bay. From there it took another twenty minutes to reach Montenegro's border crossing stations. We picked the wrong line to queue in and spent another hour clearing customs. To our dismay, cars and trailers in the lines on either side of us passed through quickly while we barely moved. When we finally reached the booth, we noticed that it was staffed by a very young woman, obviously a rookie.

Arriving in Dubrovnik in the early evening, we were surprised by how cold it had become. We had left that morning in eighty-degree weather and my cell phone now registered fifty-two degrees. Wind gusting more than forty miles per hour made it feel even colder. We moved quickly through the streets leading to our hotel and I immediately took a hot bath. Wayne followed with a warm shower.

We were glad to have taken a day to visit Montenegro but it did not live up to our expectations. The Russians had taken over the entire Bay of Kotor and the results were less than wonderful. We felt Montenegro made a huge mistake by selling out to them. I wished that I could bulldoze the many miles of shoddy construction along the bay and start all over with luxury homes, condos and resorts. The Bay of Kotor with its spectacular geographic setting deserved nothing less.

With dinner reservations at Proto, a two-star fish restaurant in the heart of Old Town, we were seated at a corner table for two in the upstairs dining area. For the next two hours we enjoyed fabulous food and attentive service. Proto met all of our expectations and then some. In spite of the chill, our walks to and from were so pleasant without the crowds from the cruise ships.

Summer weather exited and fall roared in. We were greeted on our balcony by a sunny but very cold and windy morning. After breakfast we ventured out in search of a tasteful canvas Dubrovnik bag to bring home to our daughter Liz. She had visited Dubrovnik during the summer of 1990 and it was one of her favorite memories. Her heart was broken when she learned that it had been bombed by Serbia a year later.

Wandering up and down several streets we discovered that at the end of the tourist season every shop had sold out of Dubrovnik bags. I returned to the hotel to organize my suitcase and Wayne continued up one more side street. He found a charming shop with handcrafted bags and brought me to it. Once again employing the Moscow Rule of Shopping—*when you see it, buy it because it may not be there when you return*—I purchased a hand-painted bag for Liz and several other small items.

Our game plan for today was to walk around the one-point-two-mile wall bordering the medieval city. What a memorable experience! We paid the US$24-per-person admission which thankfully discouraged most of the cruise shippers and rejoiced that the wall was relatively uncrowded. Once on the wall we had to navigate a series of 602 stone steps, some treacherously steep. The walk around the Old City was worth every step. From the wall we could clearly see the rooftops that had been repaired after the 1991 bombing.

We had a quick lunch, a slice of pizza at a small shop along the street, followed by cappuccinos and carrot cake at Café Royale on the square occupied earlier that day by the outdoor market. Noting that our selections were far too American, we both agreed that it was time to return to Santa Barbara. We packed our bags for the last time, had a delightful dinner at Nautika, a small restaurant just outside the Old City walls, and flew home the next morning. After visiting eleven countries in twenty-three days we returned home with new friendships and many treasured memories.

ACKNOWLEDGMENTS

There are so many to thank throughout the years of my journeys. A heartfelt nod goes to my husband Wayne and daughters Elizabeth and Emily, frequent travel companion Ruth Wolf, and Kaye Willette who encouraged me to put my many years of travel journals into book form. A special thanks goes to travel pal Pat Ellison who started me on my journaling in 1987 and to Pat Andersons who added helpful tips. Karen Sketch not only published this book but also designed its clever cover and my editor Sabrina Papa, a joy to work with, polished my prose to perfection. It takes a team and I had the best.

BIOGRAPHY

Barbara graduated from the University of Michigan with a BA in English and Political Science. She worked as an editorial assistant for the University of Michigan's School of Engineering Summer Conferences and for *Plays* and *The Writer* in Boston. She also taught English, journalism and creative writing, and wrote "The Time of Your Life," a two-page monthly column for seniors published in the *Pasadena Star-News*. She has two adult daughters, Elizabeth and Emily, and currently resides in Santa Barbara, California with her husband Wayne.